A Daily Dose
of
SANITY

Also by Alan Cohen

Are You as Happy as Your Dog?
Dare to Be Yourself
*A Deep Breath of Life**
Don't Get Lucky, Get Smart
The Dragon Doesn't Live Here Anymore
*Enough Already**
*Handle with Prayer**
*Happily Even After**
Have You Hugged a Monster Today?
I Had It All the Time
*Joy Is My Compass**
*Lifestyles of the Rich in Spirit**
*Linden's Last Life**
Looking In for Number One
Mr. Everit's Secret
My Father's Voice
The Peace That You Seek
Relax into Wealth
*Rising in Love**
Setting the Seen
Why Your Life Sucks and What You Can Do about It
*Wisdom of the Heart**

*Available from Hay House

Please visit Hay House USA: **www.hayhouse.com**®;
Hay House Australia: **www.hayhouse.com.au**; Hay House UK:
www.hayhouse.co.uk; Hay House South Africa: **www.hayhouse.co.za**;
Hay House India: **www.hayhouse.co.in**

A Daily Dose
of
SANITY

A Five-Minute Soul Recharge
for Every Day of the Year

Alan Cohen

HAY HOUSE, INC.
Carlsbad, California • New York City
London • Sydney • Johannesburg
Vancouver • Hong Kong • New Delhi

Published and distributed in the United States by: Hay House, Inc.:
www.hayhouse.com • *Published and distributed in Australia by:* Hay House
Australia Pty. Ltd.: www.hayhouse.com.au • *Published and distributed in the
United Kingdom by:* Hay House UK, Ltd.: www.hayhouse.co.uk • *Published and
distributed in the Republic of South Africa by:* Hay House SA (Pty), Ltd.: www.
hayhouse.co.za • *Distributed in Canada by:* Raincoast: www.raincoast.com •
Published in India by: Hay House Publishers India: www.hayhouse.co.in

Editorial supervision: Jill Kramer • *Project editor:* Alex Freemon
Design: Julie Davison

Library of Congress Cataloging-in-Publication Data

Cohen, Alan.
  A daily dose of sanity : a five-minute soul recharge for every day of the year /
Alan Cohen. -- 1st ed.
    p. cm.
  ISBN 978-1-4019-2588-8
  1. Conduct of life. 2. Life skills. I. Title.
  BJ1581.2.C537 2010
  204'.32--dc22
                              2009015220

ISBN: 978-1-4019-2588-8

15 14 13 12   5 4 3 2
1st edition, February 2010
2nd edition, November 2012

Printed in the United States of America

To Louise L. Hay,
whose life and teachings
have immeasurably blessed me
and many millions.
The world is closer to heaven
for you being here.

Introduction

If you judge the world by newscasts, economic indicators, talk radio, and conversations at the watercooler, it looks pretty insane. People are worried about paying their bills, politicians are being indicted, global warming is raising sea levels, health care is not helping people who need it, education is faltering, and the news is far more depressing than encouraging. If there is one thing we need as individuals and as a world, it is a good dose of sanity.

If you step back and view life on Earth from a higher plateau, however, you will come to several significant insights:

1. There is nothing new about weirdness in the world. Practically every epoch has been colored by fear, mistrust, and dissension.

2. Somehow we always seem to figure things out, move ahead, and parlay our challenges into assets.

3. There is a small group of people who refuse to be ruled by fear; who infuse vision, passion, and a sense of hope and confidence into the world; and who help it progress by holding a broader awareness than that of the masses.

If you would like to be one of those who maintain a clear mind and open heart while others do not, this book will give you inspiration, insight, and tools to do so. And if you have no aspiration to be a world-change agent, but simply wish to keep your head on straight and find a sense of inner peace to carry you through your day, all the better. The messages that follow will show you that you are far bigger than the news, and you have the power to live the life you choose regardless of what others say or do.

Every day your life is renewed upon awakening, and you have an opportunity to head in a new direction. Starting your day with a positive, empowering thought can make a huge difference in all that follows. The passages in this book will uplift you and help you make wise decisions at the crossroads you face during your day. If you read the message before you get into your activities, your day will surely go better. And if you read it at another hour, you will find refreshment, respite, and energy to carry on and make the latter part of your day effective and enjoyable.

Each entry contains a theme, a quotation highlighting the theme, a real-life story or parable illustrating a practical lesson, a question for you to consider, and an affirmation. The entries do not seek to provide you with answers as much as they point you to find your own. Ultimately, the mastery of your life lies in your own hands. As you take these messages in and use them, you will own them and their benefits for the rest of your life.

The principles of *A Daily Dose of Sanity* are spiritually based. They acknowledge the presence of a Higher Power behind and beyond the appearances of daily life. Call this power God, Source, Great Spirit, Life Force, Pure Love, Universal Intelligence, Well-being, the Tao, or any other name you like—it is the same. If you are uncomfortable with any term you find here, feel free to substitute your own, or just pass by it until you come upon language more to your liking. We do not need to get hung up on words; the essence of the message is far more important.

This book is not associated with any particular religion, organization, or spiritual path. It is offered to everyone in any religion or no religion, group member or solo flier, who wants to grow, make more sense of his or her life, and be happier and more successful.

All of the stories you will read are true, except for several parables passed down through a long oral tradition, which may not be literally true but represent life principles based in truth. The true-life anecdotes occurred to me personally or to someone in my firsthand experience. To honor the privacy of some of the individuals, I have changed names or identifying details.

When outer times seem dark, inner light shines the brightest. If you are experiencing a difficulty, these principles will bring you relief, healing, and a significant positive shift toward the happiness and success you seek and deserve. If you are already doing well, these messages will take you to an even better place. If that happens, or any portion thereof, I will take delight in knowing that my efforts are founded in a sanity that heals.

— *Alan Cohen*

What a Difference a Degree Makes

We have it in our power to begin the world over again.
— Thomas Paine

As you set out on a journey, the direction in which you are pointed at its outset makes a huge difference as to where and when you arrive at your destination. If you alter your course by one degree when you begin, where you end up could be changed by a hundred or a thousand miles.

So it is when you begin a new year. Be clear on where you want to go and you will get there far more rapidly and efficiently than if you harbor mixed intentions or take actions out of alignment with your true choices.

When touch-typing on a keyboard, the first step is to position your right index finger on the letter *J*. From that point, your other fingers are aligned with the keys they are intended to press. Once your fingers are on the right keys, you can type for an entire session without having to look at the keyboard again.

If you place your starting finger on the wrong key, all of your other fingers are out of position, and nothing you type will make sense. The word *hello* will be printed as "jr::p," and *love* will come out as ":pbr." Start at the right place and everything that follows will be coherent.

Take a few moments today to decide where you really want to go this year. Decide what material goals you wish to achieve, but even more important, decide which inner experience you would like to enjoy. You may wish for peace, joy, self-honoring, harmony in your relationships, or a general sense of flow in all you do. When you are clear on what you want to experience, then think, write, or speak your intention. When your statement resonates within, you know you have your finger on the *J*.

You *can* have the kind of year you choose. This can be the best year of your life. A focused moment of thought today can make a difference of many miles when you reach your destination.

What would be the best thing that could happen to you this year?
How would you most like to feel?

I claim my heart's desire, and I choose my direction. I will attain my chosen goal.

First-Class Expectations

Whatever you expect, with confidence,
becomes your own self-fulfilling prophecy.

— Brian Tracy

One day when I arrived at the airport in a city where I was to present a seminar, I told my program sponsor that on my flight I had been given a free upgrade to first class. "Oh, I get upgrades all the time on many different airlines," she responded with a light laugh. "I don't even ask. They just put me up front."

"Why is that?" I had to ask.

"I think it has to do with the fact that my dad was vice president of TWA," she explained. "As a little girl, I traveled with him a lot, and the airline always gave us first class. Now it just seems natural."

My sponsor's account demonstrates how powerfully our subconscious beliefs affect the results we generate. The image and experience of flying first class was embedded deep in her psyche. Although she did not think about it consciously, her expectation created a consistent outcome. The personnel who gave her the upgraded tickets had little idea they were agents of a system far broader than the airlines.

You can tell what you believe by what you are getting. If life is treating you well, somewhere in your mind you expect it. If life is treating you badly, somewhere in your mind you expect it. You receive as much or as little as you expect.

To improve the results you are getting, begin by upgrading your beliefs and expectations. Deeply recognize your sense of worth. Do you know that you merit kindness, respect, enjoyable surroundings, financial rewards, and success? If so, people and situations will reflect your belief.

The script of your life is etched in your mind, and the people you encounter are actors in the movie you have written. No matter what scenes have been played, this year—beginning with this day—you have the power to rewrite the story. Expect your good to find you . . . and it will.

What better conditions would you like to enjoy in your life?
Do you know you are worthy of having them?

 I expect good to come to me, and it does.

86,400 Big Ones

Each day comes bearing its own gifts. Untie the ribbons.
— Attributed to Ruth Ann Schabacker

If I were to tell you I would give you a gift of 86,400 big ones and ask you how you would spend them, what would your answer be? A down payment on your dream home? The new hybrid car you have been fantasizing about? The vacation of a lifetime with your family?

Most people would answer in terms of 86,400 dollars. But the big ones I am referring to are not dollars—they are *moments*. That is the number of seconds, or moments, in a day. Every day you are given a gift of 86,400 precious moments to spend as you wish. What you do with them determines the quality of your life.

While many people are careful about how they budget their money, they are not so careful about how they budget their time. More precisely, they are not careful about what they do with their minds and feelings during their time. You may budget your time to get everything done; but if you are stressed, fearful, resistant, or upset while you are getting these things done, you have not budgeted your time well. Take care to spend your thoughts well and you will spend your time well.

The wonderful thing about your gift of 86,400 big ones is that the gift is renewed every morning. No matter whether you spent yesterday's gift well or squandered it, each morning you have a bright new package on your table. If you made poor choices yesterday, you can make better ones today. In fact, if yesterday's poor choices have moved you to make better choices today, they have served you well.

Your 86,400 big ones include your sleep time as well. Before you go to sleep, focus on appreciative, fulfilling thoughts, and positive energy will pervade your rest. Then when you awaken, you will have received interest on the 86,400 big ones you invested wisely.

How might you better appreciate each moment
of your day and make the best use of it?

I make the most of the opportunities
that each sacred moment offers me.

Greatness Among Us

*We must not measure greatness from the
mansion down, but from the manger up.*

— Jesse Jackson

As thousands of commuters rushed through a metro station in Washington, D.C., on a cold January morning, a musician stood next to a wall playing his violin, the case at his feet open for tips. He played six pieces for 45 minutes. A few people stopped and listened for a moment, then hurried on their way. A few threw some change or a dollar into the case.

The most attentive listener was a three-year-old boy holding his mother's hand. He wanted to stay and listen, but his mom tugged him along. A few other kids tried to stop, but their parents also hurried them away.

After 45 minutes, only a half dozen people had stopped, and the violinist had collected $32. He put his violin away, closed the case, and disappeared into the crowd. No one applauded or thanked him.

Neither did anyone realize that the musician was Joshua Bell, one of the world's greatest violin virtuosos. The pieces he had played were incredibly demanding, and his violin was worth $3.5 million. Days earlier Bell had performed to a sold-out crowd in Boston for tickets priced at over $100.

The unlikely concert was sponsored by *The Washington Post* as a social experiment. Would listeners recognize and appreciate talent and beauty in an unexpected setting? Would they take a pause from their busyness to receive and enjoy it? Would their expectations of meager talent override their grasp of greatness?

Blessed are those who are open to recognizing quality and brilliance. There is talent, beauty, wonder, and inspiration in your midst right now. To pass it by is to miss the gift. To stop and breathe it in is to be the recipient of a miracle.

*Who or what around you might be offering you a majestic gift?
What would it take for you to pause to appreciate and enjoy it?*

**I am open to the gifts before me. I take the time
to receive and magnify the good offered me.**

Bigger Than You Think

Beyond the horizon . . . a great, creative impulse is at work.
— Vance Palmer

In 1949, *Popular Mechanics* printed an article describing a hypothetical computer 50 years down the road. A leading-edge expert at that time predicted, "Computers in the future may weigh no more than 1.5 tons."

The end of the 20th century has come and gone, and laptop computers have shrunk to three pounds—not to mention smaller PDAs and a universe of tiny computers orchestrating household, office, auto, and industrial gadgets. Nanotechnology is becoming a reality, in which computers perform functions at a molecular level!

The computer expert's size and weight prediction had underestimated the miniaturization of the technology by a factor of 600; if you consider PalmPilots, he was off by a factor of 5,000. So even the biggest thinker of that time had no idea how advanced the industry could become!

As you envision your year to come—and all of your life to come—consider that the good that arrives may be 600 or 5,000 times bigger and better than what you can imagine. The vision of your life that you see through the lens of history is always smaller than your true destiny. In the Bible we are told that when Abraham set out on his spiritual journey, God bade him, "Lift up your eyes." Abraham was being guided to let go of his normal limited vision based on past events and see the greater expanse of his possibilities.

Life on the planet is moving faster than ever before, including your evolution. It is very difficult to make prognostications, because we are advancing so rapidly. Your old idea of how far you may progress is being updated at every moment. You may reach your goal far more quickly than you think, and it may come through a route or in a package far different than you expect.

Believe that your future will be even better than you can imagine, and you open the door for it to be so.

*Where on your journey do you think you will
be in six months, a year, or five years?
Are you open to move beyond what you expect?*

**I allow the future to deliver me gifts
even greater than I can imagine.**

An Unlikely Theater

The world is but canvas to our imaginations.

— Henry David Thoreau

As our car waited in line to exit the parking lot at O'Hare Airport in Chicago, I wondered what was taking so long. "Probably some security measure," someone in the car surmised.

When we finally reached the tollbooth, we found a handsome Italian man with thick white hair and sparkling eyes. As he collected our fee and handed us our change, he broke into a rousing song of several verses from the opera *La Traviata*—masterfully sung. The women in the car swooned, we all applauded, the toll collector bowed, and we left the parking lot with a smile.

There are two ways in which you can change your life: you can manipulate external conditions, or you can shift your attitude. Sometimes you can change your environment; *always* you can change your mind. This parking attendant turned a dreary and monotonous tollbooth into a world-class opera house. In the midst of subfreezing temperatures and noxious exhaust fumes, he brightened the day of everyone who passed through his lane.

Sometime later I read a survey in which people were asked, "What do you think would be the most boring job in the world?" The number one answer was "toll collector." So this fellow took the most boring job in the world and made it absolutely inspiring. In his own way, he has achieved spiritual mastery.

No job or situation is too dreary or oppressive to keep you from making it into something pleasant—or even exciting. All you need is some creativity, the recognition that you deserve to enjoy whatever you are doing, and the refusal to be bored. Perhaps one day you will exit O'Hare and have your own command performance.

How can you take what you have and make what you want?

**I find creative ways to keep my
life stimulating and exciting. I do
what it takes to keep my joy aflame.**

A Crucial Balance

There's a reason you don't have pictures of your office at home.
— Citibank ad

A Nielsen survey of people in 46 countries revealed that at the top of the list of all New Year's resolutions was: *Strike a better balance between work and play.*

Work/life balance is a huge issue because most people are out of balance and longing to find it. Fortunately, some companies are recognizing the crucial relationship between health and success. The Marriott corporation, for example, has launched a huge program to help their employees create a healthier balance between home and office. The company realized that many of the health problems they were paying to correct were related to overwork, stress, and employees' lack of skill in making beneficial life choices. So their investment in their employees' well-being is ultimately an investment in the company.

Work is valuable and healthy as long as you know how to stop. When your job encroaches on your marriage, family, friendships, and physical wellness, you have stepped over the line. No job or level of success is worth the cost of your joy, health, relationships, or life. Work is supposed to *enhance* your life, not be a substitute for it.

When visiting Japan, I have observed that people in that country would benefit greatly from better work/life balance. The Japanese work too much and do not know how to stop. Several times I have stood on my Tokyo hotel balcony late at night and seen many, many lights on in offices in buildings across the street. A couple of times I have yelled into the night, "Go home already!"

It may be time for you to go home already—not just literally, but spiritually. Give your life the love and attention it deserves . . . and your work will surely prosper, along with your soul.

What could you do to create a healthier and happier balance between work, home, and play?

**I keep my work in perspective.
I place my happiness, health,
relationships, and joy above all else.**

The War Is Over

You have to wake up a virgin each morning.

— Jean-Louis Barrault

On January 8, 1815, Americans fought the Battle of New Orleans, the last major battle of the War of 1812. Under the command of General Andrew Jackson, an American army defeated British forces attempting to take control of New Orleans and the corridor to America's West. The conflict was huge, with more than 7,000 British soldiers up against about half that number of American troops. The British incurred over 2,000 casualties, the Americans a smaller number.

What neither of the warring factions knew, however, was that the war was already over. On December 24, 1814, the Treaty of Ghent had been signed, and peace officially reigned. Yet news of the treaty did not reach New Orleans until February. But the Battle of New Orleans was just as bloody as if the war had been going on.

In like manner, many of us are still fighting battles of wars long over. We pit ourselves against oppressive parents even though we are grown and completely beyond their influence. We try to prove ourselves to a father who is long dead. We are still trying to win the love of the spouse who would not acknowledge us. We try to spite or punish a past partner who abused us.

All of these efforts are as vain as the Battle of New Orleans, which had no purpose and many losses. Like the soldiers who fought valiantly but to no avail, we have not yet gotten news of the peace. We labor under ancient illusions and fight ghosts who defeat us by the reality we afford them. But they are not here.

Friend, the war is over. You need no longer struggle to defeat past enemies. Instead, turn your attention to the moment at hand and the life available to you. Release the demons that pick at your soul and stand in the blessed power of your now.

Who or what are you still fighting that is now long gone?

I release my past and I step wholly, surely, and confidently into the good of now.

Who Lost the Least?

Sometimes I worry about being a success in a mediocre world.

— Lily Tomlin

While visiting Las Vegas to present a program, I tried my hand at gambling in the casino. Meanwhile, I overheard several conversations between other gamblers. "How'd you make out?" one fellow asked another.

"Not so well," the man answered. "I lost about $400."

"Bummer," the first man replied.

Later the same fellow asked a woman, "How was your night?"

"Down $250," she reported.

"Sorry to hear that," he said consolingly.

A few minutes later he asked someone else the same question. "I dropped about $100," the man answered.

"Well, that's pretty good," the first man replied.

I scratched my head as I realized that these people defined winning by how little they lost. They assumed that they would lose, and if they lost a little rather than a lot, they felt successful. While this mentality may make sense in the world of gambling, I assure you that it is *not* sane in the course of a real life.

You cannot define success by how little you lose. The purpose of life is not to minimize your losses, but to maximize your gains. If you have lost a lot, you may become so accustomed to losing that winning seems like a fantasy. But success is not a pipe dream. It is what you are here for.

I am not referring simply to winning money. I am referring to winning joy, love, connection, creativity, and success in your chosen field. If your life is consumed with responding to emergencies, putting out fires, and damage control, consider what it would take for you to feel like you are thriving rather than just surviving. With that vision in mind, make choices from a sense of expansion instead of settling. Then when someone asks you, "How did you make out?" your answer will include a plus, not a minus.

How can you shift your focus from damage control
to expansion, creativity, and celebration?

I am here to win at life, love, and career.
I dwell in the plus column, where I belong.

Why Our Prices Are Higher

Excellence always sells.

— Attributed to Earl Nightingale

I met a man who owned a successful plumbing business. When I asked him what the secret of his success was, he told me to look at his ad in the yellow pages. I found his ad and was surprised to read at the bottom: *"Call to find out why our prices are higher."*

"Okay, I'll play," I told him. "I'm a customer calling to ask, 'Why are your prices higher?'"

He answered with authority, "Our prices are higher because all of our plumbers are highly trained. We show up on time, do the job right, and guarantee our work. We do not cut corners, and we use only the best-quality products. We do not stop until your plumbing problem is completely fixed and you are satisfied with our services."

I was convinced.

It might be said that there are two kinds of consumers: people who are looking for deals and people who are looking for quality. This is not to say that you should not negotiate for the best deal or that you should pay more than you need to for a product or service. But there is often a relationship between the investment you make and the returns you get. If you try to skimp on your investment, you will likely skimp on your returns.

This principle is as important to the service you offer as it is to the service you receive. If you spend a lot of time trying to keep your prices down, you may compromise the quality of your offering and lose business you might have gained if you gave 100 percent. So instilling more quality in your offering will likely result in larger profits over time.

The Law of Attraction governs all business deals: people who respect quality find each other, and people who are looking for bargains find each other. Bargains are cool when they are valid, but not when they undermine quality. That's why the plumber's prices are higher.

When making a purchase or offering your service,
how might you maintain uncompromising quality?

I give my best and ask for it from others.
I receive quality results for quality investments.

Age and Altitude

None are so old as those who have outlived enthusiasm.

— Attributed to Henry David Thoreau

My friend Kathy has been an elementary-school physical-education teacher for many years. She loves her work and her students, and she is an outstanding educator. Being with little children having fun every day has helped Kathy retain an upbeat, childlike energy in her own life.

Kathy told me about an illuminating exercise in imagination she did with her classes. She instructed the children to lie down, relax, and imagine that they were floating up toward the ceiling, feeling very light and free. She told them to float as high as they could, and then to come back.

When Kathy asked the children where they had floated, she discovered that there was an inverse relationship between the age of the children and how high they floated. The older children in the higher grades floated just above their bodies or to the ceiling at the highest. The younger children floated above the ceiling, beyond the roof of the building, and into the sky.

In a way, the results make sense. Children are born with a sense of unlimited possibilities, and as they are educated and socialized, they gradually adopt more and more limits. Society generally trains children into orderliness, but out of imagination.

If you wish to be as free as possible, you must unlearn the limits you have been taught. You must question what you have been told is possible. You must remember what you knew before you were trained to forget.

Most people lose altitude with age. The responsibilities of adult and family life encroach on their inherent freedom; and by the time they are old, they retain but a spark of what they knew and felt as children. This is not necessary. Some people become more vivacious and outrageous as they advance in years. If you would be one of them, vow not to stop at the ceiling.

What did you know or feel as a little child that you do not know or feel now? How can you recapture the joy you once knew and make it your own again?

I am as young as my mind is free.
I claim the possibilities I once knew.

Stranger Within Our Gates

Be kind. Everyone you meet is fighting a hard battle.
— Attributed to T. H. Thompson

When I checked into the Fort Collins Holiday Inn on a business trip, I found this laminated note on my pillow:

Because this hotel is a human institution to serve people, and not solely a for-profit organization, we strive to ensure you will experience peace and rest while you are here. This message is handed down from an ancient blessing for travelers:

Stranger Within Our Gates

May this room and this hotel be your "second" home. May those you love be near you in thoughts and dreams. Even though we may not get to know you, we hope that you will be comfortable and happy as if you were in your own house.

May the business that brought you our way prosper. May every call you make and every message you receive add to your joy. When you leave, may your journey be safe.

We are all travelers. From birth till death we travel between the eternities. May these days be pleasant for you, profitable for society, helpful for those you meet, and a joy to those who know and love you best.

It does not take a lot to make an ordinary business or personal encounter extraordinary. When you add a touch of care and a dash of humanity to your interactions, marinated with full presence, you create three powerful results: (1) you enjoy your day and your contacts, (2) your friends and customers walk away feeling nourished and served, and (3) your business thrives.

I always look forward to returning to that hotel when I can.

*How can you enrich your work by honoring
the spirit of your clients and colleagues?*

**I take every opportunity to meet and serve
people on the deepest level. My business and I
thrive on a platform of contact and connection.**

How Great Things Get Started

Imagination is everything. It is the preview of life's coming attractions.
— Albert Einstein

Every huge success starts out as a little idea. Never discount or overlook the power of one single idea. It could change your life—and the world.

Take, for example, the night that comedian Mike Myers was driving home listening to his car radio when the song "What the World Needs Now Is Love (Sweet Love)" came on. The song drew Mike's mind back to the wild and wonderful '60s. *Wouldn't it be cool to make a movie that spoofs that era?* he thought. In that moment the blockbuster *Austin Powers* series was born.

Or the day that Larry Page and Sergey Brin sat in a garage and kicked around the idea to create an Internet search engine that would supersede any that already existed. Behold the birth of Google.

Or the night at one of my seminars when I asked the audience, "What would you do if you were not afraid?"

A woman named Marge raised her hand and announced, "I would ask a certain guy to go to a party with me this weekend."

Feeling bold, I handed Marge my cell phone and asked her, "Would you phone him now?"

Marge stepped out of the auditorium and returned a few minutes later with a big smile. "I have a date!" she announced.

A year later I returned to her city and asked a mutual friend if she had seen Marge lately.

"Oh yes," she answered. "I went to her wedding on New Year's Day."

"Who did she marry?" I asked.

"The man she phoned the night of your seminar."

All good things start with one good thought. The one you have been thinking, even briefly, may be the one you and the world have been waiting for.

*What idea that you have overlooked or discounted
may be a seed for a big success? How might you act on it?*

**I value my ideas as kernels of greatness.
I open to huge success and receive it.**

Does It Grow Corn?

The practical effect of a belief is the real test of its soundness.
— Attributed to James Anthony Froude

I know a church where a husband-and-wife team of ministers took turns delivering the weekly sermon each Sunday morning. Over time a pattern became obvious: On the Sundays when the wife, a very eloquent speaker, addressed the congregation, large numbers of people showed up. On the Sundays when the husband spoke, about half the number of congregants attended.

When the couple became aware of the disparity in attendance, they decided that no matter how many people showed up, the fair thing to do was to give each minister an equal opportunity to speak. But as time went on, the number of listeners to the wife increased, and the number of listeners to the husband decreased. Moreover, the church was facing financial challenges.

The couple finally conceded that the universe was giving them a message. It was obvious that the wife was to be the Sunday speaker. Although the husband's ego was bruised, he admitted that he did not really enjoy speaking, and there were other aspects of the ministry he enjoyed more, such as working with the youth group. So the couple divided their responsibilities according to their personal strengths and the maximal results they could each manifest. Soon the Sunday-service attendance shot up every week, the youth-group attendance swelled, and the church stepped into unprecedented financial prosperity.

What seems "fair" on paper is not always effective. We may have our theories about how things should get done, but the real test of effectiveness is results. The Native Americans ask, "Does it grow corn?" In other words, does the seed you are planting generate what you intend to eat? If so, water it. If not, water the seeds that will grow and nurture them.

Are you struggling with a project?
Can you put aside your original idea of how it
should be done, and be open to what will work?

I forsake limiting beliefs in favor of effectiveness.
I base my choices on what creates tangible results.

A Soul Generated by Love

Everybody can be great. Because anybody can serve.
You don't have to have a college degree to serve. . . . You only
need a heart full of grace. A soul generated by love.

— Martin Luther King, Jr.

Today is the birthday of the great spiritual and social leader Martin Luther King, Jr. Although King departed this world at a young age, he left a legacy of wisdom, kindness, and vision that has generated waves of good to uplift our culture for lifetimes to come. King illuminated the potential of every person to be great right where he or she stands.

I used to believe that great people were those who attained fame and fortune. Now I find greatness in humble, honest people playing their roles to perfection on the turf they have chosen.

I know, for example, a marvelous waitress named Lytia who works in a little out-of-the-way restaurant with a steady, modest clientele. The first time my beloved partner, Dee, and I went to the restaurant, Lytia welcomed us as if we were long-lost family and she was entertaining us in her own home. She gave us impeccable, gracious service; touched us; called us "darling"; and told us to watch out for animals when we drove the dark rural road at night. We eventually bought a piece of property in that area, partly because we liked the kindness Lytia represented. Now our friend for years, Lytia offers the same genial welcome to all of her customers. She wants nothing more than to connect with people, and her intention makes her the perfect waitress. She is like an angel in that domain.

Then there was Raymond, the young man in a wheelchair who sat at the edge of his driveway in my town, waving to every car that drove by. I used to love to drive that road to see Raymond in his hooded sweatshirt casting a bright smile to all passersby. He was a saint in his own right.

You, too, can be as great as any statesman or healer by expressing your soul generated by love, right where you are.

Do you believe you need to be somewhere or someone else to be great?
How might you deliver greatness right where you are?

I express my unique gifts right where I am.
Greatness is where I stand.

The "Yes" Behind the "No"

How can I believe your "yes" until I hear your "no"?
— Source unknown

Many people have difficulty saying no because they feel guilty or fear they will hurt another person's feelings. But if you understand why and how to say no, it will be easy for you, and the recipient of your communication will not feel hurt or rejected, but respected and empowered.

The key to a good "no" is to remember and explain the "yes" that the no is making space for. For example, I often receive requests for endorsements for books and CDs by other authors. I used to say yes to all of them, but over time the number of requests grew to be overwhelming. Now my general response is:

> Thanks for sending me your book. I can see you've put your heart and soul into it. I receive so many requests for endorsements that I could not possibly give all of them the time and attention they deserve and still write my own books, travel for presentations, and spend quality time with my family. So I am not doing endorsements at this time. I do wish you lots of success with your book, and I hope it will touch many.

Here are some other examples of "no" making way for "yes":

- "That house is really nice, but I'm looking for one closer to school for my kids."

- "Thanks, but I'd rather not go to the party tonight. I've been very busy lately, and I'm looking forward to some quiet time at home."

- "I'd rather not have a sexual relationship with you, because I'd like to be with someone who is open and available to develop a long-term relationship."

There is a reason for "no." There is something else you would rather do that is more meaningful or effective for you. Trust and speak your truth and you will attract your true "yes." Your friends and associates will not feel rejected, and they will respect you and your decisions.

What is the "yes" behind your "no"? How might you speak it so you meet your needs and honor the recipient of your communication?

I speak "no" with confidence and make room for a more meaningful "yes."

Please Share Some Good News

. . . he was fresh and full of faith that "something would turn up."
— Benjamin Disraeli

My friends Neal and Janie have a great message on their voice mail. Janie invites callers: "Please share some good news at the sound of the beep." I always like hearing her message because it reminds me that we can set up our communication to win.

Do you know anyone who is so upbeat and forward-thinking that you would not dare be negative around that person? All communication is based on frequency. In the *Star Trek* television series, communications officer Lieutenant Uhura would send out a "hailing frequency" when contacting alien ships for the first time. She was essentially saying, *We are on this frequency, and if you want to communicate with us, this is the level at which we invite you to meet us.* A similar principle guides fax machines that send out a "handshake" signal.

You can set the tone for your communications by being clear about where you want to go with people. Perhaps you would like to be the person who is so committed to success and happiness that people who are not success- or happiness-oriented do not dare go there. Even if they do, you do not have to join them.

You do not particularly need a voice-mail message to send a signal to your friends and associates about the kind of communication you value. You simply need to be clear yourself. It is not your words that make or break you; it is your energy.

I would imagine that Neal and Janie get a lot more positive messages than negative ones on their voice mail. Wouldn't *you* like to check your voice mail knowing you will hear mostly things you would like to hear?

How can you set your tone so that people meet
you on the frequency you most value?

I am committed to success, and
I invite success-minded people to join
me for mutual empowerment.

Against My Religion

Never let your sense of morals keep you from doing what is right.

— Isaac Asimov

A Tampa, Florida, woman was arrested for hiring a hit man to rub out her husband. When asked why she did this, she explained, "I wanted to divorce him, but that's against my religion."

People do lots of strange things in the name of religion. More people have been killed in religious wars than any other kind of war over the history of humanity. Something is definitely wrong with this picture.

People often ask me about the relationship between religion and spirituality. I ask them to picture two overlapping circles. One circle represents religion, and the other spirituality. There is a portion of religion that is spiritual, and a portion of spirituality that is religious. You can be spiritual without being religious, and you can be religious without being spiritual. I have attended some religious services that are ecstatic, while others dole out death by boredom. I know deeply spiritual people who go to church, and others who are deeply spiritual and would never set foot there. God does not live in one church more than another. God lives in your heart. If you take your heart to church, there God is. If you take your heart to the woods, there God is.

There comes a time in every person's evolution when he or she must decide the truth for him- or herself. If your truth matches what religion tells you, so be it. If it does not, so be it. You are the one who has to live with yourself, and the closer you live to what you believe to be true, the happier you will be and the greater the contribution you will make to the world.

The Dalai Lama declared, "My religion is kindness." If we all lived that religion, the world would be a very holy place. Then the Tampa lady would not have had to put out a contract on her husband. She could have just loved him or left him, and that would have been okay with God.

Does the truth you know in your heart match
what others have told you the truth is?
Can you trust your inner knowing?

I trust my inner sense of the truth. I am right with God because I am right with myself.

Ducking Punches

Good instincts usually tell you what to do long
before your head has figured it out.

— Attributed to Michael Burke

I saw a film of boxing great Muhammad Ali in a championship match. To illustrate Ali's masterful technique, the film was slowed down to show Ali ducking punches *before* his opponent threw them. Ali's intuition was so attuned to the flow that he knew what was coming before it came, and he stayed one step ahead of his opponent.

A branch of psychology known as *flow* identifies a state of mind "in the zone" in which athletes, artists, and creative people act from intuition and accomplish extraordinary achievements. Jason McElwain was an autistic 17-year-old who wanted to play basketball on the high school team. Because his skills were limited, Jason was allowed to suit up for every game, but he sat on the bench. Finally, during the last game of the season and Jason's career, the coach put him in the game with minutes to go so the teenager would have a moment to remember. And remember it he would—Jason scored an unbelievable 20 points in four minutes—including six 3-point shots from *way out* on the court. Jason's amazing performance earned him national recognition and a meeting with the President of the United States.

Like Ali and McElwain, you, too, have access to the zone and can excel in your chosen field. You probably already experience the zone without knowing it. You may write, play music, dance, paint, or perform auto mechanics in a slightly altered state of consciousness in which time disappears, your mind takes a backseat to the flow, you get things done without trying, and you feel great. In those moments you lose yourself in the task at hand, and everything works perfectly.

Being in the zone is far closer to who you really are and how you were meant to live than anxious trying. When you do what you love and what you're good at, you optimize both happiness and performance and walk through the door of the extraordinary.

What do you do that puts you in the zone?
How can you cultivate being there?

I do what I love and what I am good at.
The universe naturally does great things through me.

A Little Willingness

*We've been warned against offering the people of this
nation false hope. But in the unlikely story that is America,
there has never been anything false about hope.*

— Barack Obama

We all recognize the extraordinary phenomenon of Barack Obama being elected President of the United States. A little-known African American with less than four years' experience in the U.S. Senate, he was a long shot for the highest seat in the country and the world. Yet Obama's vision, character, and desire to serve propelled him far beyond what logic and expectation would dictate.

Just after Obama's election, an interviewer asked him, "During your long campaign, did you have any doubt that you would be elected?" Obama's response was illuminating: "Yes, I had doubts that I *would* be elected. But I did not doubt that I *could* be elected."

A Course in Miracles tells us that all that is required for a miracle is a little willingness. This means that you do not have to believe for sure that something you desire will happen, and you certainly do not have to know *how* it will happen. But you do need a tiny sliver of openness that it *could* happen. That little bit of willingness, the *Course* tells us, is sufficient for the universe to orchestrate a miracle in your favor or that of another.

By contrast, the only reason that miracles do not happen, when they do not, is that our minds are shut airtight against the possibility. We simply know too much and are well fortified with reasons why our good cannot come. In such a case, we are literally our own worst enemy, for in that moment we close the door through which our success could arrive.

Take care that you do not become an expert on your limitations or those of another. Instead, be like a little child whose mind is not sullied by facts and experiences. As Obama stated to a crowd of hundreds of thousands on the evening of his election: "If there is anyone out there who still doubts that . . . all things are possible . . . tonight is your answer."

*What do you want that you believe cannot happen?
Are you open to the possibility that it* might *happen?*

**I am open to good things coming to me.
I offer willingness, and life offers miracles.**

It's Your Baby

Wanting something is not enough. You must hunger for it.

— Les Brown

In a remote region of the Andes, two tribes were feuding. One lived high in the mountains, and the other in the lowlands. One day the highlanders raided the village of the lowlanders and kidnapped a baby. The next day the lowlanders assembled a team to climb the mountain to find and retrieve the child. But they did not know the trails, and they were not skilled at mountain climbing. The search party struggled to make their way up the slope, but after a half day of climbing, they could not ascend anymore. Discouraged and disappointed, they packed their gear to return.

Suddenly, to their amazement, the rescue team saw the baby's mother coming down from the mountain, holding her child in her arms. Baffled, they asked her, "How were you able to scale this steep mountain and rescue your child when *we* were unable to do so?"

She answered, "It wasn't your baby."

Desire and motivation are the precursors of achievement. If you want something enough, you will find a way to do it. If you are not very motivated, you will either not attempt to reach a goal or, if you do make an attempt, your efforts will be halfhearted and you will attain no measurable results.

Do not assess your possibilities on the basis of the beliefs or unsuccessful efforts of people less motivated than you are. Their results are not so much a function of reality, but rather, a product of their beliefs and intentions. Nor do you require their permission to do what you want and need to do. In the story of the mother who retrieved her child, she did not ask the search party's permission or even discuss the project with them. She just knew what she needed to do, and she did it.

You have a "baby" that you love and believe in. It is a dream, goal, or intention that may seem mountain-high. But if you love your baby enough, you will find a way to bring it home.

What goal do you love enough to manifest
no matter what others say or do?

Love and intention drive me
to do what I have to do.

It Would Be My Pleasure

He who wishes to secure the good
of others has already secured his own.

— Confucius

Over the course of many years of traveling, I have stayed in many hotels, from the cheap and uncomfortable to the lavish and luxurious. I have noticed that in some of the budget hotels, staff members are often poorly trained, and if you ask them for a service, they may appear offended that you are bothering them. In the five-star hotels, staff members are trained to be professionals; and they cheerfully, courteously, do their best to make your stay as pleasant as possible.

I recall a restaurant in a world-class Cairo hotel in which I enjoyed particularly cordial service. Whenever I or someone at my table requested something of the waiter, he responded, "It would be my pleasure." Over the course of the evening, he accomplished all that we asked him, while displaying an upbeat and willing attitude.

That waiter inspired me to try to apply the same attitude of service in my work. Sometimes when workshop participants do not follow directions or coaching clients miss their appointment times, I have been tempted to respond impatiently and ask these people to please pay more attention. But then I remember the waiter whose only response was "It would be my pleasure." Holding him as a model, I consider what a five-star response would be, and I try to offer it. That attitude feels a lot better than criticizing or judging a client, and it certainly yields better results.

No one is perfect, and everyone wants to be treated kindly. When dealing with an uninformed or uncooperative customer or client, a deep breath and respectful response can make all the difference in the success of your business. And everyone will have more fun.

How could you upgrade your service or attitude to treat
clients or customers in a royal fashion?

Kindness, respect, and quality are the foundation of my business. I treat all of my clients and customers in a five-star fashion, and my business rewards me likewise.

Creating and Editing

*The intuitive mind is a sacred gift and
the rational mind is a faithful servant.*

— Albert Einstein

As a writer, I notice there are two distinct modes in my creative process. One is an act of creation, in which I get my ideas onto the page in a stream-of-consciousness fashion. In this mode I simply let ideas flow forth without judging, censoring, or editing. This process is similar to the technique of brainstorming in a think-tank session, in which all members of the group toss ideas onto a whiteboard without any discussion as to their feasibility. During the creating session, I know that I will not ultimately use all the ideas I come up with, but in order to get the best ones, I allow all to come through. Some people would call this mode channeling or receiving input from the muse. It is lots of fun and puts me in an altered state of consciousness. Hours may go by during which I have no awareness of time, and when I am done, I have the rough draft of a chapter in my hands.

Then I step away from the computer and return at a later time for the second mode: editing. During this phase, I sift through the material I have brainstormed and sort out the elements I want to keep and the ones I want to discard. I pay more attention to grammar and form, and do lots of cutting and pasting. This is the fine-tuning mode in which I switch from right-brain free flow to left-brain polishing. This phase is not as much fun for me as the creating part because it requires me to sharpen my pencil, get down to nitty-gritty details, and make deletions. But it is also deeply rewarding, since I see the final work come into a clear and comprehensive form.

Ultimate creation requires both the macro- and micro-perspectives in a healthy balance. If you lean too far in one direction without honoring the other, your work will be incomplete. But bring the two together and you have the chemistry of a masterpiece.

*How can you balance your creations by giving full
attention to both the creating and editing modes?*

**My work is masterful as I allow the flow of
big ideas and then pay attention to details.**

There's Music in There

Think you can or think you can't, and either way you'll be correct.
— Attributed to Henry Ford

When I was in high school, I played the saxophone in a rock band. I was just learning the instrument, and I could not get a smooth tone out of my sax. I decided it was simply an inferior learner's model, and I planned to take it back to the store to get it fixed or replaced.

One night our band was playing at a dance when a fellow approached and asked if he could sit in on sax for one song. Sure, I told him. The guy picked up the sax and *wailed!* I could hardly believe it was the same instrument! After the song, he handed the sax back to me, thanked me, and disappeared into the crowd. I just stood there with my jaw hanging open. For a moment I felt embarrassed that he had shown me up. But soon I felt excited, for he showed me a new possibility for myself and the instrument. Eventually I developed a decent tone.

It is tempting to blame our perceived inadequacies on people, things, and conditions outside of us. Many of us could make a long list of reasons why we are not performing as well as we might. Negative programming by our parents, a poor environment, an oppressive religion, bad karma from a past life, a depressed economy, and inferior genes are just a few of the sources to which we attribute our pain or shortcomings. While some of these factors may influence us, none of them can stop us from succeeding or making the most of our lives.

The difference between those who live happy, productive lives and those who do not has little to do with the instrument played. It has a lot to do with how you are playing it. Like the sax player who showed me my instrument's true potential, let the greatness you see in your mind or in your world inspire *you* to play like a master.

On what external conditions might you be tempted to blame your shortcomings? What greatness or happiness might you achieve by accepting the power to create what you want?

I have all the raw materials to live a happy, successful life. I achieve success by using what I have in service of my valued goals.

What to Do When Things Don't Work

I have woven a parachute out of everything broken.

— William Stafford

My buddy and I were driving along a country road when we came upon a car that had broken down. We stopped to offer the driver help, and he asked if we would push the car to get it started. As we did, we realized that he and his girlfriend were terribly drunk. The fellow could barely function, let alone drive. The car did not start, but simply rolled down the hill out of our sight. I asked my friend if he thought we should follow them, but he replied, "Maybe it's better for everyone if they can't get the car going."

Indeed it was. If they had been able to drive, they would have been in great danger and endangered the people in cars around them. The fact that the car was not working was a blessing. Its breakdown was a form of protection to them and others.

Often when things are not working, there is a message, lesson, or gift associated with the situation. At such a moment you may be tempted to rant or try to force a quick fix. But sometimes you may do better to step back and ask, "What would be my wisest action here?" There is something else more vital for you to do in that moment. Or getting what you think you want or need right then might not be in your best interest, and you are being protected. Or there is a more favorable option you do not see that will show up later. Or there is better timing that would unfold to your advantage if you waited.

Things are supposed to work, and when they do not, there is usually a reason. If you can discover this reason and see how it works in your favor, you may feel humbled by the brilliance of the universe taking impeccable care of you.

Is something currently not working in your life?
What might be the message, lesson, or blessing behind the circumstances?

**I let all situations teach me how to live well,
and guide me to my perfect path and place.**

A Reason to Get Up

*When people go to work, they shouldn't have
to leave their hearts at home.*

— Attributed to Betty Bender

I saw an inspiring video documenting the renovation of the Cathedral of Saint Paul in Saint Paul, Minnesota. Face-lifting the 100-year-old landmark was a massive undertaking, requiring huge funding and the skill of many artisans who could reinvent archaic and custom building materials and systems.

One of the craftspeople who re-formed the gold leaf on the cathedral's dome reported that he loved the project so much that "every Sunday night I start to get excited about getting back to the work on Monday morning." What a sharp contrast to the many people who start to get depressed Sunday night because they have to return to a distasteful job on Monday morning!

It may be time to rethink your purpose and experience at work. Do you feel like the craftsman who cannot wait to get back up on the scaffold, or do you pull the pillow over your head and hit the snooze button for just ten more blessed minutes before you have to face an unpleasant day?

The craftsman's attitude is far more natural and aligned with the true purpose of a vocation than taking sanctuary in the snooze button. *You are supposed to enjoy your career!* A true profession inspires you to want to get up in the morning. You do not have to be a CEO or movie star; I know chambermaids and shuttle-van drivers who take as much delight in their work as the gold-leaf artisan. The career game is about gaining energy from what you do all day, not losing it.

Take some quiet time with yourself to assess how much joy you feel in your vocation and what it would take to move to the next level of fulfillment. In some cases you may do well to change jobs, and in other situations you may find ways to reinvent what you do right where you are so you can enjoy it more. In any event, do not settle for boredom or frustration. You owe it to yourself—and the world—to do whatever it takes to want to get up Monday morning.

What would it take for you to really enjoy your career?

**I choose work on the basis of joy and passion.
My job inspires and empowers me.**

It? Or Not It?

Now all that is left is for you to become yourself.
— Johann Wolfgang von Goethe

An army sergeant was assigned a newly inducted private to work as his office assistant. On the first day of the job, the private went around picking up random pieces of paper in the office. He lifted one from the sergeant's desk, read it, and said, "This is not it!" He took a sheet out of the wastebasket and declared, "This is not it!" Then he opened up the filing cabinet, produced a document, reviewed it, and announced, "This is not it!" This went on all morning.

Finally the sergeant decided that his new assistant did not have his burritos rolled very tightly and sent him to the army psychologist, who studied the private's behavior. Finally he told the young man, "I agree with the sergeant. I don't believe you are fit for duty." With that, the psychologist signed a paper, handed it to the man, and told him, "This is your discharge order."

The private read the paper and exclaimed, *"This is it!"*

All of life's experiences are either "it" or "not it." They either match you, your spirit, and your intentions . . . or they do not. Every conversation, relationship, job, spiritual path, sexual experience, journey you take, and choice you make either brings you greater life or depletes your energy. Your role is to notice where your life force lives, or does not, and tell the truth about it.

Many people ask me, "How can I find my passion in life?" I tell them that before you can live your life purpose, you have to be honest about where your passion flows on a day-to-day basis. What would you like to eat? Whom would you prefer to be with? What parts of your job would you keep, and what parts would you change? What places do you feel most drawn to? How do you like to make love? Answering these questions, and those like them, all point you toward your "it."

Use every moment to decide what is "it" and what is "not it" for you. Be honest about where your life force lives, and everything you do will guide you in the direction of home.

What aspects of your life are "it"? What aspects are "not it"?
What can you do to maximize the "it's" and minimize the "not it's"?

I tell the truth about where my passion lives.
Every day I become more myself.

How Supportive Is Your Support Group?

Do I want the problem or do I want the answer?
— *A Course in Miracles*

Support groups have become very popular over the last few decades. There are groups for alcoholics; addicts; families of addicts; gamblers; sexaholics; codependents; people with various diseases; abuse victims; homeschoolers; mothers against drunk drivers; and many, many more. All of these groups have noble intentions to heal, and they all help many. The world is a better place for their service. Yet some support groups are more effective than others, and here is why:

If you are participating in a support group, the most important question to ask yourself is: "When I leave the group, do I feel lighter, stronger, and freer of the problem I came to heal; or do I feel more immersed in it?" Many support groups are so focused on the issue they seek to solve that the dilemma gets far more attention than its resolution. You can go over the same story so many times from so many angles that you intensify the drama and stay stuck in it. Such a group is not really supportive, since participants walk out no freer than when they walked in—and maybe even more steeped in the situation they sought to escape.

Other groups hold a stronger intention for participants to rise above their problem. Discussions are founded on progress, practical solutions, and success stories. Strengths are reinforced more than weaknesses, and pain is regarded not as a natural state, but as a temporary experience to be grown beyond. Truly effective support groups also include a graduation mechanism. Participants are encouraged to surpass the need for the group rather than stay in it forever.

All support groups support, but some help more than others. True support leads to freedom.

*How can you help yourself and others get free
of your issue rather than reinforce it?*

**I identify with strength and help others
by supporting their power and wholeness.**

Happy and Hungry

The grand essentials of happiness are:
something to do, something to love, and something to hope for.

— Attributed to Allan K. Chalmers

You have probably been exposed to two worldviews that seem to contradict each other. One states that you have everything you need to be happy right where you are, and the spiritual path calls you to find joy and satisfaction with the gifts you have been given. The other posits that life is about expansion, growth, and reaching beyond limits, so you should never settle for less than what you really want, and you should keep going for your grandest dream.

I struggled with these questions until I saw Anthony Robbins interviewed by Larry King. Anthony suggested that a healthy attitude to life is *happy and hungry.* You can find well-being and wholeness right where you stand, but at the same time you can enjoy the adventure of reaching for more. These worldviews do not contradict, but actually *complement* each other.

Consider, for example, your home, career, or relationship. You can have a nice house, a good job, and a rewarding partnership. Yet part of you may be yearning for more. Do not berate yourself for being selfish, but celebrate your natural aspiration for expansion. This does not mean you need to get a new home, job, or mate. But you may need to look for ways to improve on what you have and create your richer desired scenario.

A rewarding life embodies a healthy balance between happy and hungry. If you become too complacent with what is, you may get stuck in a rut, and life may give you a kick in the rear to keep you moving along. If you are constantly seeking more and better without appreciating and honoring what you have, some event may force you to just be where you are, with what you have, so you can learn to celebrate the good at hand.

Life is a balancing act that can be fun if you let it. Appreciation and striving both have a vital role in your well-being and success. Be at peace with what you have and what you want.

What are you happy with? What are you hungry for?

I appreciate what I have as I joyfully reach for more.

How to Pay Your Credit-Card Bill

There are so many men who can figure costs,
and so few who can measure values.

— Source unknown

I used to groan and grumble when my credit-card bill arrived, since it was usually more than I expected or wanted to pay. When I entered each item into my computer for my accounting records, I would mentally gripe about the amount of the charge, and when I was done, I felt frazzled.

One day I decided to see if I could somehow enjoy the process more, or at least not fight it. So I decided to use the procedure as a venue to practice appreciation. Instead of begrudging each of the vendors, I thanked them. Until that time, I had been negatively focusing on the money I was being charged, forgetting about the goods or services I received in exchange for the money.

To reverse my attitude, I thought, *Thank you, mortgage company, for helping me live in my home. . . . Thank you, grocery store, for good food. . . . Thank you, airline, for flying me across the ocean,* and so on. After a half dozen items, I felt pretty good, and by the time I completed all of my entries, I felt great. Simple appreciation turned the entire process around.

It is easy to fall into focusing on what goes out while forgetting what comes in. In all commerce there is an exchange of goods or services. I help you in one way as you help me in another. Money is an energy exchange that works only as it keeps flowing. Some flows out and some flows in. If you focus on what is going out by complaining about it, your attention to the outflow will increase it. If you focus on what is coming in by appreciating it, you will increase the *in*flow.

Appreciation empowers not just money transactions, but *all* interactions. Gratitude is one of the greatest meditations of a lifetime, the great multiplier. Be grateful for all the good in your life and your good will only increase, along with your happiness.

What exchange could you be more grateful for?
How can you express your appreciation?

I am grateful for all the good in my life. I bless
all of my financial transactions and appreciate those
who provide me with valuable goods and services.

Forward, Not Back

The only true statement you can make
about the past is that it is not here.

— A Course in Miracles

Ever since the Internet became popular, I have received messages from many old friends, people I never thought I would see or hear from again. I have been contacted by friends from every stage of my education, from grammar school through graduate school. I sit in awe and gratitude for the power of this technology to help people connect.

I was happy to hear from my old friends, with whom I shared many wonderful memories. In some cases we got together for dinner, and in others we just caught up a bit on the telephone or through a few e-mails. I thought we might rekindle our connection, hang out together again, and renew our friendship. Most of the time that did not happen at all; we simply said hello and then went on with our lives without much further contact.

At first I felt a bit sad that these friends would simply remain a part of my past. Yet as I thought about it, I realized that these people and I had taken new and different paths in our lives, and those paths were not parallel enough to sustain a connection at this point. Then I came to a sense of peace as I simply appreciated the good times we had, as well as their reaching out to say hello now.

I further realized that I have new friends in my life who share my current path. These individuals match me by virtue of the Law of Attraction, and it is right and appropriate for me to walk side by side with them now. So it is all perfect: great old friends then, great new friends now.

You cannot resurrect the past unless what you seek to resurrect has purpose in your current life. Sometimes that happens, but it is rare. It is wiser to celebrate the good that happened then, and the good that is here now. Trust the Law of Attraction to match you with the right people and events, and you will always be in your right place in the presence of love.

Are you trying to bring the past into the present?
Can you appreciate and release what was to make way for what is?

I celebrate my past, I release it, and
I open to enjoy the good in my life now.

The Diamond in the Mud

*The life I touch for good or ill will touch another life,
and that in turn another, until who knows where the trembling
stops or in what far place my touch will be felt.*

— Frederick Buechner

I had to telephone my mortgage company to ask them to correct an accounting error they had made. When I had called the company in the past, I had encountered difficulty getting an agent on the line, rather than a computer voice. But I was determined to speak to a real person, and finally I was connected to a cordial agent named Todd. He cheerfully rectified the error and told me the record would be changed before the next day, when he was scheduled to fly to Beijing.

"What's in Beijing?" I asked Todd.

"I'm going to see my girlfriend," he explained. "We've been dating on the Internet for a year, and I'm going meet her in person for the first time."

Well, that was inspiring to hear. I told Todd that I love relationship stories and that in my work I support people to have rewarding relationships. "Say, Todd," I remarked, "would you phone me when you get home and let me know how it went?"

"I'd be happy to," he told me, and I wished him a great trip.

When I got off the phone, I felt really good. Not just because the accounting error had been handled—that turned out to be the lesser element of the call. The greater piece was that I enjoyed an authentic conversation with a real person. I sincerely wanted Todd to succeed in his relationship, and I felt like I had made a friend.

Two weeks later I received a call from Todd from his home. "How did your visit go?" I asked.

"Even better than I expected," he reported. "I asked her to marry me, and she accepted!"

While we may see business or the mundane activities of daily life as drudgery, there is always a jewel to be plucked from the mud. That jewel has something to do with connection, support, and passion. Today, look for opportunities to connect, and you may end up mining diamonds.

What activities do you resist?
How can you use them to deepen your connections?

I make my day with the connections I cultivate.
I give the acknowledgment we all crave and deserve.

Your Passion meter

What you are stands over you the while, and thunders
so that I cannot hear what you say to the contrary.

— Ralph Waldo Emerson

A South Korean cell-phone company has announced a new voice-analysis program to enable its customers to evaluate their own sincerity and that of their lovers. After the caller speaks into the phone, a meter indicates his or her level of passion. The phone will also detect passion (or lack thereof) on the part of the person on the other end.

While the passion meter is an innovative piece of technology, I would like to suggest that *you already own one*. At every moment, your inner being is sending you signals letting you know whether or not your words and actions are aligned with your truth and aliveness and if others are speaking sincerely.

If, after you have thought a thought, spoken a word, or performed an action, you feel more energized, happy, and whole, you know that what you have just said or done is aligned with your well-being. If you feel deadened, bored, bugged, or empty, your line of thinking or action is off course with your life path. The same principle applies when listening to others. If you feel present and enlivened, you have just heard a truth that empowers you. If not, the speaker's statement or presence is not a match to your truth or path.

One night while I was having a telephone conversation with a friend at a late hour, I felt tired and began to say good night. Somehow the conversation turned toward both of us sharing our honest feelings about our friendship and our lives. This led to such a stimulating discussion that we continued on for three more hours! I went to bed at 2 A.M., feeling far more awake and alert than I had at 11 P.M. My passion meter was working perfectly, and so will yours if you receive its helpful messages.

What are you doing that enlivens you? What are you doing
that deadens you? What can you do to maximize what brings you
life and minimize or eliminate what diminishes your life force?

I trust my sense of aliveness to guide me
to my right place and right relationships.

Essence Over Form

Rather than love, than money, than fame, give me truth.
— Henry David Thoreau

Israel Kamakawiwo'ole, affectionately known as "IZ" or "Bruddah IZ," was a Hawaiian singer of now-legendary stature. A gentle giant weighing in at over 500 pounds, he had a voice as sweet as a bird's, and his heart was rich with aloha. Beloved by the Hawaiian people and all who heard him sing, he was catapulted to superstar status after his passing at age 38. His second release, *Facing Future,* was the first album by a Hawaiian musician to be certified platinum. Ten years after his death, his posthumously released album *N Dis Life* remained on the Billboard chart for a remarkable 39 weeks.

You have probably heard IZ's famous ukulele-accompanied rendition of "Somewhere Over the Rainbow," featured in many movies and television commercials. It is playful, innocent, and touching. Most listeners do not realize that IZ sang the lyrics in a mixed-up way. He reversed the verses, substituted his own lyrics, and the words do not rhyme. If you have heard the song, you may be surprised to learn this, and if you go back and listen, you will notice.

The interesting thing about IZ's lyrical errors is that *nobody cares.* He is not technically correct, but he is spiritually perfect. People do not listen to the song to analyze it; they listen to enjoy it. Because IZ came from the heart, the song is immensely rewarding. He missed the form but captured the essence.

If you are struggling to get a project technically perfect, you may be missing the point. While execution is important, the energy or spirit behind the project is even more important. If you are a singer, artist, dancer, speaker, or writer, your audience responds more to the sincerity and energy you imbue in your presentation than the letter of the law. I am not suggesting that you overlook or deny the importance of form; I am simply suggesting that you give the spirit of your offering your highest priority.

Are you struggling to get a project or presentation perfect?
How would you approach it differently if you
let realness and joy be the key elements?

I put my heart in my offerings,
and I let spirit deliver the gift.

Your True Colors

A friend is someone who sees through you and still enjoys the view.
— Wilma Askinas

When I studied with my mentor Hilda Charlton, I did a great deal of introspection. One day my self-analysis led me to confront all the ways in which I was living inauthentically. I felt overcome by a sense of hypocrisy, and I decided to make a public confession.

At Hilda's next class meeting, I took the microphone and stood before a group of about 300 students. I announced, "I am a phony. I do many selfish things out of accord with my true values, and I harbor negative thoughts and judgments I do not admit. I have pain in my relationships, I try to look better than I think I am, and I lie about certain things." I listed some more of my shortcomings, gave the microphone back to Hilda, and sat down.

Hilda followed up my confession with this comment: "Yes, Alan is a phony—but not in the way he thinks he is. He thinks he is his problems and human frailties, while he is really a perfect and beloved child of God."

Well, that took the wind out of my guilt sails. That night became a turning point in my life. That night I began to identify with my deeper spiritual self rather than my problematic surface self.

The popular song "True Colors" teaches the same lesson. Most of the time when we say, "She showed her true colors," we infer that this person's nasty or evil real self came forth. Nothing could be further from the truth. The ego, or dark side of us, is simply a complex of behaviors at a very shallow level of our being. Below and behind your errors lives a brilliant, radiant being—your soul. So the next time you refer to someone's true colors, remember that their truest colors are golden and white light—the divine essence at the very core of their being, just like yours.

What negative traits have you learned to associate yourself with? Can you recognize that your real self is an expression of pure, perfect spirit?

I accept my true identity as a whole, divine being. I celebrate who I am.

Real Psychology

There is no psychiatrist in the world like a puppy licking your face.
— Attributed to B. Williams

If you have ever studied psychology or been the client of a psychologist, you have learned that psychology is based on the study and understanding of the mind. When I visited Greece, however, I learned the true origin of psychology. My Greek friend explained to me that the word *psyche*, from which *psychology* is derived, literally means "soul." So true psychology, then, is founded on your connection with your soul.

Modern psychology, for many people, has become a head trip. It is based almost entirely on thinking, talking, and analyzing. A deeper level of psychology values feelings as a route to self-understanding and healing. The deepest level of psychology—real psychology—honors the spiritual element of a human being and respects the individual as multidimensional. When you recognize the element of spirit—or the inner being behind the thinking mind, the body, and the emotions—you gain leverage for true growth and awakening.

After graduating as a psychology major in college, I began to put the principles I had learned into practice in the field. I enjoyed moderately satisfying results, but I still felt that something was missing. Then I discovered what some call the spiritual path, and I felt deeply fulfilled as I viewed the purpose of my life and work in a higher, broader context than simply the human mind. I took a leap of faith and began to incorporate my spiritual understanding into my psychology work. Immediately I began to get richer results, and my clients moved rapidly toward healing and growth. My career took on a whole new dimension, and my work became extremely successful.

The most effective psychologists are those who treat not just the mind, but who reach the soul.

*How might you enhance your understanding of yourself
and your life by seeing from a spiritual perspective?*

**I recognize myself as a spiritual being, and
that awareness empowers everything I do.**

Your Practice Novel

Trust thyself: Every heart vibrates to that iron string.

— Ralph Waldo Emerson

Bryce Courtenay is the author of the hugely popular novel *The Power of One,* based on his life during the period of apartheid in South Africa. He is also a compelling and entertaining speaker, brimming with passion and outrageous humor.

In describing his beginnings as an author, Bryce recounts: "When I wrote *The Power of One,* I thought I was writing my practice novel. I thought that one day I might become a writer, and I would use *The Power of One* to ramp up to real writing." When Bryce showed his "practice novel" to a friend, his friend told him he thought it was really good and he should show it to an agent. "I couldn't understand why I would show a practice novel to an agent, but my friend talked me into it." The agent loved the book, pitched it to a publisher who agreed, and before long *The Power of One* became an international bestseller. "I couldn't imagine why all these people were buying my practice novel!" Bryce confesses.

Obviously *The Power of One* was far more than a practice novel. The author just did not realize it. Likewise, you may have a book, painting, song, house plan, business, service project, or relationship that you think is just for practice, but which bears far more value and potential than you see. Sometimes creative people are the most critical of their own work and in the least advantageous position to recognize the potential of their visions. Yet if the creations have value, others will recognize their possibilities and the projects will take off in ways befitting their true worth.

Never underestimate the power of one of *your* creations. The universe may be birthing a world-class gift through you.

What project or creation of yours may have more potential than you realize? How would you be approaching it differently if you knew greatness resided within it?

I open to wisdom, beauty, and service flowing through my creative impulses. Spirit blesses the world through me and brings success through my offerings.

Under Your Nose

If we could see the miracle of a single flower clearly,
our whole life would change.

— Attributed to Buddha

One of my coaching clients lost his job and spent a long time out of work. As months went on, he became concerned about sustaining himself in the absence of his former income. Then one day he casually mentioned that he had received a large check as an inheritance from the passing of a distant relative.

"Why didn't you tell me this in capital letters and an exclamation point?" I asked him. "Can't you see that you are being provided for by a Higher Power?"

You might have an idea of how your sustenance is supposed to arrive, but it might be coming to you, or available to you, or here already. Your good might be right under your nose, waiting for you to notice it.

My friend Zach quit his corporate job and was developing a career doing multimedia presentations. He was making some money, but not as much as he wanted. When he told me he was worried about his money running out, he mentioned that he had some cash in the bank from past investments. I asked him, "How much do you have in your savings?"

"About a million dollars," he answered.

Indeed!

As we discussed Zach's lifestyle, he reasoned that he could probably live for the rest of his life on his savings alone. His problem was not lack of dollars, but lack of faith. He felt insecure about money, and probably no amount of it would make him feel secure. We looked at ways to deepen his awareness of his assets, and he felt better.

You, too, may have gifts and blessings under your nose. Sometimes they are material, and sometimes spiritual—but they are there if you are willing to see them.

What good might be at your door, or right where you stand?

I am loved, cared for, and supported in visible
and invisible ways. Providence is with me.

Where Extremes Meet

I do not like that man. I must get to know him better.
— Attributed to Abraham Lincoln

On the television series *Wife Swap,* each week two women from very different families trade places to see how they fare in an environment foreign to their customs. The lifestyle polarities the wives represent are always stunning and often hilarious: a hippie mom and a materialistic yuppie; a ballerina and a Cajun swamp explorer; and my favorite, a hard-core tattooed weight lifter and a fairy princess who conducts tea parties for neighborhood girls.

The process for all the wife swaps is similar: both mothers freak out in alien environments; they try to convert the other family and meet with resistance and conflict; the host families resent the intruder; and finally both the mothers and families start to relax and learn from each other. *Wife Swap* is both entertaining and enlightening.

As I considered the Law of Attraction, which posits that like attracts like, I wondered how these so very different wives and families attracted each other. Then I realized that each wife and family harbored resistance to the opposite lifestyle. They were not just happy with their own lifestyle; they believed the opposite lifestyle was wrong, and they were proving it so by living the other extreme. This is why opposites attract when they do: there is resistance and a lesson to be learned. The Law of Attraction serves to create balance. It brings together people who do not like or understand each other so they can soften, open, learn, grow, and achieve harmony with their inner and outer worlds.

If you hold a judgment or resistance against a person or ideology, the universe will often move you to face that individual or belief. While you may fight the experience, consider the encounter a gift and an opportunity. When you can love your enemy of opposites, your world will not be destroyed. It will expand.

Who or what do you resist?
How might you benefit from getting to know this person or concept?

I welcome experiences that help me grow.
I discover value in all people and ideologies.

Love Will Have Its Way

Love burns across the infinitude.

— Attributed to Meriel Stelliger

At a seminar, a young Jewish woman named Miriam tearfully reported that she was in love with a Muslim man, but her father forbade her to see him. This created a painful quandary for her, since she could not reconcile her love for this man with her desire to honor her father's wishes. Miriam wrestled with this issue for a long time and a year later returned to another seminar, still distraught.

A few months afterward, Miriam mailed me a copy of a letter she had written to her father. The letter was a masterful communication of honesty, clarity, compassion, and purpose. She told her father that she loved him very much and appreciated all that he was to her, but she had to follow her heart and be with the man she loved. As I read Miriam's letter, I realized that she had finally claimed her power and stood up for her truth.

A year later I received a photo of Miriam's wedding; and a year after that, a photo of her newborn child. Meanwhile, Miriam's father came around to support her.

A Course in Miracles tells us: "A happy outcome to all things is sure." That may seem hard to believe if you fear that if you do not control every detail of your life, and perhaps the lives of others, things will fall apart. But when you trust the process, things usually fall together. That may seem unlikely if you are in the middle of a difficulty, yet easier to recognize over time.

Miriam's journey to marriage and motherhood, including healing her father issues, was perfect for her spiritual growth. She had to dig deep into her heart to discover her truth and live it, and she ended up with what she wanted. Love will have its way.

Do you fear that you will not get what you really want?
If you knew that a happy outcome to all things is sure,
what would you be doing differently?

I trust myself, my heart, and my path.
Everything good comes to me as I am true to myself.

Where to Find Your Other Half

Before you can know your soul mate, you must know your soul.

— Source unknown

An earthworm popped his head out of the soil one day and discovered a gorgeous worm a few inches away from him. He was so taken with her beauty that he asked her, "Will you marry me?"

"I can't marry you, silly," she replied.

"Why not?" he retorted, bewildered.

"I'm already the other half of you," she answered.

Many of us have searched for our soul mates, only to meet with disappointment and frustration. Feeling lonely, broken, or empty, we believe that if we can just find the right person, we will be complete. So we set out on a long and confusing journey to find "the One."

I have good news and bad news: The bad news is that there is no one out there who can complete you. The good news is that you are *already* complete.

If you enter a relationship to offset loneliness, the relationship will only intensify your loneliness. If you bring wholeness to your relationship, you will feel even more whole. So it is not relationships that make or break you—it is why you get into them and how you approach them.

Now for more good news: All of your relationships, even those that do not seem to work or do not last a lifetime, bring you closer to coming home to yourself. All of your trials and errors have guided you to recognize the beauty, wisdom, and love you already own, and to claim your power and peace right where you stand rather than letting your happiness depend on another.

So do fall in love, marry, and create a relationship that makes your heart sing. Just remember that it is your own self you are searching for. As you find it, all of your adventures in loving will make perfect sense.

How can you find in yourself what you are seeking from another?

As I fall in love with myself, I am in the perfect position to create a loving relationship.

The End of Guilt

*The truth in you remains as radiant as a star,
as pure as light, as innocent as love itself.*
— *A Course in Miracles*

Not long after September 11, 2001, I flew to Australia to present some seminars. In the aftermath of the terrorist attacks, American airports were heavily militarized. Soldiers with machine guns walked the terminals, and security measures were prolonged and extreme.

During my trip, I had to take a flight from Sydney to Melbourne; and in light of my experience leaving the States, I anticipated stringent security procedures. Yet the scene at the Sydney airport was much more relaxed. When I presented my ticket to get my boarding pass, I was not even asked for any identification. On my way to the gate, I had to pass through one metal detector, I did not have to remove any garments, no one searched me, and no one seemed concerned about me. My security screening took seconds, and soon I was on my way to the gate.

After such a light screening, I had the strangest feeling that I was getting away with something. In an odd way, I felt guilty. That made no sense, since I had done nothing wrong. Yet something in me felt like this was all too easy.

Then I realized that all guilt is learned. Like all air travelers at that time, I had been the subject of suspicion and regarded as a potential threat. That experience had become ingrained to the point that I accepted it as the norm. When I was treated as innocent and trustworthy, that experience felt foreign. Guilt and innocence had been reversed in my mind and experience.

No child is born feeling guilty. Children recognize their original innocence until adults teach them that there is something wrong with them and they have to earn or prove their worth. Nothing could be further from the truth.

If you feel guilty, try to trace back where you were trained in guilt, and try to remember who you were before you learned to feel guilty. Then you will remember who you really are.

*What do you feel guilty about? Can you
see how your feelings of guilt are learned?*

**I am innocent. Freedom is my
natural state. I claim it now.**

The High Road

*I always plucked a thistle and planted a flower
when I thought a flower would grow.*

— Abraham Lincoln

Imagine a man walking along a city street when a flowerpot falls from an apartment windowsill above and crashes at his feet, narrowly missing him. At this point the man has a choice of four paths of thought and action he might follow:

1. **The path of retaliation.** He could dash up the stairs, find the owner of the potted plant, and punch him or chew him out.

2. **The victim path.** He could see the experience as confirmation that life is dangerous, and things that could hurt him await at every turn. Then he might go home and hide or wear a hard hat for the rest of his life.

3. **The stoic path.** He could decide, *Well, I guess it was my karma for the flowerpot to miss me,* and just keep walking.

4. **The high road.** He could go to the flower shop on the corner, buy another potted plant, knock on the door of the owner of the plant that fell, and tell that person, "You may not know that you lost your plant. I thought you might like a replacement."

Obviously the high road is the one that will bear the sweetest fruit for everyone concerned. At this moment you stand at a crossroads in your life where you must choose which path you will take. Keep thinking about your options until you discover what your high road is.

*What choice now stands before you?
What would your high road be?*

**I choose the path that brings the deepest
reward to me and everyone concerned.**

Kissing and Driving

Be an all-out, not a hold-out.

— Norman Vincent Peale

I saw a Valentine's Day card that showed a couple kissing while the man was at the steering wheel of a moving car. The message said: *If you can kiss while driving safely, you are not giving the kiss the attention it deserves.*

Anything that is worth doing is worth doing with a whole heart. And mind. And body.

We undermine our joy and effectiveness when we approach our activities with divided intentions. Our body is doing one thing while our heart is elsewhere. We go to jobs we would rather not be at, we sleep with people we do not care for, and we go to parties we find boring or repulsive. Meanwhile, we love people we do not express our love for, we deny ourselves food we really enjoy, we sense truths we do not act on, and we do not follow our creative impulses.

I have a very simple definition of integrity: you are in integrity when what you are doing on the outside matches who you are on the inside. I respect people who live unapologetically. I know people who do things I do not agree with or would not do myself, but I honor them for being 100 percent who they are. They are in integrity.

The secret of success is to *be total.* If you are going to do something, really do it. Do not second-guess yourself, let guilt undermine your joy, or wonder if you should be somewhere else. Either do it with a whole heart or do not do it. *Be total.*

In the film *City Slickers,* a group of bumbling dudes meets a seasoned cowboy named Curly. Whenever the group is about to set out on an adventure, Curly raises one index finger to the sky. At first the dudes are stumped by his enigmatic sign. Then, after weathering trials and overcoming challenges, they realize what he means: Do one thing at a time. And do it fully.

Kissing is good. Driving is good. Both are even better when you do them one at a time.

What are you doing that is halfhearted?
How could you shift your attitude or actions so you are fully present?

I show up for life with a whole heart.
I am total in mind, body, and spirit.

Why Peacocks Honk

. . . where there is a call for love,
you must give it because of what you are.

— *A Course in Miracles*

One morning a pair of peacocks showed up at the back door of our home in the country and adopted us. We have no idea where they came from. The two were a mated pair, a peacock and peahen, inseparable, never more than a few feet apart. The two were quiet, curious, and gorgeous to behold, so we decided to let them stay. We named them Romeo and Juliet.

One afternoon I walked out onto the patio and startled Juliet. Flustered, she flew to the other side of the house, out of Romeo's sight. Suddenly she began to honk loudly, and Romeo responded. Separated, the two tried to locate each other by calling to each other repeatedly. The honking went on for about 20 minutes until Juliet found her way around the back of the house and they had a glorious reunion.

Those two birds taught me a supreme lesson about love and relationships. Their natural state, I realized, was togetherness, or intimacy. When they got separated, they were out of their natural state, and the honking began. They were each calling to their beloved.

When you feel lonely, separate, or outside of love, your pain and what you do in pain is your honk to be reunited with your beloved. Likewise for those who honk to you. What we do from joy *expresses* love; what we do from fear *calls for* love.

We have all been separated from God, love, and ourselves. In truth, we are not separate at all, but we feel that way. Our searching and reaching out is our honking to be reunited. We just want to go home, and until we get there, we will keep honking.

If you have a valentine, honk to get a little closer. If you do not have one, honk to get a little closer to yourself. The wonderful thing about love is that you can shine it at anyone or anything, including yourself. When you do, the honks stop and the great reunion begins.

How might you reinterpret your awkward or unkind acts
as a call for love? How might you reinterpret the awkward
or unkind acts of others as a call for love?

I recognize the call for love,
and I give love as the answer.

The Great Sifter

Tend to your own vibrational balance, and let
the Law of Attraction *do the rest of the work.*

— Abraham-Hicks

My friend Ralph is a firefighter by profession, and an avid metaphysician and practitioner of positive thinking. Some might even call him a sensitive New Age guy.

But sensitive New Age guys are not the norm in firehouses, so Ralph has generally kept his spiritual interests under his hat. When the video *The Secret* became popular, Ralph was excited about it and decided to take the risk of showing the DVD to the crew at the firehouse. As the film rolled on to an audience of about a dozen guys, one by one they stood and left the room. By the end of the movie, only one fireman was left watching.

After the movie showing, the remaining man approached Ralph and told him, "That was really great! I would like to learn more about these ideas!" Delighted to have someone to talk to, Ralph and the other fellow engaged in a long and rewarding discussion. They became friends, and the two men and their wives went on to enjoy social connections with lots of mutual support.

The Law of Attraction is the great sifter. When you make a statement with your words, energy, or actions, as Ralph did by showing *The Secret* at the firehouse, you send a hailing frequency out into the universe. Those whose minds, hearts, and evolution are attuned to the same frequency will hear your signal, respond, and connect with you. Those not attuned to the signal will get up and leave. Everyone is in their right place by virtue of the frequency they are generating and picking up.

If you are worried about finding your right mate, friends, home, business partner, doctor, or spiritual path, you do not need to worry at all. Just put out a clear statement and signal of what you want, and those who match it will recognize it and show up. Sometimes many will answer your call, and sometimes there may be one lone person sitting when the lights go on. But that connection will be extraordinarily satisfying, thanks to the great sifter.

How might you succeed more by clarifying your
signal and sending it out with confidence?

I make a clear statement of who I am and
what I want. The universe hears and responds.

Secret Destinations

All journeys have secret destinations of which the traveler is unaware.
— Martin Buber

As I work with coaching clients, I observe that the surface issue or question the client addresses is usually a manifestation of a core issue the client is unaware of. In most coaching calls, I find myself saying, "You think this is about _____, while it is really about _____."

For example, "You think this is about losing your job, but it is really about you getting clear on what you want to do and finding the courage to do it." Or "You think this is about your father criticizing you, but it is really about you recognizing your self-worth." Or "You think this is about losing weight to attract the right partner, but it is really about your willingness to let someone into your heart and life."

At that point the client usually has an "Aha!" and recognizes the deeper issue that needs to be addressed. When they face and master the issue at the source level of their experience, all of the problems that seem separate and unrelated are revealed to be connected, and their answers fall into place without a lot of angst or struggle.

In working with clients over time, I find that the same core issues keep showing up in different forms. In January it is a dispute with the landlord, in February a grievance with the boss, and in March a fight with the ex over child custody. Behind all of these upsets is the belief *"There are people out there who have power over me, and I cannot get what I want because they are stronger than I am."* This belief in smallness is unjustified; and as I work with the client to reclaim his or her power, the landlord, boss, and ex become less intimidating and more negotiable.

Take some time today to look below the surface of your upsets. You are mining for gold, for the answers to your problems are within you now.

*What bothers you that may be a manifestation of a deeper issue?
How might you handle your upset from the inside out
rather than trying to change the external world?*

**I improve my life by finding the truth within me.
As I heal my mind, outer situations resolve easily.**

The Genius of Ignorance

Blessed are those who are so naïve that
they do not know what they cannot do.

— Alan Cohen

When George Dantzig arrived late to his U.C. Berkeley math class, he found two problems on the board. He copied them into his notebook, worked on them as homework, solved them, and turned in his answers at the next class. The following morning George's professor pounded on his door, asking George how he had solved the problems. "What's the big deal?" asked Dantzig. "They were just homework."

"The big deal is that they were *not* just homework," the professor explained. "These were classically unsolvable mathematics problems, and you have solved them."

Sometimes you are better off not knowing what you cannot do. Knowledge is power, but too much knowledge can blind you to truth. Experts are useful only if their understanding opens doors to greater wisdom. If they are too sure what cannot be done, their expertise is a millstone.

Is there something you would like to do that others tell you cannot be done? Just because it has not been done, or the experts do not see a way it can be done, does not mean you cannot do it. Everything that has been done, at one time had never been done. So if you set out on an impossible project, you are in good company.

Trust your inner guidance more than external opinions. The voice of genius has never been a respecter of professional authority.

What idea, vision, or dream of yours seems impossible?
Would you be willing to do it anyway?

I trust my inner knowing. With the
help of a Higher Power, I can do
what others call impossible.

What an Old Dog You Are

Creative minds have always been known
to survive any kind of bad training.
— Anna Freud, Sigmund Freud's daughter

In his classic text *The Power of Your Subconscious Mind,* Dr. Joseph Murphy recounts the story of a horse that would shy away from a particular tree stump in a road that he passed regularly. His owner removed the stump, burned it, and repaired the road so that it was clean and flat. Yet, for many years, when the horse and rider reached the former location of the stump, the horse would continue to avoid it.

Like that horse, many of us feel impeded by obstacles no longer present. We carry with us ghost images from our past that haunt us. Perhaps you were subject to childhood sexual abuse, overbearing parents, a punitive religion, a disease, or a sense of insurmountable poverty. In later years, you may have had a bad marriage, experienced unfair treatment by an employer, or felt downtrodden by a government. Now, when you encounter a situation similar to the past painful one, you might generalize and expect the same results.

The only place the past lives is in your mind, and that is the only place it can be healed. If your past burdens you, you do not have to go back and fix it. You just have to change how you look at it and recognize that you are bigger than it.

When a student challenged Abraham (of Abraham-Hicks), "You can't teach an old dog new tricks," Abraham answered, "You have no idea what an old dog you are." Your identity as a spiritual being runs far deeper and stronger than any programming or imprinting you have received.

While the horse had a hard time getting beyond the invisible stump, you have the capacity to rise above your history. Core programming can be overcome. In fact, growing beyond past traumas or fears empowers you in ways far stronger than if the event had not happened. The past cannot impede you because you are far greater than it is.

What past event seems to hold you back? How can you grow
beyond that memory by realizing that you are bigger than it?

I am greater and stronger than anything that
has happened to me. I create my life now as
I would choose, and forge a new destiny.

When Judgment Falls Short

Out beyond ideas of wrongdoing and rightdoing
there is a field. I'll meet you there.
— Rumi (translated by Coleman Barks)

On the first morning of a weekend seminar, I opened the program with a group dance exercise that required the participants to coordinate steps with each other. One young woman arrived late and had a hard time getting into the moves. Although I repeated the directions several times, she was confused and kept missing the steps. After a while I grew impatient and admonished her to pay attention. I figured that her mind was elsewhere or the program was not important to her. Finally she got into the rhythm, and the dance went on.

Later that morning the young lady explained that she was tired because she had worked all night. In order to attend the retreat, she had to take the graveyard shift at the supermarket. She had attended our Friday-night program, worked all night, and then came to the Saturday-morning session. My judgment about her was completely off base. She wanted to be present so much that she had sacrificed a night's sleep to attend. So much for my assumption!

You have heard many times that you should not judge. This is so because you *cannot* judge. Like my mistaken assumption about the seminar attendee's impaired participation, you have no idea why others are doing something you do not like, and you cannot possibly know how a particular action fits into the grand design of their lives or yours. You just have to trust that life is unfolding as it should.

The Bible tells us that Adam and Eve were banished from paradise when they ate from the Tree of Knowledge. Until that time, they lived in innocent perception, trusting God and life. Then they dipped into egoistic perception of good and evil, and suddenly they were out of heaven. The same thing happens to us every time we think we know how things should go. Today might be the perfect day to drop judgment and make your way back to the garden.

Are you tempted to judge another or yourself?
Can you suspend judgment and
let things be exactly as they are?

I see through the eyes of innocence,
and my heart is at peace.

Ariadne's Thread

We came to believe that a power greater
than ourselves could restore us to sanity.

— Alcoholics Anonymous tenet

In Greek mythology, the King of Crete sent Theseus through the labyrinth to kill or be killed by the dreaded monster Minotaur. The king's daughter, Ariadne, fell in love with Theseus and, to ensure his safety, gave him a thread, which he let unwind on his way into the labyrinth. After he slew the Minotaur, he traced the thread out of the labyrinth to safety.

Ariadne's thread is a metaphor for our connection to a Higher Power. We have all left our spiritual home to wander in a labyrinthine world rife with man-eating monsters. The Minotaur represents anything in the outer or inner world that might devour us, such as a distressing relationship, a bad economy, pollution, disease, unkind people, and on and on. If we are disconnected from our Higher Power, we are vulnerable indeed, easy lunch for every beast that lurks in the darkness.

Yet at any moment we can take hold of the rope that will guide us back to well-being. Aligning with the Great Spirit brings us solace, freedom from pain, and escape from the seeming predators on the other side of the door. When we remember that the power of God sustains us, we can conquer anything. When we lose hold of that thread, we are toast.

In truth, you can never lose Ariadne's thread, because it is within you and it is who you really are. Yet you can lose your awareness of it, and in that moment, all seems bleak or lost. But it is not. With even a slight shift of attention, you open up your conduit to the Divine. This is why it is important to have a spiritual practice that connects you to your Higher Power and engage in it daily. Prayer, meditation, yoga, music, journaling, nature, dance, and group meetings dedicated to spiritual growth are all forms of Ariadne's thread in your life.

No Minotaur is more powerful than you, because Someone Who loves you very much has given you a route back home. Whenever you need it, take hold of Ariadne's thread and follow it to your safe haven.

What helps you remember your connection to your Higher Power?

Universal Love watches over me
and guides me to home.

A Reason, a Season, a Lifetime

Nature gives to every time and season some beauties of its own.
— Charles Dickens

Do you ever wonder why some people are in your life for a moment, others for a while, and others for a lifetime? Every relationship, from the briefest encounter to the longest and richest marriage, has a purpose in your life. Each person who shares your path, for an instant or forever, plays a role in the great adventure of your awakening.

Some people cross your path for a quick lesson or blessing, and move on. You might have a short interchange with someone you meet while walking your dog, go out with on a date, or sit next to at a lecture. These people may say a brief phrase that answers a question, or point you toward a book you need to read or to someone you need to meet. Like angels (the word *angel* means "messenger"), they have delivered their gift, and then they get on with their lives, as you do yours.

Others walk with you for a season. You may be friends in school, work together at a job, or be joined in a relationship or marriage for a number of years. Their purpose runs deeper than a brief encounter, as you share connections and lessons appropriate for the phase of life you are in. When the purpose of that link is complete, or you grow in a new direction, they leave your life and you are on to the next season.

A small number walk with you for a lifetime. They may be family members, a mate, or a dear friend whom you stay in touch with over many seasons. These people share a blessed, deep connection with you. Your life purposes match at a core level, and you are, in a broad sense, soul mates.

Sometimes reason, season, or lifetime partners serve you by challenging you. Their role is no less important, sometimes even more so. They help you grow in ways that you would not have grown if things were easier. They, too, are your friends.

Bless all who walk with you for any length of time. They are messengers of God.

Who are—or have been—your reason, season, or lifetime friends? What has been their purpose?

I appreciate and celebrate all who share my path and purpose, for any length of time.

Well-Adjusted to What?

Men who never get carried away should be.
— Attributed to Malcolm Forbes

You probably know someone who has struggled with alcoholism, drug addiction, or mental illness. Perhaps you have been through such an experience yourself. A teacher once explained to me that such people are deeply feeling spiritual individuals. They are so sensitive, in fact, that the harshness of the world is unbearable to them, so they seek an avenue of escape. Alcohol, drugs, or insanity provides a temporary means of relief, but obviously does not solve the problem and only complicates it.

Many people in 12-step programs such as Alcoholics Anonymous and Narcotics Anonymous have attended my workshops, and I have found most of them to be very strong and caring people. Once they came to terms with their addiction and took steps to overcome it, they became powerful individuals and inspiring teachers. They have a great deal of faith, honesty, and compassion—traits that ennoble any human being.

From a spiritual viewpoint, normality is not terribly desirable. John Mason wrote a book called *An Enemy Called Average,* and the title says it all. Most people regard being well-adjusted as a sign of mental health, but the question is, "Well-adjusted to what?" If you are well-adjusted to working every day at a job you dislike, arguing with family, friends, and colleagues, and collecting stuff so people will admire you, then you are well-adjusted to the world but maladjusted to joy. In such a case, you would do well to run like hell from normal.

People who cannot function in this world may not be aberrations, but inspirations. The trick is to find relief from the insanity most people call sanity without using a crutch like liquor or drugs to escape. If you must escape, escape into peace.

Are you well-adjusted? Would you prefer not to be?
Can you find a healthy way to escape from everyday insanity?

I am a spiritual being going through a material experience. I find value in my unique identity, regardless of who the world tells me I should be.

When It's Ready

Time is money, but timing is everything.

— Alan Cohen

After J. K. Rowling produced several books in the wildly popular *Harry Potter* series, she became the best-selling author in history. As you might expect, her publisher was anxious to receive the next manuscript in the series, which represented hundreds of millions of dollars of income. When Ms. Rowling's editor put pressure on her to submit it, she told him, "You will have the book when it's ready."

Everything has a right timing. If you pluck a fruit from a tree before it is ripe, it is hard, tasteless, and inedible. If you wait too long, it is putrid and poisonous. True artists and geniuses are sensitive to right timing as an essential element of their creations. They refuse to rush, and when the spirit moves them, they refuse to wait. There is a window through which the wind of greatness blows, and those who trust it as their guide move at its behest.

If someone pressures you to complete a project before it is ready, make a purchase you are not sure about, sign a contract you cannot live with, or have sex or marry before you feel you can do so with a whole heart, you must find the confidence to speak your truth. Do not worry about turning down someone who is motivated by greed, fear, or impatience; instead, regard your decision as an act of respect for your inner knowing. If and when the time is right, you will know it, and everything will fall into place far more easily than if you tried to force it when immature.

By the same token, do not let an action that is ripe languish beyond its fertile moment. If you sense that something is right for you, say yes without allowing your critical mind to intercede and delay a healthy step. If a project has sat on your desk for a long time, and one day you feel moved to dig in to it, your inner guidance is alerting you for a good reason.

Time is the fourth dimension of life. Creative geniuses who generate successful works in three dimensions make brilliant use of the fourth.

What are you ripe and ready to do?
What would do better to wait?

I trust my instincts on timing.
I listen to my inner guidance and
 act at the perfect moment.

A Real Teacher

The true teacher defends his pupils against his own
personal influence. . . . He guides their eyes from himself
to the spirit that quickens him. He will have no disciple.

— Amos Bronson Alcott

My partner, Dee, took an art class at a community adult school. During the first two classes, the teacher laid out some objects for the students to draw, such as a basket of fruit or tennis shoes. At the end of the second class, Dee told the teacher she would like to draw her own object next week.

"What would you like to draw?" he asked her.

"I would like to draw a picture of the cosmos, including stars and galaxies, with bold colors, like the telescope photos I've seen."

"Very well, then," the teacher replied. "Bring in one of those photos next week, and your project will be to draw it." Then he turned to the class and announced, "We have a new assignment for next week, everyone. Bring an object you want to draw, and we'll turn you loose to draw what excites you."

The students were thrilled with this assignment. That teacher was a real teacher. He recognized his role to call forth his students' potential, utilizing their passion and interests. He was not fixed on imposing his ideas or style. He was there to bring out the best in his class, and if drawing their chosen objects would serve that intention, that was the route to take.

The word *education* derives from the Latin *educare,* which means "to draw forth from within." Unfortunately, much of our educational system has fallen into the regime of "pound in from without." Real education recognizes that each student embodies genius unique to him- or herself, and the goal of learning is to set inner greatness free.

If you are a teacher or student, do not be attached to the form of the lesson, but stay true to its spirit. When you empower students to be who they are rather than trying to stuff them into a mold, they will move the world with their talent, and the journey of teaching and learning will not be a chore, but a delight.

How might you support yourself and others
to move with the flow of creativity?

I discover where passion and genius live, and
I let them guide me and others to success.

The Fifth Condition

Love can attain what the intellect cannot fathom.

— Meher Baba

Meher Baba was a beloved mystic who taught and lived the doctrine of love. He spent most of his life illuminating divine principles and helping people. Baba popularized the phrase "Don't worry, be happy," and modeled compassion and kindness wherever he went.

Meher Baba established a retreat center in Myrtle Beach, South Carolina, which I have visited and found to be a haven of tranquility. Before Baba chose the site, he dispatched two devotees to find an appropriate location. Baba gave his scouts five conditions for the retreat site: (1) It had to have a pleasant climate, (2) virgin soil, (3) ample fresh water, and (4) land that could be self-sustaining to a large number of people. The last condition, which I consider the most significant, was: (5) the property had to be acquired by the hand of love.

Before long a benefactor graciously donated the Myrtle Beach property, where it continues to refresh the souls of many sojourners.

Baba's fifth condition might be a powerful one to apply in all business projects. While it is exciting to make a deal that will net us money or advance our career, if the process is fraught with contention, upset, fear, stress, struggle, or disharmony, it is not worth it. You have probably had the experience of fighting your way to a deal and then not enjoying the result, or laboring with ongoing struggle. By contrast, you have probably had the experience of working with someone you liked and with whom you harmonized, and enjoyed the process immensely. Then everything that followed mirrored that positive energy. That deal embraced the fifth condition.

Try to apply the fifth condition to your purchases, business transactions, relationships, diet, and daily interactions. If love is the dominant theme, it is good. If love is absent, it is unacceptable. Then you will understand "Don't worry, be happy," from the inside out.

*Are you struggling to force a result with someone
you do not like or who is uncooperative?
What would you be doing differently if love and harmony
were a requirement for your dealings?*

**Kindness and care are the foundations
of my transactions. My real business is love.**

How to Get What You Really Want

I laugh when I hear that the fish in water is thirsty.

— Kabir (translated by Robert Bly)

When a coaching client asked me to help her manifest her dream home, I asked her to describe it to me.

"My dream home is a house on a hill, surrounded by tall trees, with an ocean view."

"Great," I replied. "What feeling does the house give you?"

"Security," she answered.

"And the hill?"

"The hill would show me perspective."

"Excellent. And the trees?"

"Trees represent growth."

"Now, your ocean view?" I pursued.

"The ocean attunes me to expansiveness."

"Perfect," I replied. "So you are really looking for security, perspective, growth, and expansiveness."

"That's right!" She lit up.

"And if you could feel all of those experiences, would you really need the house?"

"I guess it wouldn't matter."

I was not trying to talk my client out of her house; rather, I was trying to show her a shortcut to what she really wanted. Because we are spiritual beings at our core, it is the *feeling* of a particular experience that we crave. If my client got her house but not the feelings she sought, she would have remained unsatisfied. If she got the feelings, no matter whether the house came or not, she would have been deeply satisfied.

Be aware of the experience you seek and cultivate it right where you stand. Then you will be amazed at the manifestations that follow.

What do you want? What do you really want?
What do you really, really want?

I immerse myself in the feeling of my heart's desire, and the manifestations come naturally.

Cost and Payoff

Success is a self-fulfilling prophecy.

— H.H. Swami Tejomayananda

No one does anything unless he or she believes that the payoff equals or exceeds the cost. Everyone perceives some reward for what he or she is doing. If your value system does not agree with the sense of reward that others are receiving for their behavior, you may judge or criticize them, scratch your head at their motivation, or just decide they are nuts. But they are not suffering as much as you would be if you did the same thing, for they are finding their own version of the cheese at the end of their maze.

You may not understand, for example, why your mother enjoys complaining so much. Perhaps she is bitter and negative and finds fault with everyone and everything. "I couldn't live in her head for more than ten seconds," you tell your spouse. But your life experiences and worldview are not hers. She is receiving a payoff for her complaining. Perhaps she is getting attention or sympathy; or she has a familiar sense of identity as a victim; or she has friends who agree with her, and this makes her feel part of a club. In a way that you cannot understand, it works for her. She is happier than you know.

Meanwhile, your mom thinks you are weird for reading self-help books, going to seminars, and constantly finding the positive aspects of life. Just as you cannot comprehend why she would complain, she cannot comprehend why you do not. She tells her friends, "I couldn't live in my kid's head for more than ten seconds." *Touché!*

You can lighten up about other people who do things that you would not. They are on a different path than you are at the moment, on their own rung of evolution. They must master their life lessons from where they stand, not where *you* stand. Pay attention to your joy and next step, and allow them to figure out their next step. Help them where you can, but love them as they are.

Whose behavior do you not understand?
What payoff might they be receiving that they enjoy?

I allow others to enjoy, learn, and grow
through their experiences as I allow myself
to enjoy, learn, and grow through mine.

More Shall Be Given

For whosoever hath, to him shall be given, and he shall
have more abundance: but whosoever hath not, from
him shall be taken away even that he hath.

— Matthew 13:12

At first glance, the above statement seems unjust. You would think that God would give more to those who are without and take away from those who have a lot. That would be only fair, right? Yet the Law of Attraction is quite fair and will work for you if you use it properly.

My friend Hannah is very successful in business and quite prosperous. She enjoys making win-win deals, likes to earn money, and spends it on fun things, as well as on helping others. One day Hannah learned that Oprah Winfrey was offering a seminar for a group of about 20 deserving women, most of whom would be selected on the basis of an essay they submitted on "Why I Need a Spa Retreat with Oprah." Another handful would be chosen by a lottery. Hannah very much wanted a trip with Oprah, but knew she could not with integrity say she "needed" one, so she submitted her name to the lottery. A month later she received a phone call from Oprah's office informing her that she had won. Hannah attended the seminar, she received immense benefit from it, and the program was later shown on *Oprah*.

If you did not understand the Law of Attraction, you might argue, "That's not fair! Why should someone already successful win that lottery? The prize should go to someone who needs it!"

The answer lies in *why* Hannah is prosperous and successful. She has an abundance consciousness. She thinks and lives success, so more success finds her. People who think and live lack and failure get more lack and failure. They are exercising the power of their thoughts against themselves, while they could use that same creative power to help themselves just as readily.

No matter how long you have attracted failure, you can turn your pattern around by redirecting your energy. The Law of Attraction is at your disposal with every thought you generate. Point your mind and energy in the direction of what you want more of, for it shall surely be given.

If you knew that you would be given more of
what you focus on, what would you focus on?

God has given me the power
to create my life. I use it well.

Leap Day

No one should have to dance backwards all of their lives.
— Jill Ruckelshaus

Today is popularly regarded as the day of the year when women are allowed to propose marriage to men. The tradition began, legend tells us, when St. Bridget convinced St. Patrick that it was unfair for marriage to be proposed only by men, and women should have the chance.

Yet there is a metaphysical principle behind women's freedom to propose—on any day of the year—that we can use today's tradition to shine light on.

For thousands of years, our world has been weighted toward the power of men, or masculine energy. In ancient cultures, the goddess, or feminine aspect of divinity, was honored; but that has not been the case for a long time. (The time of prehistoric matriarchy is postulated in the book *When God Was a Woman* by Merlin Stone. Even the title is stimulating to consider!)

More recent millennia have placed women's power in a subordinate position. As explained by psychologist Patricia Sun, the right side of the body, the masculine side, is "right"; and the left side, the feminine, is "what's left." In the French language, "left" is *gauche,* and in Italian it is *sinistra*. One clear example of the patriarchal fear of the feminine and need to dominate it is the number of women who were burned as witches for expressing their intuitive or psychic gifts.

We are blessed, now, to live at a time when much of that is changing and the world is on its way to greater balance by respecting the feminine principle. Over the past 90 years, women have won the right to vote in nearly all developed nations, some countries have elected women as leaders, and the U.S. came close to nominating a female presidential candidate in 2008. The wildly popular book *The Da Vinci Code* has also brought to light a long mystical tradition of the divine feminine.

We all—both men and women—have masculine and feminine aspects within us. We have a rational, goal-oriented self and a fluent, intuitive self. Today let us allow our feminine side to come forth and invite the masculine to join with it in equal, mutually supportive power.

*How could you bring your masculine and feminine
energies into greater harmony and balance?*

**I accept and honor the feminine aspect of my life.
I join it with the masculine for success.**

What It's All About

[The human] race . . . has unquestionably
one really effective weapon—laughter.

— Mark Twain

One of my favorite cartoons portrays a classic spiritual pilgrim clawing his way to the top of a Himalayan mountain. There he finds a bearded guru sitting with his eyes closed in deep meditation. At the guru's feet the aspirant reads a simple sign: THE HOKEY POKEY. The stunned seeker raises his eyebrows and asks, "That's what it's all about?"

Enlightened beings have one characteristic in common: a light heart. The sages I have met have a great sense of humor, and they play with life. They realize that their true identity is grander than the troubles the world poses, and they teach by joy more than words. I would think twice about studying spirituality with anyone who is terribly serious. They may have intellectual wisdom, but if they are not childlike, there is a piece of truth they have yet to unearth.

My friend Ernie and I were granted an audience with the revered Swami Satchidananda, an enlightened yogi who introduced spiritual practices to America beginning in the 1960s. He opened the legendary Woodstock music festival with his invocation. My friend and I were ushered to the swami's inner chamber and seated before him. At that time, Ernie liked to make deep, heartfelt eye contact with people and he did his best to peer into the swami's soul. After a few minutes of our conversation, the swami turned to me and asked, "Why is this guy staring at me?" We all broke into laughter, including the swami's very serious disciples. It was truly a moment of enlightenment!

Psychologists tell us that one of the surest signs of mental illness is the absence of affect, or loss of the ability to laugh. Sincere laughter is a sign of the presence of love. When you can laugh about something you once took very seriously, you know you are healed.

Perhaps the Hokey Pokey cartoon is closer to the truth than most of us would imagine.

What could you lighten up about? How much better
would your life be if you played more?

I value play as much as work. I do not
need to take myself or my life so seriously.
I let joy lift me above fear.

The Big Picture

What is true by lamplight is not always true by sunlight.
— Joseph Joubert

My friend Patrice went to her health club and found a new exercise room—totally dark, with a full-length movie playing on a large screen. She decided it might be fun to watch the film while she worked out, and she stepped onto an exercise machine. The movie was so engrossing that Patrice watched it for an hour and a half while exercising. "By the time I was done, I didn't even realize I had worked out for all that time!" she remarked.

Patrice's experience demonstrates the power we gain when we stay focused on the Big Picture of our lives. If you think about how hard you are exercising, you will resist as you go, you will tire quickly, the benefits you gain will be minimal, and you will likely not return soon. If, however, you let yourself be inspired or entertained by a bigger movie than the current small one, your experience will not be a struggle, you will have fun as you go, and you will reap huge rewards.

At any given moment you have a Big Picture and a little picture going simultaneously. Both are important and require your attention. Most people get so involved in the little picture that they lose sight of the Big Picture. Then they become tense, irritable, and ineffective. They need the nourishment and inspiration of the Big Picture to remember why they are involved in the little picture.

If you are working out, caulking your bathtub, or preparing your taxes, keep the Big Picture of your life in mind. There are valuable lessons in little-picture activities that directly relate to the Big Picture. Meanwhile, get so involved in the story on the big screen that the work is over before you know it, and you have received multiple benefits simultaneously.

What little-picture activities do you get hung
up on that make you forget the Big Picture?
What is the Big Picture of your life
that empowers and inspires you?

I am here for a mighty purpose. I remember
the broader view as I take care of details.

The Self-Hatred of Envy

Envy is the art of counting the other fellow's
blessings instead of your own.

— Harold Coffin

I received a visit from my 18-year-old niece, a lovely young lady who has studied dance since she was in elementary school. While I was doing yoga, she saw me do a forward stretch I have been practicing for years. "I hate you!" she remarked with a giggle. "I've been trying to do that for a long time, and can't."

While she was joking, her statement revealed a belief behind envy. In effect, she was saying, "I want so much to be really flexible, and when I see you do that stretch, it reminds me that I cannot do it and how bad I feel about myself for not being able to do it."

While jealousy seems to be directed at an external person, it is really a disguised attack on oneself. No one who is confident and accepts him- or herself with love can experience envy. This emotion is not about hatred of another person. It is about hatred of self.

Yet there is a way to make envy work in your favor. If you feel envious of something that someone else has attained or obtained, consider that person a harbinger of good for yourself. Rework your observation in your mind so you tell yourself, in effect, *If that person can have something that good, so can I. He is showing me a bigger vision of my possibilities.* Reframe him not as a robber of your good, but as a forerunner of it.

Envy has power over you only if you believe in a world of fixed resources limited by lack. If you knew that there was enough of everything for everyone, and others receiving their good could not take away yours but only add to it, you would have no cause for envy. So if your friend finds a wonderful mate, for example, her success in no way diminishes *your* chances of finding a fabulous partner as well. Rather, it *increases* them because it means that you are attuned to the perception of a good mate, which is the first step to manifesting one.

So translate *envy* into the acronym N.V.—"New Vision," for that is what it is.

How might you reframe something you envy
as a sign of what you can and will have?

I see the good of others as my own.
I celebrate their success as a harbinger of mine.

March Forth!

We are the protagonists and the authors of our own drama. It is up to us; there is no one left to blame. Neither the "system," nor our leaders, nor our parents. We can't go out and hang the first amoebae.

— Rebecca McClen Novick

Today, March 4th, would be a very good day to march forth. March forth from old, limited ways of thinking. March forth from fear and doubt. March forth from blame and guilt. March forth from who you are not, to who you *are*.

It is tempting and easy to lay blame, but counterproductive. When you blame someone else for your predicament, you disempower yourself and remain trapped in a self-imposed prison. No one can keep you where you do not want to be, except yourself.

What most people do not realize about blame is that there is no end to it. For every person or situation you blame, there is another one behind it. Blame is problem oriented, not solution oriented. When you blame, you perpetuate the very situation you are trying to free yourself from. It matters less how you got into a situation, and more how to get out.

Great leaders do not need to make themselves right by making other people wrong. While others go in circles pointing fingers of guilt, visionaries are seeking solutions. They realize that the only purpose of a problem is to motivate you to find an answer that will lift you beyond the consciousness that created the issue.

There is a new and exciting field of corporate consulting and training called "Appreciative Inquiry." With this method, trainers invite executives and staff to look at what is working in their business, why it works, and how they can expand upon it. Little or no attention is given to what is not working or how to fix what is broken. The direction of inquiry is upward and onward, celebrating strengths rather than analyzing weaknesses.

Every time you think of today's date, make it an affirmation: today is the day to march forth!

How would you feel to drop blame and look toward positive, creative solutions and directions?

I march forth to claim the best that life has to offer.

Love How Much You Hate It

Lower your tolerance for struggle.

— Abraham-Hicks

I am not a big fan of pain. I am less of a believer in "No pain, no gain," and more of a believer in "No pain, no pain." Most people struggle and suffer a lot more than they need to, and many of us could benefit more from a dose of kindness to self rather than pushing and fighting to endure situations that rob us of joy.

Yet there is a way to make pain work in your favor if it shows up. You can use the contrast between how bad it feels to hurt and how good it feels to *not* hurt. The contrast can motivate you to make a new choice that will enable you to endure well-being rather than ongoing hell.

When you stick your finger in a flame, for example, the discomfort is a brilliant feedback mechanism. The pain receptors in your fingertips realize that this experience is not in the interest of your finger's well-being and incite you to withdraw it—*now*. Your nerve endings do not rationalize, *Suffering is noble and will get me into heaven,* or *I must pay off my karma from a previous life,* or *I am taking on the pain of humanity and relieving it.* The nerves simply recognize that this is not a healthy experience and you would be far better off to stop what you are doing that hurts. You experience a moment of pain, but once you get its message, you ensure the continuation of your finger by withdrawing it. In that case, pain is a helpful wake-up call.

We have learned to blur or deny the signals from our pain receptors when we get into distressing physical or emotional situations. Often this occurs below the level of our conscious awareness, where the pain is not acute but builds gradually over time. We linger in abusive relationships; breathe polluted air in smog-filled cities; and labor daily at jobs that leave us feeling isolated, disenfranchised, and depleted. If only we were as smart as our fingertips!

At a deeper level, you *are* that smart. You know what hurts you and what heals you. Appreciate pain as a signal that "this can't be it," and choose instead what *is* it.

What pain have you been tolerating?
How is that pain moving you to make choices to feel better?

I do not seek or endure pain, but I use it as a stimulus to choose what I want instead.

The Perception of Progress

The thing always happens that you really believe in;
and the belief in a thing makes it happen.
— Frank Lloyd Wright

While watching a panel of television newscasters debate the merits of President Obama's economic-recovery plan, one of the reporters noted, "The perception of progress is as important as progress itself." She explained that an economy can be stimulated by people *thinking* things are going well, or if things are not going well in general, focusing on the elements that *are* going well.

The commentator recalled that when President Franklin Roosevelt was striving to lift the nation out of the Great Depression, he visited and drew significant media attention to various factories the government had built and the jobs that were created there. As people grew more aware of the progress that was being made, they had a general sense of progress, and found more and more confidence to spend their money and generate *more* progress.

Faith in well-being creates well-being. Focusing on failure and lack creates more failure and lack. Whatever you look at, you get more of. If you want more of something, give it your attention even before it comes into full bloom. The flower will not be far behind.

The human psyche needs to dwell in a higher vision to stay vital and alive. For example, the board game *Monopoly* became popular during the economic downturn of the 1930s. While the game had sold modestly before then, it took off and became America's number one board game during the Depression. While people did not have a lot of money to move in their daily lives, moving around on the *Monopoly* board and getting rich with play money gave them a sense of wealth. To this day, more money is printed every day for *Monopoly* than for the U.S. Treasury!

Because we are spiritual beings at our core, the spirit of our lives creates more results than action alone. That is why the perception of progress is not just as important as progress—it is the beginning of progress.

How can you jump-start success by getting into the feeling of it?

I create my life with my thoughts and feelings.
I focus on success in my mind, and it follows in action.

One Size Fits Most

*Whenever I come upon a "one way" religion,
I know it is my cue to take a U-turn.*

— Swami Beyondananda (aka Steve Bhaerman)

While visiting Omaha, Nebraska, a friend gave me a Cornhuskers baseball cap. The first time I wore it, I noticed a notation on the label: *One size fits most.*

The statement got my attention, since all the labels I had previously seen declared: "One size fits all." This hat is perhaps more honest, since if you happen to have a really big head or a really small one, it will *not* fit you.

This label is a good metaphor for any organization, club, or religion you might join. While some organizations advertise "One size fits all," implying that everyone could or should benefit by participating, such a promotion is nearsighted. The club may fit many, but not everyone.

People struggle and suffer when they try to fit themselves into someone else's mold. The revealing documentary *Trembling Before G-d* traces the paths of several gay Orthodox Jews. Since the religion has strict edicts against homosexuality, these people had a very difficult time trying to reconcile their sexual preference with their religion.

One fellow sought the counsel of a number of rabbis in an effort to find one who would approve of his homosexuality. None did. Several had compassion and wanted to help him, but felt compelled to cite chapter and verse. Something was wrong with him, they told him by word or implication, and he needed to fix himself to get right. Eventually this fellow, after going through tremendous angst, decided that he would just love and accept himself as he was, and hope that God would do the same for him. I assure you God did, and does.

Religions, clubs, and organizations provide a huge positive service to those aligned with their intentions. There are other people whose intentions do not fit into the group at hand. If you are one of them, have faith in yourself and your process. Then you will not have to tremble before God, for God will embrace you right where you stand.

*Do you feel like a misfit? Where in the great
scheme of life are you a good fit?*

**I love and accept myself as I am.
I do not need to prove myself to anyone
or change to fit others' expectations.**

The Missing Tube

For fear is a call for love, in unconscious
recognition of what has been denied.

— *A Course in Miracles*

I heard about a fellow named Herman who was a television repairman in the 1950s. One day he was dispatched to service the TV of an old man named Jake, who lived alone. When Herman inspected Jake's television, he found that it was missing a tube. Herman replaced the tube in a matter of minutes, and spent the next 20 minutes chatting amiably with Jake before he left for his next repair call.

A week later Jake reported that his television was on the blink again, and Herman went to fix it. This time he discovered that a different tube was missing. Herman replaced the tube and chatted with Jake for a little while again.

The following week Jake called the shop again and complained that his TV was not working. When Herman opened up the box, this time a different tube was missing. Finally Herman realized that Jake was removing the tubes. He was lonely, he wanted company, and a broken television was his way of getting Herman to visit him.

You do not need to keep taking tubes out of your television to get the company you desire. You can ask for it directly. We all crave connection, and we go about getting it in different ways. Some of those ways are direct and skillful, and others are roundabout and unconscious. Yet we are all seeking the same result.

Take the initiative to create the intimacy you crave, and request the help you need. Reach out for friendship and tell the people you value that you would like their company or support. You deserve your heart's desire, and can have it. And you will not have to pay a repair bill to connect with people you care about.

What help do you want or need?
Who would you like to invite into a richer relationship?
What step could you take to receive what you are calling for?

I reach out for the love I desire,
and the universe responds.

Long Story Short

If you have anything to tell me of importance,
for God's sake begin at the end.

— Sara Jeannette Duncan

Usually when people say, ". . . to make a long story short," it is too late for that. By that time, they have missed the off-ramp and the story is on overkill. Wouldn't it be nice if we could make long stories short before we tell them?

My friend Jeremy learned this through telling the story of his breakup with his girlfriend. "When we first broke up, if anyone asked me about our relationship, I went into a long explanation of all the dynamics of our relationship and the details of our breakup," he explained. "A few months later, when I had worked through a lot of the emotions and issues around our breakup, that story was cut to half the time and details. Over time the story got shorter and shorter, until finally one day someone who didn't know about our breakup asked me how Sara was. I just told him, 'We're not together anymore,' and that was quite sufficient."

Ralph Waldo Emerson suggested, *"No man ever stated his troubles as lightly as he might."* Now there is a fabulous maxim to remember when you are inclined to relate your problems! Not just as a service to your listeners, but as a powerful service to yourself.

The more you tell a story, the more you reinforce its hold on your experience and increase the likelihood of its being repeated. So give yourself a break by shortening your old story and getting a new one.

I am not suggesting that you mechanically override your feelings or deny what you are going through or have gone through. Certainly our feelings are worth acknowledging, and we need to tell a certain amount of our story to be healed or make progress. Just take care to minimize the story of what you do not want so that you can make way for the story of what you *do* want.

How might you shorten an old story so
you can tell a new and better one?

I use my stories to get me where I truly want to go.

Misery Has Enough Company

Misery has enough company. Dare to be happy.

— Volkswagen ad

One day I walked into a corporate office feeling really good, with a smile on my face. When the secretary saw me, she snarled, "What are you so happy about?" While I was startled by her response, I have since come to understand why unhappy people resent happy people: they remind them of what they are missing.

Odd as it may sound, happiness in our culture is a radical act. So many people are so immersed in unhappiness that when someone comes along who does not share distress, he or she is criticized or rejected. *A Course in Miracles* tells us that the values of the world are upside down from those intended for us by a loving Creator; to really live, we need to think in a way entirely different from the way the world has taught us to think.

When you encounter someone happier or more successful than you are, you can take one of two courses in response: (1) you can recognize that the happy person is showing you a possibility for yourself that you have not been exercising, and use the model as inspiration to make yourself happier; or (2) you can believe that you are locked into unhappiness, with no power to change your lot, and resent the happy person for having what you do not.

Option 1 above is the truth about our possibilities, and option 2 is a self-defeating illusion. So when you encounter someone who has more happiness or success than you do, celebrate the meeting and the person for showing you a possibility that you, too, can obtain.

One of my favorite *Far Side* cartoons depicts a scene in hell. As a couple of devils watch hordes of people laboring and suffering, one fellow is pushing a wheelbarrow, smiling, and whistling. One devil turns to the other and remarks, "I just don't think we're getting to this guy."

To succeed in a world devoted to misery, you have to be that guy. And succeed you will, for your lot is not pain. Misery has enough company. Dare to be happy.

What gift do you offer yourself and others
when you are happy in an unhappy world?

I choose happiness, and bless the world
because of it. I am an uplifter.

Your Next Natural Step

Success will never be a big step in the future,
success is a small step taken just now.

— Attributed to Jonatan Mårtensson

At a prosperity seminar, I asked members of the audience to state their intentions for a goal they would like to achieve. One woman stood up and declared, "I would like to sell my book manuscript to a publisher."

"Excellent," I answered. "And how much of an advance would you like to receive?"

With hardly any thought, she blurted out, "A million dollars!"

Hmm. "That would be a wonderful advance," I replied, "and I hope you get it. Now please tell us how much you would be satisfied with."

The lady thought for a while and answered, "Ten thousand dollars."

"Very good," I told her. "Now we have something to chew on."

While wildly exciting visions are stimulating, expansive, and worth visualizing, when you get down to the business of manifestation, you have to factor in your beliefs and expectations. There was no way that woman believed she would receive a million dollars for her manuscript, so to make that her goal would relegate the possibility of her sale to the realm of fantasy, and thwart or delay it. The notion of a $10,000 advance was much more believable to her, so she was more likely to create movement by visualizing *that* as her next natural step.

In the movie *Contact*, a girl is manipulating her ham radio, trying to contact other operators at far distances around the world; but she is getting only static. So her dad tells her to take small steps. Then, as she moves the dial one frequency at a time, she starts to find receivers in the cracks she was passing over while flipping from one end of the dial to the other.

You too may find people and help in the cracks of small steps that you would not find if you were scanning to the end of the dial. A $10,000 advance may be the next natural step toward a million.

What would be your next natural step, even if it is not your ultimate one?

I achieve my goal in small steps. When I reach my greater goal, it will be solid and real.

Bank On This

Money is power, freedom, a cushion, the
root of all evil, the sum of blessings.

— Carl Sandburg

Mythologist Joseph Campbell explained that you can assess the values of a culture by the buildings it erects. In the Middle Ages, for example, the tallest edifices were churches. Come the 18th and 19th centuries, the tallest structures were government buildings. Since the 20th century, the tallest buildings have been the banks. Drive on the freeway into Orlando, Florida; and Dallas, Texas, for instance, and you will see tower after tower with banks' names on them.

In many ways, money is the god of our culture. Not because so many people have it and enjoy it, but because so many people feel that they lack it. As a result, our relationship with money is largely dysfunctional and we do not see it clearly. We do all kinds of crazy things for and around money, and it is the most common cause of arguments in relationships.

Money is not evil or the root of evil. Fear and ignorance are the roots of evil, and when we get afraid or confused, money plays out our beliefs. Money is a huge blessing if we see and use it as such. It is a way of exchanging energy, expressing appreciation, and delivering support and empowerment. Money is meaningless for its own sake, but extremely meaningful when used as a vehicle for caring and love.

The way you relate to money is equivalent to the way you relate to love. If you are generous with money, you are generous with love. If you have a hard time receiving money, you have a hard time receiving love. When considering a money transaction, see money not as a financial entity, but as a flow of positive energy, and you will get clear on where, when, and how to move your money and how to receive it.

Creating a healthy, happy relationship with money is one of the greatest challenges and opportunities of our culture. If we could see it not as a god in itself, but as a gift from God to use for well-being, all of our money exchanges would be uplifting. Maybe that's why banks are so tall. They are trying to get us to pay attention to what we most need to learn.

How would you feel and act differently with money
if you saw it as a symbol of love and positive energy?

I use money as a tool to bless and awaken. I give and
receive money as freely as I would give and receive love.

If You Don't, Someone Else Will

Opportunities are never lost; someone will take the one you miss.

— Source unknown

I once got an idea to write a unique book. This companion to the workbook of *A Course in Miracles* would contain instructions for practical applications, provide meaningful real-life examples, and be spiral-bound for easy maneuvering.

Over time I became absorbed in other projects and shelved that one until a later date. Then one day I walked into a bookstore and found that one of my colleagues, Sondra Ray, had published a book almost identical to the one I had been thinking about. Sondra did not take my idea; I had told no one about it. Yet it was an idea whose time had come, and Sondra had tapped into the vision of it and acted upon it. I was pleased to see that such a well-done book was available to benefit readers.

When the world is ripe for a new idea, a helpful invention, or a social movement, many people may tap into the idea. Usually one person gets credit for it, but it could have been credited to others. A good idea is a pipeline to a great ocean of thought that develops as a result of the collective desires and intentions of humanity. Those who are in alignment with the idea and focused on it have access to that ocean and the momentum of its waves. The first person to catch the wave and ride it to shore will be heralded as the inventor, while he or she is actually more of a messenger.

Over history, many inventions have been developed simultaneously by several inventors. While the Wright brothers were creating the first airplane at Kitty Hawk, a French team was working assiduously on the same project. If the Wright brothers had not crossed the finish line first, the French would have. While Alexander Graham Bell was moving toward the first telephone, so was a scientist named Gray. Legend has it that he showed up at the patent office hours after Bell. If he had arrived slightly earlier, you and I might be paying our telephone bills to Ma Gray.

If you have a unique idea, it may be flowing from a source of universal wisdom. If you do not bring it to life, another person will. Someone has got to get credit for it, so it might as well be you.

What idea do you have that might help someone or many?
How could you bring it to life?

I have access to an infinite number of brilliant ideas.
I act on them and reap success.

Islands

Birds of a feather flock together.

— Proverb

Jerry Hicks suggested to his mentor Abraham that one way to deal with the world's ills would be to send people of like mind and behavior to islands where they would be with others similar to themselves. "We could send all the murderers to one island, all the rapists to another, and so on; and they could all do their aberrant behaviors to each other and learn from the experience."

Abraham replied, "That is the way it already is. The islands are not physical islands, but islands of thought and consciousness. So criminals (and those who give their attention to crime) find each other and cluster together, as do people committed to helping the world, or those who share a common interest in sports, computers, or music."

You and I already live on an island of people who match our intentions, interests, and habits of thought. That is why you keep attracting the same kind of person in your dating life, work, or friendships. Your mind magnetizes people of like configuration, for better or worse. If you like the kinds of people and situations you are attracting, amp up your signal. If you do not like them, change it.

This principle explains why there are people or kinds of people on the planet you will never meet because your beliefs, values, and lifestyle are so far afield from theirs that you will never be in the same place at the same time. Meanwhile, there are people or kinds of people who are so aligned with your beliefs, values, and lifestyle that you will surely meet or keep meeting.

Internet Web pages are a good example of islands of consciousness. When you click on a Website and get involved in its material, you will usually find references and links to many other sites like it. Political sites lead to other political sites, movies to movies, and dating to dating. Whatever site you are on gives outlet to more of its own island, or unique world.

If you are going to live on an island, make it one you would choose. *Be* the company you value and seek, and those of like mind will find their way to your shores.

What island of company would you like to keep?
How can you clarify and amplify your chosen signal?

I use the Law of Attraction to bring people
and situations to my life that I value and desire.

Raise Your Antenna

Seek not to change the world, but choose
to change your mind about the world.

— *A Course in Miracles*

A short time after I bought a new car, I noticed that its radio was picking up just a few stations out of the many in my area. I adjusted some knobs and dials, with no improvement. After a while I gave up and decided I would have to take the car to the dealer for repair.

When I arrived home that evening, I approached my garage and realized that the last time I had pulled into it and then out again, I had lowered the car's radio antenna. The bottom of my garage door, when in the open position, hung down several inches below the height of the upraised antenna. To negotiate the space, I had lowered the length of the antenna by about a foot.

The next time I drove the car, I raised the antenna to its full height and instantly picked up a lot of stations. I was amazed by the huge difference in receptivity that one foot of height made!

This small but crucial difference symbolizes how much more wisdom, life, and love are available to you when you raise your antenna of perception to its full height.

You may complain about a lack of money, friends, available relationship partners, or jobs—but they may all be out there. You just might not have your antenna raised high enough to be aware of them.

The way to change the world is not by rearranging people and events. True world transformation begins with shifting your perception. If you are seeking answers or inner peace and you cannot find them, you need not scour the earth. That would be like driving your car with a lowered antenna to many different cities in search of radio stations. What you seek is being broadcast right where you stand. Your role is to receive.

The good you seek is not many miles or years away. It may simply be a 12-inch adjustment of perception.

How can you look at your life slightly differently
so that you are aware of more good?

I change my life by changing my mind.
What I seek is available here and now.

Proceed When Clear

I act freely when I am tuned in, centered, and loving, but
if possible I avoid acting when I am emotionally upset.

— Ken Keyes, Jr.

As I was about to exit the parking lot at an airport, I saw a large sign announcing: PROCEED WHEN CLEAR. Good advice for entering the main road, and even better advice for navigating life.

Decisions and acts that result from anger, fear, guilt, or retaliation usually backfire, and you will have to correct them. When you are upset, you are not seeing clearly and you are in the worst position to make effective decisions. When you are relaxed, at peace, and clear-minded, you are in the best position to make healthy decisions. For that reason, you will profit by not acting when you are riled, and waiting until you feel better before you take the next step.

The Roman statesman Seneca suggested, "The greatest remedy for anger is delay." This philosophy was echoed by a national army that had a rule that if soldiers wanted to file a grievance about an incident, they had to wait until 24 hours after it had occurred before they could do so. Usually by the time the day had passed, they had cooled down and gotten over the upset.

If you are angry at someone and want to tell him off, write a letter to him telling him everything you would like to say. Then put the letter in a drawer and revisit it a day or two later. If you still wish to communicate, rewrite the letter. Then put it away again for a while and repeat the process. When I have employed this practice, my letters grew shorter and shorter, and my communication became kinder. Usually I did not even send that particular letter. As I became clearer, my need to vent gave way to my desire to heal the issue, either within myself or by communicating more consciously with the other person.

It is not wrong to be upset; negative emotion offers opportunities for healing and awakening. Just do your best to act from strength, and you will be far more effective.

What results do you get when you act from upset?
What results do you get when you act from clarity?

I proceed when clear, and achieve far
more success than when I am upset.

Snakes Begone!

And he drove the snakes out of the minds of men,
snakes of superstition and brutality and cruelty.

— Arthur Brisbane

Many people around the world, not just the Irish or Catholics, celebrate St. Patrick's Day. Cities far from Celtic shores host parades, the Chicago River is dyed green, and pubs across the globe are burgeoning with sympathetic drinkers. The holiday has become an international celebration and an invitation for people of all faiths and nations to raise their glasses together.

Yet few people know much about the life of St. Patrick and how he became a saint. During Patrick's youth, the British Isles were overrun by Germanic tribes, and at age 16 he was captured and sold into slavery. One night while he was praying, a voice told him to escape and find his way to a boat 200 miles away. He heeded the guidance and found the ship, which sailed to what is now France. There he led a group of the boat's crew through a dangerous forest, and through prayer, escaped capture and had miraculous manifestations of food and providence.

Patrick returned to what is now Ireland, inspired many people with his preaching, and was credited with numerous miracles, including ridding Ireland of snakes. While the snake-banishing legend may not be true, it serves as a powerful symbol for St. Patrick's life, and a metaphor we may all benefit from.

We all experience being slaves of one kind or another. We may be enslaved by fear or a sense of lack, limits, or oppression. We have been captured by the small thinking and illusions of the world, and we yearn for freedom. Like St. Patrick, we may receive guidance on how to find our way home. If we trust our guidance and act on it, our faith proves itself; and we may find miraculous providence in a dark, foreign forest. As our faith becomes stronger, snakes—representing unseen threats that may slither and bite us—will disappear once and for all.

So today as you don your green attire or raise a toast with your mug of ale, remember St. Patrick as an inspiration that you, too, can be free.

How do you feel enslaved? What guidance
can you intuit to effect your escape?

I am guided and protected by the Great Spirit
in and around me. I need not fear, but trust.

Yielding Conquers Resistant

Water is fluid, soft, and yielding. But water will wear away rock,
which is rigid and cannot yield. . . . What is soft is strong.

— Lao-tzu

My friend Ron received a notice from the IRS that he owed them $18,000. He had made an honest error on his tax return, and now he did not have the money to pay. Ron's accountant did not like the IRS and fought them vehemently to get the debt reversed. But the more the accountant fought, the more Ron received nasty and threatening letters from the government.

Finally, Ron decided he was tired of fighting, and resolved to just flow with the situation and simply pay what he could. He bypassed his resistant accountant and phoned the IRS himself. Ron was pleased to contact a cordial agent with whom he had an upbeat, congenial interaction. He explained his predicament and told her that he could not pay at the moment, but his house was on the market, and when it sold, he would certainly settle the debt. The agent told him, "Let me review your case, and I'll get back to you."

A week later Ron received a letter from the agent, who informed him, "I've reviewed your case and reduced your debt to $7,000." Needless to say, Ron was very relieved and paid the sum as soon as he could. Case closed.

In retrospect, Ron believes that his accountant's defiant attitude was fueling the IRS's counter-resistance. Behold the formula for ongoing conflict. When Ron stepped in and displayed an attitude of willingness and allowance, he was connected (by virtue of the Law of Attraction) to someone who mirrored his fluent energy and wanted to help him, and did.

If you are involved in an ongoing conflict with a person or institution, consider whether your attitude of defiance or resistance is inviting a matching energy on the other party's part. If you can drop your resistance and step toward the common ground of mutual support, your gesture may be met with equivalent kindness that will resolve the conflict for good.

Are you fueling a conflict with resistance?
How might you end it with nonresistance?

I end conflict by relaxing and
trusting in a Higher Power.

The Consultant

*A consultant is someone who borrows
your watch to tell you what time it is.*

— Source unknown

A friend of mine advertised himself as a psychic counselor. He was not particularly psychic, just clever. He would tell each client to pick several cards from a tarot deck, and then he would lay them out in a formation. Then he asked the client what he or she thought the symbols meant.

"Ah!" a client would exclaim. "This confirms that I should move ahead with my business plan."

"That's right," the counselor would affirm.

His next client might survey her cards and declare, "I knew it—this relationship is killing me, and I need to get out!"

"It is so," the "psychic" would agree.

If a client did not get an obvious answer to a burning question, the counselor would ask, "What would you like to do?" When the client stated his preferred action, my friend would say, "Yes, that would be wise." This fellow had a high success rate, with many repeat customers, and his clients were happy to pay him for his services. In my opinion, he was not a charlatan. He was simply helping people tune in to their own guidance, and eliciting their confidence to follow it.

I play a game in some of my seminars, with outstanding results. If I ask participants a question about something they are struggling with and they answer, "I don't know," I ask them, "If you did know, what would you say?" You would be astounded by the wisdom that comes forth, sometimes in detail! All that person needed was permission and encouragement to *know*.

You have that permission and encouragement now. You can go to a counselor for help to access it, and a good counselor will deliver that. You can also go to the counselor *within* you. Your inner genius is your very best friend.

*Consider a question you are wondering about.
If you knew the answer, what would it be?*

**The wisdom of the universe is within me.
I know what I need to know and do.**

How to Get Everyone to Like You

*Whatever course you decide upon, there is always someone
to tell you that you are wrong. . . . To map out a course
of action and follow it to an end requires . . . courage . . .*
— Attributed to Ralph Waldo Emerson

I once sent out a newsletter with a joke in it. To my surprise, not all of my readers thought it was funny. I received several letters of complaint, and a few people asked to be taken off my mailing list. This was a mystery to me, because my intentions were innocent and I thought my readers would get a kick out of it. But not everyone did.

At a seminar, I happened to mention the issue, and several participants had interesting comments. One asked me, "How many newsletters did you send out?"

"Six thousand," I answered.

"And how many complaints did you get?" he prompted.

"About six," I replied.

"Wow, that's a really small percentage!" the fellow observed. "You're doing well."

Another fellow, Scott, told me, "One of the things I most appreciate about you, Alan, is your sense of humor. If you quit begin funny, I would stop liking you. Then what would you do?"

Hearing that, I realized that there was no way I was going to always please everyone. No matter what I do, some people will agree and like it, and others will not. After Scott's comment, I relaxed and decided to just do what I am going to do, to the best of my ability, and trust that the positive effects of my actions will outweigh any negatives.

Some of the wisest and most loving people who ever lived were confronted with lots of people who did not like or agree with them. Jesus, Gandhi, and Martin Luther King, Jr., all had critics, people who felt threatened by their message of kindness. Can you keep doing what you are doing and saying what you are saying, even if you receive criticism or complaints?

If others complain, check within yourself to see if their complaint is valid. If so, do what you can to improve your approach. If you do not believe their point is valid, march on. Not everyone will like you. But if you like you, your life is a huge success.

*Whose approval are you struggling to win?
Can you trust and accept yourself just as you are?*

**I am confident in myself and my actions.
I live for inner reward, not outer approval.**

Your Past Isn't What It Used to Be

All your past except its beauty is gone,
and nothing is left but a blessing.

— *A Course in Miracles*

During my high school years, I walked to school each morning with my buddy George. One day as an act of affection I reached my arm around George's shoulder. My friend was uncomfortable with this gesture and politely shrugged off my arm. I felt embarrassed, and we both said nothing. Before long, we were off to college and went our separate ways. For a long time, however, when I thought about George, I recalled that awkward moment.

Many years later I reconnected with George, and we began to reminisce. I confessed, "Sometimes I still feel funny about the morning I put my arm around your shoulder and you tossed it off."

George looked perplexed. "I don't remember that at all," he told me sincerely. "All I remember is that you waited for me every morning, even in the rain."

I was stunned. For all those years, one of my primary memories of my friendship with George was my perceived error. Meanwhile, all he remembered was the good. What a waste of my thoughts and energy! And how wonderful it felt to know that George had always appreciated me.

While you have many alternative futures, you also have many alternative pasts. Out of billions of experiences in your life, you have chosen to focus on only a small number of selected events as your "past." You may think of events A, G, M, and W as your past; but you could also define your past as events B, D, R, and Z. If you focus on traumatic or self-defeating moments as your past, your future will replicate them. If you focus on empowering and self-honoring events, those are the ones you will repeat.

Even if you have had painful experiences, you can reframe them as stepping-stones to where you now stand. If you learned from them, they were helpful. Bless all of your past, and your present and future will be an even greater blessing.

How could you reconsider or reframe your past so that it empowers you?

I choose a past that expands my present and my future. I am grateful for all experiences.

Magnetic Innocence

With the eyes of the mind he gazed upon those
things which nature has denied to human sight.

— Ovid

One evening I attended a screening of some video clips of paranormal phenomena. One of the more humorous segments depicted "the Magnetic Family" of the Philippines—a family whose bodies, for some unknown reason, are magnetized to such a high degree that metal objects hold fast to their skin. The audience gasped and laughed to see paper clips, forks, and even a steam iron stuck to these people by sheer magnetic force.

After the presentation, the organizer introduced me to the group, and as a joke I called myself "the Magnetic Man of Maui." Minutes later as I was socializing, a seven-year-old girl approached me with several other children. The girl took a quarter from her hand and pressed it to my bare forearm. When the coin fell to the ground, she frowned, looked up, and exclaimed, "I thought you said you were magnetic!"

I laughed, but then I realized that the child was serious. She really thought I was magnetic. With that came a striking realization: *an innocent mind is open to all possibilities.* We have been told that to get into heaven, we must become like little children. That applies not to heaven after death—it applies to heaven on Earth. If you want to be happy, you must reclaim the vision through which you saw life as a child.

Your problem is not that you know too little. Your problem is that you know too much about why things cannot or should not work. You know too much about disease, economics, war, and bad relationships. You know too much about history, statistics, and crime. You know too much about conniving businesspeople, corrupt cops, and underhanded politicians. Not to say that these things do not happen, but you simply are too aware of all the things that are not working, which stifles your awareness of how good things can and do work.

Let us be more magnetic in our expectation of good things. They might just stick.

How could you see life through more innocent eyes?

**I am open to all possibilities, and my innocent
vision paves the way for miracles.**

Can, Can

I have learned to use the word "impossible" with the greatest caution.
— Attributed to Wernher von Braun

As a resident of Hawaii, I have learned a bit of Hawaiian pidgin English, the local informal dialect. Pidgin developed organically when hundreds of years ago Hawaiian sugar-plantation owners imported laborers from China, Portugal, the Philippines, and other countries. Working in the fields together, the immigrants had to find some common language. Pidgin was it.

The result is lots of short, folksy expressions, some of which are quite humorous, like "broke da mout" (broke the mouth), referring to food that tastes delicious; "all bus' up" (all busted up), describing something broken; and "Get chance?" meaning, "Would you like to make out?"

One pidgin expression with metaphysical significance is "Can, can." It means, "If something can be done, I or we can do it." It is a statement of potential and the power to manifest. It is a good affirmation. *Can, can.*

Most people live from one of two mind-sets: "Yes, we can" or "No, we can't." I have learned this from many years of telephoning airlines to make reservations. I have found that some agents are bright and perky and will find a way to say yes to just about any request, while others seem determined to say no to whatever I ask them. If I get a "no" agent on the phone, I will politely hang up and phone again until I get a "yes" agent. Then I make all kinds of requests of this person, covering many trips ahead, and I get pretty much what I ask for. I am also amazed by the difference in the rules these agents quote. Sometimes I wonder if they all just make up the rules as they go along.

When you face a project or challenge, notice whether you are coming from "Can, can" or "No can do." Your results will prove your expectation, either way.

Are you facing a project or a challenge that
you believe you cannot accomplish or overcome?
What would you be saying or doing differently
if you were to adopt a "Can, can" approach?

If something can be done, I can do it.

Sex in the Nursing Home

*We've put more effort into helping folks reach
old age than into helping them enjoy it.*

— Frank A. Clark

A recent news article reported that a fellow went to visit his father in a nursing home and found the elder in his room getting it on with another resident. Shocked and angry, the son had his father transferred to another facility. The article referenced a survey that showed that 53 percent of people between the ages of 75 and 85 are sexually active.

Personally, I was rooting for the fellow's dad. I commend him and his partner for keeping the fires alive. The 53 percent statistic cited above denies much of what we have been told about how we are supposed to disappear from life as we age. Age, like all human experience, is a belief system. If you believe it, it will probably happen. If you believe something else, *that* will happen. That is why it is so important to keep examining our expectations, which form the platforms of our lives.

We are shifting to new paradigms in practically every aspect of life: economics, religion, education, medicine, government, and business are going topsy-turvy because the old way is not working anymore and we are reaching to find new, more meaningful ways. Aging is one of the paradigms being overhauled. What you have been told about what happens when you get old is just not true anymore.

Aging no longer has to mean that you sicken, wither, and die. We all know people who gain life, zest, and joy as they advance in years. They are a delight to be around because they have used life to expand, not contract. Until now, such vital people have been the exception. In the new paradigm, they will be the rule.

We shall all leave this world one day; how we do it is up to us. We can fade away and disappear, or we can go out in a blaze of glory. Nursing homes, watch out!

*Do you believe you have to decline with age?
Can you envision a more expansive, celebratory path?*

**I am an ageless spirit. I am in life for the distance.
I grow more alive every day and every year.**

Not Because I'm Nice

More good comes from living true than truth comes from acting good.
— Sri Neem Karoli Baba (Maharajji)

I met a fellow who spent many years presenting seminars in a genre similar to what I do. He was tired of his work and on the verge of retirement. When I explained to him that in my programs I teach people skills to be happier and more successful, he commented, "That's very nice of you."

I had not thought of it that way. I do not do things to be nice. I do things because I feel joy and fulfillment in doing them. My career is a stimulating, rewarding, and empowering adventure for me. I learn and grow as much as my clients do—sometimes even more. I do what I do because I love to do it—not because I'm nice.

When your work proceeds from joy, you are infinitely more helpful to those you serve, for two reasons: (1) the skill, creativity, and results that proceed from a happiness-based career far exceed those that proceed from drudgery; and (2) when you flow with passion, your clients catch your energy and they are empowered by your aliveness as much as by your actions. So your best service to others is to do what you love to do.

"But Alan," you might object, "if everyone just did what they wanted, the world would be chaos. People would rape and pillage, and we'd live in bedlam."

Not really. The spirit within you is intelligent and responsible, and your happiness is deeply connected to the happiness of others. Your true inner being would never guide you to hurt anyone. To the contrary, your real self loves to be helpful, and when you do what is empowering to you, you uplift others. A guilt- or obligation-based life is not God's idea for you. A *celebration*-based life is.

Choose a career, relationship, and spiritual journey that gladdens your heart and leads you to help many in the deepest possible way. Not because you're nice. Because you are *you.*

What do you do because you should be nice?
What would you be doing differently if you lived from joy?

I choose from happiness, and
I bring happiness to those I touch.

Defeating the KGB

The person who is most connected to Source
at any given moment will prevail.

— Abraham-Hicks

In the 1980s I joined several citizen-diplomacy missions to the (then) Soviet Union. We were inspired by President Eisenhower's statement "People want peace so much that one of these days governments had better get out of the way and let them have it." We went there to build bridges of trust and understanding with the Russian people. And it worked.

On one of our trips, we invited a few Soviet friends to a banquet at our hotel, where we gave them some gifts as a symbol of our friendship. This was, however, verboten by the then-ominous KGB. A tense moment arose when a KGB agent infiltrated our gathering, chastised a young Russian man for accepting gifts, and seized the packages from him. At that moment Tom Sewell, a member of our group, walked up to the KGB man, took the gifts from him, and placed them back in our friend's arms. To my amazement, the KGB agent backed off and walked away.

I saw this scenario as a lesson in the power of sincere intention to create a positive outcome. When you know who you are and what you are here to do, there is no power that can stop you. You do not have to fight anyone or anything. Just stand in truth, where drama has no claim over love, and allow a Higher Power to orchestrate the results.

The Teachings of Abraham explain that when two people interact, the person who is most connected to Source energy will prevail to achieve a positive result. By contrast, when two people go 'round and 'round in a conflict, neither is connected to Source, and no one gets anywhere. When one person gets lined up with a Higher Power, resolution is in sight.

If you are involved in a conflict or decision-making process, take some time to align with Source energy through meditation, prayer, or however you get quiet inside yourself. From that deep place you will know clearly what to do; and it will get done in a creative, healthy way.

The KGB is now history, but our friend still has his gifts.

How might you resolve a question or conflict by
connecting with your Higher Power?

I act in alignment with Spirit's will,
and positive results follow naturally.

Demanding Presence

Everything that can be counted does not necessarily count;
everything that counts cannot necessarily be counted.

— Attributed to Albert Einstein

Marti was having difficulty getting together with a friend. "Every time we make an appointment, Cynthia combines our meeting with doing other things," Marti complained. "She's either walking the dog, or she asks if I want to ride with her while she does some errands, or she invites someone else to join us. We hardly have an opportunity to get into any discussions of substance. This is really frustrating!"

I suggested to Marti, "Simply tell Cynthia that your friendship is important to you, and you would really value some one-on-one time without interruption."

The next time we spoke, Marti reported she had communicated what I suggested, and she and her friend had enjoyed a meaningful dinner and conversation.

Your presence is the most valuable gift you can offer anyone. In a society where many people are overscheduled and addictively multi-tasking, moments of real connection are precious. If you can give them—and ask for them—you will feed yourself and others on a level that really counts.

Whatever you do, show up fully . . . and you will enjoy the true reward of relationship.

How could you be more present in your interactions?
How can you ask others to do the same?

I give my full presence and ask the same.
My life is nourished by connection.

Seekers and Finders

There's a seeker born every minute.

— Firesign Theatre

After a seminar I presented, an elderly woman took me aside and asked for some help. "My husband passed away a few years ago, and I am looking for a spiritual community to join," she explained. "Can you direct me to one?"

Since I was aware of several good communities, I took some time with the lady and explained what I knew about them. She was very interested, took notes, and told me she would follow up. I felt pleased to have been able to help her.

Later that night one of the seminar sponsors asked me, "Did Edna ask you about a spiritual community?"

"Why, yes, she did," I answered. "I gave her what information I could."

The sponsor smiled a knowing smile and told me, "She asks that of all the speakers who come here. She has been asking for years. She doesn't follow up. She just likes asking."

While I am sure that Edna craved community, she had more of an investment in the question than in the answer. She may symbolize the part of all of us that would rather seek than find. *A Course in Miracles* tells us that the ego's motto is "Seek and do not find." By contrast, the inner spirit's motto is "Seek and find" or simply "Find." The illusory needful self tells us that we would be happy if only someone or something in the outer world were different. The inner spirit tells us that all that we seek is inside of us; or, as Jesus put it, "The kingdom of God is within."

Today practice shifting your identity from that of a seeker to that of a finder. Choose to be satisfied with the people around you, the conditions you encounter, and most important, yourself. If you have been asking a question, imagine you know the answer, and act upon it. If you still like seeking, follow it up with finding. You may find that what you sought . . . you already own.

How do you regard yourself as a seeker?
How can you reframe your identity to become a finder?

All that I want is already given.
I claim it now and enjoy the journey.

Gengki Des

You are loved. All is well.

— Abraham-Hicks

The Japanese culture has an illuminating way of inquiring about well-being and affirming it. If you were to ask a Japanese-speaking person, "How are you?" you would ask, *"Gengki des ka?"*—literally translated, "Is there well-being?" The response would likely be, *"Gengki des,"* meaning, "Well-being is."

I like the expression because it affirms that well-being is our natural state. To feel better, we do not have to struggle for health; more practically, we need to release whatever is blocking our natural health, which is eager, ready, and able to flow to us as we open to allow it.

If you lived in a village in merry olde England, you would hear the town crier on the hour affirm something like, "It's three o'clock, and all's well!" During every waking hour, you would receive a loud and clear affirmation that all was well, and on most days that is all you would hear.

In modern times we might do well to have a town crier that affirms on the hour: "All's well!" since at almost all hours all *is* well. As it is, at 7 A.M., 6 P.M., and 10 P.M. (and on news channels every hour), the television news crier affirms for a full hour, "All's not well!" As such, the news is misleading, since most people have a better day than the showcased events would suggest. According to The Teachings of Abraham, the news should be allowed to present information only in proportion to what happened overall for that day. So if there was one murder in a city of a million people, that story should be allowed one-millionth of the broadcast. But such news takes up 10 or 20 percent of the show (and on news channels, the *entire* show), which misleads viewers as to what actually happened that day. All is really "weller" than the news would show you.

You need to become your own town crier and remind yourself and those around you that, in general, *gengki des*—well-being is, and all is well. Then the health and well-being that you seek will find you.

How could you more regularly remind yourself that all is well?

I relax, knowing that well-being is my natural state and the natural state of life.

Undercurrents

I like to think of thoughts as living blossoms borne by the human tree.
— James Douglas

Do you ever wonder why good or bad things happen "out of the blue"? Such events are not the offspring of caprice or luck; they are governed by scientific dynamics of universal law. As you recognize the relationship between out-of-the-blue events and your unexamined beliefs, you are in a position to command your destiny.

A friend told me she was getting divorced after her husband brought his girlfriend home for the weekend. "We'd been married 13 years," she explained. "We never argued—but we also never communicated."

This shocking event was the culmination of the two drifting apart over the years, with neither one addressing the issue. My friend's husband did not wake up one day and decide, "I'm not happy, and I will seek another partner." His choice had been building for a long time, but unfortunately for both partners, it was not brought into the open.

Perhaps you have had the experience of swimming in a lake when you suddenly felt a cold undercurrent. Likewise, you may go through the outer motions of your life where everything appears to be one way, while an undercurrent is moving in a different direction. This phenomenon can work for our well-being or against it. Thus you can be apparently healthy while hurtling toward disease, and you can be apparently sick while hurtling toward wellness.

What happens to you in the outer world is not a cause. It is an effect of your interior thoughts, feelings, beliefs, and intentions. Pay less attention to how things look, and more attention to where energy is moving. The current exterior condition is a result of how you flowed your energy yesterday. Tomorrow's exterior condition will be a result of how you flow your energy today.

How might a surprise event be related to
an unexamined undercurrent of belief?

I consciously choose how I flow my energy.
I build the results I choose.

The Bigger the Front, the Bigger the Back

*I think somehow, we learn who we really
are and then live with that decision.*

— Attributed to Eleanor Roosevelt

A number of years ago a high-profile televangelist created a scandal when he was discovered having seedy relations with a prostitute. Only a few years earlier, he had launched a campaign to discredit several other ministers for their sexual indiscretions. He dramatically apologized for his transgression, but to many observers his misbehavior seemed more sincere than the apology. Several years later he was caught with another prostitute and barred from his ministry.

Individuals or religions on a campaign against evil have generally not come to terms with their shadow selves, or disowned elements of their humanity. We tend to project onto others the aspects of ourselves that we do not like or do not accept, and then wage a war to eradicate their evils. Such wars never succeed because they are based on hatred and a lack of self-awareness or self-acceptance. The most conscious way to deal with what we dislike in others is to identify the elements in our own lives we have not come to terms with and heal our minds and hearts from the inside out.

Campaigns against unwanted behavior only amplify the unwanted behavior and widen the schism of denial within oneself. If you are bent on getting rid of anything in anyone else, ultimately you will have to come to terms with the same element within yourself. You also set up a dynamic of backlash. People who band together to fight an external person or cause end up battling each other.

Many religions appear to be fighting the devil, but they *need* the devil to give them an opposing identity. By portraying something out there as all bad, they cast themselves as all good; and neither polarity is true. If the concept of the devil were removed from some religions, they would be completely at a loss for purpose. Then they might have to discover that, after all, God really is love.

*How might you withdraw judgments of others
in favor of your own self-awareness?*

I embrace all parts of me and accept my humanity.

That's So Fake!

You can indeed afford to laugh at fear.

— A Course in Miracles

As a kid, I used to watch old science-fiction movies with primitive special effects. There would always come a point in the *Flash Gordon* episode, for example, when I could see the string holding up the plastic model spaceship that was supposed to be hurtling through space. Then my buddy and I would elbow each other, laugh, and say, "That's so fake!"

Seeing through those shoddy special effects served as a good training ground to see through meaningless or threatening experiences in life. When faced with a scary or confusing moment, you may be tempted to flee, fight, or revert to an addictive or escapist behavior. But if you can stand your ground and look the difficult person or situation in the eye, you might declare (even laughingly), "That's so fake!" Then you can resolve the situation, recognizing the scary scene as simply a rudimentary effort mounted by the special-effects department.

If you look back on the people and events that once frightened you, you will realize there was always some element that was illusory about them. Why, then, when something new and scary comes along, would *it* be any more real than one of the previous impostors?

Today, April Fools' Day, might be the perfect occasion to recognize how fear has attempted to fool you into believing you are limited or victimized, and call its bluff. Every time you stand up to fear with love, courage, and trust, you expose a little more of the cheap string that holds up the plastic spaceship. Consider whatever frightens you, elbow your buddy, say with a smile, "That's so fake!" and enjoy the movie, in which the hero always prevails.

How might you disarm what frightens you by recognizing the truth behind the illusion it suggests?

I see through people, words, and events that do not have substance in love or reality. My faith is deeper, stronger, and greater than fear or illusion.

The End of Debt

Money is not required to buy one necessary of the soul.

— Henry David Thoreau

Lots of people owe money these days. One of the questions I am often asked is: "How can I get out of debt or deal with it more consciously?"

Here are several tips to undo your sense of indebtedness, in all forms:

— **Recognize** that a burdensome sense of owing is more of an attitude than a situation. There are people who owe lots of money but feel free, and there are people who owe little or no money who feel weighted with obligation. Happiness has little to do with numbers on paper, and a lot to do with thought and perspective.

— **Shift your identity** from that of a debtor to that of a whole spiritual being. You are created in the image and likeness of God, and all of the attributes of God are yours as well. The concept of God "owing" is ridiculous, and this is equally applicable to you. Affirm: *God doesn't owe, and neither do I.*

— **Make a list** of your debts and the amounts owed. Decide which is the least, and pay that debt off first. This will give you a sense of relief and begin to shift your thoughts and feelings of obligation.

— **Lighten up** about the debts owed to you—not just financially, but emotionally. If you forgive others who owe you, you open the door for the universe to forgive your debts.

— **Live and play** as if you are debt free. Many businesses have lots of debts on paper, but go on making money. Debt is a paper game. Life is a bigger game.

How can you shift your attitude to see yourself as
free and clear right now?

God does not owe, and neither do I.
I am solvent and prosperous.

If It Keeps Knocking, Answer

*Reality is that which, when you
stop believing in it, doesn't go away.*

— Philip K. Dick

When Dan Brown, the author of the megablockbuster *The Da Vinci Code*, was asked, "Where did you get the idea for this book?" he explained that it came to him when he was studying art history at the University of Seville in Spain. There he was exposed to some of the mysteries of the da Vinci paintings. Years later, while he was studying the Vatican Secret Archives, the notion returned to him. He recounts, "This particular story kept knocking on my door until I answered."

If you are one of the many millions who have enjoyed and been inspired by *The Da Vinci Code*, you are probably glad that Dan Brown answered the knock. Yet he is not the only person whose door inspiration knocks at. You, too, have ideas, visions, dreams, intuitions, and inklings that keep coming to you. The question is not "Is greatness calling you?" but rather, "Are you answering?"

A recurring idea or inspiration is quite likely a sign that the universe is trying to get your attention to follow through on it. Your ego, or sense of limited self, might deny and resist the calling with excuses like "I could never do that," "That would take a far greater person than me," "That's never been done," or "I'm too [old/uneducated/unattractive/poor/unworthy] for such a task." Yet when the ego has gone through its array of lame defenses and the vision keeps knocking, you may be certain that you are being guided and called.

The difference between those who move the world forward and those who stay stuck in a rut is that the world movers trust the voice that keeps knocking, and they act on it. You can and will be among the movers if you listen to the persistent call of greatness and move with it.

*What inspiring idea keeps knocking at the door of your mind?
If you were to act on it, what would be the first step you would take?*

**Greatness is calling to me from
within my mind and heart. I heed its call,
and the world is better for it.**

The Big Game

Anywhere is paradise; it's up to you.

— Source unknown

I know of a man who grew up as the child of missionaries in Africa, where he lived and played with the natives and went to school with them. He recounted that the local kids had an endless soccer game going. As soon as the sun was up each morning, all the children in the village would run out to the makeshift soccer field and immerse themselves in their game. When it was time to go to school, they would take turns going into the classroom and studying their lessons. As soon as school was out, they would dash back onto the field and play until dusk, when they could not see the ball anymore. In that village, soccer was the real deal, and everything else fit around it.

There are two possible relationships you can hold between work and play: either (1) life is work, and you occasionally get in some play; or (2) life is fun, and some work comes along with it. While you may automatically assume the former and accept that life is drudgery, with a few bright moments, it can be mostly enjoyable, with occasional moments when you have to bear down.

I had a business manager who had a great sense of humor. One morning when I came into the office, I found him on the telephone laughing. He stayed on the call for a while, joking and quipping. When he hung up, I asked him, "Was that an old friend of yours?"

"No, it was the IRS," he answered.

"You were goofing around with an IRS agent?"

"Well, I had to talk to him about something, so I figured I might as well have fun."

Because my manager was clear and pure in his intention, he found the place in the agent that was able, desirous, and willing to meet him there. That is how the big game works.

There are two ways you change your life: manipulate the environment, or manipulate your mind. Sometimes you can change the outer world. Always, you can change your mind. Adopt an attitude of play, and work will take its proper role in the healthy balance of all things.

*How could you shift your attitude so your life
becomes more play and less work?*

**I approach life as a game, and I constantly
win by holding a positive attitude.**

Leading to More

If you fall in a mud puddle, check your pockets for fish.

— Source unknown

I met an attorney named Andrew who had lost his job due to bankruptcy. He confided in me that he did not really enjoy the practice of law, and it was no surprise that he had gone out of business. He was more interested in computers.

During his bankruptcy process, Andrew did a lot of research on the laws of bankruptcy and recorded notes on his computer. Over time he collected a wealth of information and arranged it in a unique way. When he realized that he had created an unprecedented data bank, Andrew took his notes and program to executives at Apple, Inc. They liked the program and offered him a handsome sum of money to flesh it out. Now Andrew feels passionate about—and is well paid for—his work with Apple as a legal-program development consultant.

Nothing happens in a vacuum; everything leads to something else. What appears to be a setback or loss may simply be one event in a string of events that leads to something entirely more rewarding than the single upsetting event.

The key to Andrew's turnaround was that he did not like his law practice. How compassionate the universe was to kick him out of a place he did not want to be anyway! He ended up doing what he really wanted to do even though he did not know how to get there.

Do not resent events that move you out of your comfort zone, especially when your comfort zone was not all that comfortable. The universe is always responding to your subconscious desires and intentions. Better, of course, if you can tell the truth about what you want so that the process of growth can be conscious. But recognize that you have a friend in the Law of Attraction that is opening doors you did not know how to get through.

*How might an unexpected or upsetting change
be moving you toward your greater good?*

**I flow with change and keep my mind
and heart open to improving my position.
I journey from good to better to best.**

Steam and Tracks

The head alone is tyrannical. The heart alone is chaotic.
The head and heart together is mastery.

— Mary (guide)/Carla Gordan

I saw a documentary that chronicled the evolution of the rock group the Who, which embodied a not-unusual blend of talent and turbulence. Most of the group's legendary hit songs were composed by the gifted Pete Townshend, sung by Roger Daltrey, and backed up by bass guitarist John Entwistle and drummer Keith Moon. Townshend and Daltrey were the more stable members of the group, while Moon and Entwistle led dramatic lives and died of drug overdoses. Yet they were passionate, almost feverish, musicians.

The Who, in spite of their troubles, point to a winning formula when cultivated to advantage: visionary direction fueled by passion. A steam locomotive needs two essential ingredients to get where it is going. The fire in the engine generates steam that propels the engine, while the tracks guide it in a chosen direction. If the engine has steam but no tracks, it will flail about chaotically and get nowhere. If it has tracks but no steam, it would know where to go and how to get there, but it would sit idly, literally dead in its tracks. Combine the elements of steam and tracks and you have a powerful vehicle and useful route.

If you intend to achieve your valued goals, you need both steam and tracks. You need passion, motivation, and enthusiasm; and you need clarity, purpose, and direction. If either is lacking, you will not get where you want to go. Join the two and you are sure to arrive, and enjoy the process.

Today, think about where you are headed and consider if you have enough steam and tracks. If not, think about what it would take to add the element that is lacking or out of balance. You may need to (1) develop the lacking element, (2) invite a partner to fill in the blank in the equation, or (3) drop the project and choose another that has both steam and tracks. You can and will get anywhere you want to go if you engage the power of both head and heart.

How might you succeed more by finding a
healthy balance of passion and direction?

I get where I want to go by letting
my heart move me and my head guide me.

Why Do Anything Else?

Talent hits a target no one else can hit;
genius hits a target no one else can see.

— Arthur Schopenhauer

When composer extraordinaire Frédéric Chopin was asked, "Why do you compose only for the piano?" he answered, "That's what I'm good at. Why should I do anything else?"

Many of us have been taught that we must force ourselves to stretch into domains beyond our comfort zone. While following this practice can be helpful in many situations, you might in the process overlook the fact that what you are already good at is the ticket to your success.

Many people ask me how they can know their true vocational path—or, as Buddha called it, their "right livelihood." I ask them to consider five crucial questions: (1) What do you most enjoy doing? (2) What are you good at doing? (3) What do people most compliment you for doing? (4) What does the universe tend to reward you most for doing? (5) What would you be doing even if you were not getting paid for it?

If you ponder these questions, you will probably discover that they keep pointing you in the same direction. Your right livelihood should not be a mystery or ongoing challenge to figure out. The answer might be right before you, and if you look through innocent eyes, you may recognize it.

Do not let other people or belief systems distract you from your true calling. In your heart you know what feels good and what works, and that is your most reliable resource.

My friend Kate is a gifted, successful social worker and counselor. When she took a famous vocational-guidance test, she was directed to become a forest ranger. Nothing could be further from her reality! Fortunately, she went with her inner vocational-guidance test, and that worked out fine.

Chopin was a great composer because he let his talent pave his path. So, too, will you be great at what you were born to do when you let your inner gifts be your guiding light.

Can you trust that what you are good at will
provide for you and serve the world?

I allow my God-given talents to form
the foundation of my right livelihood.

The Provider

*Faith [is] the enabling ground of the person content
to be human and to let God be God.*

— Carter Lindberg

At a seminar, a fellow named Don confessed, "I feel bad because I'm not a good provider for my family. I work hard, but the economic downturn has decreased my business. I'm taking care of our basic needs, but we don't have enough money for anything extra or fun. My wife wanted to take our youngest child to South America to visit her family, and I hated to tell her that we can't afford it. I feel like a failure as a provider."

I told Don, "Usually people don't think they're doing enough of what they already do well. It sounds to me like you are making every effort to take care of your family and doing a good job of it, considering your current circumstances.

"You are assuming too much responsibility as the provider," I continued. "In truth, the real Provider is life, and you are but one channel through which providence comes. Consider some other possible avenues through which your good could arrive: You said that your wife has suggested that she could take on an extra shift here and there to supplement your income. Let her be big enough to contribute if she can and wants to. You could also attract income through other unexpected sources. Or you could just decide that the universe is providing beautifully for you now, meeting your basic needs, and when the cycle of economics comes around again, you will have more money for your wife to take this trip. So it may not be an issue of lack, but just timing."

I further suggested, "Reframe your role from a provider of money to a provider of consciousness. Your job is to hold the vision and faith that your family is safe and cared for. If you communicate this through word or energy to your family, you will be offering the greatest providence there is."

Do what you can to provide in a material way, but remember that your real gift is consciousness, which leads first to a sense of well-being and then to greater material good.

*How can you satisfy your needs and those
of others by holding vision and faith?*

**The Great Spirit is the true Provider.
My loved ones and I are always cared for.**

Everything's Amazing

A thousand things went right today.

— Ilan Shamir

Comedian Louis C.K. does a routine about how people do not realize how amazing life is.

"I was flying in an airplane last week when the flight attendant announced the airplane was equipped with the latest technology—Internet in the air," he reported. "I and a bunch of other passengers signed up, and within minutes I was surfing the Internet and sending e-mails from my seat on the plane. It was amazing!

"An hour later the flight attendant announced that there were some technical difficulties with the system, and the service would be suspended until it could be repaired.

"Suddenly everyone started complaining about the poor technology. 'Nothing works anymore!' someone moaned.

"*Come on!* I thought. Here you are sitting in a chair flying over the ocean at 35,000 feet in altitude, at an airspeed over 500 miles an hour, being served hot meals, watching movies, using the telephone, and now surfing the Internet. What do you mean, 'Nothing works'?!"

We take a lot for granted, sometimes overlooking the blessings and miracles that abound in our lives. Every day all kinds of astounding things happen that could be cause for immense appreciation—if we are open to see and celebrate them.

Today might be a perfect day to recognize what an extraordinary world we live in; and how much we are loved, supported, and cared for. Little children live in wide-eyed wonder at the world around them, yet adults become jaded to splendor.

You can return to that childlike vision by focusing on how well things are working. At this very moment there are many people and events conspiring to love and support you. Your job is to notice, be grateful, and pass the gifts along by applauding them.

In what amazing ways is life lifting, nourishing, and blessing you?

I open my eyes to the miracles in and around me. I celebrate all the good in my world, and it expands.

How to Goof Off

Do as the heavens have done, forget your evil;
With them forgive yourself.

— William Shakespeare

My rural trash-removal service requires customers to mark their address on their garbage cans. So I took a can of white spray paint and wrote my street number on a brown rubber can. I set the full can in the back of my SUV and drove it to the refuse-pickup spot. When I returned, I was irked to notice that some paint had rubbed off on the back of the seat; apparently it had not fully dried on the trash can. But it did dry on my car. I tried to remove the paint, but it was stuck fast.

Over the next months, every time I noticed the paint marks on the back of the seat, I felt foolish. A stream of judgment chided me: *If you had been more patient and left more time for the paint on the can to dry, this wouldn't have happened. Now you have ruined your car seat, and every time you look at it, you will remember your carelessness.* (Do you know that voice?)

Then one day I accompanied a friend to the hardware store to find some paint. On a shelf I noticed a product called "Goof Off," which removes dried paint and other hard-to-get-out stains. I bought a can and applied it to the defiant stain. To my delight, the paint disappeared instantly!

I now see this product—especially its name—as a symbol of forgiveness. The name acknowledges that you made a mistake ("goof"), but it also acknowledges that it can be undone ("off"). If you are subject to the tyranny of guilt, this name offers an important teaching: No error is etched in stone. You will always have another chance.

What you believe are your sins are simply errors. Sins require punishment; errors merely call for correction. No one punishes you for your sins more than you do. And no one can relieve you of guilt more than you can. For every indelible paint mark you leave, there is a can of Goof Off to make your car—and life—like new. Maybe even better.

What "sin" do you believe you must continue to suffer and pay for?
Can you forgive yourself and restore your mind
and heart to a sense of innocence?

I release my past in the light of grace.
I am new, whole, and free in this moment.

A Simple Question

First say to yourself what you would be,
and then do what you have to do.

— Epictetus

I had a tenant, Leslye, whom I used to chat with when I came home from work each evening. She and I would sit on the porch steps and talk about our day. One day she told me, "You always seem grumpy when you come home from the office. Why is that?"

I gave Leslye a rundown of the annoying things that happened in the office that day.

She tilted her head like a little girl and asked, "Why do you go to the office anyway?"

Immediately I wrote off Leslye's question as naïve. She obviously did not understand all the responsibilities I had. I began to go into detail about the phone calls and e-mails that had to be answered, the accounts that had to be managed, the contracts that needed to be negotiated, and the deadlines that needed to be met.

Somewhere in the midst of my explanation, Leslye's question sank in: *Why do you go to the office anyway?* When I started my business ten years earlier, the office piece was really simple. Now it was complicated. My responsibilities had crept up on me gradually, and I just assumed I had to personally handle the duties that had grown. Of all the questions I asked myself during any day, *Why did I come here anyway?* never occurred to me.

Suddenly a light went on in my brain: I was grumpy because I detested all the little tasks I believed I had to do. Leslye's question caused me to reconsider if I really had to do them. The answer was a resounding *no!* I could easily hire someone or a few people to take over the phone calls, e-mails, checkbook balancing, and stuff like that. I had drifted from my original purpose as a writer and speaker, and gotten caught up in minutiae. No one forced me to do any of it. I had taken on jobs distasteful to me, and I could delegate the ones I chose.

Soon after that conversation, I began to hire helpers, and my job and my life changed significantly. All because of one simple question. *Why do you do that anyway?*

Can you release unwanted or unnecessary tasks
so you can stay on track with what brings you joy?

I am true to my purpose. I do what I am here
to do, and I support others to do the same.

Watch Me Burn

Only passions, great passions, can elevate the soul to great things.
— Denis Diderot

When someone asked John Wesley how he inspired people so much when he delivered his lectures, he explained, "I just set myself on fire, and people come to watch me burn."

Wesley's method has tremendous practical applications for any profession. While customers ostensibly come to you for goods or services, they are more deeply seeking aliveness and validation. The huge number of tired, numb, and ill people trudging through lifeless days is a sad testament to the fact that most people's inner fire has been reduced to mere embers. When you bring vitality and full presence to your work and relationships, you are serving the world in ways far more powerful than delivering a product or service. The apparent reason for your meeting is just the springboard for a potential experience of connection and expansion.

A minister told me about a famous speaker who came to address his church one Sunday. For 20 years the guest speaker had delivered the exact same lecture wherever he spoke. It was a good lecture, but the same one. After flying overnight, the speaker took his place at the pulpit and began to address the audience. In the middle of the speech, he went silent. The minister, seated off to the side behind the speaker, assumed the man was gathering his thoughts. After the silence went on, he stood to make sure his guest was all right. To his shock, the minister discovered that the speaker had fallen asleep during his own lecture!

Be sure to stay awake during your own lecture. Surf on the cutting edge of what turns you on, and stay true to your life force in your work and relationships. Then people will drive long distances to watch you burn.

How can you live truer to your passion
so you will burn more brightly?

I express myself from the deepest aliveness
within me. I inspire myself and those I touch
with the power of my presence.

Give Atlas a Break

If you knew Who walks beside you . . . fear would be impossible.
— *A Course in Miracles*

In the garden of the Sarasota, Florida, estate of fabled circus entrepreneur John Ringling stands an impressive bronze statue of the Greek Titan Atlas bearing the world on his shoulders. The first thing I noticed about Atlas was that he was struggling dreadfully and appeared to be on the verge of caving in. Carrying the weight of the world is truly "overbearing."

While Atlas is often romanticized, his job is a cosmic drag. If you accept his role, so will your life be. If you assume responsibility for everyone and everything around you, you will get frazzled and fatigued. You will feel overwhelmed, be resentful, and lash out inappropriately. Shoulder pain, headaches, stomach problems, and high blood pressure are strong indicators that you are trying to play Atlas.

Yet it is not the universe that has piled too much on your plate. It is *you*. You have taken on jobs not assigned to you. You are trying too hard. You do not trust that others or the universe at large can handle things if you do not do it all. *Get over it.* Let go now and beat the rush later.

Letting other people and life help you will yield you major benefits: (1) you can quit doing things you do not want to do; (2) you free yourself to do the things you *want* to do; (3) your health will improve; (4) you will gain more professional success; (5) you will support and empower others to develop their gifts and talents and be rewarded for them; and (6) as you enjoy your life more, those around you will enjoy *you* more.

You are a good person. You want to do the right thing. You may be trying too hard. It is time to give yourself a break. Atlas is ready.

What tasks can you let go of to make your life easier and more rewarding?

I release the burdens that do not belong to me. I trust life to take care of me and my loved ones.

Healing Allowed

You blind guides, which strain at a gnat, and swallow a camel.

— Matthew 23:24

During a break in a program I was presenting at a retreat center, I was eating lunch with several participants at a picnic bench. One kind person in the group rose and began to give me a gentle shoulder massage. Suddenly we were jarred by a deep voice booming, "No healing allowed here!" I thought someone was kidding, but when I opened my eyes, I saw the retreat-center security guard.

"I'm sorry," he bellowed. "No healing is allowed on the campus except in the healing temple. If you want to be healed, you have to go there."

This had to be a practical joke. After all, who would make a rule against someone being healed? I looked again at the guard and realized he was quite serious. The student removed her hands from my shoulders and sat down.

On my way back to my room, I encountered the guard and decided to have some fun with him. "Sorry about that healing back there," I told him. "I can't imagine what came over me."

The fellow remained stern. "I hope you understand. If I let you do healing there, before you know it, people will be healing all over the place!"

I had to muster all the willpower I could to keep a straight face. I nodded and said, "And that's the last thing we would want to see happen, isn't it?"

"That's right," he answered firmly.

I dashed to my room and roared with laughter. This was too strange to be true. Then I remembered that Jesus was admonished for healing on the Sabbath. The Pharisees had rules, you know. Likewise, many of us have our ideas of what we must do so we can be healed. We think we need to be a better person, tithe, get the right medicine or doctor, pay off our sins, or . . .

If you are going to heal or be healed, be sure you do not miss the camel for the gnat. Rules are meant to maintain order. Love is meant to heal.

Do you believe there is a prerequisite to healing?
How can you choose healing in spite of the rules?

I am willing to give and receive healing
under the laws of love, not fear.

The Miracle of the Floating Fig

Wherever I am, God is!

— James Dillet Freeman

It was two o'clock in the morning when I arrived at Harbin Hot Springs, tired and hungry. I immersed myself in the soothing mineral waters and instantly felt my tired muscles unwind. Leaning my head back against the rim of the pool, I gazed gratefully into the vast starry night.

But I was famished. Unable to find a store or restaurant during my late-night drive through the mountains, I had not eaten for many hours and had no provisions. I began to feel anxious about not being able to get any food until the next day.

Then I looked around me and realized I was in a place of great tranquility. A candle radiated its mellow glow just above my head, while a mountain stream chanted a playful lullaby nearby. Surely the Great Spirit was in this place. Somehow I would be taken care of. Even if I had to go without food for a while, my heart was full.

Just then I felt something touch my lip. An object had floated toward me and bumped into my mouth. I reached to remove it, and discovered it was a fresh fig! The sweet delicacy had found me in the middle of a hungry night. In rhythm with the grace of the moment, I opened my mouth and received communion from a provident universe.

I looked up to see that I was sitting beneath a huge fig tree that spread its leafy limbs out over an entire section of the pool! Below the tree I found many figs, freshly fallen, floating on the surface of the water. I made a short round and gathered a handful. Then I went on to savor a most treasured midnight snack.

This experience taught me that wherever I am, God is. I am always taken care of, often in ways I could not control or plan. The miracle fig arrived at the exact moment I surrendered my sense of need and remembered that all is well. What better formula for abundant living?

How do you fear not being taken care of?
How might the presence of love be right where you are?

The Lord is my shepherd; I shall not want.

Connect the Dots

Reality leaves a lot to the imagination.

— John Lennon

Some psychologists did a fascinating experiment in which they showed their subjects a series of unrelated photographs. Then they asked them to recall the photos. The experimenters found that because the photos did not have a clear connection to each other, the subjects imagined other photos that would string together the images in some meaningful way. In psychological terms, this process is known as *rational closure*. The mind wants to make sense of what it observes, and when new information does not fit into a known reality, the mind finds ways to make sense of it, even if that means fabricating facts or experiences that close the gap between things otherwise meaningless.

Even more interesting, when the experimenters told the participants that some of the photos they thought they recalled were not presented to them, the subjects became defensive and argued that those pictures had indeed been there. That is how adamant the rational mind is about making sense of its chosen world.

Like the subjects of the experiment, you and I have our idea of reality that fits into our belief system and comforts us. Our idea may or may not have anything to do with the way reality is, but that does not matter to us. We will fight for the reality we believe in.

You can just as well connect the dots of a reality that serves you as you can connect the dots of a reality that does not support you. You can imagine photos of experiences that victimize you or ones that empower you. And you will live in the reality you argue for.

Today, experiment with making sense of ambiguity by choosing interpretations that support your happiness. Fortunately, the interpretation of well-being is closest to the truth about you, so honor yourself and your destiny of good by choosing beliefs aligned with it.

How might your current interpretation of your life be self-created?
How might you choose an interpretation that serves you better?

I make sense of my life by seeing it as supporting me.
I argue for my possibilities, not my limits.

How Easy Can It Get?

The moment one definitely commits oneself,
then Providence moves too.

— William Hutchinson Murray

The term *synchronicity* was coined by Swiss psychologist Carl Jung. It means "a meaningful coincidence," when two seemingly unrelated events occur simultaneously, with a purpose recognizable to the person experiencing the events. At such a moment, it becomes clear that the Law of Attraction is operating behind the scenes.

One day my partner, Dee, went to a spa at a hotel and received an excellent massage from a therapist named Susanna. During the course of their conversation, Susanna mentioned that she had a dog, an unusual mix of Blue Heeler and Sheltie. Dee enjoyed the treatment so much that she asked Susanna if she was available for house calls. Susanna explained that she was not allowed to set up private business through her interactions at the hotel, but if Dee got her number by some other means and phoned her, she could do it.

Later that afternoon, Dee and I were walking our dogs in a park when we met a couple of ten-year-old girls playing. They took an interest in our dogs, and we asked them if they had any. One of the girls replied, "Yes, I have a Blue Heeler/Sheltie." Dee was stunned to hear of the odd combination twice in one day, and asked the child if her mother's name was Susanna. The girl answered, "Yes, and she will be picking me up here in a few minutes."

While some would write off that meeting as coincidence, it was actually the product of intention. Dee had a very strong desire to reconnect with Susanna, and she had also surrendered the "how" of it to the universe, which is quite adept at orchestrating events we cannot.

If you really want to get something done but have no idea how to do it, worry not. The power of intention will synchronize the right people and events. If there is something you need to do, you will know it. Otherwise, just relax and walk your dog . . . and destiny will find you.

Are you worrying about how to get something done?
Can you trust the Law of Attraction to orchestrate the details?

I recognize the hand of the Divine in my significant encounters. I can let it be easy.

Your Holiness

I celebrate myself . . .
For every atom belonging to me, as good belongs to you.

— Walt Whitman

When I read that the Dalai Lama was to speak at an upcoming conference, I noticed that his name was preceded by the letters *H.H.* I asked someone what those initials stood for, and I was told, "His Holiness." It is also the respectful title bestowed upon the Pope.

I began to wonder why the Dalai Lama and the Pope are "His Holiness," and not the rest of us. To be sure, these spiritual leaders are very holy—but are they more holy than anyone else? Do the Dalai Lama and the Pope have more God in them than those who sit in their audiences? I imagine that these renowned spiritual leaders would agree that we are all holy in the eyes of God.

The "His Holiness" concept got me thinking about other appellations of respect. Take "Your Honor," the title conferred upon judges. Certainly judges merit honor, but are the other people in the courtroom less honorable? I wonder what would happen if judges addressed the defendants before them as "Your Honor" as well; perhaps this practice would bring forth the honor within *them.* Most criminals were not treated with respect as children; if they were granted this respect now, it might summon their innate integrity. Socially aberrant acts are unskillful attempts to feel love, power, and attention. Addressing criminals as "Your Honor" might begin to satisfy that call in a healthy way.

Then there is "Your Majesty," "Your Grace," and "Your Highness," offered to royalty. Does that mean that everyone else is not majestic, graceful, or high? Hopefully not.

I do not mean to demean those who merit respect. Rather, I mean to uplift those who generally do not receive it. *Holiness, honor, majesty,* and *grace* are not special gifts dispensed to a few. They are given equally to all of us. Perhaps if we called each other by the names by which God knows us, we would live in a more godly way.

Can you find in yourself the attributes of greatness
and respect that you offer others?

I am blessed with all the attributes of the Divine.
I claim them now for myself and for others.

Think Again and Grow Rich

*Great men are they who see that spiritual is stronger than
any material force; that thoughts rule the world.*

— Ralph Waldo Emerson

Napoleon Hill's book *Think and Grow Rich* is a classic text on prosperity and success. Millions of people have put its principles into action to create significant positive life changes. It belongs on the bookshelf of anyone who wishes to improve his or her life.

Many readers do not realize that the text they have read in editions published since 1960 is not exactly the one that Napoleon Hill wrote. In his original 1937 text, Hill made references to "vibrations" and "energy." The publisher of the revised edition felt that such language was too far-out for the masses, so those terms were deleted. In light of growing popular interest in metaphysical principles, it is now possible to get copies of the original text.

While the book certainly generates powerful results without the spiritual references, it is important to recognize Hill's original acknowledgment of an invisible force that lies behind success. While the publisher may have been wise to exclude such references to appeal to the readership at the time, we are living in a *new* time now. Our world is now ready to recognize and use the power of vibration as a force behind life. It would be ludicrous to deny invisible vibrations, since practically all of our technology runs on unseen wireless transmissions, from radio to radar to television to satellites to your Wi-Fi computer, and much more.

Everything you experience is based on frequency. Light, sound, touch, taste, and smell are all vibrations. Your thoughts also generate frequencies. When you recognize the unseen mental dynamics that create the obvious world, you are in a position to master your life. Success is based on a frequency of mind, and so is failure. Set your tuner and your transmitter to your desired frequency, and you can use your chosen thoughts to draw to you all that you desire.

*How might you shift your frequency of thought,
word, and action to improve your life?*

**I acknowledge and respect the presence and power
of an invisible force that creates my life. I use
this force for my good and the good of others.**

Which Lane to Drive Through

*When you have once seen the glow of happiness on the face
of a beloved person, you know that a man can have no other vocation
than to awaken that light on the faces surrounding him. . . .*

— Albert Camus

My friend Kane went to the airport to pick up a revered rabbi. As the two drove toward the tollbooth plaza to exit the airport parking lot, Kane had to choose between an automatic-payment lane and one manned by an attendant. "Take the lane where you pay a person," the rabbi urged him.

"Why is that?" asked Kane.

"Any opportunity to make contact with another human being is a blessing," the rabbi explained.

It seems that the more we fill our hunger for gadgets and labor- and time-saving devices, the deeper our hunger for human connection grows. We are well fed materially but undernourished spiritually. Many people are depressed because they miss their sense of person-to-person contact and do not know how to find it.

Anything you can do to personalize your life and work will yield rewards to you and those you touch. When I recently phoned a computer company to order a part, I was placed on hold. Meanwhile, a message announced: "Please take a deep breath and relax. We'll be with you as soon as possible."

The suggestion to take a deep breath came as a pleasant surprise to me, and I followed the advice. I recognized that whoever ran that company valued humanity, and wanted to pass ease along to their customers. This inspired me to make my purchase from this company and remember it the next time I needed a part.

Every day offers a series of choices. The next time you must decide between a machine and a person, please remember the rabbi's advice.

*What practical choice can you make today
to connect with the people you encounter?*

**I seek connection, give it, receive it, and
celebrate it. I feed my soul and that of others.**

No Right Angles in Nature

I believe that there is a subtle magnetism in Nature, which
if we unconsciously yield to it, will direct us aright.

— Henry David Thoreau

If you look out your window, step into your backyard, hike through a forest, or stroll on a beach, you will notice a phenomenon you have probably not thought about before: there are no right angles in nature.

Practically every element of nature has at least some curve to it. Even trees that grow generally straight and tall rise at a subtle yet gradual angle from the ground. If you want to experiment with this principle, take a carpenter's square and hold it to rocks, trees, and riverbeds. You will rarely, if ever, find a piece of nature the square fits.

On the other hand, walk around your house, your office, or a street downtown and you will see that practically every corner is squared off.

Gradual change is the way of nature. Radical change is the way of man. Not that there is anything wrong with square corners. They have their function. It's just not how nature operates.

The lesson nature offers is that if you want to make effective change, it is better to do it gradually. I am not a big fan or encourager of clients going cold turkey or trying to make quantum leaps. Occasionally such methods work, but more often they create a backlash, and the individual has to retrace his or her steps and make a smoother transition. If you force the pendulum of life radically to one side of its course, it will sweep just as far to the other.

If you are contemplating a big change in your life, do it in steps if possible. There is usually more grace and stability in incremental growth than revolutionary shifts. Revolutions have a place, but they must be in harmony with evolution if they are to stick.

How might you make a big change in steps?
How might gradual movement help you stabilize?

I go where I choose one step at a time.

Advanced

Go freely with powerful uneducated persons . . .

— Walt Whitman

My neighbor Marty is labeled "developmentally delayed," or in the old parlance, "retarded." He is 19 years old with the mentality of perhaps a 10-year-old. Yet in many ways Marty is like a Zen master. He has retained a childlike charm and speaks from innocence. I have come to regard him as a profound teacher.

One day when I went to visit Marty's family, he greeted me at the door and asked how I was. "Just fine," I told him. A little while later, he again asked me how I was.

"I'm still fine," I told him. "Do you remember that you asked me that when I arrived?"

"Sure," Marty answered. "But that was half an hour ago. I was wondering how you are now."

Marty is one of the friendliest people I know; he loves to connect with everyone. Once when I took him to Kmart, he walked through the aisles shaking everyone's hands, asking them how their day was going, and complimenting them on their clothes.

Perhaps Marty's greatest wisdom came one day when I passed him in my car as he was walking to the bus stop on the corner. After he greeted me, he looked up at the sun and around at the trees and exclaimed, "The world is great, isn't it?"

Now there is the meditation of a lifetime! Yet Marty had arrived at that profound truth without thinking about the issue very hard.

A lot of people tend to shun individuals with mental disabilities. Yet in many ways they are closer to innate wisdom than those of us with developed intellects. They have not strayed far from the kingdom of heaven, and this world is more of a playground to them than a workplace. We can learn a lot from them if we are open. Marty may be delayed intellectually, but he is advanced spiritually.

How might you find deeper peace by
seeing the world through innocent eyes?

I celebrate and learn from people who see the wonder in life. They are my teachers of happiness.

Passion Without Purpose

The devil can cite Scripture for his purpose.

— William Shakespeare

Mythologist Joseph Campbell tells of a man he knew who was a prisoner of war in Germany during World War II. The soldier recalled that one day Adolf Hitler came to the camp to address the troops and the prisoners. The fellow recounted, "Hitler spoke with such passion and charisma that when he concluded his speech, it was all I could do to keep from raising my hand and shouting, 'Heil Hitler!'"

The man's experience is typical of people in the presence of a charismatic leader. In such an aura, you feel awakened, stimulated, and inspired. You are moved to accept the leader's message and follow his or her action plan. In many cases, you might do just that.

Yet, as in the case of a Hitler, if the leader is motivated by ego rather than Spirit, you would do far better to listen to your own inner voice than the leader's directives. Charisma is apportioned not only to the good, but finds its way just as often to those who misuse it. If you are in the presence of such magnetism, you may feel torn, since you are hungry for life, passion, and movement. Just take care to consider where that movement is leading you.

Years ago I participated in an excellent seminar that offered many powerful and useful success principles. At the end of it, the teacher made a huge pitch for each participant to go out and enroll many more students. I went home and began to pick up the telephone to call some of my friends. As I did, I had a strange feeling that I had experienced only once before—when I had been hypnotized. I realized that along with the valuable teachings the seminar had delivered, I had been subject to some brainwashing thrown into the mix. I hung up the phone.

When joining a spirited group of any kind, check in with your gut to see if the message matches your truth. High energy is not sufficient to constitute integrity. Truth and service must be at the foundation of impassioned action.

Is the path you are moved to follow founded
in kindness as well as enthusiasm?

I balance passion with wisdom, excitement
with reason. I serve consciously, not blindly.

The Artist's Rendering

Who looks outside, dreams. Who looks inside, awakens.

— Attributed to Carl Jung

While I was walking through a terminal in the Los Angeles International Airport, I felt annoyed and inconvenienced by the massive construction projects going on around me. Squeezed between temporary plywood walls, I navigated a row of tall scaffolds and took a lengthy detour to baggage claim. I grumbled to myself about what a mess the place was, and how long it was taking to remodel it.

Then I saw a poster that stopped me in my tracks. It was an artist's rendering of what the airport would look like when the construction was complete. It was magnificent! The glass atrium roofs, sleek marble corridors, and potted palms were a delight to behold—a far cry from the current chaos. Then I relaxed. *If that is what this is leading to,* I thought, *I'm glad they're doing it.* As I dropped my resistance, I enjoyed the process, including the construction phase.

When I returned to the airport a year later, the vision had become a magnificent reality. The artist's rendering had come to life.

Construction is usually messy. You may have to turn ground over, tear an existing structure down, or pile materials all over the place. Art projects, too, are rarely neat and organized. They require some disorder and sprawl. Likewise, sometimes your life feels stable; and other times it is subject to demolition, construction, or creative chaos. Or all three. Since we are always in a state of becoming—an element of the human journey—do not resist or begrudge the messy construction stage. It is part of the deal.

If you feel overwhelmed during the transition phase, shift your attention to the artist's rendering. Behold a grand and glorious vision of where you are headed, far more beautiful and functional than the format being undone. Sometimes you cannot see the artist's rendering, and you have no idea where your life is moving. Just trust that there is a blueprint for a brilliant new creation. One day you will walk through the corridor of your new structure and marvel at its splendor.

How can you appreciate turbulence of change as leading to a more satisfying dimension in your life?

I hold the vision of new and better things to come. I trust my positive evolution.

Thank Your Critic

An insult is a boon to a sage.

— Lao-tzu

I was counseling a fellow who had been in a long, painful relationship with a woman who constantly found fault with him and laid the blame for her unhappiness at his doorstep. "She is not doing it *to* you," I suggested to him. "She is doing it *for* you."

"How's that?" he asked.

"You 'hired' your girlfriend to magnify every self-loathing thought you have had about yourself and play it back to you in such an intense and obvious way that you would have to examine your self-worth until you recognize and live it," I told him.

If others are continually annoying you with criticism, do not fight back or run away. Instead, be grateful to them. They are your best teachers. Not because they are correct in their faultfinding, but because they are serving as a mirror of your own internal critic. They have come to show you how hard you are on yourself so you can begin to love yourself and heal a long pattern of internal self-abuse.

Criticism cannot disturb you unless you agree with it. If you are clear and confident about who you are and what you do, negative feedback will not be a big factor in your psyche. But if you harbor internal doubts about yourself or your abilities, someone will likely voice and magnify those doubts. If you argue or retaliate, you have missed the gift of the experience. If you look inside and ask yourself, *Is this really true?* you are on your way to higher ground. If it is true, you can correct it. If not, you can forget it.

Your critic is your friend. Do not fight with the mirror. Use it to enhance what you see.

How might you use criticism to help you recognize
and strengthen your sense of true worth?

I appreciate all feedback to help me grow
in self-awareness and self-appreciation.

Three Baskets, Two Hands

In art and dream may you proceed with abandon.
In life may you proceed with balance and stealth.

— Patti Smith

Imagine you need to bring three baskets up a mountain. Yet you have only two hands. So you carry two of the baskets for a while and then set them down while you come back and retrieve the other one. Then you carry two again, leaving a different basket behind, and later come back to pick up that one. So goes your journey, taking turns leaving one basket behind, picking it up, and moving ahead.

This metaphor describes how we must care for the three bodies with which we make our journey through life. You have a physical, emotional, and mental body, each of which requires care and attention. The physical body must be fed, rested, and exercised. The emotional body must be nourished with inspiration through love, music, and art. The mental body must be stimulated with ideas and projects. Understimulate any of your bodies and you will starve. Overstimulate any and you will be out of balance.

But you cannot care for all three bodies at once, so you have to do a balancing act. You may feed your mind a lot, but then your physical body starts to feel sluggish, so you have to move it. Overindulge in emotion and you need to balance your choices with reason. And so on.

Most people are highly focused on one of the bodies. They spend a lot of time at the gym, at the computer, or processing their relationships. While it is good to engage in a specialty you enjoy, if you do it at the expense of the other aspects of your being, you need to retrieve the basket temporarily left behind. So weight lifters might do well to spend some more time at the computer, while geeks could use a gym membership.

Healthy, successful living is not a mystery. It is simply a balancing act.

Which body do you primarily focus on?
How can you balance the other bodies in order to feel better?

I care for the physical, mental, and emotional aspects of my life in harmony and balance.

Pulling Power

The heights by great men reached and kept
Were not attained by sudden flight;
But they, while their companions slept,
Were toiling upward in the night.

— Henry Wadsworth Longfellow

You could probably learn all you need to know about life by spending time in a garden.

I have grasped one keen lesson through growing a hedge, which starts by pruning one stem of a small plant. Two new stems emerge from the one cut; then you prune each of those stems, and four more emerge, and so on, until the plant bushes out with so many stems and leaves that you have a thick hedge.

If you severely trim a large hedge, the branches will grow back quickly, intensely, and in huge numbers. That is because the root system of the hedge is so deeply and strongly developed that when it pulls water and nutrients from the soil, it is moving a huge flow of energy up and out. When that energy reaches the tips of the recently cut branches, it bursts into many new stems, leaves, and flowers.

In The Teachings of Abraham, this dynamic is called "pulling power." The stronger you desire something, and the more deeply rooted your experience of it is, the more quickly and powerfully it bursts forth into manifestation. That is why people who have lots of money or success can lose it, but they re-create it quickly. They have pulling power. Their consciousness of success is so deeply rooted and they have so much energy moving in that direction that even if the outermost manifestation is cut off, they will bounce back with even more power than before.

That is how Steven Jobs could co-invent the Apple computer, get fired, develop Pixar Animation Studios, return to Apple and create the iPod and iPhone, and on and on. He has pulling power.

You, too, have pulling power. Just stay rooted in joy and passion and keep your energy moving. Then temporary pruning will not stop you, but instead, result in even more massive flowerings.

How can a recent setback be a setup for greater success?

I am established in my vision and intention.
Everything that happens on the way to my
goal contributes to greater achievement.

In My World All Is Well

There is a place in you where there is perfect peace.

— *A Course in Miracles*

The great yogi Sri Nisargadatta is regarded by many as an enlightened being. He was a teacher in the Advaita tradition, which affirms the eternal presence of good. He stated, "In my world all is well."

This declaration, odd as it may sound, offers an impetus for constant meditation. "How could someone who lives in a world of war, starvation, greed, and suffering say that all is well?" one might ask. "Just drop in on five minutes of any newscast and it is clear that all is definitely *not* well."

The key to the yogi's statement lies in the phrase "in my world." What world did Sri Nisargadatta live in? Is he in deluded denial, or does he know of a world that we are missing?

The latter is the case. When we toss around the phrase "the world," we make the huge mistaken assumption that there is one world that everyone on the planet lives in. We may all stand on the same globe, but the reality that each person lives in is subject to his or her own perception and interpretation of it. For the nearly seven billion people on Earth, there are nearly seven billion realities people are living in. Many of them agree and overlap, so it would appear that there is an objective, absolute reality. But some of them do not agree or overlap, and the world those people live in is far different from the one the others perceive.

Many of the people walking the earth are living in hell, while some live in heaven. What do those in a heavenly state of mind see and know that those in a hellish frame do not see? That is where the yogi's statement comes in. He has tuned his mind, heart, and perception to the frequency of well-being, which surely exists if we align with it. As you and I attune to the same frequency, we may also declare with equal authority, "In my world all is well."

*How might you shift your perception so you
see well-being where you once saw lack or emptiness?*

**I find evidence for the world I would choose
to live in. In my world all is well.**

No Kindness Too Small

Kings and cabbages go back to compost,
but good deeds stay green forever.

— Rick DeMarinis

Hairdresser David Wagner had a client who came to him regularly. One day this woman, who was young and attractive, with a life apparently working very smoothly, phoned him in between her regular engagements and asked David if he would style her hair that afternoon, since she had an important appointment soon. David kindly fit her into his schedule; and when she came, he gave her his usual thoughtful attention, laughing with her, touching her kindly, and telling her how great she looked with her hairstyle.

A few days later David received a thank-you note from the woman, with a shocking revelation: The "appointment" she had mentioned had been her own funeral! She had planned to commit suicide that evening and wanted to look good when she was found. "But," she told David, "when you were so kind, loving, and attentive to me, I changed my mind and decided that life is worth living."

You can imagine David's shock upon receiving such news and acknowledgment. This striking experience caused him to rethink his business and purpose as a hairstylist. He realized that he had the potential to change his clients' lives in far deeper ways than styling their hair. David realized that he could literally make their day—and life. So he redefined his profession as a "Daymaker," and his career has never been the same since.

Now as owner of Juut Salonspa, a network of health-and-beauty salons across America, David has trained his entire staff to be Daymakers. Serving approximately 4,000 clients per day, consider how much better a place the world is for the Juut staff regarding the clients' appointments as opportunities to make their day! (You can read David's story in detail in his excellent book, *Life as a Daymaker*.)

You, too, can redefine your profession and purpose in life as a Daymaker. You never know how far one act of kindness might go.

How might you upgrade your career by claiming
your purpose to make your clients' day?

My work and relationships are opportunities
to bring love and healing to everyone I meet.

How Motivated Are You?

Clothe with life the weak intent,
Let me be the thing I meant.

— John Greenleaf Whittier

During coaching, Cynthia asked me if I thought she should pursue a course of graduate study at a particular university. "I drove 30 miles to the college last week to check out the department, but I couldn't find a parking place," she reported. "So I just turned around and drove home."

Hmm. "It doesn't sound like you're really motivated," I reflected to her. "On a scale of 1 to 10, how motivated would you say you are?"

"If the school was next door to my house, I would say 10," Cynthia answered. "But if I have to drive to it and find a parking place, I would say 2."

"If you intend to get a graduate degree, you would have to be motivated at least enough to find a parking space," I told her.

Cynthia laughed and agreed. There were other things she wanted to do more.

Less than full intentions get less than full results. Wholehearted intentions get wholehearted results. If you are not sincerely interested in achieving a goal, you will not enjoy it and you will not succeed. Better to pursue what you are more motivated to do.

When a young man asked Ernest Hemingway if he should pursue a career as a writer, Hemingway told him, "If anything can stop you from writing, let it." Big dreams often draw forth big obstacles, or at least require big effort. If you are not deeply motivated, obstacles will put you off. You need strong intention and focus to blow past them. If you need the university to be next door in order for you to attend it, there are probably other things you would rather do, and your energy and efforts would be put to better use if you pursued what is a 10 on your list rather than a 2.

What goal is exciting enough to you that you are
willing to do whatever it takes to achieve it?

I direct my efforts to dreams that light my fire
and are worth my time and energy to pursue.

May and Might

It is your Father's good pleasure to give you the kingdom.

— Luke 12:32

There are two words you use often that have great meaning, but which you probably do not think much about. Today we will illuminate their inner meaning to liberate more inner power for you and your life.

For one, you might say, "I *may* get a new car." The word *may* indicates that you have the possibility, or permission, to get what you want. (Remember the child's game "Mother, may I?"?) Inherent in your statement is the awareness that the universe will allow you to achieve a goal if you so choose it.

You might also say, "I *might* get a new car." The word *might* indicates that you have the power to get a new car. Such an act is within your control and your ability. You know you can, and you will.

These two little words, often overlooked, indicate your divinely given ability to create. You have *permission,* and you have *power.* The universe withholds nothing from you. If anything, you withhold your good from yourself by not realizing your permission or exercising your power. Yet you can manifest anything from that vast storeroom by claiming the permission and power you already have.

It is your Father's good pleasure to give you the kingdom. God wants you to have all the wonderful things your heart desires. God does not withhold, tease, taunt, or test. God gives. It is up to you to receive. When you do, you realize that all is already given.

May and might. Permission and power. You have it. Now do it.

What do you want that you believe the universe cannot or will not give you? If you knew you had permission and power, what would you ask for or do?

I can have what I want. Life gives and I receive.
The universe rejoices in my fulfillment.

Three Graduates

I am never bored anywhere: being bored is an insult to oneself.

— Jules Renard

I once gave a church-service talk about the importance of following your joy. I suggested that boredom is a call to get creative and do whatever it takes to stay happy right where you are.

That morning one of the Sunday-school teachers did not show up, so the elders took the three eight-year-old boys in the class and sat them in the front row of the church to keep them in line. Dazzling, enlightening, and entertaining as my talk was, somehow I did not get the boys' attention, and they were fidgeting throughout the service. The next time I looked at them, however, they were sitting quietly—all with quarters in their eye sockets.

At first I was a bit jarred, but then I had to laugh. They were the only people in the audience who put my lesson into action immediately! They were not particularly interested in what I had to say, so they took the responsibility to entertain themselves. *Good,* I thought. *Three graduates of my lesson.*

If you are bored, annoyed, or frustrated in your job, relationship, home, or body, assume the responsibility to make yourself happier. If you wait for other people or conditions to change so you can feel better, that will likely not happen. But if you find some way to keep yourself entertained, two things will occur, and maybe three: (1) you will feel better, (2) you will be more present and effective doing what you are doing, and perhaps (3) your situation will upgrade so you are in a more fulfilling condition.

Children are good at keeping themselves entertained, and they need very little to do it. When I visited Fiji, I saw kids playing rugby using an empty plastic water bottle as the ball. In New York City I saw some teenagers playing basketball using a hole in a shop awning as a hoop. There is always some way to stay happy and entertained if you are willing to find it.

What creative way could you employ to offset boredom or frustration?

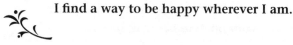

I do not accept gaps in happiness.
I find a way to be happy wherever I am.

Closer to Life

Your life is valuable not for the number of breaths you take,
but for the number of moments that take your breath away.

— Source unknown

When I drive into town from my house, I pass a lovely, well-manicured cemetery. After a tradition, there are no headstones in this cemetery, just many flowers on graves. The site is on a bluff overlooking the ocean, and I find its vista peaceful.

One day while I was rushing into town thinking about the errands I had to do, a touching sight caught my eye. An older woman and a younger man, whom I imagined were mother and son, were placing flowers on a relatively new grave. I was moved by the reverence and kindness I saw in these people. Perhaps the father in the family had passed on and the two were honoring him with their love and fresh flowers. The energy that the two people emanated was simple yet poignant. It reminded me that while we all live mortal lives, at the core we are spirit. Something about us dies, yet something about us lives.

When I went to sleep that night, I remembered little about my errands or activities that day. Yet that stirring moment stayed with me. It was the most inspiring point of my day.

Do not judge your day by what you get done, but rather, by the moments of awakening, joy, or insight you experience. Your activities are simply the template for your spiritual journey. If, in the midst of busyness, you find and absorb moments that move you, your day is successful. If you get a lot done but do not feel closer to yourself or life, the day did not yield real fruit.

You also never know how you may be affecting someone by your simple inspired acts. I am certain the family at the grave had no idea that their devotion would uplift me. Yet their kindness drifted across the cemetery like a flower's fragrance and made a significant difference in my world—and now that you are reading this, perhaps in yours.

How might you let yourself be more available
to moments that lift your spirit?

I savor the spiritual experiences of my day.
I am open to being uplifted.

All about Frequency

It's not denial. I'm just selective about the reality I accept.
— Bill Watterson *(Calvin and Hobbes)*

In his book *Inner Coach: Outer Power,* Keith Varnum tells of a metaphysical conversation he shared with a friend while dining at a McDonald's restaurant. The two were considering that there are many different realities operating simultaneously—some of which overlap, and others that do not. Keith's friend suggested, "I believe that if you and I were sitting here in a state of peace and harmony, and a bomb went off in the building next door, we might not even notice it or be affected by it because our consciousness would be functioning at an entirely different frequency."

Minutes later several police officers dashed into the restaurant, charged the table where the two men were conversing, threw them against the wall, and began to frisk them.

"What's going on?" Keith asked.

"This restaurant was just robbed at gunpoint, and you two guys are the only ones here. We suspect you may be the criminals."

While Keith and his friend had been immersed in their spiritual conversation, two gunmen had held up the restaurant. Then the crooks, staff, and other patrons had fled. Only Keith and his friend remained, oblivious to the robbery because their conversation had been in a state of mind that did not overlap with that of the robbery—perfectly proving the point they had been discussing!

The police quickly discovered that the two men were innocent and released them. Yet the lesson had run deep: Every reality is based on a particular frequency. When you are immersed in any given reality, you have access to everything that matches that frequency, and you do not have access to anything that does not match it. So take care to choose the frequency you live in by generating thoughts, words, and actions that match what you want to experience.

How do the events in your life match the frequency you are generating?
How might you upgrade your frequency and your reality?

I dwell in my chosen reality by focusing on thoughts, feelings, and words that match it.

The Law of Shared Good

That can never be good for the bee which is bad for the hive.
— Ralph Waldo Emerson

Becky rented a room in her house to her friend Tony, and the two got along very well, Tony was quiet and paid his rent on time, and in many ways the relationship was ideal. Over the years, Becky noticed that her friend was becoming a hermit. He stayed in his room most of the time, hardly went out except to go to work, and had no social life. Tony seemed depressed, his room was a mess, and he had put on weight.

Eventually Becky decided to do a major remodel on her house, which would require her to ask Tony to vacate. Part of her hated to ask him to leave, since he had been a friend and good tenant, and he liked living in the room. Yet Becky felt moved to upgrade her home, physically and energetically. So she gave Tony notice, and when he grumbled about having to relocate, she felt guilty. But Becky remembered the motto "There is no private good," and she decided to trust the process.

Tony left, Becky eventually completed the renovation, and another tenant moved in. Several months later, Becky ran into Tony while shopping, and he looked much more alive. He had lost weight, appeared to take more pride in his appearance, and seemed happier than when he had lived in Becky's house. "Thank you for asking me to leave," he told her. "I didn't realize what a hole I had dug for myself. I moved downtown, joined a health club, and I am dating someone I like. I am back in life, and being forced to leave turned out to be a huge move in my favor."

If something is not working for you, it cannot really be working for another person. When you tell the truth about what *would* work for you and you act on it, you will usually find that it helps those involved. They may grumble to be disturbed from what feels like a comfortable situation, but in the long run, they will find that a sense of greater aliveness far exceeds the slumber of routine.

How could you taking your next step serve others to take theirs?

As I move toward my greater good, I support
others to move toward their greater good.

Glad I Didn't Know Better

When I was a child, my mother said to me, "If you become a soldier, you'll be a general. If you become a monk, you'll end up as the Pope." Instead, I became a painter and wound up as Picasso.

— Pablo Picasso

When I wrote my first book, *The Dragon Doesn't Live Here Anymore*, I was blissfully ignorant about the publishing industry. I wrote for the sheer delight of expressing myself, and I published the book myself. Within a few months it became popular, and before long I was reprinting it in quantities of 10,000 and traveling around the world to present seminars.

One day I walked into a bookstore where my book was being sold, and I was appalled by the huge number of titles on similar subject matters—the self-help section was huge! It occurred to me that if I had gone to the store before writing and done an analysis of all the excellent books already published, I would have felt intimidated and probably never set pen to paper. But I was innocent and ignorant— and that made all the difference.

As I later got to know the publishing industry, I learned all the rules about what kinds of books sell, covers that attract attention, hooks to appeal to various markets, and so on. In retrospect, I am glad I did not know the rules, because most of the rules lead to the disappointing conclusion that only a small percentage of writers will succeed. Some other writers who did not know the rules were Dale Carnegie, Norman Vincent Peale, and James Redfield. *Is there a message here?*

My first book was not technically perfect or highly polished. But it was sincere. Readers tell me they felt my honesty and my heart, and that was attractive and helpful to them. I am not suggesting that you overlook technique; I am suggesting that you value inner prompting and realness more than industry formulas.

None of the authors on the shelf are saying anything new. But each has his or her own flavor, style, angle, and experiences of truth. Stay true to your own flavor and you will find your way to the bookshelf or to success in your chosen industry faster than those who know all the rules.

How might you succeed more by injecting your personal flavor rather than using a formula?

I am what I am. I express my unique gifts, and I succeed uniquely.

Ring Out the Old

Change always comes bearing gifts.

— Price Pritchett

When I saw an ad for a valuable cell-phone upgrade, I called the phone company and placed an order. The agent told me that the response to the promotion was so great that there would be a 30- to 90-day wait for the phone. *Okay, I can wait,* I figured, and resigned myself to doing so.

A week later while driving into town, I dialed a number from my cell phone. To my surprise, I received the message: "Your phone is not authorized for use. Please call the business office."

The business office had no clue why my phone would not function. My bill was paid, and their diagnostic test showed no problem. I talked to several agents, none of whom had any answers. "Try calling later," they told me. I felt frustrated and confused, but I had no choice, so I decided to just table the issue for the moment.

When I arrived home later that day, I found a FedEx box sitting at my doorstep. Inside was my new cell phone. I plugged it in, and it worked perfectly. The company had disconnected my old phone because it had transferred service to my new one.

If something in your life is not working anymore, do not fight to reinstate it or keep it alive. Hanging on to what has outlived its usefulness will create stress, confusion, and no real results. You will go in circles and only grow more frustrated. If you have to struggle or fight to keep an old thing going, it probably no longer belongs to you—and you do not need it. At some point your best move will be to simply let go and trust.

Then marshal your energy in a forward direction. Quit focusing on what was, and focus on what is next. Ask yourself, "If that was *not* it, then what *is* it?" When you can tap into that answer, you will understand why the other thing had to go. Sometimes you have to release the old before you discover what the new is. Who knows, you might just find something better at your doorstep.

How might you make room for what is new and better
by releasing what has outlived its usefulness?

I do not need to fight to hold on to anything.
I trust and let the universe deliver my good.

The Voice You've Been Waiting to Hear

. . . love from one being to another can only be that two solitudes
come nearer, recognize and protect and comfort each other.

— Han Suyin

I know of a woman who gave her baby girl up for private adoption. As the little girl grew over the first few years of her life, she seemed quite unhappy and cried a great deal. Her adoptive parents could not understand why she was so upset, and tried various tests and techniques to assess what was disturbing her, all to no avail. Finally they decided to contact the girl's birth mother and asked her if she would like to speak to her daughter.

The girl's birth mother was happy to have the opportunity to connect with her child, now three years old. When the time for this momentous call came, the mother and child met on the telephone for the first time. As soon as the child heard her mother say "Hello," she lit up and exclaimed, "That's the voice I've been waiting to hear!"

Likewise, we have all been separated from our original Source, and we long to connect with it. We walk the world feeling disconnected, alone, and abandoned, not exactly sure of who or what we are missing, yet feeling there must be more to life than the one we have been living. We try to regain our sense of connection by reaching for all kinds of things and people in the outer world, yet that fruitless search leaves us feeling only more lost and dissatisfied.

Eventually we consider that the answer to our loneliness may not lie outside of us, but within us. We were missing our connection with ourselves and our spiritual source. When we make that connection, we recognize, "That's the voice I was waiting to hear." It's our own voice or the voice of our higher or divine self that gives us comfort that our outer journeys failed to provide.

Today listen for the voice you've been waiting to hear. It may be closer than you think.

What comfort, peace, or relief do you seek?
Can you find it within you and in those you love and who love you?

I open to connect with the voice I long
to hear, and I offer it to others.

Flowers and Weeds

Whenever I step forward to claim a big new "Yes!"
all of my old "No's" come back to greet me.

— Source unknown

Have you ever noticed that when you are about to take a significant step in your life, make a major change, or approach a goal, events show up to oppose it? This is a common phenomenon, and no accident. It is a playing out of universal law, which, as you understand it, can help you overcome and move beyond obstacles that confront you.

When you set a goal or chart a course, you become keenly aware of two things: (1) everything that matches your goal and can help you achieve it, and (2) everything that opposes your goal and might stand in your way.

In my garden, when I stimulate the growth of a plant with extra water and fertilizer, the plant grows more rapidly. So do the weeds at its base. The water and fertilizer accelerate *their* growth as well, and I have to pluck them to help the plant progress.

The appearance of obstacles is not bad at all; they can, in fact, be very helpful. Like weeds that sprout as the plant comes to flower and fruit, obstacles are a sign that you and your project are growing. As you face fears, doubts, and resistance from yourself or others, remember why you want your goal and why you deserve it. Your original intention and motivation will help you pluck the weeds and let your plant grow to fruition. Even better, while you grow your project, you will also be growing yourself.

Do not be surprised when issues come up along your path. If they do not come up, enjoy the ride. But if they do, consider them opportunities for healing and empowerment that will leave you far ahead of where you would be if they had not surfaced.

What obstacles to your goal do you notice?
How might you benefit from facing and overcoming them?

I use obstacles as opportunities to
strengthen my resolve, reach my goals,
and expand my consciousness.

How Far Is the Great Pyramid?

*A penny will hide the biggest star in the universe
if you hold it close enough to your eye.*

— Samuel Grafton

I once took a group on an excursion to Egypt to study the ancient spiritual mysteries of that majestic culture. The first morning of our trip, we rose early to visit the Great Pyramid of Giza. Slowly our bus made its way through the eerie dense morning fog of Cairo. After a while, our bus came to a dead stop. One of our tour members grew impatient and asked the tour guide, "How far is the Great Pyramid from here?"

The guide smiled and answered, "About a hundred feet."

Although we did not know it, we were parked at the very base of the Great Pyramid, but we could not see it at all!

You may be extremely close to your goal, but if your vision is shrouded in doubt, fear, or confusion, you may believe you are still miles away. If you have been praying for, envisioning, or intending something for a long time, in the unseen realm you have been building your result, which is bound to manifest in the visible world.

If you spend time complaining about why your goal has not manifested, recounting your failed efforts, or commiserating with others who are disgruntled, you are manufacturing psychic fog and mentally distancing yourself from the goal.

When you hold firmly to your vision and remain steadfast in your intention, you are driving your bus to your goal, and at one point you will be able to reach out and touch it. The realm of the senses is quite deceptive. An object may remain invisible until the very last moment before it appears.

Imagine—the Great Pyramid of Giza right before you and not seeing it! Keep walking just a few yards more and you can touch it.

*How might a goal or intention that seems
far away be closer than you know?*

**I use higher vision to align with my
goal, and the object of my quest will
manifest at the perfect time.**

Rude Awakening

But difficulties are meant to rouse, not discourage.
— William Ellery Channing

"My whole life changed when I injured my hand," my client Judy told me. "I lost my career as a hospital technician, and I found myself alone for many hours a day. It was really a rude awakening!"

Judy's choice of words struck me. "You've told me about the rude part," I responded. "What about the awakening?"

"There were some major blessings," she admitted. "When I was in my job, I was on call 24/7. I would be driving home after my shift at the hospital, my beeper would go off, and I would have to turn right around. When I couldn't work, I thought about what I really wanted to do with my life. So I decided to go back to college. Now I'm studying psychology, something I've always thought about. And I have more quality time with my kids. In the long run, I'm better off."

Everyone has had rude awakenings. The question is, do you pay more attention to the *rude* part or to the *awakening?* Both are present. You will get more of whichever element you focus on. Eventually the rude part will fade into history, and the awakening will stay with you for a lifetime.

You have probably used an alarm clock with a progressively louder alarm. It begins to beep very softly, and if you do not wake up and silence it, it increases in volume until you have no choice but to rouse yourself and turn it off. So it is with life wake-up calls. First you get a whisper, and then a gentle nudge. If you do not respond, you face situations that grow more dramatic until something absolutely demands your attention. Then you say, "Ah, I should have listened to that still, small voice when I first became aware of it."

All wake-up calls are helpful. Temporary rude is an asset if it leads to permanent awakening.

If you have had a rude awakening, what has been rude,
and what has been the awakening?

All experiences lead me to greater freedom.
I use my life lessons to change for the better.

How Lucky Can You Get?

*When the bull's-eye becomes as big in your mind
as an elephant, you are sure to hit it.*

— Alejandro Jodorowsky

I met an artist who creates handicrafts with four-leaf clovers, which she uses to adorn gift boxes, bookmarks, and pendants. When I asked her how she finds all the clovers, she explained, "I just have a knack for it. On my last expedition, I found 150 four-leaf clovers."

"That's amazing!" I said. "How long did it take you to find them?"

"About 15 minutes," she answered.

I was astonished. If you have ever searched for four-leaf clovers, you have likely found perhaps one or two in a 15-minute stint. She found 150! How lucky can you get?

The answer has nothing to do with luck and everything to do with belief, expectation, motivation, and focus. The universe is abundant with all things, and it will happily deliver whatever you seek—if your mind is open to receive and you are sufficiently attuned to the object of your desire.

While many people attribute the results of their efforts to luck, fate, karma, astrological influences, and a gamut of external sources, experience is determined more by consciousness than by any other factor. The artist I described is so immersed in four-leaf-clover consciousness that they show up practically everywhere she looks.

The laws of manifestation are solid, consistent, and unbiased. They will gladly work in your favor if you understand how to use them and if you apply them consistently. Then you will not need "the luck of the Irish." You will have the consciousness of a creator.

*What would you most like to create in your life?
How could you focus on it more so you attract it by your consciousness?*

**I put the laws of manifestation into practice,
and life yields abundance to me.**

Please Take One

Forgiveness does not change the past, but it does enlarge the future.

— Attributed to Paul Boese

I know a man who, during his senior year in college, was walking past the bookstore when he saw a display of yearbooks on a table outside. The fellow really wanted a yearbook, but had no money. So he grabbed a book and kept walking.

Over the next few days he felt guilty about his theft, and he decided to return the book. He went to the bookstore manager and confessed, "I stole this book."

The manager told him, "Come with me." He led the student to the yearbook display and pointed to a sign the young man had not seen: FREE—PLEASE TAKE ONE.

This story serves as a metaphor: for every sin you can find in your life, love can find a way to reframe it in your favor. Errors you or others make motivated by pain, fear, or ignorance are not calls for punishment. They are calls for compassion. Beating yourself up for your mistakes is not the way to end them. Loving yourself is.

If you are laboring under a past misdeed, try to understand why you did it. At the time, you did not know better. You were afraid, confused, or upset; or you did not see other options. There are many reasons why people do foolish things, and we have all done plenty of them. Which feels better: to keep punishing yourself until you run your joy, health, and success into the ground; or to understand and release yourself and open a path to well-being and positive change?

To forgive yourself or another is not to condone a painful act or to encourage repeating it. It is to behold the act in a greater context. Some of the kindest and most successful people have pasts that could easily be condemned by a judgmental mind. Yet they have learned from their mistakes and have discovered how to look at their history from a perspective that makes way for a brighter destiny.

*How can you reframe a past misdeed and
regard yourself or another in the light of love?*

**I release myself and others from the prison of guilt.
I am innocent. I am free. I am as God created me.**

Drama Is a Choice

Turn your melodrama into a mellow drama.

— Ram Dass

My lawnmower repairman is an Australian guy whose attitude I enjoy as much as his skill. One day when I arrived at his shop just after closing time, I apologized for keeping him after hours. "That's okay, mate," he told me. "No dramas."

No dramas. That is one of the best affirmations I have ever heard. The notion of "drama" is built on a number of illusions. First, there are good guys and bad guys, duking it out to see who will win. Each position sees itself as good and the other bad. In the *Mad* magazine cartoon series *Spy vs. Spy,* two spies, one wearing white and the other black, were eternally trying to trick each other to gain advantage or do away with the other person. No one ever won.

Next, drama assumes a victim position on the part of the protagonist. Someone stronger is trying to hurt or take advantage of someone weaker, and the weaker one has to struggle to overcome the stronger evil. Yet the victim position is self-reinforcing. The more you see yourself as a victim, the more people and things you are victimized by. Regard yourself as a powerful creator, the source of your experience, and you grow beyond victimhood, your destiny firmly in your own hands.

Finally, drama suggests doubt about outcome. Will the bad guys win, or can the underdog triumph? *A Course in Miracles* tells us that the word *challenge* is meaningless, for it implies doubt about the outcome. Yet the *Course* assures us that everything ultimately works out.

Drama can also be an addiction. Some people grow accustomed to a certain amount of commotion, and if their drama level falls below a threshold, they find some new source of turmoil to bring their adrenaline back up to speed. By contrast, people with few dramas seem to know how to backpedal and cut back on drama if it exceeds their comfort level.

Reconsider any dramas you face and recognize that you can choose to engage in drama or let it go.

Do you have a lot of drama in your life?
How might you reframe your attitude to lighten your load?

Drama is a choice. I choose peace instead.
All is well, and life supports me.

The Story Line and the Glory Line

There is a wisdom of the Head, and . . . a wisdom of the Heart.
— Charles Dickens

A few years ago I was invited to address at a motivational conference that featured a series of speakers. My lecture was entitled "The Power Within You." I was pleasantly surprised to find that the speaker following me was a world-renowned celebrity who had accomplished an extraordinary feat of scientific skill and personal heroism.

After my presentation, I listened to this fellow's lecture, in which he recounted his life story and shared behind-the-scenes details of his adventure. Afterward, I sat at a table in the bookstore signing my books, while he sat at a table a few feet from me signing his books.

When participants asked me to autograph their journals, I noticed that most of them had a section dedicated to notes from the other speaker's lecture, and a section dedicated to notes from mine. To my surprise, most of the people had several pages written on my presentation, and few or no notes from the other speaker's.

When I asked a participant why there was a disparity in notes between the two lectures, she told me that my lecture was based on spiritual principles the participants could apply to create success in their lives. The other fellow's lecture was mainly a story line of his adventure, without highlighting life principles that could be applied. This particular audience came to the conference for inspiration more than information. They were hungry for ideas they could use, not just a historical account.

We all make two journeys simultaneously: a story line and a glory line. The story is facts. The glory is growth.

Unless the story line leads to the glory line, you will remain hungry. Lessons in "how" get far more mileage than lessons in "what." Tell your students what you have done and they will know your story. Teach them how to live and they will master their own glorious adventure.

What truths help you turn your story line into your glory line?

I use every experience to grow in awareness and happiness. I turn story into glory.

Expansive Belief

If we take people only as they are, then we make them worse;
if we treat them as if they were what they should be,
then we bring them to where they can be brought.

— Johann Wolfgang von Goethe

I've always wanted to fly an airplane, so when I saw an ad for a "You Fly" airplane flight, in which I would be able to take over the control stick for a while, I signed up and eagerly awaited my flight.

When the big day came, I drove to the Maui airport, where my pilot, Lou, guided me into the cockpit of a small Cessna. He gave me a brief rundown of the various instruments, strapped himself into the seat next to mine, and told me, "Now here's how you take off . . ."

Excuse me, I don't remember the ad saying anything about me taking off, I was about to protest. But when I looked at Lou, he was on the radio setting up our takeoff with the control tower. Suddenly I realized that *he thought I could do it.* So, in spite of my hesitation, I decided to believe in *his* belief, and I did not argue for my limits. I followed Lou's instructions, his hand on his controls as a backup, and within a few minutes we were airborne.

I flew the airplane nearly three hours that day. Over the dramatic north shore of Maui, past the thousand-foot sweeping verdant cliffs of Molokai, across the golden sand beaches of Lanai, then high above whales and dolphins cavorting in the channel. With Lou stepping in now and then for corrections, my nervousness gave way to exhilaration, my doubts to confidence.

As we approached the airport, Lou told me nonchalantly, "Here's how you land." *Now wait just a minute. . . .* But I trusted Lou, and now myself. Again, I kept my mouth shut.

I guided the plane in according to Lou's instructions, until he took over before touching down. When I left the airport later, I felt higher than our flight. Lou's belief in me brought out the best in me. The airplane flight lasted three hours; the lesson was for a lifetime.

If someone believes in you more than you believe in yourself, keep your mouth shut and give the person a chance to be right.

Who believes in you more than you believe in yourself?
Can you let them be right?

I open to see myself through the eyes of those
who love and believe in me, and I accomplish
more than I thought I could.

Shadow on the Moon

The church says the earth is flat; but I have seen
its shadow on the moon, and I have more confidence
even in a shadow than in the church.

— Attributed to Ferdinand Magellan

When Magellan set sail in 1519 to circumnavigate the globe, he believed strongly that the world was round and that, contrary to church dogma, he would not fall off its edge into space. Yet he had to buck a very strong popular and institutional mind-set to do so. Magellan was not the first innovator to swim against the tide of opinion. Practically every great world-change agent has.

Two important factors come into play when you chart your destiny or that of the world: what people say, and what you know. Sometimes the two match. Sometimes they do not. In the latter case, you are called to trust your inner knowing, which usually presents a challenge in the face of external adversity. How you handle that challenge makes all the difference in where you will end up.

I interpret Magellan's statement above less as a criticism of the church and more as a call to faith in obvious truth. Many institutions become so steeped in dogma that when an innovation comes along, they fight it. At that point the institution becomes top-heavy and no longer serves. Healthy institutions are willing to consider new evidence to help them expand service to their constituents. If they do not, they will topple and die.

You may have a project, vision, or intention that flies in the face of widespread belief. Yet, like Magellan, you may find evidence affirming that the direction in which you are headed is valid. Also like Magellan, if you base your adventure on what you know rather than what you are told, you may chart a new course and destiny for all who follow.

Do you feel conflicted between what
you have been told and what you know?
What would it take for you to follow your inner guidance?

I trust my inner knowing and expand my world
through faith in myself and my guidance.

Never the Same Trip

The cure for boredom is curiosity. There is no cure for curiosity.
— Attributed to Dorothy Parker

I chuckled as I stepped from the rental-car pavilion onto the shuttle bus to the Kauai airport. The distance to the terminal was quite short, and the shuttle went via a circle route of a half mile; if I walked the straight shot rather than taking the bus, I probably would have gotten there more quickly!

I set my bags on the rack, took a seat, and nodded to the driver. He closed the door, and the bus started to move. I joked, "I'll bet you get pretty bored making the same short circle trip all day long!"

The fellow smiled politely and answered, "I've never made the same trip twice."

Oh.

"I always meet interesting people on the bus," he added. "I like to talk to them and find out where they're from. They usually have some good stories about their vacation. I love this job!"

I see.

What a huge lesson this humble driver taught me! I was stuck in circular thinking. He was glowing with enthusiasm. He took a potentially monotonous job and transformed it into a game he just kept winning.

Boredom is not a condition; it is an attitude. Anything can be boring if you bring a closed mind to it. Anything can be fascinating if you bring an open mind to it. You can make anything out of anything, so why not make it what you want?

Today, notice if you feel bored or stuck in a rut. If so, remember the shuttle driver, who found ways to keep a circular drive fascinating. The circular movement was on a horizontal dimension only. On a vertical or spiritual level, the driver was soaring. If he can find stimulation and joy in that simple task, you and I can find greater life on our own path.

*How could you reframe something monotonous
to make it stimulating and uplifting?*

**I milk every moment for wisdom and joy.
I seek upliftment, and I find it.**

What a Drag

He that respects himself is safe from others;
he wears a coat of mail that none can pierce.
— Henry Wadsworth Longfellow

While having lunch in a Tokyo hotel, I looked out the picture window onto the street and saw a fellow walking by, wearing a little surgical mask to shield his respiratory system from pollutants, a practice common in Asian cities. What got my attention, however, was that the fellow was taking a drag of a cigarette as he ambled by.

I had to scratch my head at the inconsistency of his methodology. *Why expend the effort to protect yourself from a few stray germs from the outer world,* I wondered, *when you are inflicting far more pollution on yourself?*

I found this contradiction symbolic of the way many of us hurt ourselves with negative self-talk, self-doubt, and internal criticism. We may blame the world for attacking us or treating us unkindly, when we treat ourselves far more severely than anyone in our environment does. We don various forms of armor and construct elaborate defense systems to keep others from penetrating our well-being, when we harbor thoughts and engage in negative thinking or practices that undermine our happiness far more than anyone else can.

Today might be a good day to lay down your "sword and shield" and release the outer world as the cause of your discomfort. Reclaim your power as the only one who can make you happy or unhappy. Consider which people or events you regard as stray germs that might infiltrate your fortress of peace, as well as what you are doing to keep them at bay. Determine which thoughts and self-abrogating practices you are indulging that undo your joy far more than anyone else can. Then decide how you can give yourself a healthy dose of kindness to return to your natural state of inspiration.

How do you try to protect yourself from the outer world?
How can you claim dominion over your well-being
by bolstering yourself with more self-care?

I release others and the environment as the source of evil. I am in charge of my well-being, and I claim it now.

The Real Seminar

The eternal quest of the human being is to shatter his loneliness.
— Norman Cousins

I once presented a retreat at a camp facility on a small island near Vancouver, British Columbia. The camp caretaker, Dave, kept walking into the meeting room during our seminars, constantly seeking to fix something or make his way to the next room. At first I felt annoyed by Dave's persistent presence. Then I realized that he wanted to be a part of our group. So we invited him to join us, and he eagerly participated in our seminar.

During the program, Dave revealed that several years earlier his wife and young daughter had been killed in a car crash. He took the job as caretaker so he could hide out from life. But he found that he could not hide from himself or his heart. He craved human contact and support and yearned to give life another chance. Our group took Dave in its fold and gave him a lot of care and support, which he received gratefully.

I will never forget the day we left the island. As our boat launched from the pier, Dave stood at the edge of the dock waving vigorously to us. He was smiling and weeping at the same time. As we made our way into the bay, Dave just kept waving until he shrank from view, reduced to the size of a dot on the horizon. (I think he might still be waving.)

That weekend was a turning point for Dave and for all those present. He got back into life, and we came closer to it. While it appeared that the seminar was based on a certain format, the real seminar occurred in the "interruption." It was not an interruption at all, but Spirit's way to bring us all closer to love.

Do not be hasty to judge interruptions or people calling for love as bad. They just might be the key to the love that you, too, seek.

*What people or interruptions do you wish did
not bother you? How might they be an opportunity
to enjoy meaningful connection?*

**I recognize all situations as calls
for love or expressions of love.**

The Gap That Motivated Millions

There is just one life for each of us: our own.

— Attributed to Euripides

While many people are familiar with the inspiring books and seminars of motivational teacher Dale Carnegie, few are aware of how Carnegie began his illustrious career.

After an unsuccessful attempt at acting, Carnegie made a deal with the manager of a local YMCA to teach public speaking in exchange for a share of the proceeds. One night he ran out of teaching material before the class was over, so he improvised an exercise that invited students to come to the front of the class and talk about something that made them angry. Carnegie discovered that when students spoke honestly about things they felt strongly about, they lost their fear of public speaking. From this seminal experience he developed his world-famous courses on self-confidence, public speaking, and salesmanship based on authentic self-expression. His book *How to Win Friends and Influence People* was a megabestseller upon its 1937 release and continues to be extremely popular to this day, along with his self-development courses.

Carnegie's use of the gap in his class time proved pivotal in his life and the lives of millions who followed him. He achieved a significant paradigm leap by putting aside a standard course outline and offering the students the opportunity to simply be themselves. Carnegie withdrew the emphasis on form and reinvested it in essence. When that first student spoke from an authentic source inside himself, he came to life, and so did the entire class. They had stumbled upon the sheer power of honesty.

If you engage in public speaking—and you do, even if you are just having a conversation with one person—you can use your audience as your "truth meter." If its members are alert, sitting up, paying attention, and interested, you are speaking from the heart. If they are bored, yawning, inattentive, or making a beeline for the restroom, you have strayed from the power of truth.

Sometimes gaps in the program make space for far better programs.

How might you increase your personal and professional effectiveness by being more authentic?

**I trust who I am, and I speak from my heart.
I succeed by being myself.**

Remember the Redhead

Seek ye first the kingdom of God . . . and
all these things shall be added unto you.

— Matthew 6:33

A man approached me at the end of an evening seminar and told me, "A miracle occurred tonight." I put down my briefcase and listened.

"A few weeks ago I felt very lonely, so I went on Match.com to find a girlfriend," he explained. "I contacted several women and made a date with one to go to the city zoo. On the day of our date, I arrived early and she was not there yet. On the bench where we were to meet, a redheaded woman sat waiting for her friends. I joined her, and we began to chat. I liked her.

"My date arrived, we spent the afternoon together, and I realized this was not going to develop into a relationship. Instead, I kept thinking about the redhead, and wished I had gotten her phone number. I went home and began to feel depressed. Behold the story of my life: *I miss out on opportunities, and wind up with what I do not want.* I slipped into a funk and felt horrible.

"Then I saw the ad for your seminar called *'You Had It All the Time.'* That title reminded me that I need to find my power inside myself rather then projecting it onto a woman who will take away my loneliness. I let go of my upset about missing out on the redhead and decided to come to the seminar and trust the universe to help arrange my relationships.

"Tonight I walked into the lecture hall, sat down, and looked around the room. Across the aisle from me sat the redhead!"

When you seek a person or thing to fill your emptiness, you only feel emptier. When you recognize your wholeness and find fulfillment within you, the universe has miraculous ways of supplying what you want and need.

The Law of Attraction is constantly working to join you with who and what matches you. It's the Master Match.com.

Who or what do you seek to fill your emptiness?
What would you be doing differently if you knew you were whole?

I claim my wholeness and worth right where I stand. What I seek is inside me.

The Truth Smoke-out

Truth only reveals itself when one gives up all preconceived ideas.

— Shoseki

Are you having difficulty making decisions? Do you go back and forth between alternatives, wondering which would be better for you? If so, I have an extremely effective method for making decisions. I call it "the Truth Smoke-out."

When trying to make a decision that you are not sure about, ask the universe, *Please show me the truth about this.* Then watch for a sign. It will come.

Years ago I was considering buying a piece of real estate in a remote area. As the Realtor and I walked the land, I liked the property, but I had an uneasy feeling about it. I silently prayed, *Please show me the truth about this.*

As we were about to leave, we were approached by several tough-looking guys with a mean-looking dog. They asked us what we were doing on the property, and we told them I was considering purchasing it. The fellows went into a long tirade about how they were neighbors who had been wronged by the placement of the property line, they owned water rights to it, and on and on. Quickly it became clear they did not like the owner or get along with him, and the next owner would probably face similar issues. No, these would not be ideal neighbors.

As I drove home that day, I realized that my prayer had been answered. That property was not for me, and I was shown this clearly. While I was a bit disappointed, I felt relieved and grateful. There were other properties with nicer neighbors, and I would find one. And I did.

To use the Truth Smoke-out successfully, you must be sincere about your desire to have an answer and be open to the answer you receive. You cannot pray, *Please show me the truth about this, as long as it is my preconceived notion of what the truth should be.* Seek the answer aligned with your best interests and you will know clearly, confidently, and at the perfect time.

What question would you like to know the answer to?
Are you open to receiving the answer that is in your best interest?

I ask for guidance, I open my mind,
and I receive the answer.

One Ginger at a Time

*You can break that big plan into small steps
and take the first step right away.*

— Indira Gandhi

My neighbor Mark had a field of wild ginger he wanted to replace with an orange orchard. One day he went out to the field with a shovel and began to dig up the ginger. I shuddered as I watched him pick away at the thick, gnarly roots. As I surveyed the size of the field, I felt sympathy for him, as he faced a long, tough job.

Each day I watched Mark pick away at a new section of ginger, and each day the field grew a little clearer. "How's it goin'?" I would ask him daily.

Mark would look up, smile, and answer, "Just fine—one ginger at a time." Then he would go back to shoveling.

One day I drove past the field and saw that it was completely cleared. I was stunned! It had taken him months, but he did it—one ginger at a time.

Now whenever I find myself facing a task that seems onerous or monotonous, I remember Mark out there each day, shoveling away calmly and steadily, persevering without complaint or a sense of struggle. I once thanked him for teaching me a major life lesson. He just smiled and replied, "Sometimes that's just the way you have to do it."

Great results rarely come overnight. More often they require determination and steadfast focus. Mark probably could have used a machine or hired helpers to assist him, but I suspect he took a certain satisfaction in clearing his own land with his own hands.

Years later I purchased the property Mark had worked. On it now stands a magnificent orange orchard that produces a huge, continuous supply of delicious fruits. They are even sweeter for the hand that readied the sacred earth for them.

*Do you feel overwhelmed by a task or project facing you?
How might you relax and appreciate the journey
as you address it one small piece at a time?*

I achieve mighty things by taking small steps, enjoying the journey as I go.

Maximizing Moments

Pleasure is spread through the earth
In stray gifts to be claimed by whoever shall find.
— William Wordsworth

While Dee and I were walking our dogs in a park, we encountered a boy about 12 years old. He looked like a kid from a 1930s *Boys Town* movie: kind of rough cut—baggy disheveled clothes, long unkempt hair—with a sparkle in his eyes. And friendly beyond the norm. As he approached on crutches, we could see that one of his pant legs was pinned up, indicating his leg had been amputated from the thigh or knee down. When he saw our little dogs, the boy got very excited, let go of his crutches, and dropped to the grass to play with them. They were just as eager to interact with him and gave him lots of kisses and nuzzles. The kid was in heaven, and there was so much love in that scene that I wished I could just bottle that moment and hold on to it forever.

After a while, the boy reclaimed his crutches, rose, thanked us, and was on his way. But our day was not the same. It was the kind of moment worth living for.

Life is meaningful not for the seconds that tick by, but for the moments that fill them. Here are a few attributes of moments as compared to seconds:

Seconds are measured in time; moments are measured in experience. Seconds tick you closer to death; moments amplify your life. Seconds are navigated by the mind; moments are recognized by spirit. Seconds are fragmenting; moments are completing. Seconds are subject to humans' time; moments are subject to God's timing. Seconds are subject to planning; moments occur spontaneously. Seconds are about getting somewhere; moments are about being somewhere.

Today and every day, be open to find as many moments as possible and bask in them. There may be a lot more of them than you have recognized.

What have been the most important moments of your life?
What moments might be available to you now to bask in?

I open up to being touched by precious moments.
My good comes to me spontaneously.

Approved Chew Toys

Mind is slayer. Mind is healer.

— Hindu proverb

If you ever want a crash course in fun, hang out with puppies. They are full of joy, mischief, profuse affection, and pure play.

Puppies are also avid chewers. They love to gnaw on anything they can get their little jaws around. Furniture legs, shoes, wires, and any object lying around are attractive targets—not such an attractive prospect, however, for the home owner.

When our puppies started to chew on dangerous items, I would tell them "No!" and take the objects away. But a minute or two later, they would find something else to gnaw on. Dee, as the puppies' "mom," employed a wiser method. She would give them an object safe for them to chew on, like a stick or rawhide bone, and tell them, "Here's an approved chew toy." The pups would be just as happy to delve into these objects and, happily for us, save the furniture.

Your thinking mind is like a puppy looking for objects to chew on. Nearly every moment of the day it is scanning, scanning, scanning for things to think about. It does not stop unless you sleep, meditate, exercise vigorously, or immerse it in an absorbing activity like listening to music or watching a movie. If you leave the mind to its own devices, it will find things to think about that are counter to your happiness, such as dark news, gossip, criticism of self and others, and other subjects that leave you feeling worse and undermine your sense of peace.

For that reason, you need to point your mind toward approved "chew toys" and give it projects that uplift you. Read positive books, say affirmations, engage in a hobby you enjoy, have conversations about things that fascinate you, practice guided visualization, or do anything you can to point your mind in a positive direction and keep it there. Then your mental puppy can chew to its heart's content and serve its purpose as a helpful friend.

How can you engage your mind today in a way that uplifts you?

I am in charge of my mind. I focus my thoughts on objects that bring me happiness.

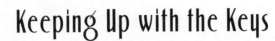

Keeping Up with the Keys

The moment you are a hollow bamboo, the divine lips are on you,
the hollow bamboo becomes a flute, and the song starts.
— Osho (commentary on Tilopa's *Song of Mahamudra*)

The inspiring documentary film *Standing in the Shadows of Motown* chronicles the careers of a dozen talented musicians who recorded the background music for the great Motown stars such as the Supremes, the Temptations, the Four Tops, and many more. The group, informally known as the Funk Brothers, contributed to more hit records than were ever sold by the Beatles, the Beach Boys, and the Rolling Stones combined.

The Funk Brothers keyboardist Earl Van Dyke described how the group would drop into a groove in which the music seemed to be playing them. "My job," he explained, "was to get my fingers to keep up with the keys that were pressing themselves down."

Any true artist will understand Van Dyke's description of the creative process. There comes a point at which you cease to play the music, and the music plays you. Or the picture is painting itself through you. Or the speech is speaking you. At that moment you happily step aside and participate in an act of creation unfolding before you—and through you. And there is no greater honor than to participate in it.

Acts of genius are less a matter of doing, and more a matter of allowing. Less trying, more flowing. Less forcing, more being. You quit being the doer and you become the vessel. When 16-year-old Sarah Hughes won the 2002 Olympic gold medal for figure skating, she described the process behind her last jaw-dropping performance: "I wasn't really trying hard. I decided to just go out and have some fun and see what I could do."

Quit trying to figure out which keys to press or forcing the ones you think should go down. Instead, watch for keys that are pressing themselves, and do your best to keep up with them.

How might you relax and step aside to
allow greatness to flow through you?

I open myself to what life wants to express
through me for the highest benefit to all.

Spiritual Phototropism

The Path that leadeth on is lighted by one fire—
the light of daring, burning in the heart.

— Helena Petrovna Blavatsky

In junior high school I did a science project on *phototropism*, the process by which plants bend toward their source of light. If you plant a seedling directly under a light, it will grow straight up. Move the light to the side and the plant will grow in that direction, and it will further adapt if you move the light to another side. A brilliant design by the Creator!

Many years later I planted some cuttings of one of my favorite plants, night-blooming jasmine. After inserting a dozen sticks in the ground and leaving them for a few weeks, I noticed that the new buds on one cutting were growing downward, in contrast to the others' growing straight up.

"Look," I pointed out to Dee, "I must have planted this one upside down; the leaves are headed toward the ground."

"Don't worry," she answered, "they'll find their way to the light."

Sure enough, after a few days the little leaves changed direction, and soon they were all moving rapidly toward the sun.

You, too, know where your source of light is, and you know how to head for it no matter what situation you are in. You may make a mistake, take a detour, or do something that runs contrary to the direction of your good. Or someone may put you in an uncomfortable or undesirable position. Yet you are not damaged or lost. Something in you knows how to find your way back to your true path . . . and you *will*.

The Creator has imbued you with impeccable intelligence. You are a love-seeking, passion-seeking, truth-seeking, and happiness-seeking creature; and you can trust your inner guidance to always keep you moving toward the light.

Do you believe your good has been compromised by something
you have done or something someone has done to you? How might
you adjust your direction to head where you need to go?

The spirit within me knows where my good lives
and constantly moves me toward it.

Who's Sorry Now?

Apology is only egotism wrong side out.

— Oliver Wendell Holmes

At a seminar retreat, a group of participants and I sat in a Native American sweat lodge. The leader began the ceremony with a series of chants and prayers. At one point he entered into a prayer of apology: "Oh, Great Spirit," he called out loudly, "I'm sorry for not being a better leader, for not making the fire hot enough, and for being so selfish." He went on to enumerate a lengthy list of his other sins. Then he turned to the group and asked, "Is anyone else here sorry for anything?" Then he waited for more sins to be confessed. And he waited. And he waited.

Finally one woman called out from the darkness, "We're not that kind of group." Immediately the participants broke into a release of laughter, along with the leader. We were not that kind of group. We had spent an intensive week reclaiming a sense of innocence, and the idea of diving more deeply into guilt, rather than stepping out of it, seemed quite the non sequitur.

Many of us grew up under the notion that there is something wrong with us, feeling sinful and guilty just for being born. Such a notion is quite counterproductive to a healthy psyche. It keeps us small, needy, owing, and controllable by those who assert our guilt.

There is another way to look at ourselves: We are innocent and whole, created in God's image and likeness. We have never done anything that could cause us to be separate from love's presence, and we need not suffer for our sins or the sins of those who came before us. We are worthy by nature, adventuring through life to rediscover the wonder of the spirit within us. Yes, we make mistakes. No, we are not evil.

You do not need to apologize for your life. You just need to celebrate it.

How might you affirm your actions and
your life rather than apologize for them?

I am here for a good reason. I belong here.
My life and deeds are valuable and worthy.

Fraud Guilt

Never bend your head. Always hold it high.
Look the world straight in the face.

— Helen Keller

In his illuminating book *Success Intelligence,* Robert Holden describes "fraud guilt"—the feeling that if people knew who you really were, they would discover you are a phony or less than competent.

Some of the most gifted, talented, and successful people I know experience fraud guilt; and I have had moments of it myself. As I have examined those thoughts, I find them to be just another variation on a sad old theme in the insecure ego's bag of tricks to try to keep us living smaller than we really are.

In a sense, you have two minds: one founded in wisdom and truth, and one founded in fear and illusion. Your wisdom mind is your natural mind, instilled in you by God, connected to everything real and worth knowing. Your fear-based mind is founded on misinformation fed to you by people who were subject to the tyranny of their own egos and who passed their pain along to you in an attempt to rid themselves of it.

The thought *I am a phony, and if people knew the truth about me, they would shun and destroy me* is illusion based and should not be indulged. The thought *I am a sincere person doing the best I can to make a contribution, and succeeding in ever greater ways* is far closer to the truth about you.

All teachers are teaching what they need to learn. Just because you have not learned everything about a subject does not make you a fraud. As long as you teach what you have experienced and you are honest about what you know and do not know, you are in integrity. If you are a few steps ahead of your students and can help them advance, you are being helpful.

Just keep doing what you are doing, and recognize that the voice that calls you a fraud is the real fraud.

Do you have thoughts of fraud guilt?
What response can you give that empowers you?

I am not a fraud.
I am an instrument for good
that helps the world.

The Ending Doesn't Matter

The way of the Creative works through change and transformation, so that each thing receives its true nature and destiny and comes into permanent accord with the Great Harmony.
— *I-Ching* (translated by Richard Wilhelm; rendered into English by Cary F. Baynes)

Billy Elliot is the brilliant cinematic saga of an 11-year-old British boy who wants to become a classical ballet dancer. Living in a blue-collar city, Billy faces the ire of his father and older brother, who want him to be a boxer and find his dance aspirations utterly abhorrent. As a result, they do everything they can to squash Billy's vision and turn him into a "real" boy.

But Billy's ambitions are stronger than his family's objections, and he pursues his dream in spite of their opposition. Eventually he gains a shot at being accepted to a prestigious dance academy, which offers him the hope of turning his dream into a real career. At first Billy's family dismisses the notion as preposterous, but over time they realize he is sincere, and they support him in his quest. In the process, his father and brother heal their deep-seated animosity toward each other, and the family is united in its efforts to get Billy into the academy.

The drama leads to a crucial scene in which Billy receives the long-awaited letter from the dance academy informing him whether or not he has been accepted. The movie does a remarkable job building and milking the tension around opening the letter; I was biting my fingernails waiting to find out if Billy had gotten in.

I am not going to tell you what happened. I will tell you what I realized as I waited to learn what the letter said: *it did not matter.* Whether or not Billy was accepted to the school was less important than the growth he and his family experienced in the process of his application. As he held fast to his ideals in the face of massive resistance, he developed immense soul strength. Meanwhile, his family experienced the healing of a lifetime as they learned to support him and resolve their deep differences. No matter what the letter said, they all triumphed, and a happy ending was assured.

Do not be fooled by waiting for the ending. The middle is usually more important.

How might your process of growth be more important than how the journey turns out?

My journey is valuable for the healing and awakening I experience en route to my goals.

What Makes Innings Count

Where there is no polarity . . . there will be much doing but no music.
— Eric Hoffer

While in Japan, I was surfing some television channels and I came upon an American baseball game. There are lots of Japanese baseball players in the U.S. major leagues now, and the Japanese are very proud of them, so they broadcast the U.S. games there. Instead of airing the games in their entirety, however, they replay recent broadcasts, edited down to the highlights. So the show jumps from the stolen base in the first inning to the home run in the fourth, to the manager's fight with the umpire in the sixth, to the Japanese player's hit in the eighth, and so on. All in all, a two-and-a-half-hour game is condensed to about 20 minutes.

While it was interesting to see all the cool plays, I found watching the compacted version far less enjoyable than viewing an entire baseball game. Somehow the innings where nothing happens make the action-packed innings more meaningful and exciting. There is something about contrast that accentuates experience.

The game of life is the same way. It is not supposed to be action packed and exciting every minute. The lulls and quiet spaces enhance the peaks and crescendos. The downs accentuate the ups, and the setbacks make the triumphs more rewarding. Hunger makes food taste better, missing others helps you appreciate them when you see them, and foreplay makes an orgasm worth waiting for. The system is pretty clever.

The next time nothing seems to be happening or something you want does not show up immediately, do not fret. The big game is far more satisfying than the condensed version.

*How can you appreciate what is not happening
as much as what you want to happen?*

**I savor the contrasts in my life.
The presence of peaks and valleys
makes each more significant.**

Good News for Crackpots

If you can't fix it, feature it.

— Source unknown

Every day an elderly Chinese woman brought two large pots to a stream to fetch water for her household. The pots hung at both ends of a stick she carried on her shoulders. One of the pots was perfect, but the other had a crack in it.

At the end of the long walk from the stream to the house, the cracked pot arrived only half-full. For a long time this went on, with the woman bringing home only one and a half pots of water each day.

The perfect pot was proud of its accomplishments. But the cracked pot was ashamed of its imperfection, miserable that it could only perform half of what it had been created to do.

After two years of what it perceived to be bitter failure, the marred pot spoke to the woman one day by the stream: "I am embarrassed because this crack in my side causes water to leak out all the way back to your house."

The old woman smiled and answered, "Did you notice that there are flowers on your side of the path, but not on the other pot's side? That's because I have always known about your flaw, so I planted flower seeds along your side of the path, and every day while we walk back, you water them. For two years I have been able to pick these beautiful flowers to decorate the table. Without you being just the way you are, there would not be this beauty to grace the house."

While you may criticize yourself for your flaws, they may serve a purpose. What you perceive as your shortcomings give you character, and may endear you to others and serve them. Do not be hasty to judge yourself for your foibles. What you think may be the worst thing about you might be the best.

How might what you see as your deficits really be assets?

**I accept, honor, and celebrate
all parts of myself. Even my
imperfections bring gifts.**

From Should to Would

Our remedies oft in ourselves do lie
Which we ascribe to heaven.

— William Shakespeare

One day my young neighbor Kenny asked me for a ride to the local grocery store so he could buy some popcorn. I told him I could drive him to the store, but since I was going on into town, he would have to walk home, a hike he often takes.

"What do you think, Alan?" Kenny asked. "Should I go with you?"

"Whatever you like, Kenny," I replied. "It's up to you."

"But what do you think I should do?" he asked again.

I thought about it for a moment, and I realized there was no "should" about it. My opinion of what he ought to do was irrelevant. His decision depended entirely on what *he* felt like doing.

"Do whatever you'd like," I told him. "If you want to go, I'll be happy to drive you. If you don't feel like going, you can stay home and play video games or whatever. It's up to you."

This dialogue went on for a few more rounds, until I told Kenny I was ready to leave. Then he announced, "Okay, I'll go!" and he jumped into the car with me.

After our drive, I realized Kenny was mirroring the part of me that tries to find out what I should do, when there is no "should" about it—only a "would." Sometimes when faced with a decision, I try to figure out how the various options fit into some cosmic plan for my destiny. But God's plan for my destiny is happiness; if something would truly make me happy, behold . . . God's plan for my destiny. Instead of asking some remote Higher Power what I should do, I need to consult the spirit within me. What I *should* do is what I *would* do.

Today, search your mind for external "should's" that came from family members, religious institutions, and social dictates. Then search for internal "would's" that proceed from your sincere choices. The journey from "should" to "would" is the most self-empowering one you will ever take.

Consider the choices before you. What would you like to do?

My guidance comes from within me.
I trust my choices, and they work for me.

Irregularity Is Not Natural

If you take enough people to the middle of nowhere,
it starts to feel like somewhere.

— Auto advertisement

I saw a TV commercial advertising a laxative. The ad was based on the testimonial of a woman who had suffered from constipation, and then found relief through using this product. At the conclusion of the commercial, an interviewer asked the woman, "So what did you learn from using this product?" The woman smiled and answered, "I learned that irregularity is not natural."

The woman's insight could be applied to all disease. Contrary to what we have been told, disease is not natural. It is the exception to the state of good health in which we were born to live. Ease is our natural state. When we drift from it, we experience dis-ease. In this sense, illness serves to prompt us to reclaim the ease we lost.

We have accepted many dissatisfying situations as natural when they are not. We have accepted bodily ills, empty or conflicted relationships, financial struggle, war, and dysfunctional institutions. We have accepted foods empty of nutrition, schools devoid of passion, and careers absent of joy. No matter how many people agree that daily drudgery is normal, it is not natural.

Many people try to work harder to offset conditions of lack. Instead, we need to shift our paradigm of thought, and define well-being as our natural condition and disease as the aberration; abundance as our birthright and poverty as the anomaly; loving connection as our truth and separateness as the exception.

Happiness is not too good to be true. It is good *enough* to be true. Irregularity of any kind is not natural, and we should not accept any condition less than well-being as our natural state. Wholeness is life's intention for us, and as we claim it, it is so by divine right.

What unhappy or unhealthy condition have you accepted as natural?
Would you be willing to question that condition in
favor of making your ideal condition natural?

My natural state is health and happiness. I claim it now.

The Faith Factor

Faith is putting all your eggs in God's basket,
then counting your blessings before they hatch.

— Ramona C. Carroll

I flew to the island of Hawaii to perform my goddaughter's wedding. In order for me to get home to Maui that evening, I had to book the last flight out of Kona and change planes in Honolulu. The airline reservation agent informed me that my connection time would be only 25 minutes, and if I missed my second flight, I would have to wait until the next morning to get home. *Okay,* I figured, *I'll take my chances.*

After the ceremony as I sat waiting in the Kona airport, a voice came over the loudspeaker announcing that my flight would be departing 15 minutes late. Hmm. That whittled my time to change planes down to ten minutes. My mind started to spin off into negative "what-if?" scenarios, but I decided to just practice trusting. Why waste precious moments of life worrying? I would use the experience as an opportunity to stay happy no matter what.

The plane took off late, and I refused to look at my watch. Instead of trying to dictate how things should go, I simply asked for peace. I looked out the window and enjoyed the sunset.

The plane landed in Honolulu 15 minutes late, I calmly exited at Gate 53, and I walked to the television monitor to find out which gate my next flight was departing from. You can imagine my surprise when I saw that my flight was leaving from Gate 53. My flight to Maui was on the same plane I had just been on! I laughed as I found my way to the very seat I had just left. No matter how late my first flight was, I would have been on the second one.

I believe there was a direct connection between my decision to practice trust and the serendipitous event that occurred. There is an Intelligent Power running the universe, and that Power responds to the thoughts you think in harmony with it. *Thinking and acting with faith changes the results you get.* The next time you start to worry, practice trust and you may create miracles.

What are you worried about?
What would you be doing differently if you practiced trust?

The universe finds ingenious ways to support
me when I trust its intelligent design.

Are You Dreaming Big Enough?

Ah, but a man's reach should exceed his grasp,
Or what's a heaven for?

— Robert Browning

I saw a large billboard displaying photos of two bottles of liquor. One was a small bottle with the caption *Regular size*. The other bottle was huge, many times larger than the tiny one—its caption said: *Fantasize*.

The only dreams worth entertaining are those greater than the life you are already living. Goals that invite you to stretch are far more empowering than goals that represent something you can do easily. Big visions call us to live larger than we thought we were.

Here is a powerful exercise that will help you step into bigger shoes: On a piece of paper write the heading *Know I Can*. Underneath, record three goals you are confident you know you *can* accomplish, and *will*. Below that section, write: *Maybe I Can*. Then list three projects you would like to embark on, but would be a stretch to accomplish. Finally, write the heading *Outrageous* and record the three most outlandish visions you can think of—the dreams that thrill you, but which at the moment you do not see how they could come about.

Then read your list daily, spending a few moments visualizing each goal. Hold each image clearly in mind, and get the feeling that you have already attained your objective. Meanwhile, take action steps toward your goals—not from pressure or stress, but with light-hearted fun.

Here is where the exercise really becomes fun! Your vision and action will attract support from the universe, through avenues you could never have predicted. As you check off the *Know I Can* section, the *Maybe I Can* section will become *Know I Can*. *Outrageous* becomes *Maybe I Can* and before long, *Know I Can*. Then you can add more to your *Maybe I Can* and *Outrageous* lists and watch them slide up the ranks. Over time you will keep stretching and growing to embrace goals you once thought impossible, and you will be glad you dreamed big enough.

How can you prime your creation pump
by stretching to reach goals beyond your grasp?

My visions take me from good to better to best.
All I desire is within my reach.

What Are the Chances?

There are only two ways to live your life. One is as though nothing is a miracle. The other is as though everything is a miracle.
— Attributed to Albert Einstein

My friend Bruce and I went to dinner at a small restaurant in a little out-of-the-way town. The eatery offers a deli counter and lots of picnic-style tables to sit at. That evening the restaurant was crowded, and we found ourselves at a table where we were literally elbow to elbow with people we did not know.

Somehow our conversation came around to education, and I told Bruce my pet theory that students who want to go to college after high school should be required to travel for a year before they do so to edify their worldly experience in ways that college does not. Bruce agreed and told me that during that period of his life he had participated in a student adventure trip to Africa. He went on to describe the sites he visited and the organization that had sponsored the trip.

At that point, the woman sitting next to me leaned over and said to Bruce, "Excuse me, but I couldn't help overhearing about your trip to Africa. I think I was in the same group you were." When the two compared notes, they realized that they were indeed a part of the same group of about 30 American students who had visited Africa 30 years earlier! A few weeks later, she mailed Bruce a photo of the two of them together.

I marveled at the astounding synchronicity of their meeting and the fact that I had brought up that subject as a non sequitur in our conversation. Somehow the universe orchestrated all of us getting together at that crowded table in that obscure locale.

The Law of Attraction has ways and means of connecting people and arranging events that you and I could never comprehend. Yet the system is always working perfectly in our favor.

*Can you relax and let life connect
you with people of like mind and purpose?*

**My life is spiced with synchronicities and miracles.
I open to receive my good wherever it comes.**

Divine Debris

*The dragons of our lives are princesses who are only
waiting to see us once beautiful and brave.*

— Rainer Maria Rilke

On the island of Kauai, I love to visit a magical stream in a lush mountain valley. I usually enter the stream at a small eddy that forms a shallow pool. When I first stepped into this pool, I noticed some natural debris in the form of small sticks, leaves, and nutshells on its bottom, which I cleared away. Then I came to a few more twigs and branches and tossed them aside. Then a few more. As I reached below the surface to get rid of the debris, I discovered that the pool floor was *made* of debris. The layer of silt covering it was less than an inch thick; everything below it was rubble. If I cleared away all of it, I would also clear away the pool's foundation.

The debris of our life does not hamper us from being what we are—it *makes* us what we are. We tend to judge ourselves and our lives for the difficulties we have experienced, when it is the difficulties that build our character. Past painful relationships, financial issues, and moral dilemmas seem to be our enemies when we are going through them, but when we glean their lessons, they become our allies. That is why it is important to embrace challenges and bless them, for they have the power to move us to a new level of life.

Manure is unpleasant to deal with, but put in its proper place—such as in a field with crops—it becomes the best fertilizer. One day the wheat that grows in that field will be milled into flour and baked into warm, tasty bread that delights and nourishes us. The bread bears no resemblance to the manure that grew it, but the relationship is intrinsic. Do not grovel in the manure, for that breeds disease. But place it where it belongs and it engenders health and life.

Take some time today to consider any disappointments, regrets, or resentment you may be holding. Each of those emotions does not recognize the gift past experiences have bestowed upon you. Accept the gift and you have the pathway to a refreshing dip in a mountain stream.

How might a current difficulty contribute to bettering your life?

**I embrace difficulties as stepping-stones
to deeper peace and richer success.**

Something Substantial

That best portion of a good man's life,
His little, nameless, unremembered acts
Of kindness and of love.

— William Wordsworth

One morning when I arrived at the Miami airport after flying all night, I was quite tired and did not feel well. I walked into a coffee shop and ordered some orange juice. The waitress, a jovial Hispanic woman, asked me, "Is that all you're having, sweetie? Why don't you have something substantial for breakfast?"

I felt very touched. Here in the midst of a highly impersonal airport, with thousands of people milling around, this dear woman took a personal interest in me. Suddenly I felt better. "Yes, I will have something more substantial," I told her, and I ordered a bagel and cream cheese—all the tastier for the care she took to serve it to me. On a deeper level, that dear woman served me something far more substantial than a bagel and cream cheese. She served me kindness and compassion, the best meal there is.

It is easy to get caught up in the busyness and doingness of daily life. Yet there are moments in every day when we take a breath of fresh air for our spirit. They are the moments we say hello to a stranger in the elevator, laugh with the fellow selling us a newspaper, or come home and have the dog greet us like a celebrity. When it is time for us to leave this life, those will be the moments we will remember. They are the ones that count.

While those substantial moments seem to come randomly, you have the power to create more of them. You can begin your business call by asking your colleague how his son is doing in college, or tell the cafeteria server she is looking especially radiant today. When a boy nearly runs into you with his skateboard, you can tell him what a cool board he has. When someone complains about the economy, you can offer a note of confidence that things will get better.

Substantial moments are the ones that make your life. See how many you can find today.

What substantial moments have touched your life?
How can you find and create more?

I build my life on values that really count.
I seek, find, and create joy wherever I can.

Is New Jersey Open?

If you don't use your mind, somebody else will.

— Source unknown

The *Candid Camera* show played a trick on drivers seeking to enter the state of Delaware. As cars approached a tollbooth after crossing a bridge into the state, actors dressed as police officers informed drivers that they would not be able to enter the state today because "Delaware is closed for repairs."

The drivers' reactions were quite telling. Some turned around and went back to Pennsylvania. Others became angry and argued with the fake cops. One woman asked, "Is New Jersey open?"

While the gag was funny, the drivers' predicament is not very different from the limits you and I may have accepted from other people telling us what we could or could not do. Great teachers have told us that *all* limits are illusory, and anytime you run into a wall or a closed door, the first place to try to open it is in your own mind.

Successful people pay little attention to what the world tells them they cannot do and a lot of attention to their inner knowing. Eighteen publishers turned down Richard Bach's book *Jonathan Livingston Seagull* before Macmillan finally published it and sold seven million copies in the U.S. alone during the next five years. Walt Disney was fired by a newspaper editor for lack of ideas. Fred Astaire was rejected at his first movie audition because he was slightly balding. And on and on . . .

The next time someone tells you that Delaware is closed, your business scheme is harebrained, you cannot finance your project in this economy, your screenplay does not have enough sex or violence, or you are too old, consider that the "limit cops" who stop you have been dressed by *Candid Camera,* and you do not need to turn back to Pennsylvania or try New Jersey as an alternative. Your first choice may be quite available if you are willing to keep driving.

What would you like to do that others have told you is impractical or impossible? What would you be doing differently if you knew you can attain your goal?

**I march on to the high calling
of what I know to be true.**

Two Sides of a Prison Wall

To forgive is to set a prisoner free and
discover that the prisoner was you.

— Lewis B. Smedes

I used to visit a prisoner named Ray. Years earlier in college, Ray had a girlfriend named Jen. One night the couple had an argument, and in a fit of rage, he beat her up. Tragically, she died. Ray was convicted of manslaughter and sentenced to many years in prison.

I met Ray when he was up for parole after nine years of incarceration. In contrast to his violent act, I found him to be a gentle soul. He was remorseful about his crime, and he had used his time in prison to advance his spiritual growth. Ray had studied *A Course in Miracles*, he was active in the prison church, and he had achieved a responsible position managing the prison laundry. I sensed no cruelty in this man, and he certainly did not seem like a dangerous criminal to me.

Ray told me that he had been denied parole repeatedly because Jen's parents had mounted a huge campaign to keep him in jail. Each year when he was eligible for release, they orchestrated a community effort to "keep this killer off the streets." Yet, looking at this man, I did not see a killer at all. I saw a basically good man who had made a heartbreaking mistake.

"I send Jen's parents love and prayer," he explained. "I know they are very angry, and I don't blame them. More than anything, I wish I could bring Jen back. But I can't. So I am doing my best to deepen my relationship with God right where I am and trying to be a blessing to the world."

I wondered who was really in prison. Ray was locked up physically, but his soul was free. Jen's parents were quite wealthy and enjoyed unlimited physical freedom, yet they were consumed by anger and vengeance. It seemed to me that their wrathful thoughts were creating walls more formidable than those encasing Ray.

Bondage and freedom are not determined by physical walls or their absence. You are as free or bound as your mind and heart. Choose freedom and it is yours.

Are you a prisoner of your anger at someone?
How could you free both of you?

I release myself and others by releasing
 resentment. I choose freedom now.

Success Without Sacrifice

Despair says I cannot lift that weight.
Happiness says I do not have to.

— James Richardson

Jennifer is a life coach who works part-time as a fashion consultant at a high-end department store. While Jennifer has an upbeat, abundance-based, service-oriented attitude and she accesses her intuition to serve customers, she reports that her supervisor and many other employees display negative, competitive, and hard-sell approaches.

Jennifer consistently ranks in the top three out of a sales force of almost 200. Even more impressive, she puts in only ten hours a week, while most of the other employees work full-time. She generates the highest amount of sales per hour than anyone else at her store.

Jennifer's extraordinary success demonstrates that we achieve more in the marketplace when we are aligned with vision, positive attitude, and inner guidance. The individual who succeeds is not the one who puts the most time in or sweats the most, but the one who is most attuned to spontaneous creative insights.

Many great works of art and literature are born in a flash and without strain. Richard Bach wrote the bestseller *Jonathan Livingston Seagull* in just a few weeks. He submitted his manuscript to his publisher, went on an extended vacation, and was stunned to come home to find over a million dollars in his bank account.

The clever romantic-comedy film *How to Lose a Guy in 10 Days* was born as a tiny cartoon booklet that two women doodled just for fun. Someone saw the book, submitted it to an agent, and within a short time their story was transformed into a huge box-office success.

Do not assume that strife and struggle are required for you to succeed. To the contrary, a sense of play and flow will net you more results more quickly. Yes, effort and perseverance may be called for, but you will gain more by trusting your creative impulses than by fighting for your good.

What job or project do you think has to be hard?
How could you approach this venture with
a light heart and positive expectation?

I let my creative impulses guide me.
I get results from working smarter, not harder.

One Light at a Time

Wherever you are is the entry point.
— Kabir (translated by Linda Beth Hess
and Shukdev Singh)

Donna sensed that she had played out her executive job, and she yearned for greater career fulfillment. One evening while working a night shift, she noticed that the cleaning crew was throwing away toilet-tissue rolls with a lot of paper left on them. Since she considered this practice wasteful, Donna took the discarded rolls to a homeless shelter. Over time she found her involvement with this charity so rewarding that she became a volunteer, then a volunteer coordinator, and eventually went on to a salaried position as director of a citywide volunteer agency. Eventually she gained national prominence and received an outstanding-service award that brought her to Washington, D.C., where she was honored at a reception and met the President, his wife, and several past Presidents and their spouses—all as a result of a spontaneous thought about toilet paper!

When you are seeking a big change in your life, it rarely shows up dramatically or overnight. More often it comes in steps or stages. You simply take the next step before you, small though it may be, and then the next and the next; and at some point you will look back and realize that your many little steps have led you to a far better place than where you once stood.

As a child, I used to watch *The Jimmy Durante Show*. Each week Jimmy would end his program by standing under a lone spotlight on a dark stage, where he would begin to sing his theme song. After the first verse the spotlight would go out, and another circle of light would appear on the stage a few feet away. Jimmy would step into that circle of light, sing his next verse, and then that light would go out. He repeated this process, one light and one verse at a time, until he finally made his way offstage and the show was over.

So it is with your life: one light at a time, showing up at just the right moment, until the train of light leads you where you want and need to go.

*What next step is your intuition guiding you to take
that may eventually lead to a big change?*

**My inner wisdom reveals my next step to me,
and I take it. Step-by-step I create great results.**

Where the Trail Gets Good

Problems are guidelines, not stop signs.

— Robert H. Schuller

One of my favorite hiking trails leads to a magnificent hidden waterfall off the beaten path. The footpath to the falls begins as an offshoot of a main trail in a county park. One day as I set out on the waterfall trail, I noticed that county officials had posted a sign: END OF TRAIL. As I stepped past the sign onto the jungle path, I chuckled to think that what was advertised as the end of the trail was really the *beginning* of the trail. If unknowing hikers simply heeded the public sign, they were led to believe that their hike was over. If, however, they knew what truly awaited them, they would not hesitate to continue.

Sometimes it appears that you are at the end of your trail when you are really at the beginning. If you plot your course from social directives, you will be programmed by what other people think for you. But many who formulate social dictates are guided by fear and small thinking; there is nothing original and little that is joyful about the well-trod way. If, on the other hand, you follow your inner voice, you will be led to experiences that far surpass any social postings.

Often the only way the universe can get you onto a new and more beneficial trail is to end the old one. While such moments can be uncomfortable and confusing, life is doing you a favor. When the old trail is useless, painful, or counterproductive, the best thing that could happen would be for you to be kicked off it. Nearsighted vision shows you that you are at the end of your trail. Broader vision guides you to a new one.

How might what appears to be the end of
a trail be the beginning of a better one?

I welcome opportunities to change and grow.
Every ending represents a new beginning.

Get Pasteurized

*My own prescription for health is less paperwork and
more running barefoot through the grass.*

— Attributed to Leslie Grimutter

Louis Pasteur is well known for the method he developed to destroy bacteria with heat. Every time you drink pasteurized milk, you are benefiting from Pasteur's legacy to the world.

Many people, however, are not aware of an insight that Pasteur is said to have voiced on his deathbed. I am told that he proclaimed, "I have come to believe that it is not simply bacteria that cause disease. Now I believe that disease is a result of the interaction of bacteria with the host organism."

This means that bacteria, in and of themselves, do not have the power to harm you. You can be hurt only if you are susceptible to them. If your immune system is strong and healthy, the nastiest bacteria could come your way but would not be able to penetrate your well-being. If, however, your natural immunity is compromised, bacteria can get to you and harm you.

While there are many medical models and explanations for how the immune system works, on a metaphysical level they all depend on your spiritual immune system. If you are aligned with your Higher Power and in the flow of life, your natural life force is more powerful than germs. Become misaligned through fear, upset, resistance, or patterns of negative thought, and you leave an open door for unwanted visitors.

While you cannot control germs floating around the world you inhabit, you can control your host organism. When you are happy, clear, and empowered from the inside out, you are an energetic match for health, and only the elements of health can touch you.

Even if you have compromised your spiritual immunity, it is easy to restore it by reconnecting with Source Energy. So be not afraid of germs. They cannot hurt you unless you are available to them. Get pasteurized.

*How can you boost your spiritual immune system
by living a life aligned with your spirit?*

**My thoughts, words, and actions are attuned
to well-being. I am safe, healthy, and whole.**

Lucifer's Gift

Many have had their greatness made for them by their enemies.
— Baltasar Gracián

My coaching client Winslow was under professional attack from one of his colleagues who engaged in a campaign to discredit his credentials and shame him before his peers. Winslow was a person of integrity and had nothing to hide, yet he was distraught and feared that this onslaught might ruin his reputation and his business.

As we explored the matter, my client revealed that his father had been very demanding, and no matter what Winslow did, it was not good enough. This left him with an underlying feeling of inadequacy. When he finally succeeded in business, he felt on some level that he did not deserve it. As Winslow recounted his critic's attempts to hurt him, he casually noted, "This guy is like the devil Lucifer."

That rang a bell for me. "Do you know the meaning of the name *Lucifer?*" I asked him. "It is related to the word *lucid,* which means 'clear.' Lucifer is the Great Clarifier. He helps you get clear on who you are and what the truth is. This fellow's attack is forcing you to look within and recognize that you are in integrity, your credentials are valid, and once and for all, *you* are valid and worthy. If he helps you accomplish this, his contribution to your life will be immense."

Winslow understood and agreed. He told me he was going to have to face his Lucifer at an upcoming conference, where he would try to practice worthiness in the presence of adversity.

After the conference Winslow told me, "It went even better than I expected. The fellow didn't bother me at all, and a number of my peers told me that they counted the man's attacks for nothing. He had been drummed out of the profession for indiscretions, and now he was trying to drag others down with him. I realize that he came to help me remember my true worth, and now I count his actions as a service."

Devils exist only in the dark. Shine the light on them and they are your allies and servants.

How do those who challenge you
help you find greater strength and truth?

I honor adversity as a gift to help me grow.
Those who challenge me are friends in disguise.

A Higher Law

You are entitled to miracles.

— *A Course in Miracles*

My friends Jack and Kendra had a beautiful baby girl named Karen, who was born with a clubfoot, which twisted inward at more than a right angle to her leg. When Karen was three months old, her doctor told her parents that the condition was correctable, but the girl would have to wear a cast on her foot, to be recast every two weeks until the age of six months. Eventually the casts would give way to a brace that the child would have to wear until she was five or six years old, at which point the foot would be straightened out.

Although Jack and Kendra did not look forward to such a rigorous and potentially distressful therapy plan, they reasoned that it was necessary for the condition to be ameliorated, and planned to go through with it.

Around that time, Kendra's sister happened to sit on an airplane flight next to a man from Guatemala who claimed he was a healer. She invited the man to her home for a social occasion that Jack and Kendra attended, along with little Karen. At one point during the evening, Kendra thought it might be helpful to ask the healer to have a look at Karen, and he did. He placed his hands over the affected foot, closed his eyes, and prayed for about a minute.

A few days later the couple brought their daughter in for her casting, and the girl was taken in for x-rays. Afterward the doctors had an animated discussion for about 45 minutes. Then one doctor came to the family and told them, "There is nothing at all wrong with your daughter's foot. We must have made a misdiagnosis."

Jack and Kendra were quite sure there had *not* been a misdiagnosis. They had seen and lived with their daughter's malformation on a daily basis. Now it was not there at all, and it has not returned in 21 years. Karen is a happy, healthy, beautiful young adult.

Miracles are possible. Prayer works. Well-being is God's will for you.

What situation seems overwhelming
to you that might be offset or healed by prayer?

I am entitled to miracles.
I open my mind and heart to receive
the good I desire and deserve.

The Healing Funeral

The excursion is the same when you go looking for
your sorrow as when you go looking for your joy.

— Eudora Welty

I attended the memorial service of a friend who was loved and respected by many. Ron was a conscious, kind man who contributed a great deal of skill, time, and money to community service. Dedicated to his spiritual path, he lived with clarity and joy. Ron moved through the process of his passing with extraordinary consciousness and peace.

Ron's service reflected his positive nature. Friends and co-workers spoke with deep appreciation for the gifts he had brought them and the world. While tears flowed and we expressed our sense of loss, the service was truly a celebration of Ron's life. As each speaker recounted fond memories, gratitude filled the room, and some laughter lightened our hearts.

The service concluded with a song of Ron's choice, "Joy to the World" (Three Dog Night version). As we exited the hall, I felt warm and inspired, as if I had been to a spiritual workshop. I encountered a friend who had just gone through surgery. She told me, "I haven't been feeling well, and I wasn't going to come. But I loved Ron, and I wanted to honor him. Strange as this sounds, I feel a lot better now than when I walked in. The love in the room and the stories of Ron's life have inspired me to be happy and get back into service."

As I considered my friend's words and observed the serene demeanor of the other participants, I realized that the general effect of the memorial service was one of healing. While we all felt a certain grief over our friend's departure, the experience of the event was the one that Ron would have wanted us to have—soul-nurturing and, in an unexpected way, joyful. So even a funeral can be healing if approached with that intention.

Everything in life is what you make it. Nothing is beyond the Great Spirit's ability to use for upliftment. Even death can be an invitation to celebrate life.

What have you been looking at through dark
glasses that you can lighten up about?

I use all events and experiences as
opportunities to practice the presence of love.

Pots and Earth

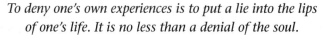

To deny one's own experiences is to put a lie into the lips
of one's life. It is no less than a denial of the soul.

— Oscar Wilde

You may have seen the poster suggesting "Bloom where you are planted," meaning that the best place for you to grow and express your gifts is right where you are. This is excellent advice we could all benefit from applying.

Yet there is another path of growth through which you end up blooming elsewhere than your original planting. If you want to grow a plant, there are two ways to do it: (1) you can plant a seed or a cutting right into the ground and let it grow where it will live; or (2) you can plant a seed or cutting in a flowerpot, nurture it in a greenhouse, and then when it is stronger and more mature, transplant it to the location where it will ultimately blossom.

I met a woman who jokingly referred to her relationship with her former husband as "my practice marriage." She wed this man at a young age and stayed with him for a few years. The couple divorced, and a number of years later she married a man whom she stayed with for a long time. In her mind the second marriage was her real one, and the first was a warm-up. In a sense, she started her marriage journey in a flowerpot; and later she was transplanted to a patch of earth where she could grow deep roots, extend long branches, and display her colorful flowers.

Likewise, you may be in a job, relationship, or living situation that is not your ideal or your ultimate position. Yet you are growing, learning, and developing insights and skills that will ultimately serve you in a situation that *is* your ideal. Your time in the flowerpot is no less real or important than your ultimate desirable situation. Do not bemoan, regret, or criticize such an experience. Instead, honor and appreciate it, for it has value in itself and prepares you for even better.

Do you regret or resent an experience that did not turn
out to be your ultimate desired position?
Can you instead bless it as a significant, helpful
time that prepared you for something better?

I am grateful for all of my relationships
and experiences, for they have contributed
to my betterment and success.

Clarity Begins at Home

We see the world not as it is, but as we are.

— Source unknown

As I was about to set out for an afternoon boat cruise on Oregon's Willamette River, I donned my hat, sunglasses, and a generous spread of suntan lotion. Curious about the water temperature, I leaned over and dipped my hand in the river. When I examined my fingers, I was shocked to find evidence of an oil slick. How dismaying to discover that a precious waterway of Oregon, a bastion of ecological awareness, was polluted! Perhaps, I considered, the slick was an isolated pocket of residue from the boat engines at the dock.

Twenty minutes later downstream I tested the water again and found it just as polluted. *How disheartening.* Half an hour later, far from the city and deep into nature, I checked again. Still the same. I began to feel depressed.

As I studied the water beside the boat, it looked pretty clear. Where, then, was that awful oil slick coming from? I opened my backpack to grab a bottle of water, and I noticed the tube of suntan lotion next to it. *Oops . . .*

The oil on my finger did not come from sludge from the river. It was the residue of the suntan lotion I had applied at the outset of the journey.

After I got over feeling foolish, I realized there was a huge lesson here: The world I saw was not polluted. The perceptual screen through which I viewed it *was.* I was not seeing reality, but an artificial version of reality based on a filter I had superimposed over my vision.

We are told that Jesus advised, "Before you attempt to remove a speck from someone else's eye, remove the plank from your own." Before going out to improve the world, improve the vision through which you see it. When you see clearly, the world may become a far better place, and you will understand more clearly how to change it for the better.

How might your interpretation of what is happening color the events you observe?

The more clearly I see, the better the world becomes and the more I improve my position to create effective change.

The Cycle of Sustenance

*Behold the birds of the air, for they neither sow, nor do they
reap, nor gather into barns: and your heavenly Father feedeth them.
Are not you of much more value than they?*

— Matthew 6:26

The inspiring documentary *The Wild Parrots of Telegraph Hill* chronicles the life of Mark Bittner, a gentle soul who nurtured a flock of wild parrots in San Francisco. Bittner spent most of his time feeding, nursing, and caring for this large flock and did not do any formal "work" for two and a half decades. During that period, people in the community recognized his devotion; and he was given free rent, meals, and whatever else he needed.

There are many different ways to be paid for your service and contribution. A direct paycheck is only one. Love always comes around, and you are subject to the laws an economy far broader than the obvious one.

I met a woman who loved Hawaii and wanted to own a property in nature but did not have the money to purchase one. Through an odd series of circumstances, she and her husband were invited to serve as caretakers for a thousand-acre pristine forest-and-oceanfront estate on the island of Kauai. The owner had passed away, and his family wanted to hold on to the property but not live there. So this lady and her husband have all the benefits of the estate without actually owning it. Yet they own it by virtue of the love, appreciation, and care they give it.

My teacher Hilda Charlton taught and helped thousands of people over decades and never charged a penny for her services. Out of gratitude, many people gave her what she needed to get by, including a wonderful living situation, a car, clothes, and money for necessities. Eventually she had to turn gifts away. There are many, many ways the universe rewards sincere contribution.

While the fearful world sees through the mentality of survival, the wisdom of faith sees through the eyes of providence.

*Can you trust that if you follow your spirit and serve,
the universe will provide for you?*

I offer good, and good comes to me.
I heed my guidance, and well-being follows.

How to Be More Like Your Hero

Don't follow me. I'm following my bliss.

— Bumper sticker

My friend Ben admired his spiritual mentor so much that he took a summer to live and study with the master at his retreat in the Northwest. One day Ben asked his teacher, "How can I be more like you?"

The healer smiled and answered, "The best way to be more like me is to be more like yourself."

This brilliant answer contains the wisdom of a lifetime! If you are trying to imitate someone else's greatness, you have missed the point of greatness. The secret is to find your own unique style and talents and bring them forth. No one has ever attained mastery by replicating another. The truly great simply replicate themselves.

Certainly you can regard gifted people as role models, learn from them, and use their skills and style as a springboard to develop your own. But at some point, like a multistage rocket, you must jettison the booster and chart your own course. Then you will be a credit to them, as they were to you.

The cute movie *What a Girl Wants* chronicles the journey of an American teenager who travels to England to find the father she never knew. When she discovers him to be a nobleman, she gives up her own delightfully animated personality to adopt stiff British ways. In the process she loses her own spirit and becomes drab and joyless. Finally, her boyfriend asks her why she is trying to fit in when she was born to stand out.

So are we all born to make a unique contribution, one that could never be copied from another.

How can you capitalize on your own greatness
rather than imitating that of another?

I claim and express my unique talents as

the doorway to success in my own right.

Taking Care of Business

*What this world needs is a new kind
of army—the army of the kind.*

— Attributed to Cleveland Amory

When people used to ask me, "Who inspires you?" I would rattle off the names of various well-known gurus and self-help authors. Lately I am even more impressed with regular people below the radar of celebrity who live in joy and service during the course of their daily lives.

Take Doug, for example, the shuttle driver at a Holiday Inn near the San Francisco International Airport. I met Doug on a hot summer day when a line of frazzled passengers were boarding his van to go to the airport.

The final passenger to board was a young woman with a splint on her knee, accompanied by her six-year-old son. Doug had saved two seats by the door for her and the boy. In contrast to the frenzy around him, he took the time to gently help the woman to her place. Carefully he set her leg on a little stool; then he turned to the boy, who was still standing outside the van, and he had a heart-to-heart talk with him. "You know your mama needs you now, don't you?"

The child silently nodded.

"She's counting on you to help her. You da man, you understand?"

Again the boy nodded. Doug gave him a friendly pat on the shoulder and lovingly lifted him onto the seat next to his mom.

As Doug slid the van door shut, took his driver's seat, and got the vehicle rolling, I realized I had just witnessed an act of extraordinary caring. In the midst of a sea of confusion and self-centeredness, this humble man had gracefully taken care of someone who needed help. I thought about all the business that the other passengers and I were jetting off to do, and realized that the real business had just been done.

*How might you remember more of what
really counts today? Who can you help?*

**I keep my priorities in order.
My first order of business is kindness.**

Misappropriated Doubt

If the Sun and Moon should doubt,
They'd immediately go out. . . .

— William Blake

My coaching client Sara is one of the kindest, most caring people I know. Gentle and compassionate, she constantly seeks to support others. She is a great mother and a loyal friend.

One day during coaching, Sara told me, "Sometimes I wonder if I'm too selfish. I could probably be there more for other people."

I was amazed! I told Sara that she did not need to worry at all about being too selfish, for I saw her as an extraordinarily generous and thoughtful person.

Sara's remark is typical of a phenomenon I have observed in coaching and in facilitating seminars. Many people believe they are not enough of what they already are. For example, a humble person declares, "I don't want to become arrogant." I would tell such a person, "You have a long, long way to go before you are in danger of being arrogant." Arrogant people never question their arrogance (while they probably should). Only humble people do so, and they are the last people who need to.

Self-doubt is one of the most insidious saboteurs of joy and success. The antidote for self-doubt is confidence in the unique gifts life has bestowed upon you. Everyone is potentially an extraordinary teacher, healer, leader, or success in his or her chosen field. Only a few believe in their talents enough to capitalize on them.

You might like to try an exercise to move you ahead in your personal and professional life. Write down the names of any traits you believe you do not have enough of: *wisdom, beauty, creativity, passion,* or *skill,* for example. Then ask several people who know you and whose opinion you respect to tell you honestly if they believe you are lacking in that dimension. You might find that the characteristic you believe you lack is the element you already own, and will be your best asset when you quit doubting your true talents.

How might you already have and be what you believe you lack?

I claim the confidence to step forward and
be and do all I was born to be and do.

Thorns and Flight

*Life's challenges are . . . supposed
to help you discover who you are.*

— Bernice Johnson Reagon

When eagles build a nest, they create the foundation with small branches and rough twigs, many of which bear thorns. Then the parents feather the nest with softer leaves that make the bed comfortable for their chicks.

As the chicks grow, they thrash about the nest and gradually displace the softer bedding. At some point the softer material is scattered away, and only the thorny foundation remains, making it quite uncomfortable for the chicks to stay in the nest. Thus they are motivated to flap their wings and take independent flight, as they are meant to do.

When you face an uncomfortable situation, you may complain or resist it. Yet, like the young eaglets being pushed out the nest, your situation may be prompting you to exercise your wings, which will help you soar in ways that you never would have enjoyed if you stayed in your familiar haven.

Life is about movement, expansion, growth, and actualizing potential. If you stay in a home, relationship, or job beyond the time it is healthy for you, the universe will prod you with thorns, as if to say, "It's time to move to a broader domain." If you do not heed the message, the thorns will feel sharper and sharper until at some point you will have no choice but to fly. When you do, you will understand why a once comfortable situation became uncomfortable.

Of course, it is important not to run away from a situation if there is still meaning and value in your presence there. Check in with your inner guidance to know "when to hold 'em and when to fold 'em." Ask for signs and direction, and you will receive them.

Life is about being all that you are and can be. Sometimes you can do that right where you are, and sometimes you need to flap your wings. When that time comes, the thorns can help.

*Is discomfort prodding you to make a change?
How might you heed its guidance?*

I use discomfort as a prompt to change for the better.

The Stable Mule

The pure love of one person can offset the hatred of millions.
— Attributed to Mahatma Gandhi

Ranchers have a trick to deal with a corral of skittish horses: they place a mule in their midst. Mules are generally more relaxed and laid-back than horses, and they exert a calming influence on high-strung equines.

If you find yourself in the midst of a tense office, family gathering, or traffic jam, you serve yourself and those around you best by being the mule. Do whatever you can to keep yourself peaceful, no matter how crazy the people around you are getting. The person who is least upset is in the best position to recognize creative solutions helpful to everyone. Regardless of what action you take, inner peace is the greatest contribution you can make anywhere, anytime.

You can also apply this principle when you find yourself getting upset. While fearful or chaotic thoughts and feelings may be running rampant within you like spooked horses, you also have a calm mule inside you that can bring a soothing energy to your world if you invite it into the corral. If you start to feel frantic about anything, bring forth your inner mule.

Your life is an interplay of different energies. You have the power to choose energies that match your intentions. Inner peace is not a random event created by outer conditions. It is a purposeful experience created by inner choice.

What situations in or around you feel frantic?
How can you help yourself and others by
calling forth and being the calm mule?

I soothe myself and those around me by
 finding and sounding a keynote of peace.

How to Write a Bestseller

Choose a job you love, and you will never
have to work a day in your life.

— Confucius

I read an inspiring interview with science-fiction master Ray Bradbury. A spry octogenarian, Bradbury remains visionary, enthusiastic, and unstoppably happy. Assessing his livelihood, he explained, "It's got to be fun. I've never worked a day in my life! . . . I've played my way through life. I've never agonized."

When asked how to remain an individual in the face of great commercialism, Bradbury suggested, "You just live your life and write your stories. If you set out to write a bestseller, it can't be done. . . . People who try to make a name for themselves are usually surpassed by people authentically expressing their joy and talents."

Those who live to see their name in lights usually miss the light within themselves. They place fame and glory at the top of the ladder of success and overlook personal satisfaction and creative expression. People who sweat to become stars rarely do, while those who live to share their gifts and enjoy the ride often find their way to the upper echelons of success.

If you are wondering which career to pursue or how to advance your current one, pay less attention to the "how" and more attention to the "why." If you are struggling, stop and ask yourself how you would proceed if you made creative self-expression the platform for your vocation rather than ambition for glory.

Ray Bradbury is not an exception to the Law of Success. He is the fulfillment of it. Like Bradbury, you need not work another day of your life. Remember that the day at hand is not just a means to an end; where you are is as crucial as where you want to go. Make joy your priority and agony will be reduced to science fiction.

What career would not feel like work to you?
What would you be doing differently if you refused
to tolerate struggle in your work?

My creative instincts light my career path.
I play my way to success.

Signs When You Need Them

*She felt again that small shiver that occurred
to her when events hinted at a destiny being
played out, of unseen forces intervening.*

— Dorothy Gilman

While driving home one day, I noticed that someone had posted some cardboard signs on poles along the roadside, leading guests to a party. Since the signs were pointing in the direction I was heading, I kept noticing them and wondering where the party was.

After I drove for quite a stretch without seeing any signs, I wondered if I had missed one. If I were attending the party, I would probably feel lost and confused at this point without more direction.

Finally, after passing a half dozen more intersections, there was another sign to turn. Good, the partygoers will not be lost, I realized.

In like manner, we receive life-course directions on a need-to-know basis. If you are wondering whether or not to make a turn and you do not see any sign to do so, just keep going straight ahead. When it is time to turn, you will know.

Just as this party organizer had posted signs at the crucial intersections only, your Source of Guidance does the same. If you are not getting a sign, you are probably not at a crucial intersection. Crucial intersections are more clearly marked than those that do not require your attention.

Your path is not a mystery, and the universe does not keep you in the dark. Higher Intelligence is communicating with you all the time, and your ability to receive direction is in direct proportion to your willingness to listen. Sometimes your guidance is to turn here, and sometimes it is to keep going. Either way, just enjoy the ride and trust that you will know when to turn.

*Are you waiting for guidance to make a move in your life?
Can you relax and trust that you will know when the time is right?*

**I know what I need to know,
when I need to know it.**

Criticism and Truth

No statue has ever been put up to a critic.

— Jean Sibelius

After the film *Patch Adams* came to theaters, I read online movie reviews by a half dozen prestigious critics. The film's grades were the worst of all the current movies, ranging from *C* to a dismal *F.* Then I noticed another column reflecting ratings by moviegoers who had seen the film. In this column *Patch Adams* received an *A*—the highest grade of all the movies.

People who sit around and criticize all day tend to be hyper-critical. They are paid to criticize, so they do. I have found that my opinions about books, movies, and entertainers rarely match the general trend of the critics. So I have learned to trust my intuition, or the opinions of people whose value system matches my own, when making entertainment or life choices.

The energy of destructive criticism is entirely different from that of constructive criticism, and you must be able to discern between the two. After I presented a weekend seminar, I received a letter of criticism from a participant. To my surprise, she found fault with me for practically everything I did, missing no area of presentation. As I tried the communication on for size, my sense was that she was simply angry in general—whether at me, someone else, or herself—and she was using me as a venue to dump. I put the letter aside and gave it no further thought.

At another time I received a letter from a fellow who took exception to some material I had included in a newsletter. He told me that in general he liked my work, but he thought that this material was off base and not up to the standard he had expected from me. When I considered this fellow's criticism, I realized that his point was well-taken, and I had indeed made an error in couching the material in the way I did. I thanked him and changed the format of my subsequent work to reflect his suggestion. I considered his criticism constructive.

Criticism, like all communication, depends on motivation and intention. When it comes from truth and kindness, it is golden. When it comes from mean-spiritedness, let it go.

How do you recognize the difference
between destructive and helpful criticism?

I know and trust feedback that resonates with me and
helps me. I let go of what is not off base or misdirected.

How Long It Took

Learning is a treasure that will follow its owner everywhere.

— Chinese proverb

One morning in the 1950s an American woman named Joan was shopping in an open-air market in the French city of Nice. When she saw a familiar-looking man holding a sketch pad, she approached him nervously and asked, "Excuse me, but are you Pablo Picasso?"

"That's right," he answered softly.

"I am one of your biggest fans!" she told him excitedly. "I don't mean to disturb you, but is there any way you would take a few minutes and do a sketch of me? I'd be happy to pay you."

Picasso studied the woman's features for a moment and answered with a smile, "Yes, I will."

The two walked to a table at a nearby sidewalk café. Picasso opened his pad, reached into his pocket for a piece of charcoal, and went to work. Fifteen minutes later he turned the pad around and showed Joan his finished work. It was spectacular—an authentic Picasso, and of her!

Joan took the portrait and thanked the master profusely. Then she took out her checkbook and asked, "How much will that be?"

"Five thousand dollars," Picasso answered in a matter-of-fact way.

Joan's jaw dropped. "But, sir, with all due respect, the picture took you only 15 minutes."

"No, madam," he replied quite seriously. "You don't understand. The picture took me 80 years and 15 minutes."

Everything you have ever done has led you to become who and what you are today, and bestowed you with what you have to offer. Assess your worth not by an isolated criterion, but by what you have learned through every job, relationship, failure, triumph, and experience. You bring to the table a huge bank of wisdom based on past learning. This moment is not disconnected from those that came before it. It stands at the apex of the pyramid of your life.

*How do you bring a lifetime of experience
to any new job, relationship, or project?*

**I am valuable not just for what I do now, but
for all the valuable experience leading to now.**

Looking Where?

*God is a circle of which the center is everywhere
and the circumference is nowhere.*

— Attributed to Empedocles

In the film *Bruce Almighty,* Jim Carrey portrays Bruce, a down-and-out reporter who is given the power of God, Whom he meets in the form of a janitor played by Morgan Freeman. When Bruce becomes overwhelmed by the responsibility of his divine powers, he longs to become a simple human being again. He consults God in an empty office building, after which the "janitor" ascends a ladder, about to disappear beyond the ceiling. Bruce desperately asks what he will do if he needs help in the future. God looks back and answers that most people make the same error: they keep looking *up.*

Truer words were never spoken. We have been taught that God is somewhere out there, above us, separate from us; while, in fact, God is really somewhere right here, inside us. We pray to a distant cosmic force when that very force is operating through us. We prostrate ourselves in worship, while what we really need, as Unity minister and author Eric Butterworth suggested, is *worth-ship.*

There are many levels of prayer, all of which work. Yet some are more effective than others. At a simple level, we feel separate from God and ask for divine help with something we cannot handle. We have all been in this position, and the call of a sincere heart is heard by God and answered.

Yet there is a higher level of prayer, one closer to the truth of who we are. In reality, we are not separate from God. We are children of God, extensions and expressions of God. The Creator did not cast us off into an alien world, alone and bereft. From the viewpoint of the illusory separated self, this gap seems very real. But from the viewpoint of the divine self, the God Who created us lives within us and through us.

If you want to find God, look not to the heavens, but within your own heart. *Bruce Almighty's* God had it spot-on: quit looking up and start looking in.

Do you believe God lives outside you? Can you find God inside you?

**I find the Great Spirit everywhere,
including within me.**

Headed in the Right Direction

Life must be understood backwards.
But . . . it must be lived—forwards.

— Søren Kierkegaard

At one of my seminars, a young woman named Abby reported that her parents had sent her there as a birthday present. At the age of 17, she had been hospitalized for an eating disorder, and she doubted she would ever feed herself again. Now, four years later, Abby was taking charge of her life and opening up to receive love and support from others. While her illness had been painful, she had grown immensely through the lessons that accompanied it. At the age of 21, she was bright, beautiful, and mature beyond her years.

During the seminar, I noticed that Abby had a tattoo of a forward-pointing arrow on each of her feet. "What made you get those tattoos?" I asked her.

Abby smiled and answered, "They remind me that I am always headed in the right direction."

Sometimes it may look as if you are not getting anywhere or you have veered irrevocably from your right course. But your inner being is always moving ahead toward greater good. Even when it seems that you have hit a dead end or are on a pointless detour, you are still on your path. Incomprehensible experiences often prove themselves to be integral elements of your journey, their gifts apparent only in retrospect. Every experience serves healing and awakening.

When a situation arises that seems to be a setback or a non sequitur, that is the time for faith and trust. Such events force you to think in broader dimensions and move ahead in ways you never would have enjoyed if everything remained stable. So bless all encounters, even those that seem adverse or incomprehensible.

Like Abby, you may use a symbol of well-being as your touchstone. Keep a photo, motto, gift you have received, or inspirational item close to you on your desk, near your bed, on your altar, or in your wallet or purse. Then whenever you look at it you will be reminded that you are always headed in the right direction.

How might you now be headed in the right direction,
even though it seems that you are not?

Everything that happens ultimately contributes to my well-being. I am on course.

The Crazy Man on the Bridge

Shovel while the piles are small.

— Source unknown

While fishing one day, two anglers saw a woman being swept down the river. *"Help! Help!"* she cried out. Quickly, one of the men jumped in the stream and rescued her. They called for medical aid, and before long the woman was taken away for care.

A few minutes later, the men heard the cries of a man being carried down the waterway. The other fisherman came to his rescue, and eventually the fellow was off to the hospital.

An hour later yet another person was calling for help, and the entire process was repeated.

Stymied as to why all of these people had nearly drowned, the fishermen hiked upstream, where they saw a bridge with a crazy man standing at its center. When another pedestrian attempted to cross the bridge, the crazy man tried to toss him into the river. The fishermen quickly realized that the insane man had intercepted everyone who attempted to cross the bridge and he had thrown them into the river. The two men dashed over to the crazy man, grabbed him, and dragged him off the bridge, rescuing the current victim and making it safe for everyone who wanted to pass.

There is a crazy person in your head who intercepts positive, healthy thoughts and tries to drown them. This is the voice of self-doubt, fear, and constant judgment. This crazy person will do everything in his power to undermine your happiness and good, as well as that of others.

There is also a wise and calm person in your head—the real you—who does not heed the voice of doubt or fear and accepts and encourages confident, healthy thoughts about you and your life.

If your life is a series of upsets, dramas, or failures, it is time to find and confront the crazy man on the bridge. If you remove him before he can sabotage your well-being, all of your loving, creative ideas can cross to the other side of the bridge and build the life you came to enjoy.

What voice within you attempts to undermine your good?
What can you do to clear the way for healthy,
successful thoughts, actions, and results?

I welcome positive, sane, and creative thoughts to manifest in my life. I will not tolerate insane, self-defeating thoughts or attitudes.

Really Free

We started out fine. Then we got de-fined.
Now we need to get re-fined.

— Swami Satchidananda

Very few people know that the Founding Fathers of the United States and the framers of the Declaration of Independence and the Constitution were very spiritual men—Freemasons, Rosicrucians, and advanced metaphysicians. The country was conceived and inaugurated not simply as a political movement, but as a radical step in living under higher spiritual laws.

If you examine the back of a dollar bill, you will find many mystical symbols, including the all-seeing eye of God; a pyramid; and the Latin phrase *Novus Ordo Seclorum,* meaning "a new order of the ages." The front of the bill contains several Rosicrucian symbols.

The Founding Fathers were champions of political freedom, but they grasped a deep understanding of *spiritual* freedom, our power to rise above circumstances and bring the light of higher wisdom to our daily lives. If you are free politically but your soul is in bondage, you cannot say you are free. If you are liberated in your mind and heart, you are truly free.

Today would be a good day to consider how free you are. If you are living in pain, fear, resentment, or conflict, it is time to declare independence. Are you tired of feeling enslaved? If you go to a job you hate, fight with people you care about, or feel shackled by economic stress, you are being moved, like the Pilgrims who left England to flee political oppression, to escape the emotional oppression of feeling limited by external circumstances.

We have all felt oppressed in one way or another, and we are all freedom-seeking beings. If we truly want to honor the United States and its Founding Fathers, today let us remember the kind of freedom they valued as men of higher thinking—freedom of the heart, mind, and spirit.

How free do you feel?
What declaration of spiritual independence would you like to make?

I claim my freedom to be happy.
I release my imprisoned power.

Synthesis

*The art of living lies less in eliminating
our troubles than in growing with them.*
— Attributed to Bernard M. Baruch

Do you have a tough decision to make? Are you contemplating whether or not to stay in a relationship, job, or living situation? Do you wonder why whenever you get a good new idea, someone or something comes along and tries to shoot it down?

Because we live in a dualistic universe where everything has an opposite, whenever you think of something, you automatically call forth the awareness of its opposite. Consider the word *thesis,* which means "an idea you put forth." Any intention you hold is a thesis.

Your thesis will usually call forth an *antithesis,* or that which contradicts the thesis. Someone else will tell you that you cannot or should not do what you intend to do, or you may find internal arguments or reasons against your vision.

If that were the end of the story, our world would just go 'round and 'round, from thesis to antithesis and back again, in an eternal frustrating loop. But when you hold both thesis and antithesis up to consciousness, you "sweat the opposites," and you are led to a solution that takes into account both thesis and antithesis. This is called *synthesis.*

Sweating the opposites is rarely comfortable, but always productive. Confusion means that your old belief or value system has played itself out, and something new or bigger is confronting it. If you can stay with this process, you will come out on the other side and realize that both opposites helped move you to your answer.

Albert Einstein said that we cannot solve a problem at the same level of consciousness at which it was created. The problem exists in order to push us to a new level. So even while you sweat out your decision, the process is taking you to a new place, better than the one from which you started. Night makes day more interesting, loneliness deepens relationship, and fear makes faith more powerful. Thesis . . . antithesis . . . synthesis.

*How might your decision-making process be just
as important as the decision you arrive at?*

**I honor the forces of opposites as divine elements
that enhance my evolution to higher awareness.**

JULY 6

Find the Stream

Life is a series of natural and spontaneous changes.
Don't resist them—that only creates sorrow. Let reality be reality.
Let things flow naturally forward in whatever way they like.

— Lao-tzu

Most of us are familiar with the *Star Wars* maxim, "May the Force be with you." While the reasoning behind this good wish is sound, its language is not a completely accurate depiction of how the Force works. The Force is already with you. The question is, "Are *you* with the Force?"

Imagine you are in the mountains and you want to get to the ocean as quickly and easily as possible. You know there is a river that can take you to your destination, and you set out to use it on your behalf. At the outset of your journey, someone says, "May the stream be with you." This suggests that you will be walking wherever you want or choose and you hope the water will leap out of the streambed, find you, and carry you. This is not how the stream helps you.

If you are going to harness the river's power, you must find it, get into it, flow with it, and let it carry you where both you and it are going. The river will not divert itself to follow the course you dictate for it. But it will become your best friend if you follow the direction in which it is already moving.

There is indeed a mighty Force animating the universe. It is one of well-being, health, prosperity, love, and all the good things you desire. The Force is happy to take you where it is going and where you want to go. But you must get with it. If you wander far from the stream, it will not help you, nor will it come to your aid if you sit at a distance from it and do nothing. If you get into the river and fight your way upstream, you will not arrive at your destination either. There is only one way for the stream or the Force to be with you: you must align yourself with it.

Whether or not the Force is with you is not a matter of luck. It is a matter of choice. The Force is already with you, trying to work on your behalf. May you be with the Force.

How can you flow more with the stream of well-being
and let it take you where you want to go?

I open up to the Force of universal good,
and I move with it to the results I desire.

Essential Nutrients

Adam and Eve ate the first vitamins, including the package.
— Squibb pharmaceuticals ad

A woman told me that after her child was born, she had the placenta frozen by a medical service. It is kept in storage until such time as the child, at any age in life, may need an infusion of blood or nutrients. At that time the placenta is thawed out and used as a source of life-giving elements, in the pure form the child had received while in its mother's womb.

This practice bears phenomenal spiritual symbolism. All healing—whether physical, mental, emotional, or spiritual—is based on a return to our original state of being. Illness and aberration are not natural to us. They are the result of mingling with thoughts, energies, or entities foreign to us that we adopt and which throw us off course. If we can get back to who we were before we got mixed up with issues alien to our nature, we can return to our inherent wholeness.

You may use a similar method to offset crashes on your computer. Many operating systems now contain some version of a "restore point." Every now and then when your computer is healthy, it notes the system's configuration. If the system becomes infected with a virus, corrupted, or in any way dysfunctional, you can press a button that returns the system to an earlier marked restore point and nullifies all the negative experience the computer has gone through since then.

Your life, too, has a restore point, or an unsullied placenta you can return to for healing. Who you were before you got mixed up with worldly dilemmas remains whole, intact, and able to offer you the healing that less profound methods of correction cannot achieve. When you pray, meditate, or act in alignment with your innate joy, you carve a path to your restore point.

The healing you seek has not been lost. It is just frozen and waiting to be thawed.

*Do you believe you have drifted too far from well-being
to be healed? Are you open to connecting with the essential
nutrients that can restore your life?*

**My original wholeness is available to me,
and given as I ask. I claim it now.**

How the Program Works

The program works if you work it.

— 12-step program motto

My friends Benny and Sue wanted to lose weight and firm up their abs, so they bought an exercise machine they saw advertised on an infomercial. A month after their purchase, I asked them how the machine was working for them.

"We sent the stupid thing back," Benny scoffed. "It didn't do what they promised."

"How much did you use it?" I inquired.

"Maybe five minutes a week," he replied.

It is easy to blame people and things outside us for failing to accomplish what only inside work can beget. I am sure that Benny and Sue would have gotten their desired results if they had used the machine more. The program would have worked if they had worked it.

Dee and I built a solar-powered retreat house in a remote location. After the structure was completed, we were away for a long time. Upon our return, we found that the solar power was not working, and I faulted the engineer for not installing the system correctly. When he came for a service call, he discovered that the batteries were drained because their water supply was depleted. He refilled the water and explained to me that the batteries need to be topped off every couple of months. My criticism of him and the system was for naught. *Operator error.*

The universe is set up to work. It is a magnificent system, with a miraculous design and infinite potential. But to get the results we seek, we have to practice the operating principles in our favor. If our lives and the world as a whole do not seem to be working, it is not because the system is flawed. It is because of operator error.

The good news is that once you begin to figure out the game and apply universal principles, you enjoy rewarding results and the journey becomes fun. The program works if you work it.

Who or what do you blame for your life not working?
How could you improve your results by using
universal principles to your advantage?

I help myself and others by applying
beneficial universal laws in my favor.

Peripheral Vision

You can assess the state of your mental health by
the number of options you are aware of.

— Source unknown

Psychobiologists have discovered a fascinating survival mechanism in nature. When an animal feels threatened—in fight-or-flight mode—its peripheral vision shrinks. It becomes fixated on finding a safe haven and does not see extraneous objects to the side. If you were a deer being chased by a tiger, you would completely focus on finding a nook to flee to, and you would not be at all interested in seeing or smelling the flowers along the way.

In human terms, when you perceive that your survival is threatened (emotionally), your peripheral vision shrinks and you see far fewer response options than when you feel relaxed and safe. Fear narrows your corridor of sight to a very limited passageway. If you were truly endangered, this response mechanism would serve you well. If you are not really threatened, this mechanism backfires, because you tend to commit desperate acts when you are not really desperate.

In reality, most times when we feel endangered, we are not. Fear can blow minor issues out of proportion so we see them as survival issues.

Your boss tells you that you have made an error, and you go into an "I'm going to lose my job" tailspin. Your boyfriend tells you he got an e-mail from a past girlfriend, and you seethe with jealousy, fearful he will get back with her. You panic, go into survival mode, and say and do things you may later regret. Your reaction to the situation hurts you more than the situation itself.

Your best response when you feel threatened is to step back, take a few deep breaths, and ask yourself what your options are. When you are relaxed, you will see far more viable solutions than simply fleeing to a cave or going for the jugular. Maybe your boss really values you, and he was just asking you to make a correction. Or your boyfriend couldn't care less about his past partner, and he will tell you that if you ask him. When you respond from a platform of confidence rather than survival threat, you generate results that affirm your well-being.

What options may be available to you beyond the ones you currently see?

I relax into strength and confidence.
I have more choices than I realize.

Upgrade

Self-respect is the noblest garment with which
a man may clothe himself—the most elevating feeling
with which the mind can be inspired.

— Samuel Smiles

A woman named Cheryl wanted to attend my Life Mastery Training but feared she could not afford it. I asked her how her life was working. "Not so great," she answered. "I don't feel well, I hate my job, and I can't seem to attract a good relationship."

"Well, then," I answered, "I don't see that you have anything to lose."

Cheryl attended the program in Maui and broke through her sense of limits. At the end of the week, she told me she had phoned the airline and asked how much an upgrade to first class would cost for her trip home. The agent explained it would cost an additional $847. "How did you respond?" I asked Cheryl.

"I booked it," she answered.

"You just graduated from the training," I told her.

When I spoke to Cheryl a few weeks later, she explained that when she came home, she discovered some funds among her assets that equaled all she had paid for the program, plus the money for the upgrade. A few years later, she sent me photos of her wedding.

This summer, and the rest of your life, have some fun with your finances. Even if you do not have a ton of money lying around for upgrades, there are things you can do with your cash that would give you more enjoyment than you have now. The more you invest in your happiness, the more happiness will invest in you.

To upgrade your airplane seat, your car, or your home, you must first upgrade your sense of self-worth. Use today and every day to practice knowing how much good you deserve. Prosperity, like all external change, is an inside job. Life will treat you as well as you treat yourself, so give it the biggest chance you can.

What upgrade would you like to make in your life?
Do you know you are worth it?

I know my worth, and the universe reflects
my knowing. My life gets better and better as
I see myself and my possibilities more clearly.

Happy for a Lifetime

If you want happiness for an hour, take a nap.
If you want happiness for a day, go fishing.
If you want happiness for a month, get married.
If you want happiness for a year, inherit a fortune.
If you want happiness for a lifetime, help somebody.

— Chinese saying

I knew an accountant named Chris who was unemployed and psychologically stressed. She felt that something was missing in her world, and she tried various therapies and seminars, which helped somewhat. But, she confessed, she still needed something more to feed her soul.

Awhile later I saw Chris, and she was glowing. "What have you been up to?" I asked her.

"I have been going to the city hospital once a week and cuddling babies of mothers with AIDS," Chris explained. "I find the experience utterly fulfilling, and I know this is the kind of activity my spirit has been craving."

Taking good care of yourself is important, yet life is incomplete unless you find some avenue through which to serve others. There is a reward in helping someone else that runs far deeper than simply helping yourself.

I have noticed this principle when I have occasionally taken six months off from teaching or coaching. At first I felt relieved and glad to have more free time. After a while, however, I became self-involved, thinking about my personal world to an unhealthy degree. When I got back into my schedule, I felt uplifted and rewarded to support others to improve their lives. I learned that I need to give help as much as others need to receive it.

If you are successful in business, well provided for, or simply bored and frustrated with your life, reaching out to lend a helping hand may be your next fulfilling step. There is just something about helping someone else that is . . . well, holy.

How might you help yourself emotionally
by helping someone else?

I find deep joy and fulfillment in supporting
others. Their happiness becomes my own.

God Did Not Desert You

The only force that can overcome an idea and a faith is another
and better idea and faith, positively and fearlessly upheld.

— Dorothy Thompson

"I nearly fell to my death on a rock climb," a seminar participant named Jim recounted. "My buddy and I were at the top of a ravine, and I slipped and fell 25 feet until I was hanging perilously over a deep canyon. I called to my partner for help. He took a few strides down, but then became frightened and ventured no farther. Then I noticed a rock I could grab on to, which stabilized me. From there I spied another rock and then another, which I clutched until I worked my way back to safety. Since that day I have harbored tremendous anger at God for deserting me when my friend chickened out. How could any loving God be so callous?"

I told Jim, "God did not desert you."

"How is that?" he asked.

"God showed you the rock that gave you a handhold to make your way to safety."

Like Jim, you may have felt let down or betrayed by someone you trusted who did not come through when you were in need. People are human, fallible, and often untrustworthy. Yet there is more to your universal support system than individual people. Often when someone turns his or her back on you, you discover a pathway that ends up being far more rewarding than the one you would have stayed on if that person had not left you on your own.

You and I have our ideas about who is supposed to be there for us, when, and how. Sometimes we are right, and often we are not. If you rigidly cling to your notion of how things are supposed to happen, and grow angry and resentful when they do not go as you had imagined, you dig a hole for yourself that is hard to escape. If you trust the process of the Big Picture, miracles happen. People may betray you, but God will not. If a person chickens out, there is always a rock. Forget about the person and bless the rock.

Can you recognize that life is supporting you
even if someone let you down?

People are not the source of my good.
Life is the source of my good, and it always provides.

Humanitarian of the Year

Nobody has ever measured, even the poets,
how much a heart can hold.

— Zelda Fitzgerald

Several years ago at a zoo near Chicago, a three-year-old boy climbed a retaining wall and fell 17 feet onto the concrete floor of the gorilla pavilion. The child hit his head and was rendered unconscious in the midst of a group of gorillas. The boy's mother became hysterical, onlookers were horrified, and several people ran to summon zoo officials. Before anyone could get to the boy, a gorilla named Binti Jua, with her own infant on her back, brushed away the other gorillas and took the unconscious child in her arms. As the astonished crowd watched, she tenderly carried the child to the door of the gorilla cage and handed him to an attendant. Later that year a magazine reportedly designated Binti Jua the recipient of its Humanitarian of the Year award.

While we often observe the savage element of the animal kingdom, an element of kindness and compassion runs through nature. In Binti Jua's case, the love of a mother for her child spilled from the gorilla world to the human domain. Dolphins, whales, and elephants are also known for their protectiveness of humans in certain scenarios. I live on the island of Maui, where great humpback whales migrate each winter to cavort in the warm offshore waters, mate, and bear their young. On any given winter day, you can see hundreds of whales.

While thousands of boats—from large tour vessels to tiny kayaks—maneuver to watch the whales each season, I have never heard of a whale harming a person. I know several people who have dived into the ocean in the midst of a pod of 40-foot, 40-ton humpbacks; and they swore the whales were very conscious to avoid contact with them. The swimmers could have easily been killed with one whisk of a whale's tail, but they noted that the humpbacks gracefully moved aside.

Even the animal kingdom, often ferocious, understands love. Hopefully we humans can live up to that standard.

Who or what inspires you to live with more kindness and compassion?

I attune to creation's gentleness and care
for my fellow creatures. I live according
to "the license of a higher order of beings."

Get Up and Leave

But what is happiness except the simple harmony
between a man and the life he leads?

— Albert Camus

When a friend of mine glowingly recommended a popular movie, I went with a buddy to watch it. After about ten minutes, I became bored and annoyed, and could not imagine sitting through two hours of an empty script. I hung in there for another ten minutes and then asked my friend if he was enjoying the film. He was not, so we just got up and left. It was the first time I had ever walked out of a theater.

Sometimes we err by staying in relationships, jobs, or living situations in which we are basically watching a bad movie. One voice in our head tells us that we need to get out, while another tells us we should sit through it. If you are in such a situation, sit a little while longer and watch what happens. If it gets better, stay. If it remains the same or gets worse, have the guts to get up and leave. I am not suggesting that you run away. I am suggesting that your time, life, and attention are valuable; and you need to invest them all in experiences that are rewarding for you and others.

Some religions and philosophies suggest that it is noble to put up with pain, to sacrifice, and to endure hardship. If you have to put up with something difficult, then find some way to keep a positive attitude. But if you have a choice, why torture yourself? You help no one when you endure pain for pain's sake. You do not add to the joy in the world. You only add to pain. What can you do to add to the sum total of joy on the planet?

It may be awkward or uncomfortable to leave something you are involved in. But if staying is more uncomfortable, it may be time to watch another movie.

Are you watching a bad movie? If so,
what can you do to either remedy it or leave?

I invest my time and energy in endeavors that
are rewarding. I release what does not serve.

When Life Happens

Life is what happens to us while we are making other plans.

— Source unknown

After presenting seminars for years, I developed the practice of taking quiet time to meditate and pray for 20 minutes before doing a program. One day before presenting an afternoon seminar, the sponsor took me out for lunch. The meal took longer than we expected, and we were returning to the seminar site just minutes before the program was to begin.

As we pulled into the parking lot of the center, I noticed an auto dealership next door. There in the showroom sat a gleaming, steaming red Mazda RX-7 convertible, exactly what I had been seeking for a long time. The showroom was open, but it would be closed by the time the seminar was over; and since I would be leaving the city that evening, if I was going to check out the car, it would have to be now. But I had my rule about inner preparation, and I felt torn between prayer and the convertible. (Can you identify?)

The convertible won. I dashed into the showroom, gave the car a quick once-over, and fell in love with it. I told the salesperson to hold it for me until I phoned the next morning. I called back, we made a deal, and a few days later the RX-7 was in my garage. I drove the car during the next five years and enjoyed every moment with it.

Even though I did not follow my ritual to meditate before the seminar, the program went impeccably well, and there was no loss whatsoever from my going to see the car. It was obviously in Spirit's plan for my good and that of everyone concerned.

We all have policies, procedures, and self-created rules for how we should do things to achieve a desired outcome. Often those procedures are well chosen, and they get results. But sometimes life calls us in another direction for good reason, and we are wise to follow.

Where is life calling you in spite of the plans you have made?
What would it take for you to follow?

As I heed my inner voice, my life unfolds with miraculous wisdom and precision.

Positive Disintegration

Bad times have a scientific value. These are
occasions a good learner would not miss.

— Ralph Waldo Emerson

I met a woman who had just come through an extremely emotionally trying time in her life. "At first I thought I was having a nervous breakdown," she admitted. "But afterward I realized I had a nervous *breakthrough.*"

We might judge or resist experiences in which something long held falls apart. A marriage, job, friendship, living situation, religious affiliation, or economic system looms as a solid reality; and when it crumbles, we may feel confused or bereft. But if something has become rigid, top-heavy, or lifeless, or has played out its purpose, it is an act of grace for it to undo itself and clear the way for better.

In college I read a book called *Positive Disintegration* by psychologist Kazimierz Dabrowski, who treated mental patients who had experienced severe disorientation due to a life change. He discovered that their breakdown was the only way they knew how to get out of lives that were not working for them. As he worked with them over time, he found methods to help them build new lives that they could not have created if their old structures had remained intact.

In the Hindu religion, Shiva is the god of destruction or dissolution. There is nothing wrong with Shiva. He clears the way for Brahma, the god of creation; and Vishnu, the god of preservation.

Life supports what works and withdraws support from what does not work. Relationships and institutions that are empowered with life force will continue naturally. When the life force is no longer there, they will blessedly disappear. Nothing dies that does not in some way give rise to new life. When something falls apart, spend no time bemoaning the loss, and quickly refocus on the gain or opportunity.

How could you view a disintegration as positive?

**I honor dissolution as a way to
clear the path for greater life.**

Personality and Character

Personality can open doors, but
only character can keep them open.

— Elmer Leterman

A dapper-looking businessman walked into New York City's Office of Land Records and handed the clerk the appropriate documents for the property he had just purchased, a $2 billion parcel at 338 Fifth Avenue. The clerk went through the title-issuance procedure, and 90 minutes later the fellow walked out of the office with his certificate of ownership in hand.

What the clerk did not know was that the "buyer" was a *New York Daily News* reporter seeking to demonstrate the laxness of the city's real estate title system. If the clerk had examined the documents more closely, she would have realized the fellow had just purchased the Empire State Building. She would have also noticed the false notary stamp and the fake witness signature of Fay Wray, the legendary actress who was snatched by the imperiled King Kong in the classic 1933 film.

Ultimately, the title in the hands of the "buyer" did not yield him ownership of the building. If he had tried to act on his "ownership," he would have gotten nowhere. The illusion of his ownership did not bestow him with the rights of true ownership.

You can sweet-talk or manipulate your way into a position, but unless you truly own it by virtue of who you are, your level of awareness, and actions worthy of it, it will disappear as quickly as the title the reporter had to return to the authorities.

All ownership is by right of consciousness. Rather than engineering the *appearance* of ownership, master the *qualities* of ownership. When you have developed your thoughts, feelings, and actions to be an equal to the object of your quest, it will come to you as the next logical step—and stay with you. You do not have to dummy documents or yourself to get what you deserve. You just need to act from integrity and be who you are.

How can you attract what you want by owning it from the inside out?

I know who I am and what I deserve.
My good comes to me and stays with me naturally.

Every Step Important

One only gets to the top rung on the ladder by steadily
climbing up one at a time, and suddenly, all sorts of powers,
all sorts of abilities which you thought never belonged
to you—suddenly become within your own possibility.

— Margaret Thatcher

I saw an inspiring presentation by award-winning photographer and filmmaker Dewitt Jones, who photographed for *National Geographic* for 20 years and received two Academy Award nominations before the age of 30.

As Dewitt showed his favorite photos, he explained that sometimes the best pictures come unplanned, as part of an unfolding artistic process. To illustrate, he shared some images he took on a shoot at Yellowstone National Park. "That day I just couldn't find a good shot," he recounted. "Frustrated, I began to randomly shoot whatever was before me." Dewitt showed some uninteresting pictures of the parking lot, grass, and shrubbery. "These photos led me to a path in the woods, which I followed. I just kept walking and shooting haphazardly. Then to my surprise, the path opened to a great placid lake, and before me was this vista." Onto the screen flashed a stunning photo of a mountain lake at dawn, surrounded by colorful autumn leaves, mist rising from the surface and two fishermen sitting serenely in a rowboat, their rods cast into the water. The image was so striking that a wave of oohs and aahs echoed through the lecture hall. "This photo was used by a large company as their premier magazine ad for years." I recognized the picture.

While Dewitt's photographer's block was initially frustrating, it was setting him up for one of his greatest works. Those random shots did not have value in themselves, but they were leading to something far greater.

You, too, may find yourself stuck or frustrated. But if you just start moving with whatever energy is at hand, you may soon find yourself standing before the greatest vista of your life.

How can you flow with the energy of the moment,
which may lead to something far better?

The process of my life is moving me to better things.
I pursue my journey with joy and trust.

Fear and Discernment

*Yea, though I walk through the valley of the shadow
of death, I will fear no evil: for Thou art with me.*

— Psalm 23:4

Many of us have been taught that the opposite of love is fear, and we should not act out of fear. Yet does fear not help you in a situation where you need to protect yourself?

I received a direct answer to this question when I was hiking with some friends on a forest trail one summer's day. As we were walking along, I suddenly noticed a rattlesnake on the path a few feet in front of me. If I had not seen it, I might have stepped on it. The moment I saw the snake, I uttered a sharp "Whoa!" and snapped back to a safe distance, all in a matter of a second. The rattlesnake slithered into the forest, and fortunately that was the end of the interaction.

What I noticed about my experience was that I felt no fear. The whole encounter happened so fast that I did not have time to think about it or be afraid. Some wise mechanism in my body recognized danger, and it took over before I could intellectualize the experience. Perhaps if I had seen the snake at more of a distance, I might have been afraid, but it all happened too quickly for that.

From this I learned that fear is always a projection of the mind into the future. If you examine your fears, they have nothing to do with what is happening now. They are always about bad things that *might* happen. If something happened that was threatening to your well-being, you, like me, would be guided as to what to do in that moment, without thinking about it much or feeling afraid.

So I learned that the answer to the question "Don't you need to be afraid to protect yourself?" is *no*. You just have to let your natural instinct for well-being take over, and that instinct has nothing to do with fear.

*Do you believe you would not be protected if you were not afraid?
Can you imagine living without fear?*

**I am protected by wise guidance
deep within me. I need not fear.**

The Sequel's Not Equal

Creativeness means to be born before one dies.
The willingness to be born requires courage. . . .
Courage to let go of certainties.

— Erich Fromm

Summer is the season of the sequel. Movie theaters are glutted with follow-ups to blockbusters of previous years, as the production studios hope Part 2, 3, or 10 will draw the same crowds as the original. Sequels, however, rarely measure up. Recently I saw a few films whose predecessors were clever and hilarious. Unfortunately, the follow-ups suffered from rubber stamp–itis, and I walked out of the theater feeling hungry for the original sparkle.

Like movies, there are two ways to live: hiding out in history, or dancing on the cutting edge of innovation. History is safe, but reeks of regularity. The cutting edge seems scary, but bestows life. You can copy what has been done, and sometimes succeed financially—but you wither spiritually. Herein lies the challenge—and invitation—to a true creator.

We all know of writers, musicians, and moviemakers who had one big success and spend the rest of their lives trying to replicate it. Yet over time, their creations grow stale, being little more than subtle variations on an overworked theme. We also know creative people who constantly challenge themselves to come up with stimulating creations. They will not settle for carbon copies of what once was. These people are fully alive, and blaze new trails of success.

Consider, for example, Carlos Santana, who, after 30 years in the music industry, tied the record for most Grammy Awards (eight) for his 1999 album *Supernatural*. Likewise, actors Meryl Streep and Dustin Hoffman refuse to be typecast and constantly throw themselves into innovative and challenging roles.

There is no end to the creativity and success available to you if you are willing to trust the new, exciting, challenging, and different.

Have you become stuck in a creative rut?
What new and different creation calls to you?

I am true to my creative genius.
I forge into uncharted territory and
live on the cutting edge of life.

Lightheart

SIN: Self-Inflicted Nonsense

— Source unknown

While exploring an ancient Egyptian tomb, I discovered a painting showing a pair of scales, like the scales of justice. On one scale was a feather, and on the other a human heart. Nearby a godly entity looked on, along with a monsterlike animal.

Our Egyptologist explained that this image depicted the Egyptian concept of the day of judgment. When someone died, according to ancient belief, the person would be accused by 42 gods of having committed various sins. If the person could deny these sins—while keeping his heart light as a feather—he would be admitted to heaven and enjoy eternal life. If he could not deny them with a light heart, the nasty-looking dog entity Anubis would send him to the underworld.

This image bears tremendous practical implications not just for facing the afterlife, but for when the dogs of judgment come at you during your daily life. When presented with a demanding situation, can you keep your heart as light as a feather? When someone projects guilt onto you, can you rise above it and remember your innocence? Can you laugh your way through challenges and maintain an attitude freer than fear? Are you bigger than your circumstances?

From time to time today, take a heart reading. Ask yourself, *In this moment, is my heart light or heavy? Am I pandering to fear or proceeding from inner peace? Have I given my power to appearances, or do I remember the truth?*

Much of the world is steeped in illusions built on fear, judgment, and guilt. If you sincerely desire to be free, you cannot afford to indulge such illusions. Stay awake, stay alert, and stay light. Then no ugly dogs can get to you; and, like the Pharaohs of old, you will ride the boat past hell and land safely on the shores of heaven. And you will not have to die to do it.

*How can you remember your innocence
when others try to cast you as wrong or guilty?*

**I am innocent. I am free. There is nothing
to fear or resist. I am light.**

How Good Can It Get?

To be what we are, and to become what we are
capable of becoming, is the only end in life.

— Robert Louis Stevenson

My friend Drake is a landscaper who used to service numerous small accounts. One of his clients, a wealthy man with a large estate, invited Drake to work for him full-time. "What would it take for you to make me your only account?" the owner asked him.

Drake told the fellow he would have to think about it. He went home and wrote down all the aspects he could picture for his ideal job, including the salary, equipment, hours, and staff. The next day Drake revisited his notes and realized that what he had written did not represent his entire vision. So he expanded the salary, equipment, and working conditions. The next day he came back to his written description and realized it was still not big enough. This process went on for a while, with Drake's dream job continually expanding on paper.

Finally Drake felt that what he had written was an accurate expression of his best vision. He took the paper to his prospective employer and showed it to him. The fellow read it, thought for a moment, and answered, "Sounds good to me." Now Drake is living his dream job. He did not stop until he asked for what he really wanted—and he got it.

How good can your income, job, house, relationships, health, and life get? They can get as good as (1) you can imagine, (2) you ask for, and (3) you accept. Take a few moments now to consider if you are doing all three of these steps toward manifesting your vision. If any of them are sagging, prop them up with a bigger truth. This process is huge fun—and you will get results!

If you are living at less than full steam, it is not because the universe refuses to supply your desires. It is because you are asking for less than what you truly want. Keep updating your list and present it to your "employer"—the Great Spirit—and you may be surprised by the response. You might not always get everything you want, but you will get a lot more than if you did not ask.

How could you envision, ask for, and receive more of what you want?

My dream is worthy.
I ask for everything I want, and
the universe is happy to supply it.

Another One Bites the Light

Never say "Oops." Always say "Ah, interesting."

— Source unknown

Several years ago I presented a Life Mastery Training at a resort in Fiji. The hotel management assigned our group to a meeting room at the top of a high hill, which required us to arrange transport for the entire group for several gatherings each day—not an attractive setup. The first evening there, we discovered that the room was cramped, had poor acoustics, and would be hot in the daytime. The space was far from ideal, and we did not look forward to pushing through the week.

The next morning the resort manager informed us that a bus had broken down on the road to the meeting room, which rendered it impassable. To accommodate us, he instructed the hotel staff to erect an open-sided tent a few steps from the beach. The moment the group arrived there, everyone breathed a sigh of relief and cheered, "Ah, this is really it!"

Our classes were blessed with an unobstructed ocean view and soft breezes under swaying palm trees, accompanied by the rhythmic sound of gentle waves and the song of birds—a perfectly heavenly setting. The group marveled at the orchestration of the bus breaking down on the first morning of the week. It was obvious that the universe had a better option for us than what the resort had offered, and our ideal situation found us. *Another one bites the light.*

Some would call this a miracle of synchronicity, and it was. I would further say that it was a demonstration of intention. The group and I held a strong vision and intention to enjoy a seminar in the most pleasant surroundings, and the benevolent universe lent us a hand. That same benevolence will carry you to your greatest good.

If something appears to go wrong, hold some space for the possibility that something bigger might be going right. You may be amazed at where the hand of love will carry you.

What has gone wrong, or is going wrong,
that you are regretting or resisting?
How might this be a setup for something to go far better?

I trust the wisdom of well-being to
deliver me to my right place and situation.

Spiritual Deficit Disorder

Diseases of the soul are more dangerous and
more numerous than those of the body.

— Cicero

ADD, or attention deficit disorder, has gotten a lot of attention over the last few decades. More and more children are receiving this diagnosis, along with many adults. Yet there is another disorder, even more pervasive and dangerous, that exacts a far greater cost on our society: *spiritual deficit disorder.*

Symptoms of SDD include resistance to awakening in the morning, boredom with work, absence of passion, irritability, fatigue, chronic low-level diseases, inclination to soft or hard addictions, a sense of lack of direction and meaning, "self-numbing" in front of a TV or computer screen, depression in the wake of watching the news, an insatiable need to acquire more stuff, and pursuing relationship partners with no lasting or rewarding results.

Experts report that far more of the population may suffer from SDD than appearances would indicate, and some of the people who claim or appear to be the happiest may in their private moments be the most devoid of joy.

While medical officials are not aware of a cure for SDD (and many are not even aware of the disease), nontraditional healing practitioners report that a number of remedies have been tried and proven effective. They include: stepping away from the computer; getting into nature; taking long, deep breaths of fresh air; spending time with people you enjoy rather than those you feel obligated to be with; choosing a career that is an expression of your passion; speaking your truth; thanking your loved ones; working less; playing more; avoiding the news or talk of it; laughing at will; and frequent lovemaking.

Members of SDDA meet at 12-step groups to share their stories of how they were addicted to fear until they realized that their inner spirit gave them more reward than anything outside them. If you suffer from SDD, it is recommended that you get help immediately.

What do you do, or can you do, to reconnect
with your spirit and revitalize your life?

I am a spiritual being at my core,
nourished and sustained by life and love.

The Great Fishing Expedition

Lift up your eyes, and look on the fields;
for they are white already to harvest.

—John 4:35

Jerry Hicks tells of one summer when he and a buddy set out on a fishing expedition. The two rented a boat at a lake, found a quiet spot, and cast their rods. From the moment the men began, fish were practically jumping into their boat until, at the end of the day, the tiny craft chugged back to the dock so laden that it nearly sank.

As the anglers approached the dock, the rental agent was stunned. "Where did you catch all those fish?" he asked excitedly.

"Right over there," Jerry answered, pointing to the locale of their windfall.

"That's unbelievable!" the agent replied, shaking his head. "Everybody's talking about nobody catching any fish in this lake all summer. I didn't want to tell you that when you rented the boat because I needed the money, but now I'm glad I didn't."

Abundance is the natural condition of life, and it yields its treasures to those whose minds are open to receive it. Yet a belief in lack is enough to create a *condition* of lack. When many people agree on lack, it seems real. Meanwhile, as you can see from Jerry's experience, those who do not know what they cannot do usually end up getting what they want.

If you are "fishing" for a house, business success, friendship, or a soul mate, pay no attention to the dire reports of those who say that what you want is not out there or cannot be done. Prophets of woe have fallen under the hypnosis of deficiency. Instead, remember that there is a lot of what you want out there, and if you just drop your line (representing your mind) into the right place in the lake (the pool of all that is available), your boat will be laden with treasure, and you will leave the naysayers with their jaws hanging.

What do you want that you believe you cannot get?
Are you open to the idea that what you want
is available and you can get it?

I open my mind to receive what I want.
The abundant universe is able
 and happy to yield what I request.

Already There

Come; for all things are now ready.

— Luke 14:17

In my book *I Had It All the Time,* I recounted a life-changing experience I had at the East Maui Animal Refuge, a private nonprofit foundation where director Sylvan Schwab and his wife, Suzie, oversee care for about 450 injured or unwanted animals. The Schwabs and their staff work tirelessly every day from dawn to dusk, feeding the animals and attending to their medical needs. Their work is an extraordinary labor of love, and the refuge is truly a holy place.

When a magazine reporter interviewed Sylvan at the Boo Boo Zoo, she noted, "I guess that when you leave this world, your chances of getting into heaven are pretty good."

Sylvan smiled and replied, "Heaven? I'm already there."

Not many people would think that taking care of injured and unloved animals 24/7 is their idea of heaven, but Sylvan is there—which demonstrates that fulfillment has less to do with conditions, and more to do with following the path that makes your heart sing.

Many religions have told us that heaven is a place you earn by suffering on Earth. The worse it is here, they teach, the better it will be there. But what if heaven is an experience you could attain even while walking the earth? We have all had moments of it. Imagine expanding those moments until they become the dominant theme of your life, rather than the exception.

Do not wait until you die to be happy. Cultivate happiness now and beat the rush later.

Are you waiting for some future event to be happy?
How could you find your happiness now by either
shifting your attitude or doing more of what you love?

Heaven is available right where I am.

I choose it, I accept it, and I celebrate it.

Soul Signals

Intuition will tell the thinking mind where to look next.

— Jonas Salk

Dr. Bruce Logan was a renowned psychotherapist who helped many patients over many years and earned the respect of his professional community. But the passion he once felt for his work just did not ignite him anymore, and he was bored. Even though he was relatively self-aware, he kept talking himself into continuing because, as he said, "this is what I've always done."

One day as Dr. Logan was listening to a patient talk about her life, he noticed he had been doodling on the margins of his notepad. Without thinking much about it, he had drawn some rough sketches of sculptures he had been formulating in his mind. Sculpting, Dr. Logan had to admit, had become more interesting to him than psychotherapy. At that moment he had an "Aha!" experience. He realized that his passion lay outside his current profession, and he needed to make a course correction.

So Dr. Logan decided to take a leap of faith. He quit his practice and devoted himself to sculpture. Over time he developed his skills, and now he is a world-famous sculptor, commanding considerable money for his artistic talents.

This man was sensitive to the signals of his soul, and he had the courage to move with them. Without knowing it, he was giving himself signs in the margins of his notepad. Sometimes when we ask for a sign for our next step in life, we expect a deep voice to boom out of heaven and tell us what to do. But that voice speaks more often through our body, mind, and inner spirit.

Pay attention to what your body is telling you. If you are sick and tired, ask yourself what you are sick and tired *of*. If you feel exhilarated and uplifted in someone's presence, your spirit is communicating with you, urging you to explore that connection.

Success and happiness are trying to reach you. Watch for signs.

What might your inner wisdom be trying to tell you?

**Divine guidance speaks to me through
my heart, mind, and body.
I observe, feel, listen, act, and succeed.**

Give Yourself a Mind-Lift

When it comes to staying young, a mind-lift beats a face-lift any day.
— Marty Bucella

A newspaper article reported that Cuba's unusually high number of centenarians say their longevity is a result of going easy on alcohol, but indulging in coffee, cigars, and sex. Of Cuba's population of 11 million, about 3,000 have lived more than a century. Most of the centenarians are mentally alert, did manual labor in rural areas, and had parents who were also long-lived.

These findings fly in the face of much of what we have been told about how to live long and well. You might not think that coffee, cigars, and sex are on the approved list for breaking the triple-digit glass ceiling. But there is one factor that many proponents of health foods or austere, medically prescribed diets do not take into consideration: the *joy* factor.

Because we are spiritual at the core of our being, it is the spirit in which we live that determines the quality of our lives. That is why the tenor of our spirit generally supersedes what we do physically.

When you do what brings you joy, you release into your body life-giving hormones and chemicals. When you do what bores or annoys you, you generate toxic hormones and chemicals that hamper your life force and diminish your longevity. So listen less to externally prescribed regimens, and listen more to your unique inner wisdom.

A man went to his doctor for a checkup and asked him, "What do you think are my chances to live to be 100?"

The doctor asked the patient, "Do you smoke?"

"No," the fellow answered.

"Do you drink?"

"Never."

"Do you run around with women?"

"No, sir," the patient replied.

The doctor shook his head and asked the patient, "Then why would you want to live to be 100?"

The secret of life is to be *in* it.

What do you do that brings you joy and life-force energy?
How could you do more of it?

I live fully now.
Happiness is my key to health.

Do You Want to Play?

Every day is an opportunity to make a new happy ending.
— Source unknown

One afternoon my friend Andrew took his five-year-old daughter, Jasmine, to the park for some playtime. At the playground Jasmine found some other children her age. She approached one boy and asked him, "Do you want to play?" He shook his head and turned away. Immediately the girl moved to another kid and asked him, "Do you want to play?" He smiled and nodded, and the two children went on to have a delightful play session.

As Andrew recounted the story to me, he observed that Jasmine wasted no time brooding over why the first boy did not want to play. She dropped that interaction immediately and went on to the next opportunity. Adults, Andrew noted, might have stayed with the first person who said no and tried to cajole, manipulate, or bribe him into saying yes. Or picked an argument. Or whined and pouted. Or employed a million other methods by which human beings try to force things when they do not go their way.

But Jasmine was more interested in getting what she wanted than complaining about what she did *not* get, so she seized the next opportunity and got her way immediately. What a lesson!

If someone does not want to "play" with you in business, friendship, or romance, do not spend a lot of time trying to force them or bemoaning why they did not go along with you. If they have made their intentions clear, why waste time when you can be cultivating a more satisfying interaction with someone else? Take their no as a signal from the universe that there is a better yes elsewhere.

Remember, too: No response is a response. If you have trouble getting an answer from someone, the person's silence usually means no. Waste no time trying to get a response if you have already made considerable effort. Let it go, and search for the yes that is waiting elsewhere. You have only so much time in the park. Why not play with kids who are available?

Are you trying to force a yes when it is not forthcoming?
Where might you turn your attention to find a real yes?

I take "no" as a sign that my good lies elsewhere, and I hasten there.

The Sin That Never Happened

Forgiveness is the attribute of the strong.
— Mahatma Gandhi

My friend Alden was a dedicated student of *A Course in Miracles*, which emphasizes the power of forgiveness. The *Course* teaches that the best way to practice forgiveness is to demonstrate to others that the "sin" for which they feel guilty has not caused the damage they perceive, and thus relieve them of suffering, along with yourself.

One day while I was visiting Alden's city, I signed up to receive a massage. The massage therapist had agreed to drive me afterward to a meeting point where Alden was to pick me up and take me to my next appointment. During the massage, I fell asleep and did not wake up for a while after it was over. When the massage therapist drove me to the place where I was to meet Alden, he had given up waiting for me and gone home. I felt pretty bad about putting him out and not showing up.

When I saw Alden the next day, I apologized profusely for inconveniencing him. His response surprised me: "That's all right . . . do you need a ride anywhere today?" Alden was putting the *Course* lesson into action by demonstrating to me that the sin I believed had hurt him in reality had no effect. To say the least, I felt relieved and healed about the matter.

Another person in Alden's position might have chosen a less enlightened response and, offended that I did not keep my appointment, not bothered to help me out again. But Alden chose the high road, and that offered me release, which has inspired me to try to offer the same to others.

Today, seek to demonstrate to others that the guilt or punishment under which they suffer is not required. Demonstrate to them that the sin they believe hurt you had no real effect. When you release them, you will release yourself, and the world will be closer to heaven.

*Whom can you release from guilt by demonstrating
that the sin they perceive had no real effect?
How can you release yourself?*

**I free myself and others by living as if
love is real and guilt is unnecessary.**

Change Your Pitch

There are a thousand hacking at the branches
of evil to one who is striking at the root.

— Henry David Thoreau

My house had a long-term leak where two rain gutters meet at the edge of the roof. Over the years I have had several repair people out to address the issue. Each time the leak stopped for a while, but returned.

Recently I asked another roofer to look at the leak. He poked around the affected area for a minute and told me, "Your previous repairmen addressed the symptom of the leak, not the cause. The real cause is that your gutter is not on enough of a pitch to make the rain run out the drain, so the water just sits in this corner." He showed me several layers of roofing sealers the previous workers had pasted over the crack. "All of these sealers did not solve the problem; actually, they exacerbated it."

Then he showed me how the quick-fix sealers had built up a little mound that caused the water to run back up the gutter rather than out of it. The fellow took some time to adjust the pitch of the gutter, and now the rainwater runs out of the drain where it is supposed to.

Western medicine is very good at damage control, but not so good at prevention. It is more of a Band-Aid than a healer. Such medicine is extremely valuable if you are injured or in pain. We know how to stop pain, but do not know so well how to keep it from starting or returning.

When President Obama's nominee for secretary of Health and Human Services addressed a congressional committee, he noted, "We need to move from a mentality of disease control to a mentality of well-being." In other words, we need to live in ways that keep us healthy rather than concentrating on being adept at dealing with the results of unwise health habits.

Health and well-being are our natural state. You will be healthy and happy if you live in harmony with yourself and the way your body is designed to work. Your body knows how to stay well and ward off disease if it approaches. Pills and quick fixes help in a moment. Right thinking, love, self-care, eating well, play, and exercise will eliminate the need for pills. Change the pitch of the gutter and you will not need to keep repairing the leak.

What do you do that helps you experience well-being?
How can you do more of it?

I live in harmony with myself and life.
Health and happiness are natural. I claim them now.

At Least We're Consistent

Nothing is at last sacred but the integrity of your own mind.
— Ralph Waldo Emerson

When Dee and I discovered we would have some free time on a trip to New York, we decided to take in a Broadway play. Dee searched the Internet for a show we might like, and she came up with a cute off-Broadway musical: *I Love You, You're Perfect, Now Change.* Since we like romantic comedies, we ordered tickets and looked forward to the show.

A few days later Dee mentioned to her sister that we were going to see that play. "Isn't that the one you saw in Maui when you and Alan were first dating?" her sister asked. Surprised, Dee asked me if I remembered the play, and when we searched our memories, we realized that we *had* seen that show on our second date eight years earlier!

We went to the show in New York anyway and enjoyed it as much as, or more than, the first time. "At least we're consistent!" I remarked. In our entire relationship of eight years to that point, we had only seen two plays—the same one!

In an odd way, our theater selection demonstrates that the choices we make consistently reflect our consciousness. The relationship partners you choose, the bosses at your jobs, and the health conditions you experience are not random. They are reflections of your inner choices, played out in the field of your external experience. While many people complain that they are being victimized by outside sources or say they are lucky to be in good situations, victimization and luck have nothing to do with who and what shows up in your world. Your consciousness does.

If you like what you are getting, keep your thoughts right where they are. If you do not like what you are getting, it's time to change your mind. Changing people and things outside you seems easier than changing your mind, but external manipulation is really much harder. One tweak in your attitude can effect a huge shift in results. Healing is an inside job. Like Dee and me, you are consistent in what you attract. Seek to be consistent in attracting what makes you happy.

Do you see patterns in what you attract?
How can you change your mind to attract better?

Universal law is solid and dependable.
I call my good to me now.

The Power of Vision

Give the other person a fine reputation to live up to.

— Dale Carnegie

Dr. William Parker was a psychologist assigned to work with a young man with a long history of drug addiction. This patient showed up with a thick dossier of dire diagnoses and failed treatments. The psychologist, however, did not focus on his patient's addiction. Over the term of the man's treatment, the psychologist kept asking the fellow, "Who are you when you're not an addict?" and "What did you do this week that was powerful and productive?" Over time the patient responded to the psychologist's vision of him as a strong, healthy person. Eventually he transformed and dropped his addiction for the first time since entering treatment many years earlier.

How you see yourself determines who you will become, and how you see others determines who they will become in your presence. If you are a psychologist, healer, teacher, or parent, you have the power to transform your clients, students, or children. If you see them as broken, needy, or impossible, that is the behavior they will manifest. If you view them as whole, capable, and talented, that is who they will become. Your vision of them is the greatest gift you can give them . . . or the greatest disservice you can do them, depending on how you choose to see them.

At a weekend workshop a fellow arrived with his 19-year-old son, whom he introduced to me as "a severe depressive." Then the father went on to describe all of his son's problems in gory detail. I felt bad for the boy, who was standing right there and being labeled as a loser. I told the father, "Let's see how big we can let your son be this weekend."

During the seminar, I addressed the young man as a worthy, capable guy, and that is how he responded. By the end of the program, he was a star of the seminar, and everyone fell in love with him. At the conclusion, he gave an extraordinarily inspiring talk about how great it felt to be regarded as good.

Take care how you see people, for the one you see is the one you will get.

Who might you help by shifting your vision of them from their deficits to their possibilities?

I create worthy, capable, and talented people around me by seeing them as whole and gifted.

No Private Good

Whoever is happy will make others happy too.

— Anne Frank

One summer evening Dee and I went to dinner at a fine restaurant, where we were seated next to an air-conditioning unit. After a while Dee began to feel quite chilly and wanted to move to another table. Since we had already been served our appetizers, we felt reluctant to ask the waiter to reseat us. But we remembered one of our mottos: "There is no private good," and we made the request. Our waiter amiably accommodated us, and we continued our meal at another table in a warmer section of the restaurant.

A few minutes later, an elderly couple entered the restaurant and were seated at the table we had vacated. As soon as the couple sat down, the gentleman took a deep breath; issued a resonant *"Ahhhh!"*; and exclaimed, "Just what I needed—good air-conditioning!"

Your good is not in opposition or contradiction to others' good, but directly connected to it. You cannot help yourself without helping others. When you act in harmony with your best interests, everyone benefits, since at the deepest level we are one, and oneness is never in competition with itself.

When considering a course of action, think less about how this might work against others, and more about how it might *help* them. Do not, of course, engage in actions that might be rash, cruel, or unkind; and never purposely hurt anyone. But if you have meditated, prayed, and asked for guidance from your inner being about something you feel moved to do . . . and you still get a "yes," trust that there is wisdom behind your action, and everyone it affects will benefit.

What would you love to do that might help others
in ways you cannot see at the moment?

I act on my inner guidance, trusting
that my well-being is connected to the
well-being of others. There is no private good.

How to Pray for Rain

Faith is the bird that feels the light
and sings when the dawn is still dark.

— Rabindranath Tagore

When a town in the Midwest was going through a long drought, the townspeople decided to gather at church to pray for rain. Among them was one little girl who brought an umbrella. Everyone thought this was very cute—but when the crowd exited the church, clouds had gathered and they found themselves in the midst of a huge downpour. Their prayers were answered on the strength of the little girl's faith.

Faith in mind is crucial, but faith in action is magnetic. Your faith is not whole unless you are taking steps to do the thing you are praying for. When you pray for one thing but act as if another will happen, you are affirming with your deeds that the opposite of your prayer will come true. If you want to manifest a chosen result, take action toward the object of your prayer.

Take a few moments today to consider if your actions are lined up with your prayers. If you would really like to live in a certain area of town, drive through it. If you want a particular kind of car, take it for a test-drive, even if you do not have the money to buy it today. If you are attracted to a certain person, quit worshipping him or her from afar, and have a conversation . . . or ask him or her for a date. You will be amazed by how much more substantial your idea feels when you take a real-life step toward it.

The world is advanced by the vision and actions of those who live on the cutting edge of faith. So it is with your life. You have nothing to lose by bringing an umbrella to your prayer session . . . and everything to gain.

What action could you take that affirms
you are on the way to your prayer coming true?

I live my faith. I act as if the best
will come to me, and it does.

You Spot It, You Got It

Whenever you point a finger at someone else,
you have three fingers pointing at yourself.

— Source unknown

While spending time in Fiji, I went to an Internet café daily to check my e-mail. While there, I noticed a boy, probably 14 years old, sitting at a table near me, immersed in his computer. After a few days of seeing him, I began to feel sad and judgmental that this kid was spending his vacation on the Internet. *What a waste of time!* I thought. *Why isn't he out having fun?*

Then a sobering thought occurred to me: In order for me to see him at the café on his computer so much, *I* had to be there, too. I was on e-mail, missing *my* vacation. My judgments about the kid were just a projection of my judgments about myself for making poor use of my time. I unplugged my computer, walked away, and did not return for a long time.

Judgments about others are always related to judgments of self. If you had no self-judgments, you would have no judgments of others. You might notice errors or ways people could be happier or more effective, but your perspective would not carry the heavy shroud of righteousness, upset, or a need to change them so you can feel better.

You can use your judgments of others as keys to your own liberation. If you find yourself upset with someone, ask: *Am I upset with* myself *for doing that?* If the answer is yes, try to find some self-acceptance, self-love, or self-forgiveness. If you can, you will liberate the other person from the onus of your judgment, but even more important, you will liberate yourself.

The world you see is a projection of your mind. You cannot imprison someone else without imprisoning yourself, and you cannot free someone else without freeing yourself.

We are all in this together. Let's get a little freer every day.

What do you most judge others for?
Do you judge yourself for the same behavior?
How could you liberate others and yourself
from your judgments through self-forgiveness?

I free the world by freeing myself. I let
myself be me, and I let others be who they are.

Spellbound with Greatness

Mediocrity knows nothing higher than itself,
but talent instantly recognizes genius.

— Sir Arthur Conan Doyle

When Paul Potts stepped onto the stage to perform on *Britain's Got Talent,* he looked entirely out of place. Wearing a modest suit and plain white shirt, he was a sharp contrast to the sexy young singers and hip-hop dancers who usually compete in the talent show. The fact that he was portly, had crooked teeth, and oozed shyness did not help. When a judge asked Paul, "What will you be doing for us?" he answered, "Singing opera." The judges heaved a sigh and rolled their eyes. If anyone was doomed for the hook before he opened his mouth, it was Paul Potts.

When Paul began to sing, the story changed. His voice was magnificent, bolstered by a sincere heart and real talent. By the time he finished the second verse of Puccini's "Nessun Dorma," women in the audience were wiping away tears, the crowd was cheering, and even the cynical judges were rapt. At the conclusion of the short performance, the audience went wild with a standing ovation, and the judges issued Paul Potts three enthusiastic "Yes!" votes.

While the judges and audience were not opera fans and likely would not have chosen to hear that piece, Paul's talent and heart were absolutely compelling. Something in those listeners yearned to feel the depth of such a performance, and when they did, they were profoundly moved.

You, too, have a talent that can and will move mountains. You just need to get in touch with it and let it come forth. People will resonate with the gift you bring, no matter how odd or unexpected. There is something in everyone, no matter how jaded or asleep, that longs to be spellbound with greatness. When you offer it, magic happens.

Paul Potts went on to win the national competition, and his subsequent CD became number one in England, a nation not known for its love of opera. Unmistakable greatness finds its right place in the hearts of those who recognize it.

What gift or talent would you like to bring
forth that can and will wow people?

I trust the gifts I am given. I express them
with confidence, and the world responds.

Setbacks Are Setups

The record books never list the score at halftime.

— Source unknown

During the 2004 Summer Olympics, U.S. gymnast Paul Hamm was favored to win the men's individual all-around, a series of six events. During the vault competition, Hamm slipped on his dismount and fell onto the judges' table. He was penalized severely and instantly dropped from 1st to 12th place. The television commentator grimly noted, "Paul Hamm will remember this vault for the rest of his life."

With two events left in the competition, U.S. fans hoped Hamm could miraculously work his way back to perhaps a bronze medal. In the final event, the horizontal bar, he turned in a perfectly stellar performance. To everyone's amazement, Hamm emerged with the gold medal by a margin of 12/1,000 of a point—the slimmest margin in Olympic history.

As it turned out, the television commentator was correct. Paul Hamm would remember the vault for the rest of his life. But not because it was his undoing. Because it represented the greatest comeback in Olympic history.

You and I, too, have made errors we shudder to think about remembering for the rest of our lives. Yet those errors do not reflect the final score, for the game is not over. Like Paul Hamm, you can still make a stellar comeback and capture the gold. You can do better next time. Or reframe the way you regard the past event so it empowers you. Or simply love and forgive yourself. No matter what you did, recognize that in the big scheme of things, it is not what you thought it was from a judgmental viewpoint. It was a platform for a stellar comeback.

*What do you regret doing that you believe
is unpardonable or uncorrectable?
How can you make a stellar comeback?*

Everything that happens to me is a gift and an opportunity for awakening and healing. I regard all experiences and situations as being in my favor.

Goat Not Necessary

Forgiveness is the economy of the heart.

— Hannah More

My friend Tom explained to me that he wanted to dump the lifelong guilt he had been carrying about his relationship with his father, who had committed suicide on the day Tom was born. Tom's mother told him that his father took his life because he did not want Tom to be born. Through word and inference, she continually pointed the finger of guilt at her son, who carried this awful pain for much of his life.

I told Tom that the relationship he needed to heal was not with his father, but with his mother, who had laid a terrible guilt trip on him. She felt guilty about her husband's suicide and projected her guilt onto her son in an effort to relieve herself of her own pain. I told Tom it was time for him to refuse to accept the dark burden his mother had laid upon him. He was not the cause of his father's death or his mother's pain. He was not guilty for simply being born. He was a good and whole person, and it was time for him to start living as such. Tom understood the dynamics of his family relationships and, for the first time in his life, felt free of the illusory burden of his father's death.

During the biblical period when the Hebrew nation was wandering in the desert, the priests performed a telling ritual. They took a goat and told the people to "send all of your sins into the goat." After the people did so, the goat was driven out of the camp, supposedly taking the group's sins with it. Thus was born the concept of "scapegoat." The people felt relieved, but they did not deal with their sense of guilt in a healthy way, by recognizing their innocence. To this day, we appoint scapegoats to help us feel better about ourselves. The process provides temporary relief, but does not dispel the self-deceptive belief that caused us to seek relief in this way.

Innocence is real. Guilt is learned. You do not serve yourself or others by projecting guilt or receiving it. Instead, extend and accept the truth about your original innocence.

How can you refuse to receive or project guilt as a scapegoat?

I am innocent. I am free. I am as God created me.

An Active Nap

Life in Lubbock, Texas, taught me two things:
One is that God loves you and you're going to burn in hell.
The other is that sex is the most awful, filthy thing
on earth and you should save it for someone you love.

— Butch Hancock

A seminar participant named Cindy was seeking support to improve her relationship with her boyfriend. As she spoke, she mentioned that occasionally the two took an "active nap" together.

"What's an 'active nap'?" another participant asked.

Cindy began to blush. "You know . . ."

"Do you mean sex?" I asked.

She looked at the floor and shyly answered, "Yes."

As our conversation went on, Cindy revealed that she had been raised in a religion that taught her that sex was evil and sinful. Now as an adult, at age 32, she could not reconcile her enjoyment of sex with the ingrained belief that she was offending God by having it.

Cindy's attitude is typical of many people, especially women, who were taught by word or example that sex is bad and they should be ashamed of doing it or even talking about it. Yet sex, like all human activity, is what people make of it. It can be a dark, unconscious event that leaves you feeling separated from love and life; or a heavenly, uplifting experience that connects you to yourself, your lover, and God.

Sex, along with eating and sleeping, is one of the most basic human instincts, instilled deeply within you at a cellular level to ensure the survival of the species. If you fight it or deny it, you will run into trouble, and your frustration will manifest physically and emotionally. Flow with it and you will be in harmony with your physical nature, which is not bad, but beautiful.

When you do have sex, do it wholeheartedly. A split mind will undermine your enjoyment and fulfillment. A whole mind will not just make your naps more active, but your entire life.

Is your sex life fulfilling? How might you open
your mind and heart to enjoy sex more deeply?

I celebrate my sexuality as a divine gift.
Through sex I give and receive love and pleasure.

So Can You

If children grew up according to early indications,
we should have nothing but geniuses.
— Johann Wolfgang von Goethe

Gifted people are not exceptions to humanity—they simply reveal our potential. Rather than idolizing people with unusual talents or stigmatizing them as oddballs, we can use them for inspiration to develop our own talents and abilities.

Stephen Wiltshire of London is an autistic savant. Known as the "living camera," Stephen has a photographic memory far beyond that of anyone ever documented. He can take a short helicopter flight over a city and spend the next five days drawing *every detail* of the skyline, down to the numbers of windows on individual buildings. He has produced mind-boggling drawings of Rome, London, and even Tokyo.

Another astonishing fellow was Ben Underwood, a master at street skateboarding, video games, and pillow fighting. Nothing unusual for most teenagers—but quite significant for Ben, since he had been blind from infancy. I saw a video of Ben defeating his sighted friends at video games. Ben's secret? He claimed he could, like a dolphin or bat, use echolocation to pick up subtle sound frequencies. Sadly, Ben left the world at a young age, but not before he demonstrated that there is far more to communication than the eyes can see.

Are these people imbued with abilities beyond those you and I have been given? Not really. They are simply tapping into their innate abilities and using them. We, too, remember everything we see, and sense many things that our eyes do not reveal to us. But since we depend on other senses, we do not utilize those of Stephen and Ben. (You can find astonishing videos of both of these gifted young men on the Internet.)

We use a tiny percentage of our potential as human beings. Occasionally someone comes along who makes fuller use of that potential, and our jaws drop in awe. Yet we would be wiser to stand in awe of the capabilities we have *all* been given.

What great person would you like to emulate?
Can you accept your ability to achieve, in your own way,
what that great person has or does?

I make full use of the magnificent capabilities
I already possess. I can do anything God can do.

Who Is the Doctor?

The wish to be well is a part of becoming well.

— Seneca

In the 1950s, psychologist Hans Eysenck did a cross-cultural study of the success rate physicians obtained with patients. He studied medical doctors, witch doctors, faith healers, and many more. Eysenck's results were fascinating: he found that across the board, about one-third of patients' health improved, one-third remained the same, and one-third worsened. This indicates that healing has less to do with the form it takes, and more to do with the belief system of both patient and doctor.

The world you see is a projection of your beliefs and intentions. You attract people who give form and expression to your desires and beliefs. If you believe that a certain doctor will heal you, he or she will. If you believe that another will be of no use, so it will be. If you sincerely intend to heal, a doctor will tell you that it is possible and you can make choices that maximize your potential to heal. If, on some level, you believe in or choose illness, you will find a doctor who will affirm that course. Doctors are your agents, and on a psychic level, they are serving your expectations faultlessly.

As a physician or healer, you will find that your patients or clients are also mirroring your beliefs, expectations, and intentions. They serve your spiritual and professional growth by acting in accordance with your belief system. Regard them as your mirrors, as you are for them.

While this paradigm of healing may be startling, it explains much that science is not yet aware of, and offers extraordinary empowerment to both doctor and patient. Examine your beliefs, choices, and intentions *before* you visit a doctor, and you can chart your most beneficial course.

How might your physician or healer be serving as
an expression of your belief and choices?

I choose healing agents who support me in healing.
Well-being is my choice, and it is so.

How Free Is Your Free Time?

He enjoys true leisure who has time to improve his soul's estate.
— Henry David Thoreau

Perhaps the greatest innovation of recent technology is an endless array of time-saving devices. Blenders, microwaves, and computers have given us more idle hours than any human beings in history. The question is: what do we do with all the free time these devices have afforded us?

If you use your free time to work more, your time is not free. If you are at the computer nights and weekends and turn down social invitations you would like to accept, your time is not free. If your relationship with your friends, spouse or lover, or kids is strained because you work too much and play too little, your time is not free. If you cannot sleep at night because you are mentally reviewing your spreadsheet, your time is not free. If your health suffers due to stress and tension and you spend your spare moments recuperating, your time is not free. How "free" is your free time?

After I moved to Hawaii, I bought a lovely property in the country. I offered a married couple a rental unit on the property in exchange for caretaking. At that time I was very busy, traveling a great deal. During my times at home, I was either debriefing from the last trip or preparing for the next one. As soon as I felt present, it was time to go out again. I was on a treadmill.

One day the wife took me by the arm and invited me to stroll the grounds with her. As we walked, she told me something that proved to be one of the greatest gifts of my life. She said, "Look at this magnificent property, Alan! There are trees, birds, flowers, and glorious sunrises. It is heaven on Earth. But how much do you enjoy it? You're hardly here, and when you are here, you're rushing to come and go. We're your caretakers, and we enjoy your property far more than you do. I wish you would experience the peace and joy that we do here."

That got my attention. That day I made a commitment to use my free time for peace, not work, and now I appreciate the blessings I have. My caretaker taught me how to take care of myself. Now I enjoy my property as much as my caretakers, and my free time is truly free.

How can you make your free time really free?

I use my free time to enjoy my life.
My self-renewal is worth every moment I devote to it.

The Critical Voice Is Not Your Own

Stop terrorizing yourself with your thoughts.
— Louise L. Hay

Do you have a voice inside your head that constantly criticizes you? Do you second-guess your decisions and find things wrong with you even when others do not? Do you wonder if you will ever overcome that nagging inner judge?

If so, I have good news for you: *the critical voice is not your own.* You were not born with that nasty inner critic. You were born with wide-eyed innocence and extraordinary confidence to explore the world as a grand adventure. You loved yourself just as you were, had no qualms about being naked, and told the truth about what felt good and what felt bad.

Somewhere along your path you learned criticism from those who disapproved of you. A parent, elder sibling, teacher, clergyperson, or other authority figure judged and perhaps shamed you for being yourself. You adopted that criticism and over time internalized it until you forgot that it came from someone else and thought it came from *you.*

Gerri's father was extremely demanding of her as a child. When she practiced her piano lessons, her father would place a 50-cent piece on the piano and leave it there for the duration of the piece she was practicing. If she performed the musical selection perfectly, she would get to keep the money. If she made even one error, he would take the coin back. Since she was just learning the piano, she rarely received the reward. As a result, Gerri developed a belief that she had to always strive for perfection, but could rarely attain it, and even her best efforts would not be rewarded.

As I worked with Gerri in coaching, she realized that it was not her own criticism under which she labored, but her father's. This insight helped her lighten up on herself and appreciate the good work she did, even if it was not always perfect.

The critical voice is not your own. The voice of love, appreciation, and self-acceptance is. Fire your inner critic and reinstate your inner fan club.

Whose voice have you adopted as your inner critic?
Can you let it go in favor of self-appreciation?

I claim my beauty, value, and wholeness.
I dump undue criticism and embrace self-respect.

Everything Comes Around

God Himself shall wipe away all tears.

— *A Course in Miracles*

When Merril had a baby at a young age, she gave up her little girl for private adoption. Thirty years later she wanted to make contact with her daughter, so she had an intermediary ask for her daughter's permission to meet. Merril and Jamie had a rewarding reunion, and Merril was deeply grateful that her child had enjoyed a positive upbringing with loving parents.

During their conversation, Jamie indicated she would like to meet her father. Although Merril had not seen her daughter's father, Tom, in many years, she was able to contact him; and she and Jamie met with him. Tom apologized for not having taken responsibility for his child, and he and Merril enjoyed their reconnection.

During their meeting, Jamie told her father about her life and her marriage to her husband, whom she described. "I know him!" Tom exclaimed. "We go to the same AA meetings."

If you are willing and ready, somehow everything comes around. The universe functions in impeccable balance, and love seeks to resolve all sense of loss and pain. You do not need to know how to accomplish all of the details; yet life has methods of healing that far transcend human understanding or manipulation.

Your quest to heal an issue may not be resolved as quickly or easily as Merril's. Perhaps someone from your past is not accessible, or he or she is unwilling to cooperate to achieve your desired result. This matters not. You can resolve an issue within your own heart. Write a letter to the other person's soul, expressing everything you would like to say and would like him or her to hear. Or simply speak the words in your mind during prayer or meditation. Whether the individual walks the earth or not, and no matter how far he or she is from you, the person's inner being will hear. There is no time or space in spiritual reality. The moment you sincerely desire healing and express it, it will come. Somehow everything comes around.

*What would you like to say to someone
with whom you have unresolved issues?*

**I am ready to come to peace with my relationships.
I trust life to take care of the details.**

Don't Confuse Me with the Facts

Facts are the enemy of truth.

— Dale Wasserman

At the conclusion of a magazine interview about spiritual growth, the interviewer told me, "You may hear from one of the fact-checkers at the magazine in case they have any questions."

I told him, "That won't be necessary, since I did not tell you any facts. I just told you the truth."

I was half-joking but half-serious. Our interview was not about information; it was about inspiration. We discussed life not in terms of what to do, but how to view it. My message was not logistical, but attitudinal.

The "facts" of life are highly inconsistent and subject to interpretation and change. Sir James Jeans noted, "Science should leave off making pronouncements: the river of knowledge has too often turned back on itself." Unlike the shifting tides of human belief, real truth is consistent and eternal and always works. It is what it is, and you cannot bend it.

When I was growing up, my Catholic friends could not eat meat on Friday because it was a sin. Later the church announced that it was no longer a sin. This puzzled me a great deal. If something is a truth of God, how could it change by a vote of men? That "sin," it turned out, was not a sin at all. It was an idea that people adopted, and it changed with human opinion.

Be more concerned with truth than facts. At any bookstore you will find thousands of diet books, many of which contradict one another. Every author has a unique idea on what and how to eat, along with plenty of scientific evidence and testimonials to corroborate the platform. These facts all make sense within the context of the author's belief system. Visit another belief system and an entirely different set of facts makes sense. If you tried to follow all the books on how to eat and how to live, you would go crazy! If, however, you discover what works for you, and you live by it, you have used temporary facts in the service of permanent truth.

What facts are confusing you? What truth bring you peace?

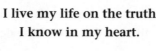

**I live my life on the truth
I know in my heart.**

Relieved

As we let our own light shine, we unconsciously
give other people permission to do the same.

— Marianne Williamson

Patrick had reached a turning point in his career. After many years of running his successful small business, he felt bored and stifled. Repeatedly using his long-standing business formula had netted his company a steady income, but he was understimulated. He did not even want to go to his own office, and when he worked with his business manager, Andrew, he was irritable. The two had enjoyed a strong relationship for many years, and Andrew had done an excellent job. But Patrick was not the same person he had been nine years earlier, and their value systems had moved the two men in different directions.

After considerable soul-searching and discussions with his wife, Patrick realized that if he continued to conduct his business as he had done, he would probably wither away and get sick; there were already signs. So he decided to reduce his business to some simple essentials and take time away from the company to renew himself and chart a new course for his life.

Reluctantly Patrick explained his choice to Andrew and told him he would be eliminating the business manager's position. Andrew was not terribly surprised, and the two, as friends, decided to just sit with the news for a few days and then revisit their options.

When they next met, Patrick asked Andrew, "How are you feeling about all this?"

Andrew smiled and answered, "Relieved, actually. I too have felt stuck and understimulated by the way we've been doing business. There are other things I've thought about doing, and this will give me a chance to stretch my own wings." Patrick, of course, was happy to hear this, and the two made an amicable severance agreement.

Andrew went on to develop a business himself, successful in its own right. Patrick took time to regroup and later moved his simplified business in a new and more rewarding direction. Both were happy with the arrangement.

When your life doesn't feel right, feel inside yourself for where relief lives.

What have you been thinking about
doing that would bring you relief?

As I move in the direction of joy,
I free others as well as myself.

Emma's Home!

*When the contrast gets greater, the desire gets
greater too, and that's what miracles are from.*

— Abraham-Hicks

A family moved into our neighborhood, bringing with them a big, friendly white dog with a black patch over its eye, like the Little Rascals' pup, Pete. When Dee and I daily drove past the dog's house, we would see her sitting comfortably on the lawn, happy to watch cars go by.

One night there was a big storm in our area, and the next day we noticed that the dog was gone. Then we saw a poster on a telephone pole with the dog's photo, explaining that "Emma" had been frightened by the thunder and lightning and had run away. As dog lovers, we felt concerned for the family and Emma, and we said a prayer for her return. Over the next few days when we passed the house, we looked for Emma, but did not see her. We called out, "Come on home, Emma! Come on home!"

Then one day we were thrilled to see the white dog back in her favorite spot on the lawn. "Yay, Emma's home!" Now every time we drive past the house, we look for Emma and say an appreciative "Hi" to her. Passing her house is always fun now because we are so happy she is home.

The contrast of Emma disappearing, our wishing for her safe return, and finding her back home gave us a relationship with her and added joy to our world. The brief distress we felt over her being gone gave way to the ongoing delight we feel every time we see her now. So the contrast of not having what we value, deeply desiring it, and then receiving it enhanced our lives more than if we had not missed it.

We live in a world of contrast that works in our favor if we let it. I am not suggesting that you need pain, drama, or struggle to make your life worthwhile. Rather, I am suggesting that the contrast generated by desire ultimately deepens appreciation and celebration. While we did not think twice about Emma before she took off, now it makes our day to see her.

How can you use your current experience of contrast to enhance your life?

**I appreciate the changes in my life as gifts that
deep my sense of joy and appreciation.**

Let Life Love You

Be a wide receiver.

— Alan Cohen

My aunt Selma lived alone in a senior-citizens' apartment complex and spent most of her time sitting on her couch watching television. Whenever I went to visit her, she complained that the sofa was old and uncomfortable. Finally I told her, "Aunt Selma, your birthday is coming up soon. I'd like to take you to a furniture store and get you a new couch as a birthday gift."

To my surprise, Aunt Selma did not light up. Instead, she shrugged her shoulders and said, "That's okay. I don't want you to spend the money. My couch is good enough for now."

I left Aunt Selma's apartment feeling disappointed. I did not mind spending the money on her couch; to the contrary, I would have taken delight in knowing she was enjoying it. But she was not able to receive it.

Many people have difficulty accepting their good when it is offered. They feel guilty for taking something from another person, even if that person offers it freely and happily. They do not recognize that it is as much a blessing to receive as it is to give. If everyone gave but no one received, there could be no giving.

Difficulty receiving is often an issue of guilt or a sense of unworthiness. You may believe you are not entitled to your good or that you will take away someone else's good if you receive yours. Or you may believe it is spiritual to sacrifice. Or you may have an ego game of "poor me" going on, in which you perceive some payoff for portraying yourself as deprived.

None of these forms of resistance can substitute for the joy you give yourself and others when you become an open receiver. At this moment, life is trying to love you and give to you in a million wonderful ways. When you say yes, you allow love to flow, which is the greatest gift you can give yourself and the universe. There is no need to sit on your old couch anymore if you do not want to. Love will make you comfortable if you simply let it.

What do you want that you could be more open to receiving?

I joyfully accept the gifts that life has to offer me.
I let all expressions of love into my world.

Stronger Than Hope

And help us, this and every day, to live more nearly as we pray.
— John Keble

I set out with a group of friends on a sailboat excursion to camp on the remote island of Molokai. Just before our ship reached harbor, we were overtaken by an unexpected storm; all we could do for an hour was tread water amid huge swells. Quite a few of us made trips to the rail, and by the time the squall abated and we reached shore, numerous would-be sailors were greenfaced and swore to take the plane next time.

Fortunately, the weather improved, and we went on to enjoy a luscious retreat on a white-sand beach kissing a clear lagoon. On the day we were ready to leave, several in our group felt anxious about the prospect of hitting bad weather again. Someone suggested we gather for a group prayer for easy passage. So we got together, held hands, and visualized a smooth trip home. I spoke an affirmation that wherever we go, God is, and all is well. By the time we finished praying, the group's apprehension had lifted and we had a sense of positive expectation.

The moment we opened our eyes, a young man in our midst, unfamiliar with the practice of prayer, blurted out, "Yeah, and let's hope we don't hit any more storms!" *Bonk!* His statement crashed against the vision we had just created. Afterward, I took the fellow aside and gently explained an important principle:

Once you have said a prayer, you must step fully into the consciousness of what you have prayed for and not backpedal into thoughts, words, or actions that underscore the condition you were praying to heal. Words and actions after a prayer must uphold it, not refute it. Prayer is not something you do once and then go back to the state of mind that moved you to pray. Rather, it is a consciousness you establish that moves your life in a new direction and then sustains it. Prayer is not the end of change; it is the beginning. So once you say "So be it!"—so be it.

What are you praying for? Do your words and actions after prayer sustain it or refute it?

I follow my prayers with thoughts, words, and actions that affirm my intention.

Dance Over Death

The goal of life is to die young—as late as possible!

— Ashley Montagu

My friend David Ault, a gifted musician, took his mother to visit his sister's grave. To David's surprise, he noticed that another grave site had been reserved next to his sister's. "Who is that grave for?" he asked his mom.

"Me," she answered. "I just want to be near my family."

The two pondered the prospect of her passing for a moment. Then David turned to his mother and asked, "May I have this dance?"

"What do you mean?" she returned.

"Let's dance on your grave."

Mom thought a moment and answered, "Why, of course!" And dance the two did. Probably one of the most memorable dances of their lives.

While dancing on a future grave may seem shocking or irreverent, it is an extraordinary metaphysical statement of vision and faith. Mother and son decided to rise above the darkness with which death is usually enshrouded, and celebrate their love, which would last far beyond their relationship in the physical world.

Death is ominous and frightening to many people, yet liberating to those who hold a higher vision. If all there is to us is our physical form, then death is final indeed. Yet if we are spiritual beings simply going through a physical experience, death is not the end of a story, just a chapter. The closing of a chapter always leads to the beginning of another.

All great spiritual masters, along with those among us who have momentarily gone beyond the brink of death and returned, have told us that death is not a cause for grief, but for celebration. David's dance with his mother signaled not the end of love, but a prelude to greater love. (After the dance, she reported proudly, "I got it on sale!")

How might you reframe your view of
death to see it as a blessed homecoming?

I am alive—I always have been and always will be. There is no death to the eternal spirit that I am and everyone is.

At Your Feet

*Grace is available for each of us every day . . . but we've got
to remember to ask for it with a grateful heart and not worry
about whether there will be enough for tomorrow.*

— Sarah Ban Breathnach

While I was presenting a program in Australia, a woman told me,
"I'd heard about your book *The Dragon Doesn't Live Here Anymore* and
wanted to read it. Yet I had a hard time finding it, since it was not
distributed in this country. I looked and looked for it, to no avail.

"Then one morning I took the bus to work and got off at my
regular stop. I had to cross a busy six-lane street to get to my office
building, and as I crossed, my foot bumped into something. I looked
down, and to my great surprise, there was your book!"

Odd as this account may sound, occurrences of synchronicity
happen more often than we realize. They are orchestrated by a Higher
Power that transcends what the human mind can fathom. They demonstrate the interaction of the Law of Attraction and grace.

A fellow told me that one day when he was feeling depressed and
needed guidance, he went out to lunch. As he was leaving the restaurant, the wind blew a piece of paper and pressed it against his legs.
When he reached down to remove it, he saw that it was a flyer about
a seminar. He decided to attend, and the program led him to a new
vista of life.

I have had all sorts of wonderfully strange things happen to me
in a similar vein. I have found jeans in my dresser drawer that I did
not buy but which were the perfect style and fit me precisely. Once I
discovered a book on my shelf that I did not purchase, but reading it
changed my life. I have heard many similar stories from friends and
seminar participants.

You, too, have gifts of synchronicity available to you . . . if you
are open to receiving them. Life can help you in ways you could not
manipulate if you tried. Your role is to get clear on what you want
and let universal intelligence fill in the blanks. The object you seek
may be right at your feet when you least expect it.

*Have you experienced instances of grace?
How can you let yourself be more open to them?*

**The universe knows what I need and delivers
it in the right way, at the right time.**

A Valuable Seminar

Life is the only school where the exam comes before the lesson.

— Source unknown

A fellow came to my mentor Hilda Charlton and complained, "An auto mechanic just ripped me off for $500! He charged me that much for a repair, and my car still doesn't work. I had a feeling I shouldn't take my car to him, and now I wish I had listened to my intuition!"

Hilda asked the fellow, "If I told you about a seminar that would help you connect with your internal guidance so deeply that you would be sure to follow it the next time it spoke to you, and the tuition for the seminar was $500, would you attend?"

"Why, sure!" the fellow answered enthusiastically.

"Then be glad you just took that exact seminar without even having to sit in a classroom for a whole weekend to learn it," she told the man.

You and I are enrolled in the wisest university ever conceived— the University of Life. While we might occasionally attend a formal seminar to learn techniques to help us live more abundantly, every day we receive lessons in the form of the people we meet and the experiences we have. A counselor once told me, "Every experience in life is to either be enjoyed or learned from. Everyone is your teacher. Some teach you what to do, and some teach you what not to do."

We all make mistakes and take actions we later wish we had not. Yet sometimes the experience, although unpleasant at the moment, imparts wisdom and insight that benefit us for the rest of our lives. In that case, we can bless the person and the event that helped us learn it. The experience was temporary. The awakening is permanent.

No one gets it right all the time. Yet if you look at your journey from the highest perspective, you cannot get it wrong. Even if you made a mistake, if you gain understanding and choose a different path as a result, you got it right.

How has a painful or difficult experience helped you in the long run?

I use every experience as a tool to awaken.
Everyone and everything is my teacher in life.

The Idiot Plot

There are three kinds of people: 1. Innovators. 2. Imitators. 3. Idiots.
— Warren Buffett

Film critics Siskel and Ebert described a classic movie type they called the *Idiot Plot,* a story that would be impossible to keep going if even one character was not a complete idiot.

A good example of the use of the idiot plot was the television series *Seinfeld,* in which most episodes were based on one character doing something stupid or telling a lie and the rest of the characters going along with it. If even one character displayed wisdom or integrity, that would be the end of the story. But it was not. Fortunately, the show was clever and hilarious. Unfortunately, similar situations happen in real life that are not so funny.

The *family systems* model of therapy explains that every family thrives on an agreement of interlocking roles. In a healthy family, the roles promote well-being. In a dysfunctional one, the roles fix everyone into ongoing pain. In the home of an alcoholic, for example, there is the addict, the enabler, the scapegoat, and so on. As long as everyone keeps performing their expected dysfunctional behaviors, the story sadly goes on as it has. And for many it does.

When one person in the system says, "I do not wish to participate anymore," and moves toward healthy behavior, this upsets the applecart, for now the dysfunctional members do not have someone to play off of, and they become very disoriented and upset. At this point they exert pressure to keep the person who is disengaging from the system from leaving. They do not realize that the family member who is getting healthy is offering them a doorway out of hell if they are willing to walk through it.

If you are involved in an idiot plot, you would serve everyone well to step out of it. You may experience pressure, demands, and threats; yet your salvation lies in making this move. You were not born to live in an idiot plot, and neither were your loved ones. Simply refuse to act like an idiot, and upgrade your script.

Are you involved in an idiot plot?
How might you serve everyone by stepping out of it?

I help myself and others by refusing to participate in a painful situation. My healthy choices promote the well-being of those I care about.

Pick Up the Phone

When you talk to God, that's prayer.
When God talks back, it's schizophrenia.

— Attributed to Lily Tomlin

I wonder what someone from the 17th century would think if he showed up on a modern city street. Among many extraordinary sights, he would observe lots of folks having conversations with invisible people. Some would be holding little boxes to their ears, more involved with their discussion with a distant unseen entity than watching where they are walking or driving. Others would be conversing through tiny clips on their ears. Others would be bopping to music no one else hears. Talk about culture shock!

People who talked to invisible spirits during such a person's time were branded witches and burned at the stake. Today we are more open-minded as we use technology to communicate with people we do not see. Yet many still resist or deny that we can talk to people we cannot see *without* technology.

Richard Bach notes that technology replicates psychic faculties that have atrophied due to disbelief and disuse. Telephones imitate our ability to converse with people at a distance, television reminds us that we can see others from afar, and airplanes re-create our power to travel in spirit to far places. If we exercised our innate abilities, we would not need external devices. But we believe in science, so it is through science that we do what we could do without it.

Clairvoyance is natural, and we can all communicate with others in spirit and with God. If this sounds spooky, it is only because such interactions have been portrayed under a shroud of fear and ignorance. Is there anything scary about connecting with those you love and the source of all good?

Yet much of that is changing. The past few decades have brought to the public eye many teachers and healers who give voice to higher and more subtle levels of communication. Such teachers will soon grow in number and respect. It is the wave of things to come.

If God or an invisible loved one calls you, pick up the receiver. You might hear something you like.

How might you open yourself up more to communicating
with unseen loved ones or your Higher Power?

I claim my power to use my innate faculties
to live up to my spiritual potential.

Acts of God

It's the best possible time to be alive, when almost
everything you thought you knew is wrong.

— Tom Stoppard

If you read the fine print on contracts, no one is liable for "acts of God." *Acts of God* are defined as disasters beyond human control, like storms, floods, lightning, and protracted visits from uninvited relatives. I find it fascinating that in such contracts, God takes the rap for everything that goes wrong and receives no credit for the things that go right.

God is responsible for far more cool stuff than disasters. Consider this morning's stunning sunrise; the stately trees outside your window and the birds that sing in their branches; your beloved's embrace; your child's finger painting on your refrigerator door; and your dog greeting you with such joy upon your arrival home that you are tempted to go out and come home again. Acts of God are pretty much everywhere, if you just look.

God is not the source of our troubles, but the source of our happiness. People have created far more pain, loss, suffering, and disaster than God ever has. We undermine ourselves with psychic self-flagellation and hurt each other with unkindness. Not because we mean to. We just forgot that God wants us to be happy.

Sure, some stuff goes wrong. Disasters happen, some dreams go up in smoke, and everyone experiences some pain. But a lot more stuff goes right. In fact, most things go right most of the time. Maybe it is time to listen less to the news and more to our hearts. In spite of the scary prognostications that abound, immense well-being is present if we are open to recognize and receive it. Even if we have denied well-being, at any moment we can change our minds. Perhaps mercy and forgiveness are, after all, God's greatest acts.

Life is an act of God. Wherever anyone lives or loves, God is acting. That act deserves not to be relegated to fine print, but splashed across the masthead of our lives in bold headlines.

Do you blame God for your troubles?
How would you be seeing God differently
if you viewed the Divine as only love?

I find immense good wherever I look.
My God is a God of love.

Blessed Are the Cage Rattlers

What the caterpillar calls the end of
the world, the master calls a butterfly.

— Richard Bach

One day I discovered that a rat had been marauding my pantry. I bought a no-kill trap and soon caught the critter and took it out to a field to release it into the wild. Yet the strangest thing happened: When I opened the door of the cage to let the rat out, it cowered in the back of the cage. I shook the cage, and the rodent clung to it. I shook harder, and it clung more. Finally, I tilted the cage and gave it a hard shake, and the rat fell out and scampered away.

We humans are not so different from the rat. We get stuck in bad relationships, jobs, or living situations; and then when life tries to shake us out of them, we cling to our cage as if it offers us security. *A bad relationship, we rationalize, is better than no relationship at all. My car is a sinkhole for money, one part breaking after another, but it gets me somewhere. My religion makes me feel terribly guilty, but it promises me heaven at the end of my road of suffering.*

While it is good to be positive about aspects of things that work, if more is *not* working than is working, you need to be honest and find your way to freedom. Perhaps you can transform your job or relationship from within it, or perhaps you need to leave. In any event, do not settle for the feeling of living in a cage. That is definitely below-standard for a divine being.

Sometimes people or situations come along that rattle your cage. You may curse or resist them, but they may be helping you get free. I had to give the rat's cage a good hard shake before the animal exited. If people or situations are rattling *your* cage, they are not your enemies, but your friends. They may be assisting you to get out of prison and on to freedom.

What person or situation is rattling your cage?
How can you shift your thinking to see this as helping to liberate you?

I thank and bless the people and situations that disturb me, for they are my keys to freedom.

Unlike Itself

Love calls forth everything unlike itself.

— *A Course in Miracles*

One evening Dee and I were having dinner with a Japanese friend visiting America, along with his translator, Maori. Dee and I tend to be physically affectionate, and we were holding hands at the table. At one point I put my arm around Dee's shoulder and drew her to me gently.

Suddenly Maori burst into tears, a behavior very unusual for a Japanese person in public. When we asked Maori what was wrong, she explained that she had been in a cold and lonely marriage for many years, and her husband never showed her any affection. When she saw Dee and me expressing affection, it reminded her of what she was missing.

We encouraged Maori to express herself to her husband and ask for what she wanted. This is also rare for Japanese women to do, as it is culturally frowned upon. Yet Maori felt heartened by our conversation. We saw her a year later, and she had initiated a divorce.

If you see someone who has something you are missing, you may also have an emotional reaction. You might get a hollow feeling in your stomach, or you could feel angry or envious. These feelings serve as a wake-up call for you to confront and address an issue that has been calling for your attention to claim and receive what you desire.

The presence of pure, positive energy in any form—such as love, wealth, success, vibrant health, a caring family, or a beautiful home—often brings up negative feelings in observers who want the same but cannot seem to achieve it. They have two possible routes to take: they could either (1) celebrate with you, enjoy your success vicariously, and see what you have attained as a positive model demonstrating that they, too, can have it; or (2) become envious, angry, and resentful, and find excuses to criticize you or try to tear you down. If they take the latter route, their reaction is more about them than about you. Hopefully at some point they will learn to make use of the experience to empower them to also have what they want.

How can you pivot on feelings of sadness to
empower yourself to move toward what you want?

I am grateful for reminders and
inspiration to ask for my heart's desire.

Tipping Points

*Masterpieces are . . . the outcome of many years of thinking
in common, of thinking by the body of the people, so that
the experience of the mass is behind the single voice.*

— Virginia Woolf

Some psychologists gave a group of crossword enthusiasts a *New York Times* puzzle to solve on the day it was published, and tested them on their skill level. A few days later they presented the same group with a *New York Times* crossword on the day *after* it was published, and the results showed a 20 percent improvement in skill level, although the participants had not seen that puzzle.

These results demonstrate the power of mass consciousness to exponentially expand results. This phenomenon has been called a watershed, the hundredth monkey, or as Malcolm Gladwell describes it, the tipping point. When many people focus on an idea, their attention builds a mass pool of thought, invisible to the eye but real nevertheless. Anyone who then aligns with that idea taps into the energy and benefits of that thought. So the people who did the crossword puzzle on the day after everyone else had done it tapped into the bank of thoughts of everyone who had solved the puzzle on the previous day, and it was easier for those who did it on day two.

This principle can work for or against you, depending on how you use it. If you tap into a field of thought that is uplifting, positive, generative, and useful, you surf on the momentum of all who have contributed to that field before you. If you tap into a field of thought that is negative, destructive, or fear based, you inherit that entire world. My mentor Hilda never read a newspaper on the day it came out, because the news is generally steeped in darkness and drama, and millions of people were concentrating on that idea and adding their emotion to it. A few days later when the issue had settled down, there was less of a charge on it in the group mind.

Your attention is one of the greatest powers at your command. Use it on your behalf.

*How can you choose what you focus on in order to
benefit from the energy of those who have gone before you?*

**I tap into fields of thought and experience
that empower me and my chosen goals.**

Beggars and Choosers

You are not a beggar at the banquet of life. You are its honored guest.
— Emmanuel/Pat Rodegast

My plane landed at the Miami International Airport just before it closed in the face of oncoming Hurricane Irene. I forged my way to my hotel, hunkered down, and watched in awe as gale-force winds humbled palm trees and sheets of rain pelted the huge picture windows. Suddenly the hotel lost electricity. I lit a candle, meditated, and savored the power of nature surging around me.

The next morning after the storm had abated, hotel guests scrambled to rearrange their flight schedules. As I stood at a public phone in the lobby, I heard a fellow on the phone next to me talking to an airline reservations agent. "I realize that beggars can't be choosers," he pleaded, "but is there any chance you can get me on this flight?"

His words reverberated in my psyche: *beggars can't be choosers*. It is true. If you think you are a beggar, undeserving of the good things in life, required to suffer to get what you want, you are certainly not in a position of choice. But if you recognize that you are imbued with the power of creation, certified by the universe to manifest according to your choice and intention, begging becomes meaningless, utterly contradictory to who you are and the way you were born to live.

Every day you must decide if you are a beggar or a chooser, for you will act and create results according to the identity you assume. If you believe you must grovel, plead, or struggle to manifest your dreams, the road to success can seem overwhelming. But if you realize that every decision before you is an invitation to remember who you are and what you want, the process of choosing becomes exciting, and the courage to claim your dreams follows naturally and easily.

Beggars can't be choosers. Today would be a perfect day to quit begging and start choosing.

If you knew you could choose rather than beg, how would you proceed?

I choose the life I want to live, and the universe accommodates my choice.

Elegant Simplicity

Simplicity is the ultimate sophistication.

— Attributed to Leonardo da Vinci

Today is the birthday of Warren Buffett, one of the richest people in the world. In a rare interview, Buffett revealed some amazing facts about his lifestyle:

- He still lives in the same modest three-bedroom house in midtown Omaha that he bought after he got married 50 years ago. He says that he has everything he needs in that house. His property does not have a wall or a fence.

- He drives his own (older) car everywhere and does not have a driver or security people around him.

- He rarely travels by private jet, although he owns the world's largest private-jet company.

- His company, Berkshire Hathaway, owns 63 companies. He writes only one letter each year to the CEOs of these companies, giving them annual goals. He does not hold meetings or call the CEOs on a regular basis.

- He does not socialize with the high-society crowd. His pastime after he gets home is to make himself some popcorn and watch television.

- When Bill Gates met him for the first time, the Microsoft founder did not think he had anything in common with the older billionaire, so he had scheduled his meeting for only a half hour. But instead the meeting lasted for ten hours, and Bill Gates became a devotee of Warren Buffett.

- He does not carry a cell phone, nor does he have a computer on his desk.

Maybe it is time to question whether all the accoutrements and complications we usually associate with success are really necessary.

How might you lighten up and simplify
your life and still succeed in big ways?

I succeed on my own terms.
I can create my life and career any way I choose.

Confidence: The Great Turn-on

When you are content to be simply yourself and don't
compare or compete, everybody will respect you.

— Lao-tzu

A few months after Harvey began dating Janet, he received a call from his former girlfriend Susan, who told him she would be in his city and would like to say hello. Harvey had remained friends with Susan over time, and the two occasionally exchanged a few brief e-mails. Since he had not seen Susan in many years and he valued their connection, Harvey agreed to meet her.

Harvey was hesitant to tell Janet he was going to see Susan, since he did not know how she would react. When he did tell her, Janet was quite relaxed. "Enjoy your time with your friend," she told him. "Call me when you feel like it."

Harvey met with Susan, and the two shared an enjoyable afternoon. No sparks flew, and he had no desire to rekindle their relationship. It was simply a pleasant, brief reconnection.

Afterward, Harvey felt far more attracted to Janet. He respected her confidence in herself, in him, and in their relationship. Other women he had known would have gotten upset and gone into drama mode. Janet later told Harvey, "I was a little anxious, but I figured that if you wanted to be with her more than with me, that was what you should do. I wouldn't want to be with someone who wanted someone else more." That moment endeared Janet to Harvey tremendously, and eventually the couple married.

Clinging to anything makes it go away. Releasing it makes it stay. It's a Zen kind of thing.

The good that truly belongs to you cannot leave you. When you trust that what is yours is yours by right of consciousness, you enjoy the most powerful form of ownership.

How can you empower yourself and others
by trusting that your good cannot leave you?

All that is mine finds me and stays with me.
My good is magnetized to me because of
who I am, what I think, and how I feel.

Higher Intelligence

I have never let my schooling interfere with my education.
— Mark Twain

Education annals tell of an elementary-school teacher we'll call Miss James who arrived at her classroom on the first day of the term and studied her class roster. To her delight, she saw high IQ marks next to each name: 121 . . . 128 . . . 138. *Thank goodness!* she told herself. *Finally a class I can accomplish something with!*

Miss James gave the students challenging lessons and freedom to create. As expected, they all excelled, and at the end of the grading period, most received *A*'s. The next day the principal called the teacher to his office. "How did you turn these low-functioning students into geniuses?" he asked.

"What do you mean?" Miss James replied, pointing out their IQs in her register.

The principal studied the register and shook his head. "Those are their locker numbers," he explained.

Excellence in any educational arena is based largely on (1) the passion of the student, (2) the passion of the teacher, (3) the student's self-image, and (4) the image the teacher holds of the student. The role of a true teacher is not to cram facts into empty brains, but to see the students as capable and powerful, and ignite the fire of purpose.

If you are not enthusiastic about what you are teaching, you are robbing your students as well as yourself. If you are enthusiastic, you are giving them the gift of aliveness. Education is not just about facts. It is about life force.

In the movie *E.T.*, young Elliott has met his extraterrestrial friend and hidden him in his bedroom closet. Elliott's older brother, Michael, discovers E.T. and befriends him, too. On their way to school the next morning, Michael asks his brother if he explained school to their friend. Elliott answers by asking how you explain school to higher intelligence.

Many schools have become little more than holding tanks and babysitting institutions. Yet some teachers and administrators remember that the goal of education is expansion of the spirit. Students, they realize, do not come to school to be contained, but to be inspired.

*How can you draw forth the greatness in your
children, students, employees, or friends?*

**I regard people as intelligent and capable, and
I ignite their potential by acknowledging it.**

Good News for Procrastinators

Only Robinson Crusoe had everything done by Friday.

— Source unknown

Do you put things off until you absolutely have to do them? Do you judge and criticize yourself for not being more prompt about getting your tasks done? If so, I have some good news for you: you may be closer to wisdom than you know.

Esther Hicks tells about how she had been putting off making airplane reservations for an upcoming trip that she and her husband, Jerry, were planning. Every now and then Jerry would ask, "Did you book that trip yet?" and Esther would answer, "Not yet," feeling a bit self-critical for not having taken care of it. Yet she did not feel moved to do it, and did not.

One night late in the evening Esther had an urge to pick up the telephone and book the flights. To her pleasant surprise, her call was answered by an unusually cheerful and helpful agent who got the Hickses good seats at excellent fares. "The agent was so helpful," Esther recounts, "that I made arrangements for several trips, all at great prices."

In this case, Esther's waiting to act was not a result of procrastination, but of attunement to right timing. If you criticize yourself for a delay in getting things done, some of your waiting may be based on intuitive guidance.

You could probably do some things earlier and feel better about finishing them than you would have felt putting them off. But there are other things that, if done sooner, will not prove as effective as if you do them later. How do you know the difference? As it is with all decisions, you have to practice tuning in to your intuition to sense the right time to act. You will know.

Do you judge yourself for procrastinating?
Can you lighten up on yourself and trust that in
some cases your intuition is guiding you?

Using my intuition, I know when to act,
and my timing is perfect.

The Connection Factor

Each contact with a human being is so rare,
so precious, one should preserve it.

— Anaïs Nin

Consider this scenario: You wake up one morning and feel like having some French toast for breakfast. You look in your refrigerator and realize you need bread. So you go to the local grocery store, pick up a loaf, and chat with the cashier for a minute before you check out.

What was the purpose of your trip? While the obvious reason was to get the bread, the deeper purpose was your moment of connection with the cashier. The bread nourishes you physically, but your connection nourishes you spiritually. And because you are spiritual at your core, that is the level that *truly* feeds you.

As the world becomes more and more automated and depersonalized, the value of human connection increases like a rare jewel. Many corporations would rather have you talk to a computer or make your purchase over the Internet, which saves the company money but, in a way, costs its soul. As more and more people feel lonely, objectified, and alienated, human connection and caring go a lot further than they did when human relationships were an integral element of business. If you can offer your presence and receive that of others, you are participating in a healing exchange.

There is no such thing as an insignificant interaction. Paying for a paper at a newsstand or phoning the cable company about a billing question is of minor importance to your physical world, but of paramount importance to your spiritual world. The way you speak to someone can make their day—or if you are gruff or rude, influence them to pass the negative energy along to other customers. Never underestimate your power to uplift the world with your daily interactions.

In what interactions can you use the power of connection to
turn a mundane activity into a rewarding relationship?

There are no small moments.
All interactions are opportunities for me to shine.

Hiding in Complexity

The ability to simplify means to eliminate the
unnecessary so that the necessary may speak.

— Hans Hofmann

I once traveled cross-country with a buddy. We got along pretty well, but whenever we argued, I found myself extremely frustrated. My friend had a way of complicating arguments so that they would go on for a long time and nobody would win. He would drag in all kinds of irrelevant information and inappropriate analogies and go off on tangents that left me scratching my head, wondering, *What were we talking about anyway?* Eventually I gave up trying to win arguments, and just prayed to resolve the issue at hand. Even that was difficult.

My friend had developed a propensity to hide in complexity. He had grown up as a child of an alcoholic and needed to feel safe from being hurt. So he learned to weave tangled webs around himself to keep people at a distance and avoid being wounded. He is not alone in this diversionary tactic. Many in our society have gone that route.

In his book *Success Intelligence,* Robert Holden cites the following statistics:

- The number of words in the Lord's Prayer: 56

- The number of words in the Ten Commandments: 297

- The number of words in the Declaration of Independence: 1,322

- The number of words in the Directive of European Economic Community import of caramel and caramel products: 26,911

The closer a statement is to truth, the fewer words are needed to express it. By corollary, the more words, the more hiding and room for manipulation.

Today, and every day, practice saying the most with the least words. You may be amazed by how crystal clear your communication becomes, along with your results.

How can you clarify your communication and
your life by simplifying your words and acts?

I trust simplicity and truth
to get me what I want and need.

That's About It

When you speak from your heart, everyone
listens, because God is speaking.

— Source unknown

In college I took a religion course taught by a rabbi. On the first day of class, he announced, "There are two kinds of learning: 'It' learning and 'About It' learning. This is a course in 'It.'"

Some forms of religious education stay above the neck—intellectual pursuits that leave the heart hungry. They study people who had religious experiences, but do not inculcate a direct spiritual experience within the student. Other teachings go below the neck and touch the student's heart. They do not teach *about* life, but draw the student to the very center of it.

I had a roommate named Lou Chalupa who taught English in a public high school. Recognizing that most educational offerings were above the neck, Lou appealed to his administration to let him teach a new course called "Humanities," and they agreed. The subject of Humanities was the students and their lives. Lou would place two director's chairs in front of the room and invite students to sit with him and have a heart-to-heart conversation about what was going on in their lives. He organized Thanksgiving food drives, and on Halloween invited a group of senior citizens, dressed as teenagers, to the class—while the students dressed as seniors.

When word about Humanities got around, it became the most popular elective in the school. Lou eventually left English teaching and taught six periods of Humanities each day. The course was so popular that two other teachers were hired to teach it full-time.

Lou developed lifelong relationships with his students. I remember one fellow phoning our apartment to tell Lou that he had just returned from the military service, and Lou's class had prepared him for life more than any other. Another time my roommate took a day off from work to go rowboating with a student whose father had just died. Lou was a real "It" teacher.

"It" is a far more powerful education than "About It." That's about it.

How could you live more in the "It" of your life?

I choose to live, rather than study how to live.

The Left Side of the Class

Attitudes Are Contagious: Are Yours Worth Catching?
— Title of a book by Dennis and Wendy Mannering

"I just don't know how to deal with my mother," Rebecca told me. "She phones me regularly, and all she does is complain. I try to be patient, listen, and help her, but she seems committed to using our phone calls to vent. It's no fun for me, and I don't look forward to talking to her. I've been calling her less and less, and I fear that we no longer have anything to talk about."

I explained to Rebecca that she was not helping her mother or herself by listening to hour-long tirades. I suggested that she set an intention that her conversations with her mother focus on subject matters truly rewarding to both of them.

I told Rebecca about a college psychology class in which the instructor had a habit of pacing back and forth in front of the classroom. The students of the behavior-modification course decided they would do their own experiment, using their professor as the subject. When the professor stood on the left side of the classroom, the students looked directly at him, paid attention, took notes, asked questions, and laughed at his jokes. When he stood on the right side, they paid no attention to him, did not engage with him, and looked bored. It was not long before the professor was teaching from the left side of the classroom only.

If you have friends, relatives, business colleagues, or clients who are steeped in negativity, you serve neither yourself nor them by indulging misery. You must become established on a higher ground of interaction and let them know that if they want to engage with you, they will have to meet on a more positive frequency. You can state this overtly, or simply become so established in the energy *you* prefer that they pick it up.

The next time I spoke to Rebecca, she happily reported that her conversations with her mother were becoming shorter and more positive. Mom was staying more on the left side of the class.

What relationship could you upgrade by establishing
yourself in the energy you prefer?

I use my interactions to uplift myself and others.
I choose to dwell in healthy, positive
conversations and connections.

Passionate Engineers

When you discover your mission, you will feel its demand. It will fill you with enthusiasm and a burning desire to get to work on it.

— W. Clement Stone

My friend Doris is a division manager for a large software company. When she was assigned to oversee a department of engineers, she shuddered, since the members of this department were notorious for not getting along and were not completing their tasks. Yet Doris had been studying Joseph Campbell's maxim of "Follow your bliss," and she decided to put the principle into practice.

At her first meeting with the engineers, Doris had to designate tasks for a project. Rather than giving the staff members assignments based on their history or skills, she asked each of them, "What aspect of this project would you most like to do?" The engineers expressed their preferences, and she assigned roles based on joy and choice. To her delight, at the end of the meeting the engineers walked out of the room smiling and shaking hands. They told her this was the first successful meeting they had ever had.

In the corporate world, and perhaps in your personal life, the factor of joy is often low on the list of important elements when it comes to deciding who will do what and when. Yet it deserves to be very high on the list. People do well what they *want* to do. People do not do well what they do *not* want to do. If you can match jobs with passion, you are on your way to success.

Certainly there are things we would each rather not do that we have to do. But there are also things we would like to do that we put off. Try doing the things you enjoy first, and you may be surprised by how the other tasks fall in line.

If you were to do more of what you really enjoy, what would you be doing differently?

I honor joy as a significant factor of success. I make passionate choices, and I thrive.

In His Own Quiet Way

You can recognize a saint by his utter ordinariness.
— Source unknown

For nearly 20 years I have patronized a small video store near my home, where I have gotten to know the proprietor, an amiable senior named Don. The store is more of a family affair than a business. Don keeps a stash of treats for all the patrons' dogs (some of whom find their way to the store without their owners). On one wall a tall, thin Disney movie poster contains penciled lines recording customers' kids' heights, showing growth from year to year. Once, when I checked out 20 videos to prepare a seminar on inspirational cinema, Don did not charge me because, as he noted, "It's for educational purposes." And he has never charged me for late returns.

One day Don, now age 86 and just through several knee surgeries, announced he would be selling the store to live with his family across the ocean. The day before he left, Dee and I went to visit him at his home. He answered the door spryly in his wheelchair and ushered us to his couch, where he showed us photos of his going-away party at the store. Parents, kids, and dogs showed up; ate unlimited popcorn; and contributed to a scrapbook with notes of thanks, poems, and kids' crayon drawings of Don and the store. In his own quiet way, Don had touched many lives.

Suddenly I realized that our friendship had crept up on me, and Don had a place in my heart. I was going to miss him. The time came for us to leave, and although we tried to hold back, we all shed a tear. Then Don told us in a chipper tone, "I guess I'll see you in heaven."

His candor struck me. "Yes, I will look forward to seeing you in heaven," I replied as we left. As I drove home, still choked up, I realized I had been privileged to know a sacred man who has lived with extraordinary kindness, presence, and generosity. In a world where fear, greed, and protectionism seem to rule, Don reversed those conditions in his little shop.

Maybe I do not need to wait to get to heaven to see Don again. Every time I experience an act of kindness, I go to the place he lives.

Do you know any incognito saints?
How might you uplift the world in your own quiet way?

**I find beauty and riches in simple moments
of connection and kindness. Heaven is where I stand.**

Fear Under Pressure

If you knew there was infinite supply,
you would have no need to demand.

— Alan Cohen

Many people struggle with issues of anger. Either they are angry themselves or they deal with angry people. You might wonder, *Is it better to express anger or keep my mouth shut?* The answer is: *neither.* It is better to understand where the anger comes from and heal it.

Anger is fear under pressure. Behind every angry upset there is a fear. If you attempt to deal with anger at the level of anger alone—by either venting it or repressing it—you are manipulating the symptom without addressing the cause. If you can discover the fear behind the anger and dismantle it in the light of awareness, the anger dissipates. The next time you are angry, ask yourself, *What am I afraid of?*

For example, if you are angry at your wife for spending more money than you believe you can afford, you are dealing with fear of lack. If you are angry at your boyfriend for looking at another woman, you are facing a self-confidence issue, the fear of not being enough. If you are angry at a government for not being fair, you fear that you are powerless. Certainly all of these situations may call for attention, but they will not be resolved through anger.

To dismantle fear, get in touch with the truth that it overlooks or denies. If you know that you are a prosperous being living in an abundant universe and you can generate abundance by your skill and attitude, you could never feel poor or lacking. If you know that you deserve a partner who loves you and is true to you, you could attract someone of that caliber. If you recognize that you have power over your life no matter what the government does, that institution would not be the target of a misappropriated sense of powerlessness.

Anger is not a bad emotion; to the contrary, it is a powerful tool to get your attention to make a correction. That correction always begins with an internal shift from fear to power.

If you feel angry, what is the fear behind the anger?
What is the truth that offsets the fear?

I am whole, abundant, and empowered.
I heal my life by recognizing the truth.

Résumés and Results

Good luck is another name for tenacity of purpose.
— Ralph Waldo Emerson

Tim had been out of work for a while and wanted to get back into a career. He spent a lot of time thinking about his ideal position and what he had to offer, and he worked and reworked his résumé. Finally Tim felt that the résumé represented him and his vision, and he printed numerous copies. Tim searched the Internet and found a few dozen prospective employers, he addressed an envelope and cover letter to each of them, and inserted the packets.

Just as Tim was about to leave his house to mail his queries, his phone rang. The caller was a former business associate looking for staff, and he had thought of Tim. The two discussed the position and found it an excellent match for Tim—at a good salary.

Tim never made it to the post office to send out his résumé because he had already sent it out psychically. He did not purposely sit down, close his eyes, and advertise himself through invisible thought waves, although that was the dynamic that occurred. Tim did spend a great deal of time, thought, feeling, and energy getting clear on what an ideal position would look and feel like. In a sense, the psychic résumé he sent out was more powerful and meaningful than mailing papers, by virtue of the Law of Attraction.

When you are clear about who you are, what you want, and where you are going, you will achieve results aligned with your intentions. If you are getting no results or wishy-washy ones, you are being called to clarify your identity, passion, purpose, and visions.

I am not suggesting you just sit at home and think, without taking any action (although in many cases that may help you more than acting without clear purpose). I *am* suggesting that you do your inner homework and let the universe save you postage.

How might your current results reflect your intentions?
How might you clarify your intentions so your
results can reflect your ideal situation?

I get to the heart of who I am and
what I want, and the universe generates
 results that match my vision.

Never Anything Good to Say

Nothing splendid has ever been achieved except by those who dared believe that something inside of them was superior to circumstance.

— Bruce Barton

My "developmentally delayed" neighbor Marty always has a bright smile, loves to connect with everyone he meets, and often utters profound truths you might expect to hear from a Zen master.

Once when I visited Marty, he showed me his skill on a video game. I was amazed to observe how quickly and masterfully he overcame foes and obstacles and worked his way to the top of the mountain the game required him to scale. At the apex, he was confronted by a huge fire-snorting dragon who puffed himself up and threatened in a booming voice, "Go no farther or I will destroy you!"

But Marty was not daunted. He turned to me, laughed, and advised, "Don't listen to that guy—he never has anything good to say!" With that, Marty pressed a few buttons on his joystick, grabbed the dragon by the tail, twirled the beast several times, and hurled him into the abyss, thereby winning the game.

When dragons confront us in life, we might do well to remember Marty's comment: *Don't listen to that guy—he never has anything good to say.* The voice of fear takes many different forms, but if you trace it back to its essence, it is by nature weak and paltry and has no power in the face of truth. You need not be intimidated by people, news, or events that threaten to hurt or annihilate you. Instead, stand tall; laugh; and using the fulcrum of your identity as a spiritual being, toss the impostor into the abyss.

What person, situation, or voice is trying to intimidate you? How might you respond if you recognized that you are more powerful than any adversary that confronts you?

I answer fear with confidence, truth, and integrity. I am greater than any threat I perceive.

One Good Idea

Give me a place to stand, and I will move the world.

— Archimedes

People are paid far more for their ideas than for their actions. One good idea can affect more people and earn more rewards than many actions. If you want to change the world and be successful, leverage your career with good ideas.

When Bill Gates developed the computer disk operating system (DOS), no one recognized how profoundly the personal computer would change the way we live and do business across the globe. When Steven Jobs fleshed out Apple's graphical user interface, he was at the forefront of a mouse revolution. 3M researcher Art Fry was singing in a church choir when he noticed that the little pieces of paper he used to hold his place in the hymnal were falling out. He remembered a weak adhesive that Spencer Silver had invented six years earlier . . . and behold, Post-its were born.

If you have a good idea, you must be true to it rather than getting bogged down in the details of it. Visionaries channel ideas, and executives put them into action. Both are important. It is rare that a visionary and an executive live in the same brain. If you try to do the other's job, you will be frustrated and ineffective. Do what you do best, and leave others to do what they do best.

When Bill Gates was CEO of Microsoft, if he had been walking down a hall of that company and he saw a $1,000 bill on the floor and bent down to pick it up, he would have been wasting his time. That is because he was making more money than that thinking up ideas for Microsoft. He let other people carry out these ideas, and everyone emerged triumphant for it.

Never underestimate the power of one good idea. Every great invention, work of art, and social change began with a seed idea. The only difference between geniuses and ordinary people is that geniuses take their ideas and run with them.

Do you have ideas you do not act on?
If you knew you might change the world and be
highly successful, what idea might you develop?

I respect my ideas as seeds of huge success.
I act on them, and the world is better for it.

As Thyself

Some people have so much respect for their
superiors they have none left for themselves.

— Peter McArthur

"I am a fund-raiser for the Red Cross," a woman at a seminar re-ported. "When a hurricane or other disaster hits, I mobilize, and within a few days I collect millions of dollars for the victims. Meanwhile, I have trouble paying my rent. Something is wrong with this picture. What do you think it could be?"

I told her, "When you recognize that you are as worthy to have what you need as you know the disaster victims are worthy to have what they need, then your rent will be paid easily."

Many of us have a double standard: We believe that others de-serve more than we do. As a result, we watch others prosper, and we even *help* them prosper, while we stand in the shadows wondering why we do not have enough for our basic needs or fun. Something is indeed wrong with this picture.

We are all familiar with and probably try to practice the biblical teaching "Love thy neighbor as thyself." Yet a lot of us are better at loving our neighbor than ourselves! Unless you are loving yourself as much as your neighbor, the equation is out of balance, and you are not practicing this noble lesson.

The Red Cross fund-raiser stood at a significant threshold in her life—one at which you, too, may be standing. Can you find the same beauty, deservingness, and value in yourself that you find in others? When you do, the good you observe in their lives will come to you. Then your disasters will be relieved by a universal agency that has its headquarters in the center of your soul.

What have you done for others, or would like
to do, that you have not done for yourself?
Would you be willing to give yourself the gift that
you delight in seeing others receive?

I am worthy of love, abundance, health, and good.
I am generous enough to give and receive.

Up the Down Escalator

Your Arms Too Short to Box with God
— Title of stage play conceived by Vinnette Carroll

In Chicago's O'Hare Airport I saw a little boy, about three years old, trying to forge up a down escalator. The child would make his way a distance up the moving staircase, but the apparatus was moving faster than his little legs could go, so eventually he would lose ground and end up back where he started.

The child's frustrating journey reminded me of the times when I, perhaps like you, have attempted to buck the current of life and ended up back where I started. You seek to negotiate a contract with a desired company, create a relationship with a particular person, or buy a certain piece of real estate, and no matter what you do, you get nowhere.

At such a point you can either fight harder or you can step back and look for an escalator moving in your desired direction. Such an escalator represents the great current of life. Lao-tzu called this current "the Tao," and in more modern terminology, it is known as "the Force." No matter what you name it, there is a river of energy that will take you where you want to go. You just have to place your canoe in it and let the stream take you rather than trying to fight your way upstream.

To succeed in life, you must embody a sort of "reverse paranoia." Paranoia traditionally means that you believe that life is out to hurt you. Reverse paranoia means that life is out to help you.

The next time you find yourself losing ground, come back to where you started and have a look, for there is a staircase moving where you want to go.

Are you fighting your way upstream?
How might you align with the current?

The universe is trying to help me.
I open to let it.

The Cases You Don't Take

*Have the courage to say no. Have the courage
to face the truth. Do the right thing because it is right.
These are the magic keys to living your life with integrity.*
— Attributed to W. Clement Stone

A successful lawyer told me that he had just turned down a request by a potential client to take his case. The client did not seem honest, and his demands did not seem justified. "You build your practice on the cases you *don't* take," the attorney explained to me.

This advice applies to all professions and life choices. If you accept everything that comes your way, agree to do what you would rather not do because you are afraid you will lose business if you do not, or say yes because you feel too guilty to say no, you will end up doing things that grate against you. Then you will either not enjoy them or not succeed because you were out of integrity with yourself.

I know a landscape-materials supplier who had a client he did not like. But the client was the source of 20 percent of the supplier's income, so he forced himself to continue with the account. Finally he found the courage to cut the client loose, and he took on new accounts to fill the gap. At the end of the year, his income was 30 percent higher than the previous year's! His success demonstrates that the universe rewards us for making self-honoring choices.

Think of your career or life as a computer disk with a fixed capacity. If your disk is full of data you do not use or want, when it comes time to add data you *do* want, you will get a "disk full" message. Then you have to delete the unwanted or the unnecessary files to make space for what you really desire or need.

When you say yes to a case or client, you are setting the tone for more of the same energy to come. So if you would rather not work with a particular project or person, the time to say no is at the beginning. If thinking about something does not feel good, doing it is probably going to feel worse. If thinking about doing something feels good, doing it is probably going to feel better.

*How might you succeed more by releasing
clients or projects you would not choose?*

**I work with people and projects that empower me.
I release those that do not empower me.**

Getting and Being

Why get rich quick when you can be rich now?

— Alan Cohen

The popular DVD and book *The Secret* were originally inspired by an obscure 1910 work entitled *The Science of Getting Rich* by Wallace Wattles, a masterful overview of the relationship between thought and results, and how to expand your abundance by proper use of your mind.

Not obscure anymore due to the attention cast upon it by the author of *The Secret,* Wattles's text has resurfaced in both print and electronic formats. If you search for it on the Internet, you will find the same book also titled *The Science of Being Rich.* This distinction is absolutely fundamental, and the principle behind it is as important as the book itself.

The secret to getting rich someday is to be rich *now.* We have been taught that life works on a "Do-Have-Be" model: You do something, you get the result, and you become it. You work to make money, you have stuff that money gets you, and so you are rich. While this model works if you believe in it, it is essentially backward. There is a far more direct path to wealth.

The real wealth paradigm is "Be-Have-Do": You find the place within you that already *is* what you wish to be, then you experience ownership of it, then you end up doing the things that someone who has that quality of life would do. You know you are rich, you have the feeling of wealth, and the things that a rich person does follow naturally. The idea of *getting* rich is counterproductive. If you think that you are not rich now, but you will become rich by doing A, B, or C, then you have overlooked the identity that makes you rich by nature, not by action.

So your best way to get rich is to *be* rich. Meditate on, contemplate, visualize, and feel the riches you already own; and from that knowingness outer riches will flow. If there is something you need to do, you will recognize it, but that action will spring from a *consciousness* of wealth, which is real wealth that all the gold in Fort Knox cannot buy.

How can you increase your wealth by recognizing that you are already wealthy?

I am rich by nature. Material wealth springs from my awareness of the wealth I already own, and am.

Don't Sweat the Petty Stuff

Don't pet the sweaty stuff and don't sweat the petty stuff.
— Source unknown

On an episode of the TV show *Dog Whisperer,* canine behaviorist Cesar Millan was summoned to rehabilitate a dog with the odd obsession of chasing beams of light. The owner had gotten the dog from a shelter after the animal had been abused. At home with his new pet, the man flashed a small laser beam on the floor, and the dog made a game of chasing it. Before long, he was chasing the light constantly, and then he generalized to any beam or reflection of light he saw. What began as an innocent game developed into a neurotic obsession the owner could not stop.

After observing the dog's behavior, Cesar explained that the obsession was a control issue. Because the dog had felt out of control of his world when he had been abused, he sought to have power over the small dot of light. When he pounced on it, for a moment he was bigger than something and in charge of it. So he did not stop doing it. As usual, Cesar intervened and reprogrammed the dog.

The case made me wonder if a similar principle applies to people with computer or cell-phone addictions. I noticed that I was habitually going to the computer and checking e-mail or surfing the Internet. At one point I realized I was spending more time online than I would choose. Considering the neurotic light-chasing dog, I wondered if I found the computer satisfying because sitting at it I was in charge of my world.

At the keyboard, you assume the role of creator and god of your own little universe. You press a button and things appear; you press another button and they disappear. If you are a writer or graphic artist, you can spin worlds from your fingertips. Surfing the Internet takes you virtually anywhere you want to go.

I overcame my computer addiction by recognizing that there were bigger and better things I wanted to do with my day and my life. Being in charge of a small world was far less satisfying than participating in a greater one.

Only magnitude and expansiveness befit us as divine beings. Play with the light if you wish, but at the end of the day, it is more fun to *become* it.

Do you get enmeshed in smallness?
How can you remember and practice expansiveness?

**I invest my energy in what connects me with
a larger universe. I am the light I seek.**

The Crucial Intersection

The place God calls you to is the place where your
deep gladness and the world's deep hunger meet.

— Frederick Buechner

Life is like sex: it works best when both people want to be there, choose to be there, and are enjoying themselves.

If you apply this formula to the way in which many people approach their work, you will find parts of the equation missing. Either the person giving service is lacking in deep joy, or the work is meaningless and not feeding a deep hunger. If you are involved in either element of this equation, I suggest you step back and seriously consider what you are doing or how you are going about it.

I remember sitting at the ferry terminal one afternoon in Tiburon, California, watching commuters disembark after their workday in San Francisco. They looked beat, frustrated, and lifeless. *Is this really what a career is supposed to do to you?* I asked myself. *Deplete your life a little bit more every day until you die of joylessness?*

You need not sacrifice joy for success. The very *foundation* of success is joy. Karen Drucker was tired of singing at weddings after many years, and she launched a career singing uplifting music. Now she is in huge demand, working with people who crave her talent. She is simultaneously living her dream and helping the world.

I read a magazine article on "the best company to work for in the world—period," describing the phenomenal benefits given to employees of a software firm called Motek. Employees must take at least a three-week vacation, for which they receive a $5,000 travel benefit, and they also get two weeks in paid holidays. Innovative CEO Ann S. Price sends everyone home at 5 P.M. without laptops, and the doors are closed on weekends. Ten-year company employees get a luxury leased automobile. The firm's revenue per employee tops competing firms by 10 to 25 percent.

Joy and success are not mutually exclusive. They are as natural as making great love.

What career path would be an expression of your joy?
How could it fill the world's hunger?

I follow my inner calling to the intersection
of deep joy and powerful service.

Your Secret Smarts

I am convinced all of humanity is born with more gifts than we know.
Most are born geniuses and just get de-geniused rapidly.

— Buckminster Fuller

As I was strolling through the grounds at a conference center one morning, a woman sitting beside the path asked me, "Do you know what time it is?"

Not having a watch, I took my best guess and answered, "I think it's about 9:15."

"I don't think so," she came back quickly. "It was 9:15 about half an hour ago."

Hmm. "Then why did you ask me?" I had to inquire.

"I guess I was just looking for confirmation," she replied.

You know more than you think you know. You were born wise, but your awareness and confidence in your inner wisdom has been obscured by training to the contrary. You have been hypnotized to believe that you do not know who you are and how to live, when you really do. How would your world change if you acted on the wisdom you already own? How would you proceed if you were smart enough to know which foods to eat to keep you happy and healthy, your right career path, and whom to date or marry; as well as to answer any question you would ask a wise person?

In bookstores I see hundreds of books for "Dummies" and "Idiots" on every possible subject, from computers to dating to out-of-body experiences. People buy millions of these books because we have learned to identify with stupidity. If I wrote a book titled *Public Speaking for Geniuses,* it would probably not sell as well as *Public Speaking for Dummies.* We live as if other people are smarter than we are, and the cycle goes on.

Certainly you may reach out for learning and advice. Just feed the information to your inner genius, who knows exactly what to do with everything you learn.

Do you feel or act stupid? How would you be feeling
or acting if you knew you were a genius?

I embody the wisdom of the universe.
I honor my inner genius and let it guide my life.

Where the Flame Doesn't Flicker

In the light of his vision he has found his freedom.
— *The Dhammapada* (translated by Juan Mascaro)

When I began to learn meditation, a teacher taught me to envision an image that has been supremely helpful in my practice, with tremendous applications to my daily life. This may be helpful to you, too: Imagine yourself in a sacred room where a white candle burns brightly. This room is a sanctuary from the bustling activity of your busy day. The energy inside this room is so still, safe, and protected that when the outer winds of change blow, the candle flame does not flicker.

There is a place of peace inside you that is unaffected by the "slings and arrows of outrageous fortune." It is calm, pure, whole, and unswerving. It is not altered by the highs of worldly achievement or the lows of external loss. Nothing anyone says to you or about you can dampen it. No financial ups or downs can move it. No heady falling-in-love experience or relationship breakup can sway it. Bodily challenges cannot undo it. Even the death of a loved one cannot extinguish it, as you realize that your loved one has not disappeared, but has simply returned to the refuge of his or her own soul.

You will never find perfect peace in the world. By nature, the world is built on ups and downs, comings and goings, triumphs and failures, victories and defeats, war and relative peace, life and death. It offers many blessings and adventures, but none as profound as the discovery of perfect peace within yourself, and the recognition that you carry well-being with you.

Today and every day, take some time—preferably at the beginning of the day and again at the end—to visit and dwell in your inner sanctuary. There you will be cleansed of the debris of painful thinking and emotional upsets. Your heart will be opened and your soul restored. You will remember who you are and what your purpose in life is. You will recognize the beauty and value of your loved ones and, most important, yourself.

Go often to the place where the candle flame does not flicker. It is your true home and the source of the soul nourishment that can and will satisfy you more than anything outside you.

*What place can you touch inside you that
delivers respite and healing to your soul?*

**Within me dwells a domain of perfect peace.
I go there and renew my mind, heart, and spirit.**

Closer Than You Think

All creations are 99 percent complete
before you see their manifestation.

— Abraham-Hicks

I saw a fascinating series of photos that illuminated the process of creation. The first picture showed a fishing boat entering the field of a mysterious substance floating on the surface of the ocean. As the boat penetrated the field, the crew could see that the substance was a vast layer of pumice. Each succeeding photo showed the boat maneuvering deeper into the field until the captain spied a plume of smoke in the distance. As the boat approached the plume, the crew saw a mass forming atop the ocean, creating an island. Closer inspection revealed a volcano erupting, just breaking through the surface of the ocean and growing new land before the astonished crew's eyes.

This process symbolizes how manifestation occurs in our lives. At first we conceive a simple inkling of something we would like to create. This stage is like the seminal moment when a volcano pierces the ocean floor. Then, as we focus on our idea and nurture it, the volcano builds from the ocean floor up, invisible at the surface. Over time the undersea mountain grows until one day it pierces the surface and it is visible to everyone, along with a landmass—often huge—that accompanies it.

When you seek to bring a creation into the world, most of the work occurs beneath the surface before you can see tangible results. You must build your creation in your consciousness, sometimes for a long time, before it is real. But when it becomes real, it is very solid and will last for eons.

You may be closer to your manifestation than you know. The tip of your volcano might be just below the surface of visibility. Do not be discouraged or give up because your dream is taking what feels like a long time to come true. One day it will pop into reality because you built it carefully, lovingly, over time in the invisible realm of your mind and heart.

What projects are you impatient to bring into reality?
Might you be closer than you think?

I build my consciousness, and the results show
themselves at the perfect time.

How Much Would You Pay to Be Yourself?

Self-confidence is the first requisite to great undertakings.
— Samuel Johnson

The film *Being John Malkovich* tells of an unhappy guy named Craig who discovers a portal into movie star John Malkovich's mind, where he can live vicariously for 15 minutes. When an opportunist hears about Craig's discovery, she devises a scheme to charge customers $200 to enter the portal. Soon there is a long line of people anxiously waiting to be John Malkovich.

Like Craig's customers, many of us pay dearly to be someone else. We spend time, energy, and money trying to live as someone we admire or idolize. Fashion trends are thus born, fan clubs thrive on worship, and teenagers' bedroom walls are altars to stars who offer borrowed worth and identity. Yet identity cannot be borrowed. Either you find it within or you find it not at all.

Wouldn't it be wonderful if we were equally motivated to discover truth through our own eyes? Life's gift to us is our unique vantage point, and our gift to life is expressing from it. A real friend or teacher reminds you that your true power and joy lie in authenticity, not imitation. It is said, "A friend is someone who remembers your song when you have forgotten it, and reminds you to sing it." No one can perform your song as well as you can, so sing it loud and clear.

Occasionally people have asked me to certify them to teach my work. I prefer not to do so, as I encourage people to express their own insights. Once a woman inquired if I would certify her to teach from one of my books. "Which book would you like to teach?" I asked her.

"Dare to Be Yourself," she replied.

"I cannot certify you to be yourself," I told her. "You already are."

Two hundred dollars to be John Malkovich for 15 minutes. What would it be worth to you to be yourself for a lifetime? Authentic power is free. You do not have to invest a penny to become who you are. All you need to invest is yourself.

From whom do you seek to borrow worth or identity?
Are you willing to claim your own worth as yourself?

I am perfect in my uniqueness. I express authentically
and have a corner on the market of me.

The Law of the Vital Few

The secret of success is constancy of purpose.
— Benjamin Disraeli

Do you ever feel like you are wasting time and energy, spinning your wheels, with no results? Do you wonder why some people just keep winning while others cannot catch a break? Would you like to maximize your returns while minimizing your effort?

If so, your answer may lie in understanding the 80/20 rule, which states that for most events, 80 percent of the effects proceed from 20 percent of the causes. The rule is called "the law of the vital few."

This principle reveals itself in many businesses, where 80 percent of the income derives from 20 percent of the clients. A publisher told me that 80 percent of company book sales come from 20 percent of its books. A hotel marketing director revealed that 80 percent of its group-sales income derives from 20 percent of its accounts. A minister reported that 80 percent of church donations come from 20 percent of its parishioners.

The practical implications of this rule are immense: to amplify your results enormously, give your attention and effort to the vital 20 percent, and do not waste your energy on the less vital 80 percent.

On an intrapersonal level, 80 percent of your success and forward movement comes from 20 percent of your thoughts. Lots of niggling counterproductive thoughts ramble through your mind in the course of a day. You also have a smaller number of uplifting, creative, expansive thoughts. If you give more attention to the creative thoughts and less to the diminutive ones, you will reap huge rewards.

According to The Teachings of Abraham, "The secret of genius is focus." That is also the secret of all success. Give your attention where it is deserved and your business and life will soar.

Which thoughts and actions take you to places you truly value?
How can you focus more on your good ideas and capitalize on them?

I give my energy and action to the portions of my life that I value and that pay off.

Your Message Service

When your body talks, listen.

— Source unknown

Cartoonist Scott Adams (of *Dilbert* fame) states: "In Japan, employees occasionally work themselves to death. It's called *Karoshi*. I don't want that to happen to anybody in my department. The trick is to take a break as soon as you see a bright light and hear dead relatives beckon."

Although tongue in cheek, Adams captures a key principle: When you hit a point of overworking, it is time to stop. In our culture, we tend to ignore physical or emotional signals that it is time to quit, and we keep pushing on (or take a pill to numb the pain telling us to ease up). The result is usually greater stress, irritability, strained relationships, and often illness.

Your body always alerts you when you are about to step past the line of well-being, or already have. Each of us has a unique body part that signals stress as soon as it comes on. Some people get a headache; others indigestion, shoulder pain, a cough, allergy flare-up, cold, flu, or eliminative irritation. While you may be able to treat these symptoms with medicine, the ailment needs to be addressed at the core level rather than overridden. It is giving you a signal to step back and take care of yourself. If you try to deny or mask the symptom, you are shooting the messenger bearing a most helpful message.

While many of us have been taught to regard the body as our enemy and subdue it, it is really our best friend, always seeking to help us maintain or return to our natural state of well-being. Too much work—or too much of anything—puts our system off balance.

Sniffles or a cold sore are life's way of telling you that you have just gotten off balance, and it is time to reclaim your equilibrium. You do not have to quit what you are doing forever; just take whatever time you need to return to a poised state. From that position, you will feel better and accomplish far more than you would have if you just kept pushing yourself.

Thank your body for its signals. It is the best message service you could have.

What bodily irritation is your signal to stop or slow down?
How could you heed it better?

My body teaches me how to feel good.
I thank it for its wisdom, and I listen to its messages.

Success and Happiness

You don't have to go looking for love when it is where you come from.
— Attributed to Werner Erhard

USA Today conducted a survey in which a number of successful people were asked, "Which came first: success or happiness?" The results are striking: 65 percent of the respondents reported that happiness led to success, while 35 percent said that success had made them happy.

These findings run significantly contrary to much of what we have been taught. They demonstrate that happiness attracts success far more than success attracts happiness. Stated another way, happy people are twice as likely to be successful as successful people are likely to be happy.

The survey's results have two very practical implications:

1. Happiness is an experience you generate from the inside out. It is not something that happens to you; it is something you *choose*. Happiness is not the result of external conditions; it is the result of personal intention. Your relationships, job, living situation, car, weather, astrological alignments, bank account, and stock-market portfolio can go up or down, but you do not have to go up and down with them. It is quite possible to maintain joy in the face of outer change, because joy is an inside job.

2. When you are happy, the Law of Attraction will draw more success to you than when you are unhappy. So while you may think you need to work harder to be successful, the exact opposite may be true: you may need to drop struggle and get happier. Think about it: when you are considering buying a product or doing a project with someone, don't you feel more drawn to work with someone who is positive and fun? Joy is a magnet for good things that match it.

It might be time to rethink the road to success. It may, after all, be paved with delight.

How might your sense of happiness attract more good to you?

Happiness is mine because I choose it.
My inner peace draws good to me.

One Sentence Away

One must steer, not talk.

— Seneca

I took a media-interview training with Joel Roberts, an expert in radio and television interviewing. In this program Joel taught a group of authors how to maximize the impact of our appearance on interview shows.

One of Joel's most incisive lessons was: "You are never more than one sentence away from delivering your message." A good interviewee can take any question an interviewer asks, and with a one-sentence segue, use the question as an avenue to proclaim a message or sell a product.

You, too, can use this principle—perhaps to sell your product, but more important, to move a conversation into a zone that you find meaningful. If you find yourself conversing with someone who is negative and critical or seeks to take a discussion in a direction adverse to your intentions, you can get it back on track with a wisely chosen bridge of words.

For example, your partner begins to complain about the economy. You might respond by saying, "I know things may look bleak at the moment, but I'm sure they will turn around at some point. They always do. In the meantime, let's enjoy each other and all the blessings before us."

Or one of your friends begins to gossip about how bad another friend looks. You might answer, "Maybe it's because she has been under a lot of stress lately. She's had some difficulties with her kids, and her brother passed away. I think some time and love will bring her back around."

Or you might use humor to defuse a barb. If your mother asks you why you are not in a romantic relationship, say, "I've decided to become a missionary instead. Have you been saved?"

If you are dealing with someone who is disconnected from peace and *you* remain connected, you are in a more powerful position to take the interaction to a positive place.

How might you shift a mundane interaction
by taking a more uplifting approach?

I am connected to wisdom, and I easily
move my conversations to a rewarding place.

Your Ideal Day

The greatest achievement was at first and for a time a dream.
The oak sleeps in the acorn; the bird waits in the egg; and
in the highest vision of the soul a waking angel stirs.

— James Allen

In my seminars I lead an exercise called "My Ideal Day." If you would like to try it, write down in detail the most wonderful day you can imagine. The only requirement for each activity you list is that you choose it from a sense of joy and delight rather than routine or obligation. When seminar participants go through this process, they become very animated and inspired.

In one seminar, a woman read aloud her ideal-day essay. After relating many rewarding experiences, she read: "In the evening my husband and I go into Toronto to see our favorite opera performed by world-renowned singers. We ride in a big limousine, which allows my husband to stretch out his arthritic legs."

Clunk. "Why," I asked her, "would you include arthritis in your ideal day?"

"I guess my husband has had arthritis for so long that I can't imagine him without it."

"Perhaps," I suggested, "you can change that condition by not continuing to imagine it."

Be careful to build your intended experience upon your visions, rather than building your visions upon your experience. It is tempting to gauge what *could be* based on what *has been,* but that only perpetuates what has been. *Your history is not your destiny.*

If you have had a health challenge, a dysfunctional relationship, financial distress, or emotional pain for a long time, you can improve your situation by not including it in your plans. Abraham-Hicks teaches that every moment is changing to something new if you let it. If you are still getting what you have been getting, it is because you keep focusing on what was, so the new moment keeps changing back to replicate the old one. In any moment you can change to something *new,* not old. So if you are going to ride in a limo to the opera, stretch out your legs because it feels good, not because you have arthritis.

What would your ideal day look and feel like?

**I build my life on my loftiest visions, and
they become living realities in my world.**

A Big Chunk of Your Grade

What are we here for, if not to make life easier for each other?

— Source unknown

A college business student sat down to take his final exam, ten questions that would largely determine his grade. When he came to the last question, he could hardly believe his eyes: "What is the name of the cleaning lady in this building?" Since he did not know her name, he challenged the teacher as to the validity of the question. The professor answered, "If you intend to get anywhere in business, your success depends not just on spreadsheets, but on relationships."

Successful business leaders will tell you that you build your business by building relationships—which means you constantly ask, "What can I give?"

My friend Carla Gordan was a highly successful counselor. When I visited her home, she showed me the room where she did her sessions, mostly over the phone. Taped over the face of the telephone was a reminder note to herself: *"How can I help?"*

We are undergoing a major shake-up in the business and financial structure of our world. One of the reasons economics has gone awry is because individuals and corporations have allowed self-serving greed for money and power to overshadow integrity and care for people. When the bottom line of profits overshadows healthy relationships, corporations falter because they have lost heart.

Making money is an excellent goal to pursue. What many people do not realize is that in the long run you make the most money by recognizing the people who make your business. So knowing the cleaning lady's name is good for the business as well as the soul, and will always prove to be a significant part of your grade.

How might you build your success by
acknowledging and supporting people more?

I keep my heart in my work, and I seek to serve.
The more help I give, the happier I am
and the more my career thrives.

Don't Pray Yourself Short

We must learn to . . . keep ourselves awake . . .
by an infinite expectation of the dawn.

— Henry David Thoreau

While I was a guest on a radio talk-show interview featuring my book *Handle with Prayer,* a caller shared an inspiring story.

"When my daughter was scheduled for surgery, I asked my prayer group to pray for a positive outcome to the surgery," he recounted. "At the prayer group, someone asked, 'Why accept the surgery as a done deal? Let's pray that your daughter be healed without the surgery.' So we prayed for a natural healing. When I took my daughter for her next exam, the doctor informed me that her condition had cleared up and she no longer needed the surgery."

Sometimes when we pray or set goals, we make assumptions about what is available to us. We plot our route based on what we think we can get or on the options that others tell us are available. If you are not altogether satisfied with the options before you, it might be time to step back and question your assumption about the options. Very often if you think or pray outside the box, you will find vast terrains that you did not see from your previous level of thinking.

A problem may arise not so much because of the obvious issue before us, but to stimulate us to think more deeply. Seen from this vantage point, problems exist to move us to a higher level of thinking. Then the solution becomes obvious, and we have attained a new rung of consciousness that we can apply to all future issues and decisions.

The preceding story does not mean that you should not get surgery. It means that you should not settle for a solution unless it takes into account options grander than those you have noticed.

What options may be available to you that are bigger
than the ones you have been considering?

I seek and find a solution that truly answers
the question. I will not settle for less.

Reducing the Bylaws

There is much in the world to make us afraid.
There is much more in our faith to make us unafraid.
— Attributed to Frederick W. Cropp

A friend of mine was hired to be a church minister. Soon after she began, she called a meeting of the board of directors. "We are going to review the church bylaws," she announced. "Let's sift through them to find which elements proceed from fear and mistrust, and which come from trust and love. We will remove those motivated by fear and keep those inspired by faith."

The board dug into the bylaws, which at the outset comprised 44 pages. After the minister and board removed the fear-based elements, the bylaws were reduced to 18 pages.

You might like to do a similar cleanup on the rules you have created around your home, business, organization, or life. You may be surprised that many of the laws you have prescribed around your world are fear based. Consider how you might lighten up by letting them go.

When I first began presenting seminars, I worked with no contract. Then, after sponsors did things not to my liking, I created a contract that would hold them to their agreements. Every time something went wrong—such as the sponsor not charging the agreed-upon ticket price, or putting me in undesirable accommodations—I added a clause to make sure that did not happen again. Every year the length of my contract grew until it felt cumbersome.

One day I realized that the contract was largely fear based, so I cut it back to the bare minimum. That felt a lot better. I realized that sponsors messing up was the exception rather than the rule, and I would rather work from trust. Everyone liked this format better, and the programs suffered not in the least for it. They went even better.

Rules are helpful as long as they engender success and well-being. Once they become overbearing, cut them away like a piece of rotten wood.

Are the rules you live by motivated by fear or inspired by love?
Which fear-based rules could you let go of?

I live my life from a deep sense of trust and faith. I stand on integrity.

At Your Command

Once you make a decision, the universe conspires to make it happen.
— Attributed to Ralph Waldo Emerson

Evelyn was tired of the consulting job she had taken on in addition to her regular work. In a coaching session, she told me, "I wish I had the courage to say no to my boss Tom when he calls me back to consult. But I am afraid of losing the extra income, about $10,000 a year."

After we discussed the situation, Evelyn decided that the stress and strain of an extra job was not worth the money. She decided that the next time Tom called her, much as she hated to turn him down, she would tell him she was not available. She also decided to trust that her finances would be taken care of even if she did not take on this additional job, which was draining her.

During our next session, Evelyn was ecstatic. "You'll never believe what happened!" she exclaimed. "When I went into Tom's office, he told me that there's a new government rule that requires that the job I was doing as an outside consultant be done by someone inside the company. So I was off the hook without any effort. Then I received a memo from my supervisor at my regular job telling me that I had been given a $10,000 merit increase!"

I laughed with Evelyn as we marveled at the tangible result of her putting faith into action. Her desire to quit the consulting job was in alignment with her highest good, and she did not need to exert any struggle to rearrange her position. How easy can it get?

I joked, "Look how powerful you are! You got the government to make a rule that removed you from the job you didn't like, and saved you the trouble of saying no to your boss."

In a way, the government and Evelyn's company were at her command, playing out the intention she clearly held. The same result could have manifested itself through another channel. It does not matter. When Evelyn got clear about her intention, the universe got clear about the result.

You, too, can have any person or institution play out your intentions. They already are. Upgrade and clarify your intentions and watch miracles unfold.

How could you get clearer about your
intentions and attract what you want?

My role in creating results is real and powerful.
I make my choice, and the universe supports me.

True Victory

*Where there is compassion even the most
poisonous impulses remain relatively harmless.*

— Eric Hoffer

A young Japanese man named Shui was riding on a crowded train when a belligerent drunk made his way through the train car and began to bully the passengers. Shui had studied martial arts for many years, yet never before had he been forced into a public confrontation. He felt his blood begin to boil and realized the ruffian needed to be stopped before he hurt someone.

Shui stood up, blocking the fellow's path, and the two exchanged angry words. As the men were about to square off, Shui felt a hand on his arm. He looked down and saw a frail old man. "Let me handle this," the elder suggested.

Shui watched in amazement as the old man invited the thug to sit next to him. Strangely, he acquiesced. The elder began to engage the fellow, asking him questions about his life as he looked him in the eye with kindness and compassion. After a while, the man confessed that his wife had just died and he was in great pain; he had gone out and gotten drunk to numb his agony. The old man placed a comforting hand on the fellow's shoulder, and he began to weep. Before Shui's eyes, the ruffian was transformed from a villain into a vulnerable child.

When the train arrived at the next station, the tough guy thanked the old man and exited the car. Stunned, Shui sat down next to the elder and asked him, "Why did you stop me?"

"You were about to meet that man's violence with your own," he answered. "In true martial arts, if you hurt your opponent, you cannot call your act a victory."

We have all encountered people we feel we must protect ourselves from. Yet there is a way to keep ourselves safe without violence. We have been taught that we must wield pain as a weapon to keep others at a distance, but it is not so. The true master can disarm another without hurting him or her. Compassion is a far more powerful weapon than violence.

How might you end a conflict with compassion rather than resistance?

**I connect with an opponent on the level
of our sameness. I disarm hatred with love.**

I'm Starting to Like This Guy

Well-ordered self-love . . . is right and natural.
— St. Thomas Aquinas

At a seminar a fellow named Ted reported, "As a child, I saw my wealthy parents struggle, fight, and get greedy over money. As a result, when I became a civil trial lawyer, I resisted accumulating lots of money. Over my career I have done a lot of *pro bono* work and billed clients for fewer hours than I have put in. My peers criticized me for undercharging, but I have felt good about my practice. Now I need to send my children to college, and I'm having financial difficulties. I wonder if I should have charged more over the years. What do you think?"

It was obvious to me that Ted's judgments about his parents' relationship with money and his painful associations with it set him up to keep money at a distance. Now he needed to reframe money as his friend and recognize that he was worthy of having what he needed.

I invited Ted to come onstage, along with another fellow, who sat in a chair beside him. "Ted, imagine this is you sitting in the chair," I suggested. "Now imagine you are facing a jury to summarize your case for why this man, Ted, deserves to have all the money he needs to send his kids to college."

Ted was a good sport and agreed to enact the scenario. He began an eloquent argument highlighting Ted's positive qualities and deeds, and why he merited the needed funds. Then he suddenly interrupted his summation, pointed to "himself" sitting in the chair, and whispered, off-the-cuff, "I'm starting to like this guy."

That admission was more powerful than his statements to the jury. Ted had talked himself into appreciating who he was—and that was absolutely compelling.

Self-love and self-honoring are absolute prerequisites for success in the world and, more important, peace of mind and heart. When you accomplish those, the essential elements of your life line up in wondrous ways.

How might the results you are getting in your career
and life be tied to your sense of self-worth?
How might you open more to receive your desired good?

I love and honor myself and recognize that
I deserve all the good things my heart desires.

The Devil Goes to Church

Life is God's novel. Let him write it.

— Isaac Bashevis Singer

I attended a seminar on healing at a lovely little holistic health center near my house. The center is also an independent church that honors all faiths and spiritual paths. The sanctuary is decorated with flowers and inspiring photos of great leaders from various traditions.

During the seminar, I looked across the aisle from me and was surprised to see a woman dressed in unusual attire. Most striking was her sweater with a large embroidered image of a devil's face on its back. Her black spandex pants were covered with images of skulls and crossbones.

At first I was put off by her radical garb for a healing temple. *What's she doing here in that outfit?* my judgmental mind railed. *This is a place for love, not some devil!*

Then, as I relaxed and got over my judgments, I had a fascinating realization: She was in this place and wearing that outfit by the power of God. God is the intelligence by which the material of her outfit was designed and woven together. God created the colors in her devil sweater. God was the love and grace by which her heart was beating, her lungs breathing, her eyes seeing, and her mind thinking. Everything about her originated in the God of love.

I looked again, and she seemed like a nice enough person. She was participating in the seminar and not doing anything weird. She was there for the same purpose I was—to learn about healing. She wanted to feel better and maybe help others feel better. Perhaps she and I were quite the same at a fundamental level, and our differences were quite superficial.

God is the only power in the universe. The level of the devil, good and evil, conflict, and socially defined aberration is extremely superficial and not worth indulging. If you know Who God is, who you are, and how the universe operates, you need not fear or fight the devil. If you find him sitting next to you at church, at a seminar, or in your office, just love him and admire his outfit.

How can you reframe your vision of evil so you are not upset by it and do not fight it?

I see past superficial illusions and pierce to the truth of love.

What Are You Doing Back Here?

*You are prepared. . . . It would be far more profitable now merely
to concentrate on this than to consider what you should do.*

— *A Course in Miracles*

One Sunday a Unity church minister gave a talk on the importance of recognizing our connection to universal wisdom. "You already know everything you need to know," he told the congregation. "If you understood the depth of your true self, you could just go home and live a happy life, and you would never have to come to this church or another again."

The following Sunday when most of the same group showed up at church again, he asked them, "What are you all doing back here?"

The minister was kidding, but also teaching a lesson. Beware of any organization or belief system that teaches that you are dependent on it, and that horrible things will happen to you if you do not keep participating. By contrast, teachers or organizations that encourage you to find truth, strength, love, and direction from the God inside you are serving you in the highest way. They are empowering your wholeness and strength rather than your emptiness and weakness.

Does this mean you should not go to churches, seminars, meetings, or support groups? Not at all. The crucial issue is not whether or not you go, but *why* you go. If you feel uplifted, inspired, and connected to yourself, your friends, and your Higher Power by attending, then your time is well spent. Go because you would, not because you should. Then you will be there by joyful choice, not guilt or fear.

Sometimes in the early stages of healing or awakening, it is important to attend a group regularly to effect a desired behavioral change or new life direction. In such a case, your attendance may be more crucial than at a later stage when you have mastered the lessons more. Go if you need to temporarily, but ultimately any good organization is only as helpful as it gives you wings to fly.

*Are you attending any group due to fear, emptiness,
or guilt? What would you be doing differently if you
were choosing from wholeness and joy?*

**I am whole, strong, and clear,
as God created me.**

The Price of the Omelet

Ask for 100% of what you want 100% of the time.

— Stan Dale

While passing through the lobby of an Embassy Suites hotel, I noticed a large poster proclaiming: "You should be thinking about the omelet, not the price of the omelet." I smiled when I saw the ad, for it put into practical terms a key prosperity principle:

When faced with any purchase decision, one of the best ways to choose is to momentarily take money out of the equation. Ask yourself, *What would I be doing if money were not a factor?* The answer to that question may determine your next step.

While money is potentially a symbol of abundance and expansion, for many people it has become associated with fear and constriction. When we factor finances into a choice, it often obscures our vision. When we temporarily set aside the money issue, we begin to get clear about what we really want.

Someone gave me a gift certificate for a dinner for two at a fine Italian restaurant. I invited a friend, and we sat there perusing the menu. I told my friend, "Don't look at the prices. Just order whatever you want." Then I realized that I needed to take my own advice, for I have often made choices based on the price of the entrée. *How silly,* I thought, *since a few dollars here and there would make no real difference in my life.* At that moment I made a commitment that I would always make dining choices based on true preference, not price.

I am not suggesting you make decisions that will cause you anxiety about money or throw you into financial distress. I am suggesting, rather, that (1) you recognize that you are an abundant being living in a universe that supports you to have what you want, and (2) you spend time and energy focusing on your authentic goals so they become the driving force to attract the money you need. Money should be the servant of your visions, not their master.

What would you buy or do if money were not a factor?

I ask for what I sincerely want, and I receive it.
Money is my servant, not my master.

You've Got to Believe Me

*What could you not accept, if you but knew that everything
that happens, all events, past, present, and to come, are gently
planned by One Whose only purpose is your good?*

— *A Course in Miracles*

I dreamed that a friend of mine had just gone through a painful breakup. She felt devastated because she had thought for sure that this fellow was the man of her dreams and they would be together for life. Now she was heartbroken and discouraged, and was afraid to face her future.

In the dream, I was telephoning my friend from two years ahead in the future. From that vantage point, I knew what had happened since her breakup. During that time, she had met and married a wonderful man, and she was very happy. The breakup was of no consequence now; in fact, it had put her in a position to meet this fine fellow.

On the telephone in the dream, I told my friend, "I know this sounds crazy, but I'm seeing your life from two years ahead of where you are now. Your future is already history to me. Within the next two years you will meet an awesome man and be happily married. You've got to believe me."

My dream represents a powerful lesson for all of us. A wise sage could call any of us up and say, "Please listen to me. I am standing in your future, and I can tell you with perfect assurance that the thing you are worrying about now is going to turn out all right. You will have what your heart desires. You've got to believe me."

How wonderful life would be if we could each walk ahead with the faith that everything will turn out all right! From a higher perspective it is already so.

*How would you be feeling and acting differently if
you knew that everything would turn out all right?*

**Momentary setbacks cannot stop my good from
coming to me. I trust in the grand process of my life.
I will have my heart's desire.**

Disengage Mechanism

*. . . pause a while, extricate yourself from the maddening
mob of quick impressions ceaselessly battering our lives . . .
the viewer must be willing to pause, to look again, to meditate.*

— Dorothea Lange

In the film *For Love of the Game,* Kevin Costner portrays Billy Chapel, an aging major-league baseball pitcher who will soon be forced to retire, but faces one more crucial game to pitch in his career. When Billy takes the mound for his final performance, he is under tremendous pressure to thwart the opposing team.

As the game progresses, Billy, without really trying, is on his way to pitch a perfect game, which would be the crowning achievement of his lifetime. Toward the later innings, as tension mounts, the crowd goes wild, both for and against Billy, and the roar in the stadium is deafening.

Yet Billy has a technique to stay focused on his pitching. He tells his mind to "disengage mechanism," and instantly the clamor goes silent and disappears from his awareness. Then it is just him and the batter, a far more manageable forum than a house of crazed fans.

You and I might do well to develop our ability to "disengage mechanism." If people or situations around you start to get crazy, step back for a moment, take a deep breath, and do whatever you can to detach and release from the "movie" at hand. You can use the phrases *disengage mechanism* or *peace, be still* or any other affirmation, prayer, or technique that helps you gain a sense of calm and clarity away from the storm. Then, from this platform of strength and poise, you can act with mastery that was not available to you when you were caught up in the fray.

Each of us has a perfect game within us, but we must establish ourselves in a consciousness of perfection from which to execute it. Billy Chapel found his pitch . . . and so will you.

*What can you do to find clarity in the moments
when you need to rise above outer challenges?*

**I step back from the chaos of the world and
connect with my inner wisdom and peace.**

I Wouldn't Wish This on Anyone I Loved

Give yourself abundant pleasure, and you will have abundant pleasure to give others.

— Neale Donald Walsch

My friend Tricia is a brilliant businesswoman who has upon occasion worked herself almost to exhaustion. At one point her travel schedule was as onerous as 250 days a year. As a friend and coach, I had been encouraging Tricia to lighten up on her travels as an act of mercy to herself and as a contribution to her health and well-being.

One day Tricia told me that she was about to set out on a horrendous series of business meetings that would keep her hopping around the globe for nearly a month. I suggested that she take her right-hand assistant, Laura, who could ameliorate a great deal of the stress.

"Oh, I wouldn't wish such a trip on anyone I loved," Tricia answered firmly.

"Then why would you wish it on *yourself?*" I had to ask her.

Tricia agreed that she had a double standard in her work and life. While she was kind, considerate, and supportive to her staff, she would force herself to do things she would never ask of others. "Something is definitely wrong with this picture," I told her. Later Tricia told me that she was taking her assistant with her, and as a result her travels were easier.

Psychic self-injury is neither heroic nor practical. You cannot say that you have mastered love until you include yourself in its embrace. If you make everyone in your life happy but yourself, you have missed the point of living and loving. Self-honoring is the beginning of true service. When you practice self-nurturing, others around you will catch the energy and you will create a wave of well-being that far supersedes the illusory benefits of self-sacrifice.

Do not do anything to yourself that you would not wish on anyone else. Instead, do everything for yourself that you would do to make others happy . . . and the world will be a happier place for everyone.

What are you doing to yourself that you would not wish on anyone else?
How could greater self-care on your part be a service to others?

I take care of myself so I can be in the best position to empower others.

I Don't Play Hurt

I am not the victim of the world I see.

— *A Course in Miracles*

I began to feel irritated when the limo driver was late. After a long flight on the eve of an intense book-promotion tour, I was tired, and anxious to get to my hotel. Finally the limo arrived and the driver emerged. He was a tall, husky African-American man who resembled a cross between George Foreman and *Goldfinger*'s Oddjob. I decided not to get in his face.

En route, the driver, Terry, apologized for being late, explaining that he had been involved in a minor fender bender on his way over. When he asked me what I was doing in L.A., I told him I was promoting my new book, *Why Your Life Sucks and What You Can Do about It.*

Terry chuckled. "I can use that book."

A few minutes later, I heard Terry reporting the mishap to his dispatcher over the two-way radio. "Was there any damage to the car?" asked the dispatcher.

"None," Terry answered curtly.

"Did you get hurt?" was the next question.

"Not really."

After a silence, the dispatcher replied, "You know, there could be some cash in this for you."

When I realized the dispatcher was suggesting that Terry file a false insurance claim, I waited for his response. A moment later Terry answered in a low, sober voice, "I don't play hurt."

Now there is an affirmation to file in a conspicuous place: *I don't play hurt.* That is exactly the principle I have been striving to live and teach for my whole career. Stunned, I placed a hand on Terry's shoulder and told him, "You don't need my book, man—you're already living it."

None of us can afford to play hurt. When you do, you undermine your true strength and you live a lie. Do not play small. Do not act like a victim. Do not seek rewards for pain. Be magnificent. Be powerful. If you are going to play any role, play strong and whole, for that is who you truly are.

Are you playing hurt in any area of your life?
What would you be doing differently if you played whole and strong?

I am strong, whole, and empowered.
I don't play hurt.

Get Off the Runway

Slow down and everything you are chasing
will come around and catch you.

— Attributed to John De Paola

Do you ever wonder why something you have been praying for has not come? Are you frustrated that your efforts have not shown a return? Have you been working hard to achieve your dreams, but they keep eluding you?

If so, imagine you are at an airport where an airplane you are waiting for is about to arrive. This plane contains all the good you have been asking and striving for. It holds your material good, in the form of money and things; your relationship good, in the form of a wonderful love partner; vibrant health; inner peace; and everything you deeply desire.

The moment you catch sight of your airplane of blessings, you dash out onto the runway and yell, "Here I am! This is the runway! Hurry up! Land here!" Then you run up and down the runway, pointing to the landing spot, fervently beseeching the aircraft to land.

But the plane cannot land while you are dashing frantically around the runway. It needs you to get out of the way first. Your best move at that point is to quit yelling and step aside for a moment.

According to The Teachings of Abraham, there are three steps in the manifestation process: (1) you ask, (2) the universe answers and sends your requested good, and (3) you receive. The first two steps occur naturally without a lot of thought or stress on your part. The zone that requires your care and attention is step 3, in which you receive.

Are you a good receiver? Many people are good at asking for themselves or giving to others, but not so good at receiving for themselves. They are so busy trying to *make* good things happen that they cannot *let* good things happen. Try relaxing, trusting, and making space. After you have done what you can on your own behalf, take a seat beside the runway and you will have the pleasure of watching the airplane of your good arrive gracefully, without exhausting yourself to tell it where to set down.

How might you relax more about
what you seek and let life help you?

I do *my* part, and I let the universe do *its* part.

Open to See

*Become a possibilitarian. No matter how dark things
seem to be or actually are, raise your sights and see possibilities—
always see them, for they're always there.*

— Norman Vincent Peale

Today is the day acknowledged as the one on which Christopher Columbus set foot in the Americas. When Columbus's three ships arrived in the Bahamas, a fascinating phenomenon occurred: While his ships were anchored at a distance offshore, because the vessels were not in the natives' known reality, the people did not see them for quite a while. One day a shaman, whose mind was open to realities beyond the obvious, saw the ships; and when he told his people about them, they saw them for the first time.

There are realities available to you that you do not see because you are unfamiliar with them or do not believe they are there. You might search a room for your car keys and not find them because you believe you left them someplace else. You may pass over the spot several times and overlook the keys even though they are in plain sight. When you call a family member over to help you find them, the other person sees them instantly. That person found them because he or she did not expect them to not be there.

Reality is not limited in any way, except in your expectations and beliefs. If you sense that there may be more to life than the world you are seeing, the first step is to open your mind to the *possibility* that there may be more. The second step is to quit arguing for why things are the way they, or resisting or complaining about what is. "What is" is highly subjective and generally fraught with limiting illusions. "What can be" is also subjective, greater than your familiar world, and available if you are open to seeing and claiming it.

There may be ships offshore that can deliver the good you have been seeking. Ask the shaman within you to open your eyes, and your ship may soon come in.

*How might you be sustaining an unwanted reality by focusing on it?
How might you experience a more satisfying reality by being open to it?*

**I lift up my eyes to see what is available
to me, and I claim it now.**

What Channel Are You On?

*We either make ourselves miserable, or
happy and strong. The amount of work is the same.*

— Attributed to Francesca Reigler

My friend Kathy told me about a clever method she uses to keep her elementary-school physical-education class in a healthy state of mind and behaving well. She tells them, "There is a Happy Channel with programs you really like, and a Sad Channel with programs that make you feel bad. You can watch whichever one you want, and you will feel like the channel you are watching." Kathy posts the names of both channels on the chalkboard for reference.

When students get into a negative behavior pattern, she points to the Sad Channel term on the board and reminds them that they have slipped into being mean or uncooperative. The kids understand the concept and usually shift their behavior quickly. Even at a young age, these students recognize the importance of tuning to a healthy, rewarding frequency.

While this method may sound simplistic, it represents a principle we can use as adults. At this moment there are countless invisible communication channels rippling through the room you are sitting in. Hundreds of television channels are beaming unseen, along with many radio stations, cell-phone signals, and wireless computer frequencies, to name just a few. You will be the receiver of the station you are attuned to.

Thoughts and emotions, too, have frequencies, and every thought and emotion you focus on leads you to more of the same. If you are angry and upset, you will find more and more reasons to be angry and upset. If you are appreciative and expecting good, you will find more and more reasons to attract success. You will always hear more of the station you are tuned to, so take care where your dial is set.

Kathy is teaching her students far more than physical education. She is teaching them life.

*Which channel are you watching at this moment?
Is it getting you what you want?
If not, which station would you rather watch?
How can you switch your channel?*

**I am conscious about the thoughts and feelings
I entertain. I choose my frequency.**

I Know This Sounds Weird

Knowledge is power, but enthusiasm pulls the switch.

— Attributed to Ivern Ball

While Dee and I were perusing the stock in a granite warehouse, the owner showed us some samples for our desired kitchen counter. Russell's face lit up as he described the unique qualities of each piece. Then he picked up one and explained with boyish pride, "When I saw this style, I just had to get some! I know this sounds weird, but I buy certain pieces just because I love them."

"That doesn't sound weird to us at all," I told him. "That's a great reason to buy stuff—far better than simply because you think it might sell."

How significant a factor is enthusiasm in your decision-making process? When considering a purchase, career, date, relationship partner, or vacation, do you base your choice on what you should do, what you have historically done, what other people advise you, what the formula says will work, or what is the cheapest? Or do you tap into the flow of life force and move from that?

The words and actions of people who enjoy what they do are far more compelling to customers than those who trudge through their day and work simply for money rather than joy. Salespeople who choose careers and items to sell because they love them have a huge edge over sellers who are not excited about their product or service. If you want to be successful in sales, sell what you love.

If you want your career to grow—and to enjoy it—let enthusiasm lead. I know stockbrokers, corporate managers, and excavators who make decisions more from the gut than the head. As a result, they are among the most successful in their trade. Even more important, they are among the happiest.

No, Russell, we don't think buying granite you love is weird at all. That's why we bought yours.

Do you choose the goods or services you offer
on the basis of the joy they bring you?
How could you choose differently to
align your work with your enthusiasm?

I make choices based on joy and intuition rather than obligation, history, or standard procedure.

Jet Packs and Wingtips

. . . I hope our wisdom will grow with our power . . .

— Thomas Jefferson

While most people would like to win a lottery, few who do so manage their winnings well. Studies show that most people who win large sums of money in a lottery revert to their former level of wealth (or lack thereof) within five to ten years.

Besides the financial issues, many winners face emotional challenges. Suddenly they have "friends" they never knew they had, family feuds erupt, and they fear for the safety of their children (who might be kidnapped). A certain number of lottery winners become alcoholics, some commit suicide, and many states provide support groups for lottery winners to help them maintain their mental health. So winning the lottery is not necessarily a dream come true—it can turn into a *bad* dream.

Meanwhile, other winners enjoy their money, and it enhances the quality of their lives and relationships. An accountant who studied the lives of lottery winners concluded, "People who were happy before winning the lottery are happier after winning. People who were unhappy before winning are unhappier after winning." So it is not money that makes or breaks you; it is how you think about it.

Receiving a massive infusion of energy like money, fame, or power is akin to adding a jet pack to your airplane. Suddenly you are going faster and farther, and everything you do is intensified. If your wings are straight and stable, you will have a speedy, fun ride. If your wings are twisted, your ride will be chaotic. So you cannot blame high energy for enhancing your trip or wrecking it. The shape of your wings, or attitude, determines the quality of your journey and where you end up.

Do not just pray for money, fame, or success. If you get these things without wisdom, they will be booby prizes. Instead, pray for the wisdom to use what comes to you in a way that enhances your life and the lives of those you love. Then you will really be a winner.

*How might you upgrade your attitude so that
you handle influxes of energy to your advantage?*

**I use spiritual wisdom to
manage my material good.**

The Last Time I Did Good

It is far more impressive when others discover
your good qualities without your help.

— Attributed to Judith Martin (Miss Manners)

I once went to Toronto to visit some new friends, a couple whom I respected and wanted to impress. After our dinner I headed for the kitchen to do the dishes, largely to demonstrate what a good person I was. As I was washing the dishes, I made noise and whistled once in a while to let them know I was doing good.

The last item to be washed was a large wok, the belly of which was dark with oil from cooking many stir-fry dishes. *Here is a chance to really do good,* I thought. *I'll clean the wok thoroughly.* I found a piece of steel wool and scrubbed the metal to the bone, until it was spotless and shiny as a mirror.

If you cook, you are probably wincing right about now. You know that a wok is *supposed* to have lots of oil in its base, which means it is well seasoned and produces tastier dishes. But I did not know that— I was busy doing good.

Just as I was finishing cleaning the wok, the hostess walked into the kitchen. I proudly held up the wok to show her, like a five-year-old presenting his mom with the finger painting he did in kindergarten. "Look, I cleaned the wok!" I bragged to my hostess.

To my surprise, she did not light up, hug me, and offer effusive thanks. Instead, her eyes bulged and her jaw dropped. "It took me three years to season that wok!" she exclaimed.

That was the last time I ever did good. If you are a do-gooder, I suggest you stop right now, before you really get in trouble.

What are you doing now to show that you are good that
you might not do if you trusted your inner worth more?

I do not need to prove I am good.
I am already good as I am.

Move to Top of Queue

My will shall shape the future. . . . I am the force; I can clear any
obstacle before me or I can be lost in the maze. My choice; my
responsibility; win or lose, only I hold the key to my destiny.
— Attributed to Elaine Maxwell

I belong to Netflix, an Internet service that mails me DVD rentals upon request. When I log on to my Netflix account, I see a list of movies I have ordered but which have not yet shipped. If I learn of a movie I want to see before waiting for it to work its way up through the list, I can click on a box entitled "Move to Top of Queue." Then that film becomes number one on the list, all the other selections move down a notch, and I receive my chosen DVD the next day.

You have the same power to reorder your life priorities at any moment. No matter what choices you have made in the past, what is happening now, or what you have set in motion for the future, when you change your mind about what you value and intend, your new choice takes precedence over former decisions and begins to stream your way.

Life is more liquid than it is solid, more an energy flow than a fixed entity. The people, events, and circumstances that show up in your experience are a result of the thoughts and intentions you have launched in the past. If you launch new thoughts and intentions now, then new people, events, and circumstances will show up to reflect your updated priorities.

You and only you are the one in charge of your queue. When you accept responsibility for the items in the queue you have chosen and claim the power to alter it based on what you now know and desire, your life will reflect your predominant intentions. Then your good will arrive as quickly and efficiently as a DVD showing up in your mailbox.

What value or choice would you like to move to the top of your queue?

I set my priorities, and the universe
helps me manifest them. My life is
an expression of my true choices.

Retire Before You Have to Work

*Before you embark on [a path] you ask the
question: Does this path have a heart?*

— Carlos Castaneda

In a hotel elevator I encountered a young boy, perhaps six years old, dressed in a dapper suit. "Are you a businessman?" I asked him.

"No, but I hope to be," he answered resolutely. "I intend to retire before I have to work."

When I recounted that story at a seminar I presented the next day, a fellow stood and reported, "I was a physics professor for many years, and I enjoyed myself for a long time. I retired when it became work."

Perhaps it is time to rethink the concept of work. The very idea of "work" suggests that you have to do something you would rather not do. What a horrible attitude to begin each day with and carry through the hours! I suggest you remove the concept of work from your mind-set and replace it with "career," "livelihood," or "vocation." The word *vocation* proceeds from the same Latin root as *voice,* indicating that your true career is the one you feel called to do by your inner voice. Then it is really a livelihood, not a deadlihood.

Certainly there are some aspects of any career that you would prefer not to do. But if your overall joy and intention is an expression of your spirit, these aspects are minor in comparison to the Big Picture of your vocation. Is your vocation generally joyful, with some pieces that are distasteful, or generally distasteful, with some happy moments?

Do not settle for a career devoid of joy. Keep telling the truth about your heart's desire until you find a path that feels less like work and more like fun. In some cases, you can transform your current situation to become more satisfying. In other cases, it may be time to move on. When your day starts to feel more like work than play, stop and ask yourself where your inner voice is calling you. Then you can retire before you have to work.

*What career path would you choose
if you followed your inner calling?*

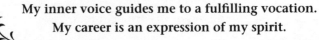

**My inner voice guides me to a fulfilling vocation.
My career is an expression of my spirit.**

That Look

Wheresoever you go, go with all your heart.

— Confucius

During a coaching session, Bonnie asked me for some suggestions about how she might more effectively discipline her eight-year-old son. "He's basically a good kid," she explained, "but sometimes he just doesn't listen, and it frustrates me to no end!"

"Are there any times when you can get him to listen?" I asked her.

"Well, yes . . . when I give him that look," she explained.

"'That look'?"

"If I really want him to do something, like put away his toys, and he doesn't comply, I give him a look that lets him know I really mean business. I don't even have to say anything. When he sees that look, he listens."

Bonnie was demonstrating the crucial relationship between intention and results. She admitted that lots of times when her son did not listen, part of her did not care that much. But when she really cared, he got the message and obeyed.

If you are not getting what you want in your family, relationship, or business, consider that the less-than-solid results you are getting are a match to your intentions. Do you really mean business, or do you have some leeway in your expectations? If so, your leeway in intention will play itself out in the recipient taking leeway in action. If you were really serious about getting something done, it would happen.

You can tell what you believe by what you are getting. If you are not getting all you want, revisit your beliefs. If something is really important to you, get clear and send the message. Then, like Bonnie, you may not even have to say a word. "That look" may do the trick.

In which situations have you been getting less-than-desirable results?
How might you improve your results by
clarifying and communicating your intention?

I am clear about what I want.
I state it, and I receive it.

Historical Documents

The difficulties of life do not keep you
from greatness. They show you to its door.

— Alan Cohen

The movie *Galaxy Quest* chronicles the adventures of a washed-up crew of actors whose popular sci-fi TV series has run its course. Their careers have dwindled to signing autographs for nerds at cult fan conventions. One day the crew is kidnapped by some genuine extraterrestrials, who take them for a (long) ride and explain that their distant planet is under siege and they need the courage and expertise of the crew to save their world.

"What makes you think we can help you?" asks the captain. An extraterrestrial explains that the aliens know of the crew's heroism because for years they have been reviewing transmissions of the crew's historical documents.

The "documents" he refers to are not historical at all. They are the television transmissions of *Galaxy Quest* reruns, which the aliens assumed were fact rather than fiction. When the crew tries to explain this, their hosts do not believe them; all they know is that they desperately need help, and they believe the crew can handle the job. So, under siege and with little choice, the crew members throw themselves into the task at hand. Although they are at first inept and bumbling, eventually they rise to the occasion and succeed in extricating the aliens from their predicament. Their "historical documents" were closer to the truth than their meager self-images.

Sometimes life pushes us to find strengths and abilities we did not know we had. We thought we were awkward, inept actors; while in truth we have the wisdom and power to handle any task that confronts us. We thought our greatness was fictitious, but it is literal. We might even be tempted to argue for our limits and explain why we are not who admirers think we are.

But such an occasion is a great opportunity to keep your mouth shut and just go ahead and be great. All you have to lose is your identity as a loser.

How might you actually be up to the task
at hand, and able to master it?

I believe and act on the truth of my strength,
not the illusion of my weakness.

Not Gonna Take It Anymore

To tolerate everything is to teach nothing.
— Frederick Joseph Kinsman

In elementary school, a group of three boys bullied me daily, intimidating and embarrassing me in front of my peers. I put up with their heckling for a long time, but inwardly I was seething.

One day I walked to the front of the class for show-and-tell, where I held up and described a model boat I had put together. On my way back to my seat, one of the boys stuck his foot into the aisle and tripped me, sending me to the floor and the boat crashing to pieces. Instantly all the frustration and rage I had suppressed in the wake of these boys' harassment exploded. I lunged at the one who tripped me, then went for the other two and chased them around the classroom, jumping over desks and banging against lockers. Finally the teacher corralled me and marched me to the principal's office, and I was sent home. The teacher told my mother, "Alan just went berserk."

I was back in school the next day, and those boys never bothered me again.

Sometimes you have to get to a point where you refuse to put up with the intolerable. Usually that refusal comes forth dramatically, an expression of all the moments you *did* put up with it and wished you did not. But when it comes out, it is powerful and often ends an ongoing issue.

Breaking free of unwanted patterns does not have to be violent. I am not encouraging you to go berserk. I *am* encouraging you to tell the truth about what is unacceptable so you do not have to get to the point of rage or violence before you express yourself and call for what you really want.

Are you putting up with the intolerable?
What truth would you have to tell to change it?

I refuse to accept that which demeans me or others.
I speak my truth and stop what is intolerable.

Who's Really in the Band?

Cherish forever what makes you unique,
'cuz you're really a yawn if it goes.

— Bette Midler

The video of *The Beatles Anthology* offers some fascinating insights into the minds and hearts of the renowned band. Ringo Starr revealed that at one point he wrestled with whether he was worthy of being in the band. "I decided that the other three guys were the *real* Beatles, and I was the odd man out," he confessed. So Ringo went to George Harrison and told him that he was thinking of quitting the group.

"Odd you should tell me that," George replied. "I was just thinking that *you* three are the real Beatles, and *I* should quit." Later the pair told the story to Paul McCartney, who revealed that he, too, had misgivings about whether he really belonged in the band.

You might chuckle to hear this account, since the Beatles were, well, the Beatles, and it is hard to imagine the band without any of those four talented musicians. Yet each in his own way went through a dark night of the soul, feeling less than and "out of the in crowd."

The ego, or self-doubting mind, will play all kinds of tricks on you to make you question your value and your sense of belonging. It will tell you that there is something wrong with you; that others know what they are doing, while you do not; and that you are a phony who will be discredited and ostracized if the truth about you were exposed.

Believe none of this. You have as much to offer as anyone else, and when it comes to your unique gifts and talents, you have *more* to offer than others. The next time you start to doubt yourself or your worth, remember that even members of the Beatles at one time wondered if they were *really* Beatles. Then dismiss their foolish doubts, as well as your own.

Is your mind telling you that something is wrong
with you or that you do not belong?
How can you recognize and acknowledge
your genuine value and contribution?

I have as much to offer as anyone,
and in some cases, more. I belong.

The Trip of a Lifetime

There is no end to the adventures that we can have,
if only we seek them with our eyes open.

— Jawaharlal Nehru

While perusing the lavish buffet at a resort hotel, Dee and I met the restaurant's master chef, a portly Austrian fellow named Hoerst. As he enjoyed schmoozing with his customers, Hoerst recounted the exotic details of his recent full-month trip to Africa. His eyes brightened as he described the magnificent flamingos, elephants, gazelles, and birdlife. In moments he was transformed from a 70ish man to a little boy.

"That sounds like the trip of a lifetime," I commented.

But not for Hoerst. "Oh no," he countered. "Next year my wife and I want to go to Machu Picchu."

I realized then that I had jumped to a conclusion. Hoerst was not an almost-retired senior who had gotten in one good trip before he croaked. He was an ever-youthful spirit who was in life for the distance, and the moment he finished one exciting adventure, he was on to the next. You will not find Hoerst sitting on his plastic-covered couch showing his bored grandchildren crinkled photos of his long-gone days in the sun. His life is a long, *brilliant* day in the sun, every new adventure a stepping-stone to a greater one. Hoerst is one of those rare people who live in constant, total amazement.

When I departed from the buffet later that evening I felt deeply nourished—not just from the food, but from my conversation with Hoerst. In our brief encounter, he taught me that the goal of our journey on Earth is not to have the trip of a lifetime, but to remember that all of a lifetime is the trip.

How might you appreciate more of your journey
rather than focusing on the highlights or a goal?

I open my eyes to the gifts, blessings,
and miracles around me. My life is an ongoing
adventure that keeps getting better.

Wow 'em

Man is only great when he acts from the passions.
— Benjamin Disraeli

Charlene was a skilled caterer who wowed participants with delicious, healthy meals at our residential seminars. Over time, however, the variety and presentation of her cuisine became blander, and we were receiving less favorable feedback about the meal service. Finally I had to tell Charlene that her catering was not what it used to be and ask her why.

Charlene explained that she had different things going on in her life than when she had started working for us. Catering was not as exciting to her as it used to be, and she had enrolled in a program to earn a social-work degree, a career into which she planned to transition.

I told Charlene that I appreciated the turn her life had taken, but we still required the high quality of catering she had demonstrated when she began her stint with us. I explained that if she could strive to wow people at every meal as she once had done, we would love to keep her on. If not, we would need to seek a new contractor.

Charlene thought for a moment and asked, "How about if I wow them for dinner but serve them a regular lunch?"

That answer did not quite hit the bull's-eye. Charlene's heart was no longer in her meal service; and for programs that taught participants to put their whole heart into whatever they did, she was not a match to our intention. We found a new caterer who was a 10 at wowing, and the participants were again inspired not just by word, but by experience.

Later Charlene thanked me for letting her go. She had quit catering, and she threw herself into her social work, where she felt more rewarded. So my commitment to passion served her as well as our program.

When you work with full passion, you create huge success for yourself and your clients. When you act with less than a whole heart, everyone remains hungry. Be honest about where your energy is streaming, and go there. Then you will wow everyone around you, along with yourself.

Where does your passion live?
What would it take for your life to reflect your passion?

I allow enthusiasm to lead me to my right place.
My passion uplifts me and everyone I influence.

Not Rich Enough to Buy Cheap

My old father used to have a saying, that,
"If you make a bad bargain, hug it all the tighter."

— Abraham Lincoln

At a prosperity seminar, I met a woman who had grown up in Russia. She quoted a famous Russian proverb, which she translated as: "I'm not rich enough to buy cheap things."

When I asked her about the meaning, she explained, "When you buy cheap things, cut corners, or do anything with an intention of less than full quality or integrity, you think you are saving money. But in the long run, such an act will cost you more." I could see her point. Cheap things break, and you have to repair or replace them. Buying from people who offer you a hot deal usually costs you more peace, joy, and money in the long run than if you had claimed excellence when you began. Acts that proceed from poverty thinking propagate poverty conditions. So you cannot afford what living from a poverty mentality will ultimately cost you.

As I consider my own business dealings, I realize that every time I have tried to get something for nothing or struck a bargain with a shady character, it has cost me more than if I had just stepped up to the plate and paid what a quality product or service was worth. When you make a stand for integrity, the universe gets behind you in ways far more rewarding than when you play games.

Consider which acts in your current life proceed from a wealth mentality and which acts proceed from a poverty mentality. Think, also, of how you are dealing in your friendships, family, and other relationships. Practice thinking abundantly and acting from an expansive mentality. You are not rich enough to buy cheap, but you are rich enough to buy quality.

What acts are you engaging in from a poverty or scarcity mentality?
What would you be doing differently if you
proceeded from abundance and integrity?

I prime wealth by
making quality purchases.

Identity Theft

. . . be free, all worthy spirits,
And stretch yourselves, for greatness and for height.

— George Chapman

Identity theft is a troublesome issue for lots of people. Every day unscrupulous individuals impersonate unknowing people and bilk millions of dollars through credit-card fraud and other illicit means. As a result, credit-card companies and banks go to elaborate security measures to protect their customers' true identities.

There is an even more insidious form of identity theft of which you are already a victim, one that has hijacked far more than your credit-card account. This theft has caused you to forget who you really are and assume a false identity that has been laid upon you by others.

"Grand theft identity" begins soon after you arrive on Earth and intensifies with age. Parents, teachers, siblings, and religious authority figures told you that you are small, limited, stupid, inept, insignificant, and sinful. Over time you began to believe them; and the day came when you forgot your innate wisdom, beauty, strength, and innocence, and adopted an identity contrary to your divine nature.

This erroneous identity is the only thing that keeps you from living your true purpose and being all you can be. To step into your power, you must shed this illusory identity like a coat that is too small for you. Make it your foremost priority to discover and remember who you really are and live confidently as that wonderful person.

To do so, pray or meditate each day with the intention of re-membering and reclaiming your wholeness. Never speak words about yourself that affirm smallness or lack. Act on your intuition, and re-fuse to do what insults your soul. Over time you will feel less and less like the broken person you were taught you were, and more and more like the whole being you *are.*

Protect your identity today. Let no one steal your greatness. It is given to you by God and is rightly yours forever.

What erroneous identity have you adopted?
How can you reclaim your true self?

I remember who I am.
I am as God created me.

Honesty or Brutality?

*People who are brutally honest get more satisfaction
out of the brutality than out of the honesty.*

— Richard J. Needham

We all encounter situations in which we need to tell someone something he or she will probably not want to hear. Perhaps you need to end a relationship, let an employee go, or confront someone about a financial issue. When the time comes for the uncomfortable conversation, many people err in one of three ways: (1) they avoid the confrontation, and the unwanted situation goes on and gets worse; (2) they deliver a meek presentation, and the recipient of the communication does not take them seriously; or (3) they bludgeon the recipient with a brutal onslaught of judgment or cruel remarks.

None of these situations yields the result you desire. Yet there is a way to say what you need to say and resolve the situation peacefully. As an Arabian proverb suggests, "When you shoot an arrow of truth, dip its point in honey."

The more kindness you add to your communication, the more likely the recipient will receive your message. You can say just about anything in a way that leaves the other person feeling like you are not the bad guy and he or she is going to ultimately succeed. In the course of my career, home ownership, and relationships, I have occasionally had to break off some associations. While none of these situations is attractive, I have developed the habit of praying before addressing the person, asking, *What is the kindest way I can deliver my message? How can I show the recipient that this change may be in everyone's best interest?* I am happy to report that I have been able, for the most part, to resolve these situations with a sense of mutual support.

Remember why you are saying what you need to say, and try as much as possible to see beyond your upset. How would you like to receive the communication if you were in the other person's place? Then speak from your heart, clearly and lovingly; and trust that honesty and kindness are not mutual enemies, but a winning partnership.

*How might you succeed at a potentially difficult
conversation by blending truth and kindness?*

**I skillfully merge honesty and love, and
create results that work for everyone.**

Just One More Room

The more you live, the less you die.

— Source unknown

Sarah Winchester believed that unless she kept adding rooms to her San Jose mansion, she would die. So the house was under construction for 38 straight years until it comprised 160 rooms!

While Ms. Winchester's building practices may seem neurotic or superstitious, her action illustrates a certain principle of ongoing growth. We all need a purpose, a project that gets our juices flowing and keeps our life force moving. Without something to focus on with passion and purpose, we shrivel up and die, literally or spiritually.

The notion of retiring from work is deceptive. While it may be attractive to quit a job you dislike, a life of pure leisure is less beneficial than a life with purposeful pursuits. Statistics show that people who retire from work but stay active with community or family projects live longer than those with nothing much to do. Activity with intention yields life. What you do with the time you have is more important than the time you have to do it.

There is a time for work and a time for rest, play, and renewal. Most people work too much, and in professions they dislike, so they dream of a time when they will not have to go to work. But the key is not to quit working; the key is to quit doing what you hate. Do not wait until you retire to decide to do something you like. Instead, be honest about where your joy lives, and pursue it at any age. Then you will see that passion is not just a part of life. Passion *is* life.

If you are bored, sick, or depressed, your healing will surely be facilitated by immersing yourself in a project that stirs you. I have seen many people overcome depression and illness by pursuing creative endeavors. The most direct path to a long and happy life is one that inspires you and challenges you to grow. Then you will trade a rocking chair for a rocking life.

What project stirs you?
What step could you take to do it, or do more of it?

I direct my time, skill, and energy to
purposeful activity. I do what brings me life.

Dangerous Moments

People who fly into a rage always make a bad landing.

— Will Rogers

A Tibetan Buddhist monk was incarcerated for 18 years as a political prisoner of the Chinese. After he was released, an interviewer asked him if he had ever been in serious danger. "Yes, about three times," the monk explained.

"How so?" the interviewer asked him. "Were you tortured?"

"No," the monk replied. "Those were the times I grew angry."

What happens to your spirit is far more significant than what happens to your body. We all know people who have great material wealth but are miserable spiritually. We also know people who have little in the world, but are *soaring* spiritually. You can, of course, be wealthy materially as well as spiritually. It is all a matter of attitude.

You live life simultaneously on two dimensions:

1. On the horizontal dimension, you move through your story line in the world. You were born in a certain family, you went to school, perhaps you got married and have your own family, you go to a particular job each day, and so on. This is the story that most people would relate to if they were asked, "Tell me about your life."

2. At the same time, you also live on a vertical or spiritual dimension. You have ups, downs, joys, sorrows, a sense of connection or disconnection, and a whole realm of experiences invisible to the eyes of most observers.

While your horizontal dimension is important, because you are a spiritual being at your core, your vertical dimension is even more significant. So no matter what occurs in your worldly story, your real quest is to maximize your sense of well-being, which is independent of any particular form on the horizontal dimension.

When the monk noted that he was in danger when he became angry, he was affirming that his primary commitment was to inner peace, and he evaluated his success in life by how much he stayed connected to that peace. His body could be incarcerated, but not his soul.

If inner peace is the real measure of success,
how much danger are you, or have you been, in?

The life of my spirit is my real life. I evaluate
my success based on my degree of inner peace.

How to Produce a Classic Scene

It is a mistake to look too far ahead. Only one link
in the chain of destiny can be handled at a time.

— Winston Churchill

What would you say are the three most memorable scenes in cinematic history? My answer would be:

1. The chariot race in *Ben-Hur*
2. Moses parting the Red Sea in *The Ten Commandments*
3. Meg Ryan's faked orgasm in *When Harry Met Sally*

When I did some research on the Internet Movie Database (**www.IMDb.com**), I learned some fascinating facts about these famous scenes:

1. The *Ben-Hur* chariot race occupied about 12 minutes of the movie, but required five weeks to shoot. The scene holds the record for film-shot-to-film-used ratio—263:1. For every 263 feet of celluloid used to shoot the scene, only one foot of film was included in the final cut.

2. Over 300,000 gallons of water were poured into a tank to create the special effects for the *Ten Commandments* Red Sea–parting scene. Then the film was played in reverse to create the illusion.

3. Although the *When Harry Met Sally* orgasm scene occupied but three minutes of the movie, it took an entire day to film until director Rob Reiner felt it was just right.

These facts tell me that sometimes it takes lots of tries and angles before you get something right—but when you eventually *do* get what you want, the final product is spectacular.

So it is that greatness is built—not overnight or in a flash, but through the steady development of skill, consciousness, and heart. So you need not be discouraged if you did not get your first marriage(s) right, you have had a career setback, or your health issue did not clear up overnight. Like the great movies above, you may have to walk through many takes to get the scene just as you would like it. But when you do, what a scene it will be!

On what project or area of your life would you be willing to persevere
if you knew you would eventually end up with a spectacular ending?

My faith, patience, and perseverance
yield outstanding results.

Banishing Boggarts

Fear grows in darkness; if you think there's
a bogeyman around, turn on the light.

— Dorothy Thompson

The film *Harry Potter and the Prisoner of Azkaban* depicts a group of young wizards in training standing before an imposing armoire—a boggart box—which contains terrifying shape-shifters assuming the form of whatever a person fears the most. Luckily, instructs Professor Lupin, a very simple charm exists to repel a boggart: "Riddikulus!" After the students practice the chant, the professor explains that what really finishes a boggart off is laughter. One by one the boggarts come forth, and when the students proclaim them "Riddikulus!" and laugh at them, they shrink to humorous, nonthreatening forms.

A truer teaching was never revealed.

On Halloween you may behold a parade of monsters, goblins, and ghouls walking along your street or knocking at your door. You are not afraid of them because you know they are just kids in costumes. You may even enjoy them, have a laugh, and give them a treat. You do not run and hide with fright, because you know they are not real and they pose you no threat.

Imagine how much lighter and freer your life would be if you related to the monsters and ghouls that show up in your daily experience in the same way. Perhaps we would all be wise to take Professor Lupin's advice to face these scary images, shout "Riddikulus!" and have a good laugh.

A famous poem declares:

Fear knocked at the door. Faith answered. No one was there.

Love is real, and the voice of fear is ridiculous. Remember this and nothing will ever hurt you again.

How could you dissolve a fear by lightening up?

Wherever I am, God is. There is no greater Power and no other Power.

An Excellent Dinner

Excellence . . . is not a capacity, nor a feeling, but a habit.

— Aristotle

My friend Terry took his daughter out to dinner on the eve of her wedding. Since this was the last father-daughter time he would have with her before she got married, he made reservations at a five-star restaurant and spared no expense.

As the two were finishing dessert, Terry decided to give his little girl a bit of fatherly advice on the threshold of her new life. "Whatever you do in your marriage, or your whole life, imbue it with excellence," he suggested.

"What's your idea of excellence, Daddy?" she asked.

Just then the waiter delivered the leather wallet containing the credit-card slip for Terry's signature. He picked up the enclosed pen and began to sign the slip. Terry hesitated for a moment and held up the pen. "Do you notice anything unusual about this pen?" he asked his daughter.

The young woman studied it and shrugged her shoulders.

"This pen is an advertisement for a cheap hotel chain," he noted as he pointed to the promotional writing on its side. "It is not a match to the quality of a restaurant like this, and I imagine it got here by mistake. When you're committed to excellence, all the elements of your presentation are equally excellent, and you don't make compromising exceptions. That's what I wish for you in your marriage and your life."

Excellence in any domain implies the integrity of all of its components. If you cheapen one aspect of what you do, you cheapen your entire product. Do your best to walk the high road of excellence in all you do and you will draw unto yourself excellent customers, an excellent income, and an excellent quality of life.

How could you upgrade your work and life to walk the high road of excellence?

I imbue all I do with the highest level of character, integrity, and excellence.

Not Crazy After All

Sometimes you just have to look reality in the eye and deny it.
— Garrison Keillor

Popular author and lecturer Wayne Dyer once mentioned that an excerpt from one of his books was included as a reading comprehension module in a scholastic aptitude test. For fun, Wayne took the test himself. You can imagine his surprise when he received a grade of *B*.

"How do you explain that the author of a book got only a *B* on his own material?" he asked the test administrator.

"Sometimes even authors don't fully understand what they wrote," the administrator replied.

The administrator's response was an evasion. Authors know their material. The interpreters of Dr. Dyer's writing had their own take on it—yet for them to assume that they knew what he meant better than he did is ludicrous.

If you have spent your life following what other people believe you *should* do, after a while you may think you are crazy for the path you feel guided to walk. But you are not. If anything is crazy, it is the idea that others are smarter about you than *you* are. So you are not crazy after all.

I saw an old movie in which a married man was having an affair with another woman, and the adulterous couple set out to convince the man's wife that she was insane. They manufactured a reality and did everything they could to make her believe that there was something wrong with her because she did not live in that reality. But their intentions were far more flawed than her sanity.

Most people are not malevolent like the scheming couple, but they do have their idea of how things are or should be. They have every right to live in the reality they choose if it works for them. But if their reality does not work for *you,* you cannot afford to live in it. You must make choices based on what you know rather than what others think you should know. Then, when you come to the end of your day or your life, you will receive a well-deserved *A*.

What do you believe but have doubted because others disagree?
How can you be more confident to live according to what you know?

I trust who I am and what I know.
I act with confidence on my intuitive guidance.

How Long Healing Takes

In a moment, in the twinkling of
an eye . . . we shall be changed.

— 1 Corinthians 15:52

When my neighbor passed away and his house came up for sale, our family bought it and set about the business of cleaning it up. While my neighbor was a dear fellow, he collected lots of junk. When I opened up his garage, I was appalled to find 20 years' worth of gnarly odds and ends. *Am I in for 20 years of cleaning?* I wondered.

Finally one Saturday morning, I rolled up my sleeves and hired two guys to help me dig into the mess. We found broken furniture, hardened paint in cans, and rat skeletons. (Did I wander onto an *Indiana Jones* set?) Yet we just kept plowing through the mire, tossing old rugs into garbage cans; trucking rusty scaffolding to the dump; and sweeping, sweeping, sweeping.

Around early afternoon I stepped back and realized, to my amazement, that the garage was mostly clean. I looked at the clock—it had been just about four hours since we began. How could that be? Twenty years of junk and only four hours to clean it?

The process of healing does not take as much time as it took to get sick. While you may have experienced many years of emotional or physical dysfunction, when you get onto a healing track, the issues that long bothered you can be dissolved and resolved in a far shorter time than it took to create them.

If you turn on a light in a room that has been dark for ten years, the room is just as illuminated as if the light had been turned on in a room dark for only ten minutes. The moment you shine the light, darkness flees. Transformation is not a function of history. It is a function of the powerful now.

Do not become discouraged or dismayed if you are seeking to heal a longtime issue. If a garage that has grown awfully messy over 20 years can be tidied in four hours, you can undo years of sleep in a moment of awakening.

How might you solve or offset a longtime issue
with a short period of focused positive attention?

Anything in my life can be healed
quickly as I sincerely set my mind and
heart to it and act accordingly.

Launch and Release

He who cannot rest, cannot work;
he who cannot let go, cannot hold on.

— Harry Emerson Fosdick

President Barack Obama has employed an interesting custom on election days: he plays basketball. From his first primary until the day he was elected President of the United States, he has stepped away from his home and office on nearly every Election Day and gotten into a vigorous game on the court with his friends. (Interestingly, he won the election on every day he played basketball.)

While someone superstitious might make a correlation between playing basketball and winning elections, a powerful metaphysical principle is operating behind the scenes of Obama's victories: *launch* and *release*.

During a launch phase, you do everything in your power to bring your project to life. You set goals, make contacts, take action, and accept responsibility for creating your desired results. This is an active, hands-on, I-can-do-it approach.

Then, when you have done everything you can, it's time to release. You let go, knowing you have done your part, and you trust the universe to do its part. You invite and accept the presence of a Higher Power that has the wisdom and wherewithal to accomplish the pieces of your project you cannot control. You also trust that if this project is in your best interest and the best interests of those involved, it will fly. If it is not in everyone's highest good, you are willing to let it go and make space for something better.

Barack Obama campaigned diligently, and when Election Day came, he let go. He did not keep pushing or sit at home anxiously wringing his hands. He was playing a higher game.

Many of us are so used to launching that we forget to release. Yet letting go might be just the action required to win.

After you have done your part, can you let go?

I act responsibly and then leave
space for the universe to help.
Together, we are a winning team.

Contagious Passion

Enthusiasm is the leaping lightning, not to be measured
by the horsepower of the understanding.

— Ralph Waldo Emerson

When a fellow at my luncheon table told me that his hobby was restoring military aircraft, I prepared myself for a long, boring diatribe. I could not imagine a subject further from my interests.

Yet as the man described his latest project, the museum he was establishing, and his ardent fascination with old planes, his passion was so strong that I began to catch it. While the subject was immaterial to me, his love for it was electric. The more he spoke, the more excited I felt. I thoroughly enjoyed the conversation, and when it was done, I felt uplifted and renewed.

Words mean little. Energy means everything. Because you are a spiritual being by nature, it is the spirit of an activity, or its lack, that fulfills you or leaves you cold. When you are afire with passion, you inspire everyone you touch, and you get results.

Some psychologists did an experiment to determine which kind of music affects people most profoundly. They invited musicians of many different genres to play for an audience, and then they measured the audience's response. The experimenters found that no particular kind of music affected listeners more than another. They did, however, discover that the key factor that moved the audience was the amount of passion with which the musicians were playing. Musicians who were absorbed in and excited about their music grabbed the audience's attention more than those who were playing by rote or seemed bored.

If you want to be a successful teacher, salesperson, coach, healer, or leader, the key element you must bring to your work is passion. Your clients will catch it from you and receive the message you intend to deliver. With passion, you are a dynamo; without it, you are lifeless.

Today and every day, monitor yourself and those around you for the passion you and they are exuding. Then gravitate to where the life force lives and it will carry you with a mighty power.

How passionate do you feel about what you are doing?
What would it take for you to be more passionate?

The passion of my spirit guides
me to my right place in life.
I go where the life force lives.

Most Like Yourself

*What you thought was wrong with
you may be what's right with you.*

— Alarius

Have you ever felt like a misfit in this world? Do you sometimes think you were dropped here by some otherworldly source, and you cannot relate to most people or what goes on around you? Do you feel like a pair of brown shoes on a tuxedo?

If so, you may have more company than you know. You may be a part of a very large group (perhaps over 50 million in the U.S.) called *cultural creatives,* a term coined by sociologist Paul H. Ray and psychologist Sherry Ruth Anderson to describe people who are disenchanted with traditional religion and societal roles, hold visionary values, and seek a lifestyle unlike the masses.

If so, one of your major life lessons may be to find and claim your right place in the great web of life. If you have felt guilty or weird for being spiritual, gay, uninterested in a corporate position, bored with television, unwilling to sell your soul for a mortgage, or bashful about revealing your psychic experiences, you may be closer to home than you know. You may be living exactly the life you came to live, and you simply need confidence to claim it without apology or compromise.

In the film *The Lake House,* one character feels lost and confused and does not know where to go. A friend advises her to go where she feels most like herself. So, too, must you go to the place where you feel most at peace and be with people who feel most like family. You do not need to attend perfunctory family gatherings, church services, or business meetings where you do not belong. They may be right for others, but if they are not right for *you,* you must seek people who match you at your core. Those who truly belong to you will greet you with open arms, and you will feel like you have finally come home after a long trek in the wilderness. Then your jigsaw piece will fit, and you will realize that the universe has a place for you.

*Where would you go or what would you do if
you were true to your unique preferences?*

**Who and what I am is perfect. I belong
to the universe. I go where I feel at home.**

Everything Comes Around

There is a destiny that makes us brothers:
None goes his way alone:
All that we send into the lives of others
Comes back into our own.

— Edwin Markham

Do you feel indebted to someone? Is someone is indebted to you? Do you fear that you will be unable to repay this person, or vice versa? If so, consider that everything comes around.

My photographer friend Ted took some excellent publicity shots of me. When I asked him what I owed him, he told me that he would not charge me, but perhaps we could trade. I offered Ted free tuition to an upcoming seminar, and he was happy with that.

During the following year, I eliminated his chosen program from my schedule. I felt bad, since I would no longer be able to offer Ted what I had promised. Later that year a mutual friend told me that Ted and his wife were divorcing. I knew this had to be hard for Ted, so I phoned him. Our call turned into an intensive coaching session, which my friend said helped him immensely. So the opportunity to return his favor came around in a way that worked for both of us.

Another time, a longtime coaching client named Sheri wanted to participate in an in-depth residential program for which the tuition was $2,500. Since Sheri was out of work, I told her to join in and pay me what she could, when she could. She participated and reaped a lot of benefits.

Time went by and Sheri did not pay. Then one day she mentioned to me that she had just bought a new flat-screen TV for $1,000. I was tempted to say, "Well, how about my $2,500?" but I figured it would come in its own way—or not—and I released the issue. The following year Sheri volunteered to organize a program for me in her city, with no payment to her. The program netted $10,000, and I considered the account happily settled.

Sometimes, of course, debts linger or are not repaid so amicably . . . or at all. Yet if you trust the grander process of the Big Picture, somehow everything comes around.

How might you relax about a debt, knowing that the
universe will provide a way for it to be repaid?

I trust that all debts will be settled in due time,
and I let the universe take care of business.

Inspiration and Motivation

Motivation is when you take hold of an idea.
Inspiration is when an idea takes hold of you.

— Dr. Wayne Dyer

I saw a video about a high school student named Jed who was failing his classes and getting into trouble. His parents, teachers, and counselors tried hard to motivate him to do better in school, but their efforts were to no avail. Nothing they did could get Jed out of his rut.

Then Jed discovered a sanctuary that rehabilitated injured hawks and birds of prey. Something about this work stirred him, and he began to visit the sanctuary every day after school. Before long he became a volunteer and learned a great deal about the winged creatures.

The final scene of the video showed Jed giving a lecture at the sanctuary, adeptly explaining the habits of these birds and the methods the sanctuary used to rehabilitate them. The camera panned to the audience, composed of several classes from the school at which Jed had been having such a hard time. The students in the audience were enthralled with Jed's presentation—he had become a local expert in the field, and he was shining.

I would not waste time trying to motivate people (including yourself) to do something they do not want to do. Instead, I would find out what moves them from the inside out, and assist them to bring forth their unique joys and talents.

When in a lecture I quoted Joseph Campbell, who encouraged everyone to "follow your bliss," someone asked me, "If everyone just followed their bliss, what kind of world would this be?"

My answer was simple: "It would be a very blissful world."

If everyone lived truer to their inspiration, everything would get done and everyone would be happier. While you may not be inspired to wait tables in a restaurant, there are people who would be completely happy to do so. Meanwhile, they could not imagine doing what you are doing. Somehow it all works out.

You cannot instill joy. You can only find where it lives and call it forth.

What inspires you the most?
How could you more fully express your unique calling?

I trust and follow my natural inclinations as
I support others to trust and follow theirs.

Everything I Need to Know about Meditation I Learned from My Jewish Mother

Knowledge is a process of piling up facts;
wisdom lies in their simplification.
— Attributed to Martin H. Fischer

When I first began meditating, I tried to convert my mother. But Jewish mothers have arsenals of truth that young meditators cannot begin to fathom.

"I already know how to meditate," she told me.

"Really?" I asked. "How do you do it?"

"I sit at the window of my apartment with my coffee in one hand and a cigarette in the other," she explained. "Then I just look out at the world going by, and my mind doesn't function. I don't think happy thoughts, and I don't think sad thoughts. I don't think any thoughts. It's the best part of my day."

Now, many years later, I recognize that my mother was far closer to real meditation than I was. In her own way, she had mastered the wandering mind—something I am still trying to do.

If the Jewish-Mother Meditation is valid—and it is—any activity that takes you beyond your intellect and connects you with your inner spirit is a good meditation. If you write, paint, dance, play music, or engage in sports, you know there is a state of awareness you enter where the small sense of self disappears and Something Greater moves through you. Or you may sit in silence, watch your breath, say a mantra, or become absorbed in the light within you. Anything that helps you find peace is worthwhile. It is your true source of happiness.

It has been a long time since my mother taught me the Jewish-Mother Meditation. Since then she has gone to heaven, and I am still learning to deal with a restless mind that tells me all kinds of things that are simply not true. When it is my turn to meet Mom in the afterlife, if I find her sitting with a cup of coffee in one hand and a cigarette in the other, I will not be surprised.

What do you do that connects you with inner peace?
How can you maximize that experience each day and in your entire life?

I do what it takes to quiet my mind.
In peace I know truth.

The Purpose of a Suitcase

Your treasure house is within; it contains all you'll ever need.

— Hui-hai

While waiting for my suitcase at an airport baggage-claim area, I noticed a conspicuous sign:

THE PURPOSE OF A SUITCASE IS TO PROTECT THE CONTENTS. SMALL CUTS, SCRAPES, AND SCRATCHES ARE A NORMAL PART OF TRANSPORTATION WEAR AND TEAR, AND THE AIRLINE IS NOT RESPONSIBLE FOR THEM.

Hmm. To follow the airport-sign analogy, your body is like a suitcase for your spirit. It is a focal point through which your inner being expresses. So damages or alterations to your body cannot affect the precious cargo it contains—your true self.

Yet we become hypnotized by values the outer world dangles before us, and we believe that the game of life is about the body, not the spirit. We go to elaborate measures to keep our physical selves looking perfect, unscratched and untarnished by the wear and tear of our transit through Earth life. Yet it is virtually impossible to keep the casing from getting bumped and bruised here and there. Or old. One day it will outlive its usefulness, and you will choose to discard it.

Yet when the suitcase is opened, it reveals and releases its priceless contents. The more we focus on the contents and the less on the container, the closer to truth and happiness we are.

A Course in Miracles likens the spirit/body relationship to a beautiful picture and its frame. If you have a magnificent painting, you want to set it in a frame that highlights the grandeur of the picture. If you go to elaborate measures to build a heavy, gaudy frame that draws more attention to itself than to the picture, you lose sight of the gift the frame was intended to highlight.

It is important to keep the body healthy and happy; indeed, there are those who err by denying it or attempting to crucify it into submission. Yet real happiness lies in the recognition that the joy you seek is available far below skin level. Then you can retrieve your baggage with a couple of bumps and scrapes and still rejoice, because what the suitcase contains is far greater than what is containing it.

How can you refocus so you find more value
in your inner self than in your social presentation?

My body is the vehicle through which
I express my true self. I am whole and eternal.

Brush with Greatness

I do not care so much what I am to others as I care what
I am to myself. I want to be rich by myself, not by borrowing.
— Michel de Montaigne

I received a voice-mail message from a friend who is a massage therapist at a luxury hotel. "Call me," she requested excitedly. "I have to tell you about my brush with greatness."

When I returned her call and asked her what had happened, she told me, "I massaged Dustin Hoffman today."

Well, that was cool. Yet something about her phrase "my brush with greatness" did not sit well with me.

"Dustin Hoffman is a great actor," I told her. "But when you say 'my brush with greatness,' it sounds as if he is great and you are not, and you were lucky to touch greatness for a moment. In my opinion, you are just as great as he is. You are an outstanding massage therapist and an awesome person. Who knows, maybe after his massage he phoned a friend and reported, 'I have to tell you about my brush with greatness . . .'"

My friend thanked me for my affirmation of her worth. Yet the lesson goes far beyond that one encounter. We have all been taught that greatness lives outside of us, and we need to rub up against it or import it so we can become great. That is exactly the opposite of how true greatness operates. Magnificence resides within all of us, and we need but tap into it and bring it forth. We do not need a brush with greatness; we need to simply brush *from* greatness.

People who idolize greatness constantly seek it outside themselves and remain on a frustrating quest, like the goat that pulls a cart in order to get a taste of a carrot that is hung just beyond reach. Those who look within for greatness realize that greatness is in them as a gift of life. Then they share it with quiet confidence and transform the world from the inside out.

Do you idolize anyone as greater than you, or
seek to become great by importing worth?
How would you proceed differently if you knew that
greatness already lives inside you?

I accept the gifts I have been given, and
I express greatness through my unique talents.

A Perfect Preparation

Evil is an interpretation, not a fact.

— Source unknown

I met a man who was a devotee of the miracles that took place near San Sebastián de Garabandal, Spain. Beginning in 1961 four children were regularly awakened during the night and mystically drawn to a small glen on the outskirts of their village. There they beheld an apparition of Mother Mary, who gave them prophetic messages and performed miraculous healings. This extraordinary phenomenon continued for four years, with more than 2,000 apparitions.

The devotee, Joe, was so moved by this inspiring phenomenon that he dedicated his life to sharing its message. One evening, Joe came to my study group, where he showed a film of the events and offered his narrative. After his talk, I asked him how he got into all of this.

"As a young man, I went to parties and told off-color jokes," he explained. "Eventually I was invited to men's clubs and banquets to recite my risqué stories. Since I had been shy before all this occurred, my performances built my confidence, and I gained public-speaking skills.

"When I learned of the Garabandal miracles, my life changed and I stepped onto my spiritual path. After a while, I gave up my dirty-joke career and channeled my public-speaking skills into this ministry. Needless to say, this work is far more meaningful. Yet I have to acknowledge that my career as an off-color comedian was a crucial stepping-stone to the service work I now do."

If you or I had met Joe during his risqué-comedy stint, we might have judged him as a crude or sordid character. Yet we would have had no idea that this phase was not an end in itself, but a preparatory step for lifework that would bring illumination and solace to many.

Do not be hasty to judge yourself for what you believe are your sins or guilty errors. Evil is an interpretation, not a fact. Everything that happens is ultimately in the service of awakening and may be seen as good.

How can you reframe your past or current
events so you see them as a blessing?

I interpret events so they empower me.

I am grateful for all my experiences.

Talk to the Hand

People see God every day, they just don't recognize him.

— Pearl Bailey

Keith Varnum recounts that when he was an intern on the set of the fabled television show *Mister Rogers' Neighborhood,* some of the stagehands made fun of Fred Rogers behind his back. The big, tough guys, Keith surmises, seemed threatened by Mister Rogers's gentle ways.

Their mockery evaporated, however, when during rehearsal Mister Rogers disappeared behind the puppet stage and worked a set of puppets. Something about the puppet theater was comforting to the stagehands, and they interacted amiably with the characters. They even delved into rather sensitive discussions and asked the puppets for advice. Meanwhile Mister Rogers was behind the scenes, delivering wisdom and compassion to these fellows through the puppet venue.

This odd scenario symbolizes how we relate to God. Since we have been taught that God is a wrathful, punitive entity to be feared or because we blame God for misfortunes, we may have difficulty relating to a Higher Power. Yet when someone appears in a body as a person we *can* relate to, we are more likely to communicate with the Divine through that familiar form. In this sense, a Jesus, Buddha, Krishna, Mohammed, or any great prophet or guru may serve as a comfortable way for us to connect with God.

Can we have a personal relationship with God and communicate directly? Indeed, as easily as the stagehands could have had a relationship with Mister Rogers if they were not threatened by him or they did not hold judgments about him. Is it okay to relate to a divine guide in the form of a person? Absolutely. That may be precisely why he or she has shown up.

Each of us has our own relationship with our Higher Power. Take comfort in yours today as you support and allow others to take comfort and find healing in theirs.

*How might you communicate more intimately
with the God of your understanding?*

**I relate to God in the way that is most
comfortable to me, and God responds.**

The Long Drive Home

*I am unable to understand how a man of honor could take
a newspaper in his hands without a shudder of disgust.*

— Charles Baudelaire

One of my coaching clients is the director of a psychiatric hospital. During one of our sessions, he asked me if I had some ideas about why he was exhausted at the end of his workday. "I go into work around 7 A.M., do my paperwork, meet with my staff, visit patients, and go through my administrative tasks. I work until about 7 P.M. Then I drive home for about 45 minutes, and when I get to my house, I fall on my couch, exhausted."

"It sounds like you're working too hard," I surmised. "Can you shorten your workday?"

"Actually, my work energizes me," he explained. "When I leave the office, I still feel good."

"Then what happens between when you leave the office and when you come home?"

"I listen to the news," he replied.

I found it fascinating that a brilliant man could work a long day, enjoy his endeavors, and regularly have his joy wiped out by media broadcasts. The implications are clear: the news sucks.

The news sucks life out of listeners because what is presented as the news runs contrary to who we are and how we were born to live. We are illuminated beings here to create, find joy, and uplift the world. The news, on the other hand, culls the planet for the worst of what happens each day, exaggerates it, dramatizes it, and presents it as reality. Yet most news is not a valid representation of reality. It is a highly slanted and precisely concocted spin on reality.

If you want to live a more positive, fulfilled, happy, healthy, and peaceful life, I suggest you withdraw your attention from the news. You will not miss anything important that you need to know about. To the contrary, you will remember what is really important and create good news by virtue of the aliveness you exude and the actions you undertake from a platform of inherent well-being.

How can you withdraw your attention from the news so you feel better?

**I focus my attention on the good, the beautiful,
and the true. The better I feel, the better position
I am in to help others and the world.**

Don't Sell Yourself Short

Whatever games are played with us,
we must play no games with ourselves.

— Ralph Waldo Emerson

A number of years ago I noticed a drop in attendance at my Life Mastery Training in Hawaii. To make the program more attractive, I decided to lower the price of tuition. When I reprinted the brochure advertising the program, I added a banner announcing in large letters: NEW LOWER PRICES.

Soon afterward I showed my brochure to a business consultant. After perusing the material, he told me, "This sounds like a great program, and I think the brochure is really excellent. The only thing that bothers me is the phrase 'New Lower Prices.' I believe this kind of advertising cheapens the quality of the offering. Discount stores use this kind of come-on, but the program you are presenting is far classier than that. I suggest you drop it from the brochure."

The consultant's feedback hit home, and I deleted the phrase from the next printing of the brochure. His advice reminded me that I was offering a program that changes people's lives in a most significant way, and the price I was charging was well justified. His feedback got me back on track to recognize and ask for what the program was worth. Soon more and more people began to sign up for the Life Mastery Training, and the attendance swelled to numbers far beyond what they had been.

What you charge for your goods or services, and how you advertise them, reflects what you believe they are worth. If people are not patronizing your business, the answer may not be to lower the prices or create more glitzy marketing. The answer may be for you to remember the value of what you offer, or enrich its quality.

People are willing to pay for goods and services they value. When you value what you do, you will attract customers who agree with you.

How could you more deeply recognize the value of what
you offer so you attract customers who agree with you?

I participate in a rewarding financial
exchange for my product or service.
I offer a quality product that attracts customers
willing to pay for the value they receive.

How Are You Really?

When people talk, listen completely. . . . Most people never listen.
— Ernest Hemingway

At a residential seminar, I passed a participant on my way to the program. I politely asked, "How are you?" expecting she would smile and answer, "Fine," and I would continue on my way. Instead, she took my query seriously and began to tell me about some health issues she was experiencing. While at another time I would have been pleased to chat with her, I needed to get to my program. The woman sensed my impatience and asked if I was really interested.

"To be honest, I am on my way to give a lecture, and I need to get going," I explained.

"Then why did you ask me how I was if you weren't ready to hear my answer?" she retorted.

She had a point. Since that time, I do not ask "How are you?" unless I am ready and willing to hear the answer.

I notice that when most people ask "How are you?" they really mean "Hello." I see strangers passing on the street or sharing an elevator exchanging "How are you?" and "Fine, thank you; how are you?" without meaning that at all. I understand that this is a polite way to make a pleasant brief connection, but I have found that a sincere "Hello" is more direct and honest.

In his book *Success Intelligence,* Robert Holden underscores the importance of shifting from "thin conversations" to meaningful ones. While thin conversations are generally accepted as the norm in our culture, you may be craving more substance and be ready for it. Not that every interaction has to be cosmically significant, but why waste time talking about things that are empty or boring? Why not generate the kind of conversations you prefer and invite your communication partner to meet you there? You may not hit a bull's-eye every time, and you may even get a blank stare or nervous look, but you could strike up a meaningful connection often enough to make your effort worthwhile.

How could you make your conversations more meaningful to you?

I set the tone for my interactions and
create relationships with substance.

The Thought That Gave Birth to Billions

Yesterday I dared to struggle. Today I dare to win.
— Bernadette Devlin

When media mogul Ted Turner donated $1 billion to the United Nations, in his donation speech he declared, "The world is awash in money."

"Easy for him to say," you might scoff if you are having trouble paying your bills. "He has billions of dollars." But if you understand *why* Ted Turner has billions of dollars, you can make a major stride toward his financial status.

The key lies in the answer to this question: *does Ted Turner say "The world is awash in money" because he has billions of dollars, or does he have billions of dollars because he believes the world is awash in money?* The latter is certainly the case. There is no way that someone who does not believe the world is awash in money could generate such a bank account. And there is every way that someone *with* that belief could grow rich.

The trick to getting more money is not to work harder, but to open your mind. You have heard that the most crucial sex organ is your brain, and the same brain is equally your most crucial prosperity organ. Everything you create falls between the upper and lower parameters of your belief, so if you want more good stuff, the place to start is by stretching those upper parameters.

Begin by thinking and talking about things you would like to attract rather than things you have attracted that you do not want. Do not think or talk lack. Every time you focus on lack, you get more of it. Instead, focus on supply, creativity, expansion, and abundance. Quickly you will find that where you once saw insufficiency, you now find enough and more than enough.

Gradually you will raise your set point for what you believe is available to you; and after some rewarding manifestations, you too will be able to declare, "The world is awash in money."

How might your beliefs be limiting what you are receiving?
How could you open your mind to receive what you want?

The universe is abundant and capable
of supplying me with all I want and need.
I accept greater good now, and more every day.

My Big Fat Greek Lunch Date

Trust yourself. You know more than you think you do.
— Dr. Benjamin Spock

During a weekend seminar I presented in Greece, a fellow named Gregory invited me to lunch. I told him I would go, but when the time came, I realized I needed to rest. I felt a bit guilty about changing my mind, but I knew I had to take some quiet time. So I politely cancelled my appointment and suggested that as an alternative we sit together at the celebration party that evening at a nightclub. Gregory graciously agreed, and he went off to lunch.

That night at the club, I saved a seat for Gregory, but he did not show up. Hours went by, and I imagined that he had decided not to attend. Later that evening, though, I saw him sitting at a table in the corner with an attractive woman.

"I didn't know you were here," I told him.

Gregory smiled and said, "I've been here all evening with Anna." The two raised their glasses and giggled. "When you and I didn't go to lunch today, I went with some other folks and met Anna. We are having a wonderful evening. Thank you for cancelling our appointment!"

I smiled as I walked away, glad that Gregory had found himself a lady friend. No matter how interesting our lunch discussion might have been, I assure you he was having more fun with Anna than he would have had with me.

The Law of Shared Good stipulates that our good is not separate. When I followed my right path by taking my needed rest, I opened the door for Gregory to find *his* good. There was no need to feel guilty or be apologetic about the way things went. It was in everyone's best interests.

If you feel guilty about taking care of your well-being, today would be a good day to get over it. Your happiness is linked to the happiness of others. I certainly do not suggest that you hurt anyone. I do suggest that when you nurture yourself, you are in a good position to help others.

Gregory and Anna might agree.

*What would you like to do for yourself
that might also help others to be happy?*

**My good is connected to the good of others.
I follow my path and support them in following theirs.**

The Best Eater I Know

What nourishes you is not vitamins in food.
It is the joy you feel in eating it.

— Ramtha

Down a country road from our home lives a lovable potbellied pig named Snoopy. Every day around dinnertime we walk our dogs and visit Snoopy in a pasture he inherited from some horses. Along our way we pick some fresh guavas to feed him as a bedtime snack.

I have never seen anyone enjoy food as much as Snoopy does. Watching him eat is one of the highlights of my day. When he sees us coming, his face lights up, his tail wags, and he runs to the pasture fence about as fast as a pig can run. He receives the guavas with gusto and downs them as fast as we can toss them to him. He is not dainty or polite, and often leaves remnants of the fruit around his piggy lips. Snoopy loves to eat, and he is unapologetic about it.

Observing Snoopy enjoy his snacks, I realize that unlike most humans, he is completely at one with eating. We humans, in contrast, have been trained to have a double-edged, self-defeating attitude toward food. On the one hand, we love to eat, since it is the basic instinct of all living things. On the other, we have been told that there is so much wrong with practically every food, we suffer from fear, guilt, or resistance while ingesting it.

If you are into health foods or are on a diet, you can cite a long list of reasons why just about any food is dangerous. It has been grown with pesticides, overrefined, tainted with preservatives, genetically altered, or heated to the point of killing nutrients; or it will make you fat, raise your cholesterol, or throw off your insulin level. Water is polluted. Even if the food is pure, it may have been processed by someone with bad vibes or who is not on your religion's approved list. And on and on and on, until all you might be able to eat is a lettuce leaf you grew in your backyard.

Snoopy, after all, may be the best teacher of conscious eating you or I might find. He derives deep joy from eating, which is more than most people do. If you want to come and watch him, he is offering seminars every evening around sunset.

Do you fully enjoy your food?
Can you enjoy eating even if the foods you eat are not perfect?

Eating is a delight. I bless and
savor my food as a gift from God.

The Best and the Rest

Every saint has a past, and every sinner has a future.

— Oscar Wilde

A friend told me that he had just come from a motivational conference where he attended a seminar presented by his favorite self-help author. "I was flabbergasted by the attitude she displayed," he confessed. "She was rude and abrasive and shamed some of the audience members when they asked questions. I'm never going to see her again. How can someone be so brilliant in a book and so unkind in person?"

I explained to my friend that it is not unusual for famous and talented people, even in the self-help industry, to have ego issues. Having presented at numerous conferences where top authors and speakers were on the ticket, I have found that while they are indeed gifted with wisdom and the power to uplift, many of them also display behaviors far afield from the principles they teach. At one conference on "The Path of Happiness," a well-known speaker walked into the teachers' room after his keynote and confessed, "I don't know how I gave that lecture. I've never been happy a day in my life."

Motivational teachers are not perfect, I told my friend, just human like the rest of us. Yet there is a way to understand and accept their human foibles without throwing out the benefit of their helpful teachings. Sometimes people become gifted authors, speakers, and teachers because they have wrestled with their own pain, fears, relationship problems, conflicts, and money issues. The lessons they teach are based on the insights and victories they have gained in dealing with their own shadows. Just because they have a number one book or were on *The Oprah Winfrey Show* does not mean those shadow selves or egos disappear overnight. (Sometimes they become exaggerated!) We would be foolish to write such teachers off because we observe their egos in action. They also offer brilliant gifts. You can pay attention to the ego or to the greatness and you will receive more of what you focus on. So, I advised my friend, just take the best and leave the rest.

Everyone has both divinity and humanity within them. Let us bless the positive, and while it is important to discern the negative, let us not dwell on it.

How can you learn from both the beneficial teachings of a mentor as well as the person's humanity?

I bless all my teachers as I focus on what I need to learn. I take the best and leave the rest.

Mistake Salad

A man of genius makes no mistakes.
His errors are volitional and are the portals of discovery.

— James Joyce

When my friend Dorothy goes home to visit her family each Thanksgiving, her mother serves the traditional "mistake salad." The dish was born many years ago when Dorothy's mother was using a cookbook to prepare a salad. In the process, her mother accidentally included half the salad ingredients from a recipe on the left page of the open cookbook, and half the ingredients from a different salad recipe on the opposite page. Everyone enjoyed the salad so much that she continues to serve it every year. So it was really no mistake at all.

Likewise, your apparent mistakes may not really be mistakes. There are two levels at which mistakes serve in an unseen way: (1) they might be leading to a success even more significant than the one your course is currently headed toward (like pharmaceutical drugs such as Viagra that have been discovered while searching for a cure for an unrelated ailment), or (2) a material foul-up or setback may give you the impetus to make life changes that benefit you far more profoundly than if you had not "erred" on the issue.

Everything is part of something bigger, and mistakes are no exception. Every minus is half of a plus, waiting for a stroke of vertical awareness. In his brilliant book *Illusions*, Richard Bach explains that every problem comes to you with a gift in its hands. If you focus only on what went wrong, you miss the gift. If you are willing to look deeper and ask for the insight, the problem dissipates, you are left only with the learning, and you advance on your path.

The next time you make a mistake, do not berate yourself. Instead, look for some opportunity in it. Since everything is what you make it, you can create successes by focusing on what has gone right when it seems to have gone wrong.

What error or failure have you recently berated yourself or another for?
How might the apparent error lead to a success or better result?

I use every experience as a stepping-stone to something greater.

Yes, and . . .

Argue for your limitations, and sure enough, they're yours.
— Richard Bach

I have noticed an interesting phenomenon when working with coaching clients: Some people are eager and willing to move ahead in their lives and embrace suggestions for movement forward. Others argue for their limits. One of my clients was aware of her propensity to make a stand for what she could not do, and she called this her "Yeahbut and Costello Show."

For example, a client states a problem she feels stuck with. After restating the issue so the client understands that I have heard her, I might say, "Maybe we could look at it like this . . ."

The client responds, "Yes, but . . ." and presents a reason why that approach would not work.

Then I might say, "Something like that happened to me, and I was able to resolve it by . . ."

Then another "Yes, but . . ."

Finally I might say, "Shall we pray about this so we can enlist the help of a Higher Power?"

Then I might hear another "Yes, but . . ."

I sometimes joke that I will give clients three "Yes, but's" and then I kick them in the "Yes, but." I have been tempted to call some of my seminars "Reducing the Size of Your 'But.'"

We all have our own version of "Yes, but . . ." and we need to recognize that in such moments we are standing in our own way. Your spouse, friend, counselor, or God may be willing and able to help you, but if you fight for your limits, you will keep them.

One way to change a "Yes, but . . ." pattern is to consciously substitute the phrase "Yes, and . . ." The word *but* automatically negates what was said before it and empowers what is said after it. "Yes, and . . ." acknowledges both the problematic situation *and* a possible solution to it. Even a slight sliver of willingness to change something for the better is a sufficient opening for greater good to come.

Do you have any "Yes, but's"? Can you change them to "Yes, and"?

I make a stand for my possibilities, not my limits.
I embrace invitations to create positive change.

It Wants You, Too

Don't ask yourself what the world needs; ask yourself
what makes you come alive. And then go and do that. Because
what the world needs is people who have come alive.
— Attributed to Howard Thurman

I saw a billboard with a marvelous advertisement for the lustrous BMW Z4 sports car. The ad simply showed a photo of the sleek car and proclaimed, "It wants you, too."

The sign was teaching a paramount life lesson: *The good you seek is seeking you.* If you have a house to sell, someone is in the market for a house like yours. If you need a job, an employer needs someone with your unique skills. If you deeply desire a mate with certain characteristics, someone just like that is looking for someone like you.

The universe functions in perfect balance. The voices of fear and lack tell you that you are small, alone, and abandoned, and you have to struggle to get what you want and need. The voices of trust and prosperity remind you that all is well, you are being supported by a Higher Power, and you are provided for in a million ways you do not understand and cannot manipulate. Fortunately, the voice of trust speaks truth, while the voice of fear is couched in illusion, so you need not pay a moment's attention to the ranting of desperation.

During a lecture, I mentioned one of my favorite films, *Standing in the Shadows of Motown.* After the talk, a fellow from the audience told me, "My brother produced that movie. Before the story became a movie, it was a book. Author Allan Slutsky searched for years for a producer, to no avail. Then one day he was sitting next to my brother on an airplane, and he told him about his dream to turn the book into a movie. My brother liked the idea and produced it."

You have no idea how or when a dream might come true. Just keep showing up, and your heart's desire will meet you at the appointed intersection.

What do you most want now?
How might what you seek be seeking you?

What I want and need is on its way to me.
I hold my intention clearly, and the Law of Attraction
cleverly arranges a means to its fulfillment.

A Visit with Grandma

*The human spirit needs places where nature
has not been rearranged by the hand of man.*

— Source unknown

I met a Hawaiian man on the beach who told me that his grandmother had just died at the age of 117. She lived in the remote, undeveloped Maui town of Hana, where she had given birth to 33 children. In her lifetime, Grandma had never ridden in a car, watched television, or gone to a doctor.

Anomaly that Grandma is in modern times, she offers us some striking lessons in long life, health, and happiness. While you and I are not ready to move to a pristine, remote location and renounce cars, television, and doctors (unless you *are*), Grandma may be pointing us in some directions that can improve quality and length of life right where we stand.

Grandma was subject to the healing influence of natural surroundings. If you can get into nature regularly—even taking a walk in the park—you will find refreshment and renewal. If you can spend a weekend or vacation in places untouched by outer industrial development, you will enjoy *inner* development.

Grandma was surrounded by close family. One of the great tragedies of our culture is the isolation, alienation, and loneliness many of us experience because we feel cut off from loved ones. When I lived in New Jersey, I interacted with my neighbors only when we shoveled our cars out of the snow. Even if you are not close with your biological family, you can huddle with a family of friends.

Grandma was saved from the mind suck of most television programming. She missed nothing of life because she did not sit in front of a screen for hours a day. She also ate homegrown foods. While you may not be able to grow your own provisions, you will be healthier if you can find foods in as close to their natural forms as possible. Finally, Grandma did not experience the stress of driving many hours to and fro a day. She found her delight where she was.

While Grandma is the exception to many of the rules and routines we experience, she may serve as a model for how to get back to the Garden.

*How might you reclaim more of a natural lifestyle,
including connection to your loved ones?*

I live in harmony with my nature.

Feet on the Ground

How come we put a man on the moon before we figured
out how to put wheels on suitcases?

— Stephen Wright

A number of years ago I was invited to present a seminar for an organization that specialized in psychic skills and mediumship (communication with departed spirits). Although this subject is not my specific area of expertise, I wanted to learn more about it, and I thought working with this group would be an adventure.

My initial observation of the group was that it was difficult to nail down a contract. Although we had verbally agreed on the terms of my program, every time the contract came to me, something was missing or had been changed. Finally we came to terms, and the date of the program was set.

When I arrived at the local airport on the evening before the event, no one from the group was there to pick me up. I phoned their office, where a representative apologized, saying, "Oh, we thought you were coming in tomorrow!" I checked my records and confirmed that I had given them the correct date. "Take a cab to a hotel near the airport, and we will come for you in the morning," the representative directed me.

I went to the hotel, flopped on the bed, and wondered, *What is my lesson in working with this group?* My answer came thus: *What's the use of communicating with the dead if you can't communicate with the living?*

I had to laugh. These people were experts at dealing with spooks, but when it came to dealing with real people . . . well, that was a challenge for them.

Many people seek to communicate with the world beyond the senses, which is a very real world indeed, and can offer rich lessons. But if you are out of this world at the expense of being *in* it, your efforts are for naught. Real mastery lies in navigating the Earth plane as you walk it. Explore higher truth, but remember your zip code.

How might you develop greater mastery
by taking charge of the details of your life?

I walk with my head in the clouds
and my feet on the ground.

Gargoyles

Prosperity lets go the bridle.

— George Herbert

Have you ever started a relationship with someone you thought would be your perfect mate, only to find that something was wrong with him, or he was unavailable? Did you find a wonderful home you could not pull off a deal to buy? Have you lost a good job or business opportunity?

If so, you may blame the universe for teasing you with unavailable goods, or you may criticize yourself for missing or botching your golden moment. But this is not so. There is a bigger picture than you realize.

In olden times, tall buildings were adorned with statue heads of gargoyles at the edge of their roofs. When rain came, the water would rush down the roof into gutters and then pour out of the gargoyles' mouths. If you did not know better when you looked up from the street, you would think that the gargoyle was producing the rain. But it was not. The rain was coming from the sky, and the statue's mouth was the last orifice through which the rain was channeled before it was delivered to Earth.

So it is with your good. You may believe that a particular person, home, or job is the source of your good. But each of these entities is simply a gargoyle through which a far broader universal source pours. If the rain ceases to flow through one channel, there are many others by which it may arrive. Do not confuse the delivery service with the source. The source of your good is infinite universal supply. Remember how vast is the source of the rain, and you will recognize how vast is your well-being.

Are you fixated on one person, place, or job as the source of your good?
How might you recognize that your source is far
broader than the channel that delivers it?

I trust in universal supply.
My good can come at any time, in any way,
through any channel. I welcome it now.

Dynamite Transformation

It takes great learning to understand that all things,
events, encounters, and circumstances are helpful.

— *A Course in Miracles*

Alfred was stunned to read his own obituary in the newspaper! His brother Ludvig had died, and a French newspaper had mistaken the other man for him. It was 1888, and Alfred was a famous Swedish engineer known for his invention of dynamite. He was astonished to read the headline "The Merchant of Death Is Dead," followed by a discourse about how he, who "became rich by finding ways to kill more people faster than ever before, died yesterday."

Shocked and saddened that this is what he would be remembered for, Alfred decided to devote his money and his life to create more peace, not destruction, on Earth. So he revised his will to donate the bulk of his earnings from explosives—the equivalent of $110 million today—to establish a fund to honor individuals who furthered the causes of science and peace. His full name was Alfred Bernhard Nobel, and his fund became the most respected award on Earth: the Nobel Prize.

What begins as a force of destruction can be rechanneled to become a force for redemption. Energy is neutral, neither good nor bad; it is how we use it that determines its value. Money, electricity, atomic power, the Internet, and the mass media can all be used to debilitate humanity or to uplift it. In the hands of ego, anything is dangerous. In the hands of love, it becomes divine.

Do not be hasty to judge your negative acts or those of others as permanent or absolute. What you thought was a sin or a huge error may ultimately be an element of great good in the grander picture of things. It's all what you make of it.

What have you negatively judged in yourself or others, which could
be a source of good when considered from a higher vantage point?

I use my mind and talents to make the world a
better place. I reframe the evil I perceive in myself
and others as potential good.

Don't Think Human

One who has come into a knowledge of his true identity . . .
makes it possible for laws higher than the ordinary
mind knows of to be revealed to him.

— Ralph Waldo Trine

In the film *The Last Starfighter,* Alex Rogan lives in a trailer park, bored out of his mind. He spends most of his time at the one video game in the park, *Starfighter,* developing his skill shooting alien starships out of virtual space. He becomes so adroit that he breaks the all-time record for ships destroyed.

One night a mysterious stranger arrives at the park and invites Alex for a ride. When the car levitates above the road and shoots off into the heavens, Alex realizes he is in for an adventure. The driver, Centauri, peels off his mask and reveals himself as the denizen of a distant planet under siege from the evil empire of Xur. Centauri explains that he designed and planted the video game, which replicates the control panel of a real starfighter ship, in order to recruit someone who could save their civilization from extinction. As the champion of the game, Alex is qualified and Centauri's people need him.

When Alex argues that he is just a kid from a trailer park, Centauri answers that if that is what he thinks he is, that is all he ever will be. The boy thinks over his situation and decides to help, but he is faced with overwhelming odds—it is just him against a vast armada. Again he wants to turn back, but his mentor advises him, "Don't think human." When Alex comes upon a starfighter who has been killed, his advisor tells him that death is simply an illusion, and he prefers to think of the fighter as battling evil on another dimension.

If you intend to do great things, you cannot afford to think of yourself in limited human terms. To create extraordinary results, you have to think in a higher dimension. You are not just a kid from a trailer park. There is a greater adventure for you if you are willing to accept it.

How could you reframe your vision of who you are
to enable yourself to accomplish great things?

I am empowered with wisdom, strength, and
spirit sufficient to do anything I set out to do.

Roots and Leaves

To be interested in the changing seasons is . . . a happier state
of mind than to be hopelessly in love with spring.
— George Santayana

Bamboo is a fascinating plant, the fastest growing in the world. A bamboo stalk can grow six inches or more in one day! I know a fellow who swore he actually *saw* it growing.

One of the clever adaptive qualities of bamboo is that it grows its leaves in the summer and its roots in the winter. It takes advantage of each season, and while it appears dormant, it is not. The roots grown in winter prepare for rapid branch and leaf development in summer.

We, too, go through seasons, all of which afford us opportunities for different kinds of growth. In a prosperous economic season, there is a lot of building and external expansion. When an economic winter comes, with little activity in the outer world, that is the time for inner deepening.

Many blessings and opportunities are available when money is not flowing. You can catch up with aspects of your life that were on hold when you were involved with external development; enrich your introspective and spiritual life; deepen your relationship with your family, friends, and home; envision, research, and plan a more meaningful business than the one that is not supplying you the way it once did; and explore creative hobbies. Economic winter is a time to grow the roots that will serve you well when the summer comes again, as it surely will.

Similarly, after a relationship breakup or divorce, or during a romantic winter, you are in a perfect position to go inward and get to know yourself, your true choices, and your life in ways that were not obvious or available when you were involved with your partner. You can feed your soul so that when you enter a relationship again, you will be in a position to make it even better than the last one.

All seasons are helpful if you know how to use them.

How might you benefit from the current economic,
relationship, or spiritual season you are in?

I accept the gifts available where I stand.
Every season empowers and blesses me anew.

Men of Lofty Genius

The minds of men of lofty genius are most active in invention
when they are doing the least external work.

— Attributed to Leonardo da Vinci

There is a well-kept secret of success that only some geniuses will reveal. The secret runs counter to popular belief, so even when it is told, few people understand it and even fewer use it. If you can grasp this nugget of wisdom, you will advance toward your goals with haste and joy.

The secret is this: Great ideas come to the world in flashes of inspiration, without struggle. Many geniuses receive their best insights when they are relaxed, playing, and in the flow of life. World-changing inventions, works of art, and social and religious movements begin not in an atmosphere of trying, but in the womb of allowing. Many great people flash on their best ideas while napping, walking in nature, listening to music, playing with their children, or making love. It is through the window of joy that God shines the light of truth.

In the early days of his illustrious career, Steven Spielberg said, "Once a month an idea crashes into my brain, and I can't do anything else until I've acted on it." The Queen in Lewis Carroll's *Through the Looking-Glass* noted, "Why, sometimes I've believed as many as six impossible things before breakfast."

My mentor Hilda Charlton studied with a metaphysical teacher who spent a long time each day sitting at his apartment window, smoking a cigarette, and looking onto the city street below. He told her, "My personal form of meditation is far more effective than simply doing, doing, doing and going, going, going, without knowing why I am here or where I am going. Those people on the street are caught up in the franticness of life. I am pondering the why of things, and when I act, my acts shall be more effective for it."

One good idea can set into motion changes that rock the world far more than a tepid notion. Quit trying to be great or do great things, and let greatness find and recruit you in your quiet moments.

Are you struggling to accomplish something?
Can you relax and let greatness find you?

I offer wisdom and genius a quiet space
to alight in the chamber of my soul.

Striking the Keynote

A good beginning makes a good end.

— English proverb

How will your holiday season go? Will you be stressed, rushed, and worried about getting the right gifts, traveling, and attending parties and family functions? Are you concerned about overeating and gaining weight? Or will you flow with the events that come your way, enjoy your person-to-person connections, and remember the spirit of the holidays?

You can make a huge difference in how your holidays turn out by setting your tone, or establishing your intention, *before* you get busy. It's very easy to get swept up in busyness and doingness. If you want to stay in your right mind and in your heart, it is up to you to decide to do so now.

Here are some qualities of experience that you may wish to choose as your holiday keynote: *Abundance. Aliveness. Appreciation. Celebration. Connection. Ease. Flow. Fun. Generosity. Heart. Innocence. Joy. Love. Play. Reverence. Spirit. Togetherness. Wonder.*

Now choose one of these qualities of life, and take a minute or two to close your eyes and picture yourself moving through your holiday activities with this feeling as your dominant experience. Picture not so much the activities themselves, but the kind of energy you would like to maintain in the process. Continue your visualization until the feeling becomes real in your experience. Then go about your day and your season, and as much as you can, keep coming back to this feeling. You may lose it for short or long periods of time, but the more you consciously remember it—even for a few moments—the more your desired theme will be real and rewarding. At some point, your chosen tone may become your dominant tone, and then your season will truly be one of joy.

What is the most important tone or experience that you would like to enjoy through the holiday season?

I set my tone and reap the benefits of my intention. I choose to enjoy the best holiday season ever.

The Healed Healer

Who understands what giving means
must laugh at the idea of sacrifice.

— *A Course in Miracles*

I attended a seminar on healing where one of the students asked the teacher, "Why do I feel burned-out when I offer my healing services?" The teacher answered, "Because you think you are the healer."

Burnout is a huge issue in all of the healing professions. I work with many doctors, nurses, psychotherapists, social workers, ministers, massage therapists, and coaches. Many of them—especially those in more traditional modalities, like medicine—get fried and become stressed, ill, and less than effective. This need not be.

If you think it is up to you to fix, heal, or change a patient or client, you are taking on an unreasonable responsibility. Yet at a deeper level, your job is to invite the patient to rise to a healing consciousness. Hold the high vision of the patient no matter what vision he is holding for himself. Certainly you want your patient to be healed, and there are tools and methods you can offer to move the process along. Yet they are secondary to the power of consciousness.

No loss is required of you for your patient's gain. To the contrary, the lighter you can stay, the more optimal the environment you offer for your patient to find release and relief.

I saw a movie that depicted Jesus as returning during modern times and healing people. After he performed a healing, he would wince and sometimes almost fall over with pain. The film suggested that Jesus was taking on the suffering of his patients. Nothing could be further from the truth. You cannot get sick enough to make someone well. You do not remove illness from the world by transferring or adding to it. You inculcate wellness by the experience and model of wellness. This leaves both healer and patient empowered and feeling whole and good.

Burnout is not required. Let the spirit of life do the healing, and both you and your clients will benefit.

How can you reframe your healing practice
by allowing life force to do the healing?

I offer healing by recognizing the power and presence of wellness. The Great Spirit is the true healer.

On Higher Ground

Never wrestle with a pig. You both get dirty, and the pig likes it.

— Source unknown

If you were to ask our dogs why God invented cats, they would answer without hesitation: "Highly stimulating moving targets." Although our pooches are generally loving and well behaved, the minute our cat makes an appearance, they believe it is their solemn duty to chase it. They mean the cat no harm, but the sport is just too enticing to pass up.

At first the cat would just run to a corner, and we would have to rescue it. But eventually he learned that if he jumped to a high counter, the dogs could not follow him there. Now he just hangs out on higher ground and smugly watches the dogs from an untouchable vantage point.

This escape dynamic is symbolic of how you and I can find relief from the struggles of worldly life. If someone attempts to engage you in a battle, or you are involved in an ongoing war, you are trapped as long as you remain at the level of warfare with your opponent. All human interactions exist on the basis of frequency and agreement. If you are attuned to the same frequency as someone who wants to duke it out, you will keep going 'round and 'round with them. You also have the option to raise your frequency and refuse to go there with them. Then they will have to either meet you at a higher, more satisfying level of interaction, or go away.

You are not required to attend every argument to which you are invited. At any moment you can jump to a counter where the other person cannot reach you. If they want to fight, they can find someone else or change their mind. You, however, remain at peace and secure on higher ground.

You have the power to end any war in which you are immersed. It takes two to fight, but only one to end the conflict.

*How are you perpetuating an ongoing struggle
by matching energy with your opponent?
How could you end or transform the issue by moving to higher ground?*

**I choose the frequency at which I live.
I elevate all of my interactions to harmony.**

Happy to Ride in Cargo

*From speaking to many cancer survivor groups,
I have learned that the watch on your hand no longer says,
"tick, tick, tick." It now says, "precious, precious, precious."*

— Steve Sobel

As Dee and I took our bulkhead seats on our flight home to Hawaii, we noticed a young couple seeking their seats in the row across the aisle from us. They were on their honeymoon, very much in love, and excited about their adventure. When they realized that they were assigned to sit apart from each other, both in middle seats, one behind the other, their countenance dropped like five-year-old kids whose ice cream cones had fallen on the sidewalk.

The passenger seated next to the husband, a woman probably the age of the bride's mother, sensed their distress and kindly offered to switch seats with the bride so she could sit next to her husband. The young lady was delighted, and the women changed places. As the older woman took her new seat, I told her, "That was very generous of you to trade your bulkhead aisle seat for a middle one farther back."

The lady smiled and answered, "I was a newlywed once, and I know how she feels. Besides, I'm going to Hawaii! I'd ride in the cargo compartment if I had to!"

Her comment caught me by surprise. Dee and I are generally fussy about where we sit, and we make extensive efforts to get roomy seats on airplanes. This woman, however, was in such a state of joy and appreciation that she was just happy to be on the plane. Her exhilaration was so great that she created a miracle for the newlyweds. She reminded me that happiness has little to do with conditions, and a lot to do with attitude.

As the plane hurtled skyward, I began to reconsider my fussiness. My happiness was conditional upon getting my chosen seat. That woman's happiness was *un*conditional because she chose it. Even though the plane we were both on leveled off at 35,000 feet, she was flying closer to heaven.

*How could you make yourself and others
happier by appreciating what you have?*

Happiness is a choice I can make wherever I am.

A Jewish Santa Delivers

Angels have no philosophy but love.

— Attributed to Adeline Cullen Ray

When Jay Frankston grew up Jewish, he wished he could participate in the Christmas holiday. So when he became an adult and had his own family, he brought home a tree with all the trimmings. But that was not enough. Jay wanted to be Santa Claus.

Jay went to the main post office in New York City and asked to see the letters that kids had written to Santa Claus, c/o the North Pole. There he found thousands of letters from children wanting things. Some were selfish and demanded lots of toys. Others were more altruistic, asking for a blanket for their mom or gifts for their brothers and sisters. Jay was touched by the heartfelt requests and decided to fulfill them.

Jay took home a number of the letters and purchased the items requested. Then he dressed up as Santa, and his wife drove him to the poorest section of the city. There he found the homes of the children whose letters he had chosen, and he personally delivered the gifts. You can imagine the astonishment of the children and their families when Santa showed up at their door and gave them what they had written to the North Pole to request!

Jay chronicles his adventures in his heartwarming book *A Christmas Story*. Every holiday season, I read it aloud with friends. Every time, it brings me to tears. If you care to read it, you will find it one of the most touching holiday accounts ever.

The word *angel* means "messenger." This holiday season you can be an angel by bringing love to others. You do not have to find North Pole letters and deliver Santa's gifts (although that might be a lot of fun). You just have to be fully present with the people you are with and keep your heart open. You may find that the door you leave open to give love is the very one through which love arrives.

How can you be an angel this holiday season?
Whom can you surprise with a gift of love?

**I seek to bless others, and
in that blessing, I am blessed.**

Confluence

Nothing is as real as a healthy dose
of magic which restores our spirits.

— Nancy Long

At the beginning of my Life Mastery Training residential seminar, a woman named Sonia arrived to drop off her boyfriend, Eddie, who was about to participate in the program. As Sonia and I spoke, she got interested in the seminar and asked if she could attend. We had a place for her, and without any planning, she was on board.

Also attending this program was an Egyptian fellow named Mahmud, who had written to me and asked if we had any scholarships available. Although we usually do not offer scholarships for that program, his sincerity and desire were winning, so I decided to follow my intuition and make an exception, allowing him to attend for simply the cost of room and board.

During the seminar, Eddie and Sonia announced that they were in the process of breaking up. The other participants and I supported the couple as they expressed their feelings in the presence of the group and said a mature and loving good-bye.

Two years later I saw Sonia, and she told me that she and Mahmud had gotten married. I was amazed! "We got to know each other a bit at the retreat," she explained, "and a year later we began to exchange e-mails. We fell in love, and now we are together."

I marveled at the synchronicity and confluence of the whole scenario. Mahmud was at the program on a rare scholarship, Sonia decided to attend on the spur of the moment, and she and Eddie processed their breakup among us. At that time no one had any idea that the couple would get together.

You never know how your good will show up. Be yourself, trust the process, and divine timing will take care of the details.

How might right timing be leading you
to your greater good even when you do not realize it?

I follow my spirit, speak my truth, and trust.
Divine timing is taking care of me.

You Deserve Better

*The important thing is this: to be able at any moment
to sacrifice what we are for what we could become.*

— Charles Du Bos

The award-winning documentary *Born into Brothels* chronicles the humanitarian efforts of Zana Briski, who went into the seamy red-light district of Calcutta and taught children the art of photography. Zana took painstaking efforts to enroll the children in a private school where, through better education, they could escape a life of prostitution, drug abuse, and early death.

The last step of Zana's school plan required getting permission from the children's parents or guardians. Some agreed and some did not. Several parents wanted their girls to stay home so they could go "in the line" and earn money for the family. One girl's grandmother refused to allow her to go to the school interview because it was scheduled for a Thursday and the grandmother's father had died on that day of the week. Grandma never did anything on a Thursday because it was bad luck. Once she had done something on a Thursday, she noted, and she was still suffering because of it.

Grandma's attitude symbolizes the part in all of us that fears to move ahead. We hold tenaciously to the known, even if the known sucks. To the resistant mind, this makes perfect sense. To the enlightened mind, this makes *no* sense.

Fortunately, the little girl in Calcutta overrode Granny's edict and went anyway. Something in her knew that she was being offered a great gift, and the voice of hysteria was not convincing enough for her to deny herself this opportunity. Bravo.

At this moment you are being offered an opportunity for a better life. A voice inside or outside you may try to intimidate you into staying because the known seems safe. Another voice is showing you an open door.

You were not born to live in squalor or prostitute yourself with activities that demean your true vision, joy, or talent. Respect yourself by saying yes to your higher good.

*What fears or beliefs make your old world seem safer
to you than the unknown? What opportunity calls to you that
could make your life better if you stepped forward?*

**My life beckons me toward greater success.
I release the familiar to make way for better.**

More Alike Than Different

Come out of the circle of time and into the circle of love.

— Rumi

On an airplane I heard the head flight attendant announce that one of the crew was celebrating her 40th anniversary as a flight attendant. I was impressed by such a long career of service and thought I might learn something from this professional. I made my way to the galley, congratulated the flight attendant, and asked her, "In all your years of flying, what has been your most important lesson?"

The woman thought for a moment and answered, "I have flown internationally for many years and dealt with people of many ethnic, racial, and cultural backgrounds. Over that time I've discovered that people are basically nice, and we all want essentially the same things. We are all more alike than we are different."

A poignant lesson, indeed. I discovered the same truth when I made citizen-diplomacy trips to the Soviet Union in the 1980s. Growing up during the Cold War, I had been taught that Russians were evil, they wanted to dominate the world, and they were out to annihilate Americans. When I spent time with salt-of-the-earth people there, I found the exact opposite to be true. I found the Russians to be a warm, generous, and openhearted people, just as eager for peace as we were. They loved their children, enjoyed laughing and toasting, and displayed immense passion for life. While the government espoused atheism, the nature of the people was deeply spiritual. Those trips were some of the most enlightening spiritual workshops I have ever experienced. I learned that fear and separateness are illusions, and love and connection are real.

Perhaps we can all learn from the veteran flight attendant. We are all more alike than different. People are basically good, and we want the same things.

What beliefs in separateness keep you in fear or pain?
What beliefs in sameness bring you peace?

I am one with people of all walks of life.
We all share the goal of happiness.

Stay with Life

We must not demean life by standing in awe of death.
— Attributed to David Sarnoff

When my friend Robert passed away suddenly through odd circumstances, I felt shaken and saddened. Robert was healthy, happy, and very much in life. For several days I felt disturbed by the thought of his death, trying to figure out how this could have happened.

A few days later I went to a cliff overlooking the ocean to meditate at sunset. In my meditation I asked for some guidance to help me understand Robert's passing. When I opened my eyes, I saw a large brown frigate bird gracefully coasting on the thermals just offshore. With that sight, a knowing came to me, as if a voice was saying, "Behold the grace and magnificence of life. Don't be distracted by thoughts of death. There is only life."

Immediately I felt a sense of peace and relief. I knew that Robert was okay, and my job was to look for evidence of the presence of love and life rather than dwell on thoughts of death.

A few days later I received this e-mail from a friend who had been hiking with Robert's girlfriend:

> *The day he left his body, I took a walk to a cliff, where I saw a frigate bird in the distance sailing the thermals. It was so smooth, peaceful, and easeful. Of course I thought of Robert as I watched it slowly disappear from sight. Just then a rainbow appeared behind the bird. I knew it was Robert crossing the rainbow bridge.*

How strange and wonderful that we both received the same message at different times yet in similar places through a frigate bird! I am certain that this was guidance from above.

If you have lost a loved one, or fear such a loss, know that you and your loved one are in the hands of a Great Spirit that knows only life. Those who leave us physically remain very much with us, as close as our thoughts and hearts. They want us not to become preoccupied with death, but dwell in the awareness and appreciation of life.

Can you find the presence of life and love,
even in the face of the appearance of death?

I trust life as the truth of my being and
the essence of all whom I love.

Your Miraculous Supply

It is better to light one candle than curse the darkness.

— Chinese proverb

This is the season of the Jewish holiday of Hanukkah, known as the "Festival of Lights." The holiday derives from a miracle that occurred over 2,000 years ago when the land of Judaea was occupied by an army of Syrians. The invading forces attempted to eradicate the Jewish religion and brought their own idols and religious artifacts into the sacred temples.

A man named Judah led an army called the Maccabees to resist the Syrians. After a long war, the Maccabees drove the Syrians out of Judaea. Upon their victory, they reclaimed the great temple in Jerusalem, where their first act was to light the eternal flame. Their dilemma, however, was that they had but one small container of oil sufficient to fuel the flame for one day only. It would take them a week to find and press olives to make new oil.

The flame, however, burned for eight days, giving the Jewish people time to replenish their supply. In celebration of this miracle, Jewish people to this day light a *menorah* with eight candles on it, starting the first night with one candle and lighting an additional candle each evening. (One further candle is used to light the others.)

The holiday of Hanukkah (meaning "dedication") bears a positive message not just for Jewish people, but for all of us: We are sustained by God. When we believe that we do not have enough, or are not enough, our Higher Power can replenish our supply and keep us thriving as long as necessary. We are not limited to the resources our eyes or other senses show us. We have a vast, unlimited source of good. When it seems that we will run out, the universe has wondrous ways of running in.

Let us all use this day and this holiday to remind us, "The Lord is my shepherd. I shall not want."

What do you fear running out of?
If you knew you had access to a vast, unlimited supply of good,
how might you be feeling, speaking, or acting differently?

I trust in universal supply. God is my source.

Law Enforcement in Action

Miracles occur naturally as expressions of love.
The real miracle is the love that inspires them.

— *A Course in Miracles*

One Thanksgiving I hosted a gathering at my home. A friend brought a large turkey, but since most of the guests were vegetarians, a lot of it was left over. The real beneficiary of the day was my dog Munchie, who received leftovers for a couple of weeks.

When the supply of turkey finally ran out, the dog refused to go back to eating his former diet of dry pellets. (I can't say I blamed him.) I then realized that I would have to get Munchie some more turkey, but being a vegetarian, I was not thrilled by the thought of buying one.

A few nights later, I was driving home when I was stopped at a police roadblock checking for holiday drunk drivers. Lieutenant K. approached me and asked to see my documents. I handed them to him, he studied them for a moment, and he asked, "Would you like a turkey?"

"Excuse me?"

"We are giving away turkeys as a reward for not being a drunk driver. Would you like one?"

Well, bless my giblets. "Sure, thanks!" I told him.

A minute later Lieutenant K. was handing me a huge Butterball turkey, while his assistant officer photographed me receiving it for the local newspaper.

I laughed all the way home. When I arrived, Munchie greeted me at the door with a knowing smile. "You are the best manifester I know," I told him. "You got the cops to give you a turkey!"

This incident was an extraordinary lesson in intention and providence. My dog's newfound love for turkey and my love for him sent out a strong signal that the universe heard and responded to. Sure, I could have gone to Safeway for a turkey, but it was much more fun to have it personally delivered by law-enforcement officials. In this case, they were enforcing the Law of Attraction, which can find all kinds of clever means to deliver what you want and need.

Are you open to having your prayer or intention
answered in a clever, unexpected way?

I place my needs in the hands of a loving
universe, and providence delivers my good.

How to Heal the World

Only those who see the invisible can do the impossible.

— Source unknown

Dr. Ihaleakala Hew Len is a psychologist who was assigned to be a therapist in a ward for the criminally insane at a mental hospital. When Dr. Len showed up at the ward, it was beset with major violence and a high staff turnover. The doctor soon realized that if he was going to survive in this position or help the patients, he was going to have to do something more effective than the treatments the patients had been given.

Dr. Len was a practitioner of the Hawaiian healing method called *ho'oponopono,* which literally means "restoring balance and harmony." One of the principles of *ho'oponopono* is to accept full responsibility for the world you see as a creation of your thoughts and beliefs. So Dr. Len sat in his office each day and took each patient to mind and heart. He told each one mentally, *I'm sorry. I love you.* He was using metaphysical principles to accomplish physical healing.

His results were extraordinary. Over time the violence decreased significantly, patients improved, and they were discharged. In fact, after a while the entire ward was shut down due to attrition! Dr. Len attributes this significant transformation to his willingness to accept responsibility for creating the ward of unruly patients with his beliefs, and then for altering the situation by shifting his thoughts about them.

Metaphysicians have told us throughout the ages that we see the world not as it is, but as we are. The world we see is a movie we have produced with a script we have written. At any time we can change the script and the movie by changing our thoughts about it.

You have the power to heal the world. Today would be a perfect day to do it.

What situation do you believe you are powerless to change?
How could you transform the situation by changing your mind about it?

I heal the world by healing my mind.
I expand well-being by beholding it.

Time Enough

Time is like the wind, it lifts the light and leaves the heavy.
— Doménico Cieri Estrada

Right about now you may feel a time crunch for purchasing holiday presents, sending out cards, and fitting in social and family engagements. Shopping reaches a maddening fever pitch, roads and airports are crowded, and lines at the post office are long. You may feel frustrated or guilty about not being able to take care of everyone. You wish there were more hours in the day, or more days in the year, and that you had ordered presents long enough in advance to be ready now. Your joy goes out the window because there is too much stuff to do first.

Stop! This can't be it.

If you feel pressed for time, here are a few tips to find more and feel better:

1. You can maximize time by relaxing your mind and emotions. When you are relaxed and in the flow of life, the hours have a way of expanding to allow you to do all you need to do, often in ways that seem to defy the laws of time. When you are relaxed, you get more done than you would expect possible in a given time frame. When you are stressed and uptight, time has a way of contracting so you end up with even *less* time: "The hurrieder I go, the behinder I get."

2. A sense of not enough time is not a logistical issue. It is an abundance issue. You can use this season to practice abundance. Affirm: *I always have enough time to do the things that Spirit would have me do.* Check in with yourself often and ask, *Is this something I really need to do, or is it an obligation I have created in my mind?*

3. Remember that this is the season of joy. Keep joy at the top of your priority list. When you start to rush or fret, ask yourself what it would take for this particular day or activity to be fun.

4. Stop when you feel tired. Quit shopping or wrapping when you feel drained, and leave the party when you've had enough. Your inner being has an impeccable sense of timing.

Time is not your enemy. It can become your friend if you approach it consciously.

How can you relax more about time and trust that everything will get done?

 I always have enough time to do the things that Spirit would have me do.

Say "Ah!"

God's Will for me is perfect happiness.

— *A Course in Miracles*

If you grew up in a traditional religion, you were probably taught that the path to heaven is paved with suffering. Yet there is a hidden code in the names of many prophets and spiritual expressions that demonstrates the opposite.

The sound *"Ahhhh"* is a universal note of relief. When you lie down after a long day, taste delicious food, receive a massage, or hold your lover in your arms, you spontaneously exude this sound of release and homecoming.

You will find this same sound in the names of spiritual masters, chants, and uplifting words—for example: God. Yahweh. Jehovah. Jeshua (Aramaic name of Jesus). Rama. Krishna. Buddha. Mohammed. Mama. Papa. Lao-tzu. Shalom. Aloha. Aum. Yoga. Hallelujah. Amen. And the spontaneous expression of discovery, *Aha!*

The purpose of therapy or healing is to get to *"Ah!"* and find a sense of relief in contrast to fear, stress, and resistance. Although religion has in many ways been a source of guilt and worldly strife, its true purpose is to bring us release from fear and guilt. You might say that anything that delivers you relief from pain is a spiritual experience.

If you are struggling with an issue, a good question to ask is, "What would it take for me [and the other person involved, if there is one] to get to *'Ah!'*?" You may be so involved in the complexities of your question or issue or so sure that it requires hardship that you overlook the simplest answer right before you.

Certainly there are moments in life when tension is inevitable. Yet that tension has purpose when it gives way to peace. Say "Ah!"

Regarding a question or issue you face,
what "Ah!" would you like to get to?

God wants me to be happy, and so do I. I seek and find relief.

Never Alone

By all means use sometimes to be alone.
Salute thyself: see what thy soul doth wear.

— George Herbert

While the holiday season is a time of social festivity, many people feel lonely. Some feel alone because they do not have a significant other. Others do not feel close to their family. Others have experienced a breakup or the loss of a loved one, and the season reminds them of the person who is gone. Others just wish they had more friends.

While all of these situations may bring up feelings of loneliness, they also offer gifts. Being alone is a powerful opportunity to recognize your connection with your inner being. During a time of disconnection from a loved one or group, you can find self-fulfillment in ways you could not achieve in a crowd.

Here are some tips to help you feel more connected to yourself and others:

1. Acknowledge your sad or lonely feelings, and let it be all right for you to feel them. Journal them or speak them to a trusted friend or counselor.

2. Use your alone time to deepen your relationship with yourself. Find out who you are without needing someone or something to stimulate you.

3. Create self-nurturing activities. Walk in the park, read inspirational words, listen to your favorite music, play with your pet, get a massage, or take yourself to dinner at a nice restaurant.

4. Buy a present for yourself. Who can know better than you what you would most like?

5. Remember that "this too shall pass." Before long you may get so busy that you wish you had more time alone. Savor this chapter and extract the blessings it offers.

We all feel alone at some time or another. You have done nothing wrong, and the universe has not erred in putting you in this position. You might just fall in love with yourself and recognize the presence of love right where you stand.

How can you use the experience of aloneness
to find inner strength, joy, and wholeness?

I am never alone. God is within me, and I am loved.

Bridging the Gap

I felt it shelter to speak to you.

— Emily Dickinson

Yesterday we looked at how to use feelings of holiday-season loneliness to build inner strength. Today we will illuminate another way to offset loneliness: using the experience as an impetus to reach out to give and receive love.

At one point in my life I felt quite lonely, isolated from friends and the world. I picked up *Emmanuel's Book* by Pat Rodegast and Judith Stanton, in which a student asked life guide Emmanuel about loneliness. Emmanuel explained that loneliness is a powerful feeling not to be denied, but rather used in one's favor. It is the call of the soul to reach out and connect. Reading that wisdom, I realized that I had isolated myself from others, and my loneliness was a call for a course correction. I began to phone some friends and make plans for dinner, walks, talks, movies, and other social activities. That was a significant turning point for me. From that time on, I began to value loneliness and all of my feelings as motivators to change direction for the better.

If you feel lonely, your inner being may be calling for you, too, to reach out to loved ones. Your family and friends may want and need to connect with you as much as you want and need to connect with them. A phone call or two, or a well-placed visit, may make a huge difference in your experience and that of your loved ones.

Every experience in life has its reason and season. There is a time to be alone and a time to be connected with others. If you are ready to step back into the world of social connection, listen to your heart. It knows you, loves you, and speaks to you through your deepest feelings.

Who would you like to reach out to connect with?
How might you take that step?

I heed my inner call, and
I connect with people I love and care about.

I Don't Think I'll Be There

The pen that writes your life story must be held in your own hand.
— Irene C. Kassorla

When I was about to be ordained as a minister in a church of the Hawaiian spiritual tradition, I invited my eight-year-old goddaughter, Shanera, to attend the ceremony.

"What's an ordination?" she asked me.

I explained the ritual to her, she thought for a few moments, and she replied, "I don't think I'll be there."

"Why not?" I asked her.

Shanera shrugged her shoulders and answered, "Because I'll be bored."

I had to laugh; the girl's honesty was disarming. I could not blame her. Why should she go someplace where she knew she would be bored?

I began to think of all the weddings, bar mitzvahs, and board (bored) meetings I have attended where I wished I had to courage to say, "I don't think I'll be there. I'll be bored." Of course, I could refuse such invitations more diplomatically, but I have attended far too many functions to which I would have done better to say "No, thank you."

Once I was invited to a wedding of some friends I knew casually. I did not want to go, but I felt a social obligation, so I accepted. Then I wrestled with my conscience. I had made a vow to be true to my intentions, and here I had violated them. *The next time I have a choice that requires me to be true to myself, I will act on it,* I rationalized.

On the day of the wedding, I decided to take a short nap before driving to the event. When I opened my eyes and looked at the clock, it was an hour past the wedding's start time. My inner being had commandeered my actions and did what I would have chosen if I were in integrity with myself. Since then, I just say no when I know it is a no, and save the hassle of being dishonest with myself and others and needing to lull myself to sleep in order to do what I wanted to do anyway.

What are you now doing out of social obligation
that you would prefer not to do?
What would it take for you to be true to your real choice?

My words and deeds reflect my honest choices.
I kindly say no, and make way for my yes.

Focus and Blur

Do what is important, not what is urgent.

— Stephen Covey

Motion-picture cinematographers use a clever technique to high-light key actions. When the director wants to call your attention to a particular character or interaction, the camera will shift the focus from the foreground to the background, or vice versa. For example, if two people are having a conversation in the foreground and a forth-coming love interest appears on-screen in the background, the people in the foreground will become a blur and the background character will snap into sharp focus.

As you move through the holiday season, you have a choice as to what will be the focus and what will be the blur. If you are not care-ful, all the busyness of the season—social obligations, family issues, financial considerations, time crunches, weather, end-of-year details, and many more—will become the focus, and joy will become the blur. If you *are* careful, happiness, connection, and celebration will be the focus, and all the *other* stuff will be the blur.

Stephen Covey, the author of *The 7 Habits of Highly Effective People,* describes "the tyranny of the urgent." When you set a goal that is meaningful to you, there always *seems* to be something more important that you have to do before you can have or do what you really want. This holiday season might be a good time to identify and rise above the tyranny of the urgent. If you can keep your priori-ties in order, you will find that things get taken care of in ways more powerful—and peaceful—than when you give your power away to apparent emergencies.

A Course in Miracles asks us to remember that inner peace is the only goal that really matters. If you have it, you have everything. If you do not have it, you have nothing. This season, let us all do our best to focus the camera on the part of the movie we really want to see.

What are you focusing on that robs your peace?
What could you focus on to restore your peace?

I set my priorities, and I stay with them.
I value inner peace above all else.

Call Me When Your Brother Leaves

A man can't make a place for himself in the sun
if he keeps taking refuge under the family tree.
— Attributed to Helen Keller

My coaching client Melissa is generally an upbeat and positive person. Our telephone coaching sessions move along fluidly, and she has made significant progress in her life.

During one session, however, Melissa seemed despondent and depressed. She fell into a "Yes, but . . ." mode of response, highly unusual for her. Perplexed, I tried to explore with her what had shifted her attitude.

Finally Melissa mentioned casually that her brother had been staying with her for a couple of weeks.

"Tell me about your brother," I said.

"He's been clinically depressed most of his life," she explained. "He's been in and out of mental institutions. Our whole family has tried to help him, but our progress has been minimal."

"And how long have you been feeling depressed?" I inquired.

"Since a couple days after my brother arrived," she explained.

"And when is he leaving?" I asked.

"On Tuesday."

"Then let's stop here for now," I said. "Let's talk again Wednesday."

When we picked up our conversation on Wednesday, Melissa was her enthusiastic self again. She had allowed herself to be influenced by her brother's energy field of confusion and upset and had adopted his feelings as hers. When he departed, she regravitated to her true self.

If you do not maintain your chosen energy, you are prone to being influenced by the energy of others. Sometimes you may be experiencing an emotion that has nothing to do with you and a lot to do with someone around you. I am not suggesting that you run away from people with bad vibes or that you not try to help them. But if you have gotten steeped in an adverse energy field, your best move may be to step back until you get your head on straight. Then you will be able to act in a way that is helpful not just to you, but to the other person as well.

How might you have allowed another's energy to affect you?
How can you renew your own?

I choose the energy I wish to live in, and
I maintain it no matter what others are doing.

A Tale of Two Fliers

The only true measure of success is joy.

— Source unknown

It was a hectic day at Chicago's O'Hare International Airport. Adverse weather conditions had delayed most flights, and the sitting areas were crowded with frustrated travelers. I had a pass to the executive lounge, where I went to wait for my flight. As I took my seat, I noticed a woman sitting across the aisle from me. She was dressed like an executive, talking on her cell phone loudly, giving orders to her subordinates. She seemed demanding, rude, and generally irritated and upset. She went on for quite a while in this manner over a number of calls to different people.

After a while, a cleaning lady came through the lounge. A Hispanic woman, roughly the same age as the executive, she bore a kind smile and offered a pleasant "Hello, how are you?" to the folks she passed. As she picked up the trash and wiped down the counters, she seemed at peace with herself and her work, a sharp contrast to the executive and many of the other travelers.

I marveled at the irony of the scenario. Here were lots of business travelers in a club lounge that cost a lot to enter. Most of those present likely made significant salaries, lived in upscale houses, and were important professionals. Weaving among their midst was a humble cleaner, wearing a smock with the company name "Scrub," probably earning minimum wage and living in an apartment. Oddly, she seemed like the happiest person in the room. If ever there was a teaching that happiness comes from the inside out, here it was.

Over the past few years, I have been reexamining my value system. What are we doing with our lives, our homes, and our work if they do not bring us true happiness? It's fine to make good money and have lots of nice stuff, but only if we keep our souls alive. Today let us think about where our true joy lives and whether it comes from inside or outside. Then one day maybe we can attain the extraordinary success of that cleaning lady.

When are you the happiest?
What priorities could you reorder to be happier more of the time?

My happiness does not depend on outer things.
My happiness depends on what is inside me.

From Night to Light

he world is round and the place which may
...eem like the end may also be the beginning.

— Ivy Baker Priest

Each year around December 21 in the Northern Hemisphere marks the winter solstice, the shortest day and the longest night of the year. After today, the days will get longer and the nights will get shorter. At this juncture, we are heading to only more light.

I find it fascinating that Christmas, Hanukkah, the winter solstice, and the New Year nearly coincide. I believe that all of these events represent one holiday. They celebrate the end of the darkness and the beginning of the light. They remind us that darkness goes just so far before it begins to revert to the light that dispels it. They demonstrate there is new life, hope, and a Higher Power that dwells among us.

Many of us have gone through dark times, but we are still here. Something inside of us is greater than our circumstances. Difficulties call us to remember our power and magnificence in the midst of appearances that would tell us we are small and limited. Yet if we look within, we will find that we are whole and complete, and nothing outside us is greater than the wisdom, strength, and vision we embody independent of any external events. Stephen Longfellow Fiske wrote a wonderful song with the refrain, "There is nothing to need, hide from, or fear. We are whole and complete, right now and right here."

If you have gone through a dark time, or are going through one right now, rejoice that the light is near and expanding. A sense of stuckness or challenge can help you clarify your choices and motivate you to take your next step. Confusion is the last stop on the train to clarity.

Meanwhile, there is comfort and beauty in the darkness. Wintertime is a healthy phase when we can step back from outer doing and, like the hibernating bear, turn within for renewal. Every season has a purpose, and winter bears its own gift. Enjoy it and make use of it. Then, when the time is right, the leaves shall return to the trees, the flowers will open in vibrant glory, and the sun will shine. Today that process has begun.

How can you appreciate and be empowered by darkness?
Can you capture the vision of how the
light will expand and spring will come?

I honor the seasons of my life and trust
that the light is now increasing.

How Much Is Heaven Worth?

The "kingdom of heaven" is a condition of the heart.
— Friedrich Nietzsche

A *USA Today* survey asked a group of wealthy people how much they would pay for various life experiences, if money could buy them. The fascinating results revealed that people would pay an average of $640,000 for a place in heaven, $487,000 for true love, and $407,000 for a great intellect.

While money cannot deliver these experiences, the priorities indicated by the respondents are quite telling and well chosen. A great intellect will get you just so far, but if you do not have true love, your life will be empty. If you have true love but not inner peace, you are still wanting. If you have inner peace, symbolized by a place in heaven, you have it all.

Heaven, as it has been portrayed by religion, is quite misleading. The happiness part is accurate. The timing is not. Heaven is not simply a place you go after you die. It is a consciousness you choose right where you are. The experience of heaven is just as available to you now as it ever will be. This moment is the intersection of time and eternity. Heaven is not a faraway place beyond your reach. It is the purpose your reach was made to grasp.

Heaven is your natural state, and you will live in it unless you trade it for experiences far less joyful. Some common substitutes for heaven are fear, anger, loneliness, conflict, a vendetta against some person or group, busyness, or distraction with stuff.

The good news is that just as you exercised your power of choice to choose something *other* than heaven, you can exercise your choice to *choose* heaven. And you will not need $640,000 to do so. All you will need is the recognition that you deserve happiness, and the willingness to accept it.

What have you traded heaven for?
How can you reclaim happiness by reversing the trade?

I do not need to struggle or wait for happiness.
I choose love, here and now.

Around the Campfire

Love in its essence is spiritual fire.

— Emanuel Swedenborg

After presenting a seminar, I attended a reception party for the participants. In the corner of the room a young mother sat with her one-year-old baby girl playing on the floor in front of her. Dee and I sat with the child, and a few minutes later another person joined us, then another, until a cluster of about eight people were sitting in a circle surrounding the baby and savoring her innocent delight.

The scene, I realized, resembled a group of friends circling a campfire. The child was light and warmth to our spirit, and we were gathered to bask in her energy. So it is with children, who clearly emanate the spark of the Divine. As adults, we, too, own that spark, but the illusions and distractions of the world cause us to overlook it and grow cold outside the circle of its radiance.

As we stand in the crescendo of the holiday season, we might take a few moments in the midst of our busyness to try to recognize that spark in the people we encounter. It is all too easy to get so caught up in the doingness of the season that we overlook the reason for it. We can become so focused on the social and material aspects of the holidays that we lose the warmth this time of year was intended to radiate.

If you are a parent, you might want to remember the "campfire" that your children are. As they have grown past infancy, you may have gotten distracted to the point that you remember less and less the light they emanated as little children. Whether your kids are 5 years old or 40, they are still your "campfire."

There is one more "campfire" to remember: your own. You, too, remain a child of God no matter your age or history. You still have the warmth of your own fire to bask in, a radiance that you take with you wherever you go, enlivening the world as you let it glow.

How can you bask in the life force of those you encounter today?

**I recognize the light of my soul
and the souls of those I meet.**

Stories Worth Telling

The birds are moulting. If man could only moult also—his mind once a year its errors, his heart once a year its useless passions!
— James Lane Allen

At the apex of the holiday season, Dee and I went to a liquor store to purchase a gift of wine for a friend. There we asked the store owner, a congenial fellow named Ali, for some recommendations. We were pleasantly surprised to find that Ali was a world-class wine expert. He went into fascinating, poetic details about each wine, describing its subtlest nuances and mesmerizing us with stories about the history of each winery, some of which went back over a thousand years. I was rapt.

Finally I commented, "I guess all wines have a story."

Ali smiled and shook his head. "Not exactly," he replied. "All *good* wines have a story."

There are some stories worth telling and some stories not worth telling. We have all told lots of stories, some of which empower us and others that disempower us. Many people have been stuck on a self-defeating story for so long that their lives stay in a rut, and they wonder why. Others have latched onto life-giving stories that keep making their world better.

The end of this year might be a good time to assess which stories you wish to quit telling and which ones you would like to continue, amplify, or replace the old stories with. Any story that portrays you as a creative, whole, and blessed being living in an abundant universe with infinite potential is a worthwhile one to tell. Any story that portrays you as a limited, unloved, or victimized person living in a world that does not honor or support you will undermine you. The choice is yours.

Think of your story as a train you have been riding on. If it has been taking you to places you want to go, it is worth continuing the ride. If it is delivering you to undesirable places, it may be time to get off and board a vessel that takes you to where you'd rather be.

Which story would you like to let go of?
Which story would you like to replace it with?

I have a choice about my story.
I choose one that takes me where I want to go.

Gentle Jesus

Christmas, children, is not a date. It is a state of mind.

— Mary Ellen Chase

The film and stage play *Whistle Down the Wind* tells of an escaped criminal who holes up in a deserted barn in the country. Two children stumble upon him and imagine that he is Jesus Christ. They call him "Gentle Jesus," treat him as God, bring him gifts, and play with him. Although he is hardened and resistant at first, over time the criminal softens and grows kind, thoughtful, and playful. Eventually the children's innocent love and respect for the man transforms him, and he becomes Christlike.

Christmas celebrates the birth of Jesus the man, but even more significantly, it honors the birth of the Christ, the divine spirit that animated Jesus. It is easy to get overly involved in the details of the man or worship him as a person. Yet his real gift is the level of consciousness he represented. He showed how to live in divine ways even while walking in a body on Earth.

Jesus is not a god to be worshipped, but a model to be emulated. He does not want us to bow down to him, but to walk straight and tall, with dignity and grace, by his side. He does not want followers, but peers. The same Christ light that shone through him shines through you. The greatest gift you can give Jesus is to join him in his wholeness and divinity.

Today let the Christ, or illumined one, be born in you. It is already there, seeking avenues of expression. If you let it come forth, it will bless you and everyone who looks upon you. Just as Christ was not limited, neither are you. If God is the sun, you are a ray. Every attribute of the sun is in the ray. The only difference between Jesus and us is that he knew who he was, and we are in the process of remembering. Today is the day to shift your sense of identity from an escaped criminal to a divine being.

Merry Christmas, Gentle Jesus.

*How can you use Christmas and the model of Jesus
to lift your own life to the level of expression he demonstrated?*

**I celebrate my own divinity and that of
everyone I know. I let my true light shine.**

DECEMBER 26

A Week for You

. . . be quite still and solitary. The world will freely offer itself to you to be unmasked, it has no choice, it will roll in ecstasy at your feet.

— Franz Kafka

The week between Christmas and New Year's Day is a precious and meaningful one if you choose for it to be so. In our culture many businesses shut down or slow down, and many employees are on vacation. Most people put projects or purchases on hold until the new year, and little gets done in the business world.

I used to try to keep my business momentum going during this week, but eventually I learned that this is not what the week is about for most people. I ended up leaving more unreturned phone and e-mail messages than at any other time of the year, and felt like my efforts were counterproductive. So I took the hint and closed my business for the week.

Since that time I have learned to use this week for purposes other than business. I clean out the clutter, old files, and stuff from my office and house; I think about and envision next year's direction; I connect with friends and family; and I meditate and pray. I go in instead of out. As a result, I feel better and set up my mind and energy for the new year. Pulling back from activity does not defeat my business success, but ultimately enhances it.

This period reminds me of times when I lived on the East Coast and snowstorms brought commercial activity to a halt for a few days. Schools, businesses, and roads were shut down; and you could not go anywhere or do anything even if you wanted to. At that point I surrendered and decided to just stay home, relax, read, write, and be with myself and my family. What a gift that was!

In a world hell-bent on doing, this week offers a pleasant opportunity for being.

*How could you use this week for quiet joy, reflection,
vision, and connection with loved ones?*

**My time is precious. This week is precious.
I use it to strengthen my inner self.**

Eliminate Your Worst Score

His heart was as great as the world, but there was
no room in it to hold the memory of a wrong.

— Ralph Waldo Emerson

Not long ago the International Olympic Committee revised its scoring system for athletes competing in Olympic gymnastic all-around events. It chose to retain a safeguard in which the panel of judges throws out the best and worst score of each athlete, calculating the average of the other scores to arrive at the athlete's final score.

We might do well to apply the principle in our lives. As you look back over this year, you probably made a number of mistakes that you wish you could just erase from the record book of your life. Take a moment now to consider which blunder you would most like to have eliminated from your memory and the memories of those involved. If it were gone, would you feel relieved? Lightened? Liberated?

If you feel even a moment of the release this exercise offers, you have a taste of true forgiveness. Forgiveness does not mean that you are pardoned from a terrible sin, thus underscoring the gravity of the sin. It means that you review the experience without the heavy burden of judgment you have laid upon yourself or that others have laid upon you. Forgiveness also releases you from fear of the pain or punishment you believe your sin will bring upon you. Real forgiveness enhances the quality and buoyancy of the rest of your life—like eliminating your worst score.

You cannot change what you did this year, or in any previous year, but you can change how you think about it. That is where your true power lives. Would you be willing to try another way of looking at your blunders so they are less important than your successes? If you do, you are well on your way to gold that lasts far longer than a medal.

What gift of pardon can you give yourself?
What gift of pardon can you give another?

I free myself by changing my mind.
I drop judgments and embrace love.

Your Shining Moment

*Human life is purely a matter of
deciding what's important to you.*

— Source unknown

In the Japanese film *After Life,* a group of people who have just passed away find themselves in a sort of way station. There, a team of counselors gives them the assignment to choose a moment of their lives that they would like to live in for eternity. Each person embarks on a soul-searching expedition to decide which memory he or she would want to experience forever.

Which moment from this year or your whole life would you like to sustain forever? Was it falling in love for the first time? Making passionate love with a partner with whom you had fantastic chemistry? A special moment with your children? A sports achievement? A flash of spiritual illumination?

The message of *After Life* and the above inquiry is closer to truth than you might imagine. At the moment of a peak experience, you tap into the reality of who you are and how you were born to live. Your peak experiences are far closer to your nature and purpose than your valley experiences. The only purpose of the valley experiences is to provide contrast for you to seek, create, and value the peaks. So the question offered in the movie, applied more practically to your life, would be: *What experiences have brought you feelings you value so much that you want to expand on them for the rest of your life?* Now *there* is a meditation and a mission!

You have a choice about your future, based on what you learned from your past. While many people focus on what went wrong in the past, the secret of success is to recognize what went right and expand on it. Which blessings from the last year would you choose to be coming attractions for the next one . . . and the rest of your life? That is the movie to watch, and you do not have to wait until after life to experience it.

*How can you focus on the best things that have
happened, to attract more and even better?*

**The best of my life is a preview of even better to come.
My peak experiences are mine forever.**

Validation

*There is no effect more disproportionate to its cause than
the happiness bestowed by a small compliment.*

— Robert Brault

The film *Validation* tells the story of a fellow named Hugh Newman who works in a parking garage validating tickets for patrons. Yet Hugh's validation goes far beyond stamping parking tickets. When customers arrive at his station, he enthusiastically compliments them on their smile or their attire, or he simply tells them they are a great person. One by one, tired patrons light up and step away with a sense of joy, confidence, and spryness absent just a few moments earlier.

Hugh's reputation as an uplifter spreads far and wide, to the point that people come to park in his garage and stand in long lines just to receive the validation from him that they are missing in the rest of their lives. Hugh is a true healer, using his worldly occupation as a venue to feed the soul of the world. (*Validation* is available on the Internet if you care to download it.)

While Hugh's story is presented as fiction, the principle it highlights is real. Most people have been criticized and verbally or emotionally whittled down to a self-image far smaller than they are and deserve. When someone comes along who affirms their beauty, gifts, and worth, they come to life and walk taller, freer, and happier. There is no gift greater than seeing people as magnificent and reflecting their innate strength to them.

You, too, can be a validator and create results on par with Hugh's. Today you might consider the people who have supported you this year and contact them to deliver your appreciation. You can make their day—or year—with a short phone call or e-mail in which you acknowledge them for the good they are and have given you. This act will be especially potent with anyone you have been out of touch with or have not gotten along with.

Meanwhile, do not forget to validate yourself. The first ticket you stamp should be your own.

How could you bless the world by being generous with your validation?

**I empower others and myself by
expressing sincere appreciation.**

Farther Than You Know

You are always doing better than you think you are.

— Source unknown

For many years my I have done a pre–New Year's ritual that I find rewarding and illuminating. I take a few minutes to write down what I have accomplished during the preceding year and then set forth my intentions for the coming one.

As I review my notes, I am usually amazed by how far I have come during the past year. If I try to evaluate my progress toward my large-scale goals on a day-to-day basis, it usually seems like I am not getting very far. But when I look back and take stock of the whole year, I see that I was moving along even when I did not know it.

Once in a while I find one of my goal lists from two or five or ten years earlier. I am surprised that the goals I set long ago have come to pass. The Big Picture in review yields insights and reveals successes that the mind absorbed in the little picture rarely notices.

Perhaps you have advanced more than you know during the past year. The ego, or limited idea of self, wants you to think that you are not getting anywhere. It thrives on an illusory sense of being small, stuck, and powerless. Yet your inner being recognizes and rejoices in movement forward. It recognizes who you are, what you have done, and what you can and will do. At every moment you are listening to the voice of the ego or that of your higher knowing. As you choose which voice to hear, you will experience more of what it is telling you.

While you may be tempted to judge or berate yourself for not accomplishing more this year, today would be a good occasion to celebrate movement. Then one day you may pick up a long-buried piece of paper and realize that everything you wanted has come to you.

*In what ways might you have accomplished
more than you believe during the past year?*

**I am grateful for the progress I have made
this year. I am always moving forward.**

The Great Art of Ending

Great is the art of beginning, but greater the art is of ending.
— Henry Wadsworth Longfellow

As we approach the end of this year, you may look back and decide it was a great year or a tough one for you. None of that matters now. The only thing that matters is that you complete it with style, dignity, and grace. Celebrate the successes and capitalize on the mistakes. Imagine that everything that has happened has worked in your favor, for it has.

The most powerful tools for healing, transformation, and evolution are *appreciation* and *blessing*. "Thank you" is the highest prayer that can be said in words or feeling. Say "Thank you" for everything that has happened this year, and the next one will be even better.

How has this year served you? Where have you progressed in your soul's journey? What riches do you own that you did not own a year ago? What people and experiences are you grateful for? Who has helped you by supporting you? Who has helped by challenging you? What would you do differently next year? How can you use the difficulties as stepping-stones to greater success? This year was not so much about getting it all right as it was about learning *how* to get it right. When you value all your experiences, you *are* getting it right.

Today is your springboard to enter a bright new year with the confidence that who you are is enough, and that life will support you to have all that you deserve. Miracles await. Now you will not need any New Year's resolutions. Your New Year's *evolution*, prompted by a stylish completion, will be quite sufficient.

What have been the gifts of the past year? What mistakes
can you learn from? How can you bless it all?
How can the coming year be a soaring success?

I appreciate and celebrate the blessings
of this year. I receive its gifts and make way
 for the best year of my life to come.

Acknowledgments

I am most grateful to my beloved partner, Dee, who has supported me in innumerable ways to discover and extract the lessons in this book and record them. Dee's patience, care, and love have uplifted and empowered me throughout this writing in so many ways. How blessed I am to walk with someone who can look at life with me and find miracles.

Thank you to Kathy McDuff, whose office skills, friendship, and camaraderie have made it so much easier and more joyful to do what I do. The good words that reach you have all passed by her watchful eyes and received the benefit of her editing and feedback.

I appreciate the belief and support of the staff at Hay House, who hold the high watch for service and quality. Louise L. Hay has been supremely encouraging with her appreciation of *A Deep Breath of Life*, as well as her model of generous giving and living. CEO Reid Tracy is consistently affirmative and attuned to what wants to happen, echoed by his always-helpful assistant, Stacey Smith. The editorial team, headed by Jill Kramer, make it a delight to publish. Special kudos to my editor Alex Freemon, whose watchful eye, thoughtful comments, and stellar attitude have made the book stronger, clearer, and reader friendly. Thank you, too, to Jenny Richards for her excellent cover design, and Julie Davison for her interior layout. It sure is fun to work with people who know what they are doing, and care!

Finally, my deepest thanks to all of my mentors, friends, seminar participants, coaching clients, and the films I cite here. The world is my school, and all of you are my teachers. Thank you for the lessons you demonstrate and the wisdom I have gained through walking by your side. We are all in this together.

Wisdom for Today

Daily Inspiration and Guidance via E-mail Directly to You

If you have enjoyed and benefited from *A Daily Dose of Sanity*, you can continue to be inspired by receiving a lesson each day via e-mail. Just like the daily entries in this book, each message contains a theme, a quote, a story and related lesson, a question for introspection, and an affirmation. For a nominal fee, you can subscribe for a 3-, 6-, or 12-month period and enjoy an uplifting new message every day.

You may also want to explore other programs by Alan Cohen, including his free inspirational quote service; Life Mastery Retreats; Life Coach Training; and All About U., a school of higher learning for the higher self, which offers online courses, personal coaching, teleseminars, and much more. Alan's free monthly e-newsletter contains articles; media recommendations; and announcements of his new books, CDs, DVDs, and programs near you.

For information about all of these programs, visit:
www.alancohen.com.

About the Author

Alan Cohen, M.A., is the author of many popular inspirational books, including the best-selling *The Dragon Doesn't Live Here Anymore* and the award-winning *A Deep Breath of Life*. He is a contributing writer for the #1 *New York Times* best-selling series *Chicken Soup for the Soul,* and his monthly column, "From the Heart," is published in magazines internationally. His work has been featured on **Oprah.com** and in the book *101 Top Experts*. His books have been translated into 23 foreign languages. Alan keynotes and presents seminars in the field of life mastery and vision psychology. He resides with his family in Maui, Hawaii.

For information on Alan Cohen's books, CDs, videos, seminars, and online courses, contact:

Website: **www.alancohen.com**
E-mail: info@alancohen.com
Phone: (800) 568-3079
(808) 572-0001 (outside U.S.)
(808) 572-1023 (fax)

Or write to:

Alan Cohen Programs and Publications
P.O. Box 835
Haiku, HI 96708

Hay House Titles of Related Interest

YOU CAN HEAL YOUR LIFE, the movie, starring Louise L. Hay & Friends
(available as a 1-DVD program and an expanded 2-DVD set)
Watch the trailer at: **www.LouiseHayMovie.com**

THE SHIFT, the movie, starring Dr. Wayne W. Dyer
(available as a 1-DVD program and an expanded 2-DVD set)
Watch the trailer at: **www.DyerMovie.com**

❧ ❧ ❧

DAILYOM: Learning to Live, by Madisyn Taylor

*THE EYES OF FAITH: How to Not Go Crazy: Things to Bear
in Mind to Get Through Even the Worst Days,* by Ben Stein

*FINDING OUR WAY HOME: Heartwarming Stories That Ignite
Our Spiritual Core,* by Gerald Jampolsky, M.D., and Diane Cirincione, Ph.D.

*HAPPINESS NOW!: Timeless Wisdom for Feeling
Good FAST,* by Robert Holden, Ph.D.

*IT'S NOT THE END OF THE WORLD: Developing Resilience
in Times of Change,* by Joan Borysenko, Ph.D.

THE LAW OF ATTRACTION: The Basics of the Teachings of Abraham®,
by Esther and Jerry Hicks

*MAXIMIZE YOUR POTENTIAL THROUGH THE POWER OF
YOUR SUBCONSCIOUS MIND TO OVERCOME FEAR AND WORRY,*
by Dr. Joseph Murphy

THE PRESENT MOMENT: 365 Daily Affirmations, by Louise L. Hay

*WHAT IS YOUR SELF-WORTH?: A Woman's Guide
to Validation,* by Cheryl Saban, Ph.D.

All of the above are available at your local bookstore,
or may be ordered by contacting Hay House (see next page).

❧ ❧ ❧